PENGUIN CLASSICS

THE ANALECTS

CONFUCIUS (551–479 BC) was China's earliest teacher and
moral thinker, and his name is most closely associated with China's past. A man from a modest background, Confucius relied
on his learning and his practical skills to secure positions first in
the aristocratic families and then in the government of his home
state of Lu. A falling out with the chief counselor and the ruler
of Lu forced him to spend his mid-life in self-exile, wandering
from state to state, with a few disciples, in search of a government job. His conversations with disciples and rulers, political
operators, and people he happened to meet laid the foundation of
a teaching, which, through time, came to shape the Chinese idea
of what is moral and what is politically viable, what is a good
government and who has integrity. Confucius returned home
toward the end of his life at the invitation of his ruler. The number of his disciples grew during those last years, and the people of
Lu accorded him the kind of respect he had not known before—
they addressed him as the "elder statesman." Confucius' description of himself as an old man suggests that he had finally found
calm and spontaneity. Yet this is someone who remained careworn about the future of humanity and about the possibility that
men and women might lose their way if they become morally
unmoored. Confucius died at the age of seventy-two.

The Analects, compiled by his disciples and their disciples, is
the source of what we know about Confucius' conversations
with his contemporaries and his observations about the world
and about men from the past, and it is the book the Chinese
have returned to repeatedly for reflection, renewal, and valida-
tion of their own views.

ANNPING CHIN teaches in the history department at Yale and
is the author of *The Authentic Confucius: A Life of Thought
and Politics* and *Four Sisters of Hofei*. She lives in West Haven,
Connecticut.

T0025730

CONFUCIUS

The Analects
(*Lunyu*)

Translated with an Introduction and Commentary by
ANNPING CHIN

PENGUIN BOOKS

PENGUIN BOOKS

Published by the Penguin Group
Penguin Group (USA) LLC
375 Hudson Street
New York, New York 10014

USA | Canada | UK | Ireland | Australia | New Zealand | India | South Africa | China
penguin.com
A Penguin Random House Company

This translation first published in Penguin Books 2014

Library of Congress Cataloging-in-Publication Data

Confucius.
[Lun yü. English]
The analects = Lunyu / Confucius ; translated with an introduction and commentary by Annping Chin.
pages cm. — (Penguin classics)
Includes bibliographical references and index.
ISBN 978-0-14-310685-2
I. Chin, Ann-ping, 1950- translator. II. Title. III. Title: Lunyu.
PL2478.L338 2014
181'.112—dc23   2014010222

Printed in the United States of America
15th Printing

Cover design by Nick Misani
Cover art (from outside layer inward): *Shufangxuan hezuan sishu tizhu*, commentary by Zhu Xi and
subcommentaries by Fan Xiang, et al. (published sometime between 1692 and 1722); *The Morals of
Confucius, A Chinese Philosopher* (London: F. Fayram, 1724); *The Chinese Classics, Vol. 1, Confucian Analects*, translated by James Legge (London: Truber & Co., 1861); *Lunyu zhengyi (Collected
Commentaries of the Analects)*, edited with commentary by Liu Baonan (Sibu beiyao edition, Zhonghua
reprint, 1936); *Zhengshizhu Lunyu jicheng (Excavated Handcopy Manuscript of the Analects from
the Tang Dynasty)*, edited by Kanaya Osamu (Tokyo: Hebonsha, 1978); Confucius image taken from
Sheng ji tu by Zhenduo Zheng, 1898–1958.

Contents

THE ANALECTS

Preface

The *Analects* is the single most important book in the history of China. Yet for the uninitiated, this fact is hard to grasp because the principal figure in the book, Confucius, is often seen to be responding to a question, offering a comment, or just thinking aloud. He refrained from "putting forth theories," the *Analects* says, and "did not think that he must be right." His approach is personal, so that even when a simple fellow asks him a question, Confucius has "to knock at both sides [of the question] until everything has been considered."

In the introduction to his translation of Montaigne's essays, Donald Frame tells us, "Montaigne resists definition. . . . Yet this very difficulty points to one answer: that the book is the man." Perhaps the same is true of Confucius and the *Analects*, but the *Analects* is not a record of what Confucius wrote, only of what he said. It is, in hindsight, the way Confucius represented himself to the world, though he never intended for that to happen, since it was his disciples and generations of disciples following them who compiled the book. How then did such a work end up being the central point of reference for scholars, thinkers, rulers, political counselors, and just about anyone in the last twenty-five hundred years of Chinese history? And how did Confucius' voice become a source of authority for the Chinese, even for the leaders of the present Communist government? Through a combination of hard work and chance, one might say.

In the years right after his death in 479 BC, competitive interpretations of what Confucius had taught helped to keep his name and his ideas alive. Then, in the next two hundred years, two followers, Mencius and Xunzi, took his teachings in different directions, and between them much ground was covered, from the self to society and nature. These men's disquisitions on man's inborn dispositions, on his private and public duties, on what is fair and what is misguided judgment, and on the many moral conundrums of life could seem like a long stretch from what Confucius had originally put forth, but the world had changed by their time. People demanded more from the wise and learned because there were more variables in human relationships and in one's relation to the state. Also, more contenders had entered the field—but Mencius and Xunzi were not just eyeing the opposition. They had to be ready, of course, to spar with the quickest and most discerning minds of their day, but, more important, they were looking to satisfy their yearning for knowledge. In the course of their endeavor, Confucius would grow in name and stature.

Imperial patronage in the Han dynasty, after China became a unified country in the second century BC, helped Confucius secure a permanent place within China's institutions. Bureaucracy, law, education, social organization, and ritual practice—all stood on principles that bore the influence of Confucius' assumptions and beliefs. This, however, does not mean that Confucius' teachings did not go through periods of decline. The longest of these lasted nearly seven hundred years, from the beginning of the Six Dynasties (220–589) to the end of the Tang dynasty (618–906), during which time Buddhism, a foreign religion, captivated the Chinese imagination and the Chinese, in turn, shaped the foreign religion to look like their own. It was in response to the imminent threat of losing their cultural distinction that the Chinese in the beginning of the Song dynasty (960–1279) saw a need to revive Confucian teachings. The movement unfolded gradually, and by the end of that dynasty nearly everything was being addressed by this new Confucianism, from the arcane to the practical, from metaphysics to spiritual cultivation, from scholarship to learning and education, from the selection of officials to principles of government.

The Confucian counselors in the next dynasty, the Yuan (1279–1368), managed to persuade their Mongol rulers to tighten the focus of the civil service examinations, limiting them to four books from the Confucian canon and a set of commentaries sanctioned by the imperial court. The *Analects* was one of these Four Books. In a society where, for most men, succeeding in the examinations—and thus securing a government post—was the only avenue to raising one's social standing, what this meant was that the *Analects*, along with the three related texts, became a fixture in the studies of all those who were able to get an education. These hopeful aspirants would memorize the text when they were very young and then return to it repeatedly almost as a daily exercise. In time, the book would have helped them to shape their views and might even have helped them to find a moral anchor. But the story of the *Analects* does not end there. If competition against a foreign religion fueled the Confucian revival in the Song, disagreements within the tradition about how to read the *Analects* kept the book alive, and the man who started it all vigorous and relevant, until today.

Most of the translations in English, however, do not reflect this rich tradition in reading the *Analects*. Instead, they tend to favor one commentary, Zhu Xi's from the twelfth century, that had become standard through five hundred years of imperial support and the only interpretation the state would accept in the civil service examinations. My work follows a different approach. I relied on the scholars from the last three hundred years—scholars who put research before ideology—to show me the competing interpretations and the possibilities of understanding a word, a sentence, or a passage, and my translation is what I arrived at after I had considered the range of choices before me. My hope, of course, is to recover some of the ambiguities and nuances in what Confucius says, which are often lost if one comes to trust a single voice or a single vision.

In the introduction to this translation, I offer a brief account of Confucius' life and some guidance about how to read the *Analects*. I also explain why one would need traditional commentaries to make sense of this book and how I have tried to handle the bulk of this knowledge and scholarship from the last two thousand years. A chronology of China's dynastic history follows the introduction.

Very few chapters, called "Books" in the translation, have a prefatory synopsis, because often there is no thread to bind the ideas together in any given section; therefore, unless there is a good reason to suggest one, I have refrained from providing a synopsis lest it become an obstacle, a limitation or misdirection, to reading. Glossaries of names and terms carry the same risk, I feel, and so my approach is to provide in the commentary a thorough description of a name or a term when it first appears in the text, and then to gloss it each time it shows up again. This is my attempt to think aloud about the character of, say, a disciple like Zigong or Zilu and about what Confucius means by *ren* (humaneness) or *ming* (destiny). My hope is that by the end of the book the reader will have come to his or her own conclusion about a given person or idea. I have, however, drawn together, in Appendix 1, an index of the disciples of Confucius and of historical individuals that appear in the *Analects*; in Appendix 2, an index of terms and of topics; and, in Appendix 3, an index of Chinese scholars and thinkers cited in the commentaries. I have also included, following my English translation, the Chinese text of the *Analects*, because more and more readers in the West have shown an interest in having it, and it is also the right thing to do in a work in which exegesis—as a discipline and by way of translation—is the principal mode of operation.

For a book as old as the *Analects*, many questions remain—about its origin and development, and about the work that went into producing its early redactions before it took its present shape. We have, through archaeological discovery, a version of one early redaction, dated to the first half of the first century BC. Written on bamboo strips, the text was found in 1973 in Ding prefecture, Hebei province, in the tomb of a Han dynasty nobleman, but it was in bad shape. A fire from long ago in the tomb—which bore the vestiges of a botched robbery—had destroyed more than half of the bamboo strips and left the remaining ones gravely damaged. It took scholars two decades to have the transcription of the Dingzhou *Analects* published. Comparing this and the received version, we notice variants in the usage of particles and characters and in the partition of the passages but no fundamental differences that would alter our thinking about the standard text.

Since the discovery in Ding prefecture, many more excavated texts have come to light. Some of these have been dated to the first hundred years of the Han dynasty. Others are from 300 BC or earlier, in a period of Chinese history known as "the Warring States." Confucius appears in eight of the forty-five Warring States texts from the Shanghai Museum collection, most of which are records of his conversations with disciples or political figures. They add to our knowledge of Confucius and his world and have contributed to my own consideration of the *Analects*, but answers to questions regarding the formation of the *Analects* still await the emergence of more evidence. A correction in approach, however, has already taken place. It had been widely accepted that a work with a long history, like the *Analects* or the *Laozi*, even before it became stabilized, must have evolved linearly from a single mother source. But more and more scholars are giving up this theory, because the excavated materials, especially those of the *Laozi*, suggest that at inception there were many threads and mutual influences. What this means for the *Analects* is that the search for its beginnings will be more difficult than we thought, but the odds of finding more early examples may be on our side. In the meantime, we still have a lot to absorb from the book that we have right here.

Acknowledgments

I am indebted to my grandfather, Jin Yufu, and to scholars like him whose passion for research is big and constant and infectious.

I am grateful to my editor, John Siciliano, who always had time for me to talk through a point, an idea, or a change of mind about form or content. Many thanks to Janet Fletcher for being the most rigorous of copy editors. It is my good fortune to have been able to put a manuscript in her hands again. My thanks also to Yulia Bereshpolova and Shao Xiaofang for allowing me to intrude into their lives any hour of the day to get me out of my trouble with computer technology.

My family has been a part of this journey from the beginning. Mei and Yar helped to keep me on the road. And Jonathan was my constant companion—my "friend and dear friend"—through every stage and turn. He has read every draft and pored over every word, and to him this translation is dedicated.

Introduction

I have been exploring the *Analects* of Confucius for most of my adult life—more obsessively in the last ten years—and though the journey has not gotten easier, the pleasure never diminishes. This is because the more I burrow into it the more generous the text becomes, the more knowledge it is willing to give away. Confucius, too, allows himself to be that much more palpable when I search for him with extra effort. But this is what I always wanted, to find him not as an elevated idea but as someone who thinks and speaks and responds to the world with human instincts and an awareness of his own limitations. And in my long relationship with the *Analects*, something else—something even more important—has happened. It seems that somewhere along the way the book has shed its earlier identity as an object of my studies. In fact, as I read it now, I plunge deeper into my own life. I feel more acutely those things that make up this life: family, friends, students, my country, her politics, memories of childhood, and memories of my parents.

The eighteenth-century scholar Cheng Yaotian says this about literature: "Its influence can be more inspiring than being in the presence of a great man because it calls upon us to articulate our ideas and it beckons us to draw analogies. And so what literature offers is more than just something to rely on: it takes us by the hand and bolsters us up; it holds us by the arm to get us on our way." The *Analects* is that kind of literature, yet it is also a book with few points of access. To find a way in can be discouraging even for the most earnest beginners, and it is not because the language is abstruse. The *Analects* is not a store of esoteric knowledge. It is a work about Confucius' life and teachings, but the records stand piecemeal—as a bit of a conversation Confucius had with a disciple or someone he knew or as part of a remark he made about a contemporary or a figure from the past. And the fragments are often isolated from one another even though they may be bundled together as a single chapter. This is one reason why the book is difficult to approach. Names of people pose another problem. Of these, there are many, and rarely does the text explain who these people were, and only in a few instances are we told why a person was mentioned or why a conversation took place at all. The heaps of commentaries written over the last two thousand years to help us get through the opaque passages and work out the enigmas can paralyze the reader with their sheer weight and volume. And this is where I would like to come in: to bring clarity to this work with a new translation and commentaries that reflect centuries of scholarship but without the heft. And my hope is to be able to take readers through each chapter and entry, without ever losing them. One example from Book Fourteen may help to illustrate this point:

> A young boy from Que took on the task of being a messenger [for the people] of this district. Someone asked Confucius, "Do you see him as someone who is eager to make progress in his learning?"
> The Master replied, "I have seen this boy sitting down [in a gathering of adults] and walking abreast of his elders. He is not someone who seeks to make progress [yi]. He simply wants to grow up fast [cheng]."

The two words yi and cheng are critical to our understanding of Confucius' assessment of the young boy. But before he pronounces the boy to be cheng and not yi, Confucius says that he has seen this child "sitting down with" his elders and "walking abreast of" them, which, according to the mores at the time, was a violation of ritual propriety. Thus the boy, in Confucius' view, could not have been someone who was "eager to make progress in learning [yi]": "He simply wants to grow up fast [cheng]." Evidence is crucial to judgment. Confucius

applied this principle to the judgment of character, and scholars later on extended it to the reading of a text. But the idea is
the same, and this is how we get the moral thinker and the
exegete. There is one other thing the record shows, and that is
just how closely Confucius observes a person's—even a mere
boy's—conduct. And the fact that the boy was from Que,
which was Confucius' home district, suggests that the knowledge was firsthand.

A more difficult kind of exegetical work involves searching
for a thread among the records in the *Analects* to tell a bigger
story about Confucius' thinking on a broader subject. And if
the subject is politics, one could start with Book Thirteen.
There, Confucius comments on how to govern and who is fit
to govern; how politics works and what it should serve; when
to be flexible and when to get tough; what is an ordered society and whether capital punishment has a part in it. His view
on the principles of government appears in 13.3, where he says
that rectifying names is what he would attend to first if he
were to take charge of a government, because, "If names are
not rectified, what is said will not seem reasonable. When
what is said does not seem reasonable, nothing will get accomplished." What this means is that if a government does not
restore the integrity of names and words before everything
else, then no one will trust what is being said, and consequently nothing can get done. Punishments, too, will become
arbitrary, Confucius observes, and so "people will not know
where to put their hands and feet." And once a government
has ceased to function, the state will come to ruin.

Confucius always held on to this belief, that a government
runs on trust and on all of its moral capital, but he did not
clench it too tightly. In practice he allowed flexibility, and he
urged those in office to act with common sense. In 13.2, he
tells one disciple, after this disciple has received an appointment as a district steward, to assemble his staff first and
"assign them to the right positions." "Try to overlook their
minor shortcomings," Confucius says. "Promote those of outstanding talent." The disciple asks, "How can I recognize
those of outstanding talent in order to promote them?" And
Confucius responds, "Promote those you recognize to be

outstanding. . . . As for those that you missed, will other people let them slip by you?" And when asked in 13.9 what a ruler should do first when he has already attracted a multitude of people to his state, Confucius says, "Make them rich," and then "instruct them."

Examples like these may give the impression that pragmatism is the driving force in Confucius' political thought, but a closer look at the records—just those in Book Thirteen, for instance—shows that even when Confucius lets moral issues take a backseat, he never loses sight of where he is going—that his aim has always been to achieve greater benefits for a greater number of people. And if he seems inconsistent at times, it may be that he is thinking aloud about the pull and counterpull of an argument while searching for that precise point of balance. Thus he stands firm against killing people for their transgressions, no matter how serious the offense, because he believes that self-reform can come about only through the influence of moral instruction and exemplary virtue. But he also points out that "only after good men have been in office for a hundred years is there the possibility of winning the war against cruelty and doing away with capital punishment." In this example the pragmatist in him takes a long view of how to reach a goal, and so even when he is in a hurry to get there, he refrains from taking extreme measures, which, he knows, may introduce other kinds of cruelty.

This is how Confucius works out most of life's questions. Thus you, as the reader, have to feel the tug going both ways before you are able to hear what Confucius says about trust (*xin*) and humaneness (*ren*), learning (*xue*) and knowledge (*zhi*), rightness (*yi*) and petty loyalty (*liang*). And it is the search for his distinct voice that promises the most satisfaction. This is the reason why, in my task as translator and commentator, I concentrate on Confucius—on gathering evidence about his life and on placing him in his own world. I want us to be able to imagine him thinking or speaking or mulling over a question. And so I do not treat his ideas as a set of concepts and categories that could find their counterparts in the Western philosophical tradition. The latter approach, in a book like this one, could have spoiled the pleasure and the surprise of discovery.

Besides, Confucius himself stays away from "putting forth theories" and making conjectures. He does not speculate about man's inborn propensities or debate the nature of knowledge. But he is happy to talk about poetry and the rites, for they are inseparable from the speech and conduct of everyday life. An education in both, he proclaims, can give a man discerning eyes and ears, moral acuity and a sense of propriety. In 16.13, Confucius tells his son, "Unless you learn the *Odes*, you won't be able to speak." What he means is that you may be able to string together a few words, but this is not the same as speaking because it will have neither the measured voice of a fine poem nor the poem's transforming power. Of the earliest anthology of poetry, Confucius says, "The *Odes* can give the spirit an exhortation and the mind keener eyes. They can make us better adjusted in a group and more articulate when voicing a complaint." He compares the kinetics in these poems to driving a team of horses in the wild: "They never swerve from the path." The balance in the act of spurring on and reining in is the point of the lesson. That it should become the gauge of one's conduct and judgment was what Confucius hoped, but he was also eager for this knowledge to be put to use. He says in 13.5, "A person may be able to recite the three hundred poems, but if he is unable to put [this knowledge] to full use when he is given a political assignment, or if he is unable to hold his own in a diplomatic exchange when he is sent abroad on a mission, no matter how many poems he has learned, what good will it do?" In early China, a man acting as the representative of his ruler on a foreign mission was expected to understand the aesthetic elements and the political implications of the poems his host had selected for their entertainment. And in response, the emissary would ask the court musician of his host to recite, on his behalf, poems of his choice. The test in these functions was whether the emissary could "hold his own." If his selections were equally forceful and fitting, then he would not have brought "disgrace to the mission his ruler had entrusted to him." This form of diplomatic exchange, where one's knowledge of poetry was a means of assessing each party's strengths, had been around long before Confucius was born, but it was Confucius who noticed a moral dimension in these performances, and he wanted to amplify it in his teachings.

The same could be said about his teachings of the rites. According to his earliest biographer, the Han dynasty historian Sima Qian, Confucius, in his childhood games, liked "to set up ritual vessels and orchestrate a ritual performance around them." Even though there is no record to support this claim, we can well imagine the scene. For how could a precocious child, destined for great things, not be awed by the weight of bronze implements and the sound of bronze bells and stone chimes? The ritual wares Confucius played with were wooden ones and modest, but he must have witnessed ancestral rites being performed. He would have been drawn to the solemnity of the occasion, and he must have found satisfaction in the fluidity and the balance of a given movement or act. Thus he also told his son in 16.13, "Unless you learn the rites, you won't be able to find your balance." "Balance" here refers to a person's deportment and conduct, but if the person were to try to achieve it for the sake of a good name, he would be missing the point. Confucius says in 17.12, "To assume a dignified exterior with only a soft pith for an interior—that kind of person, to take an analogy from the riffraff [of the world], is like a thief who makes his way into a house by boring a hole through the wall." If a person were the genuine article, he would want the rites to effect an inward change: "Being human and yet lacking in humaneness—what can such a man do with the rites?" The fulfillment of humaneness (*ren*) is the beginning and the end of one's journey through life, Confucius teaches, and to "restrain the self and return to the rites" is "the way to be humane." This idea is easier to visualize when Confucius construes it as a guide to proper political behavior. He says, "When abroad, conduct yourself as if you were receiving an honored guest. When employing the service of the people in your state, deport yourself as if you have been put in charge of a grand sacrifice." The acting principle in these instructions is "Do not impose on others what you do not desire for yourself." That is a heavy burden, and no one who has "only a soft pith for an interior" can hope to carry it off.

Confucius—Latinized from Kong *fuzi*, or Master Kong—was born in 551 BC, toward the end of an era in Chinese history called "the Spring and Autumn" (770–481 BC). His home was in Lu, a regional state in eastern China in an area now known as the Shandong peninsula.

The Kongs of Lu were common gentlemen (*shi*) with no hereditary entitlements and privileges. The common gentlemen—in the social hierarchy of the Zhou dynasty (1045–221 BC), just a notch higher than the common folk—could boast of their employability in the army or in any administrative position because they were educated in the six arts of ritual, music, archery, charioteering, writing, and numbers. Confucius' father had been a military officer and later served as a district steward in Lu, but he was already an old man when he fathered Confucius. A previous marriage had given him nine daughters and a clubfooted son, and so it was with Confucius that he was granted a healthy heir. But he died soon after Confucius was born, leaving his young widow to fend for herself.

Confucius was candid about his family background. He said that because he was "poor and from a humble station" he could not enter government service as easily as young men from prominent families and so had to become "skilled in many menial tasks." He found employment first with the Jisun clan, a hereditary family, whose principal members had, for many decades, served as chief counselors to the rulers of Lu. A series of modest positions with the Jisuns—as keeper of granaries and livestock, and as a district officer in the family's feudal domain—led to more important appointments in the Lu government, first as minister of works and then as minister of crime.

Records of the time suggest that, as minister of crime, Confucius was effective in handling problems of law and order but was even more impressive in managing diplomatic missions: he knew when to flex his muscles and when to yield, and how to bring a tough negotiation to a successful conclusion. But his involvement in the internal politics of Lu cut his tenure short. In 498 BC, in an effort to restore the authority of the ruler, he came under suspicion of being the mastermind of a plot to steer the hereditary families to self-ruin, and when the case was unraveled, even the ruler was unwilling to offer his support. Thus Confucius had no choice but to leave his position and his home.

His self-exile took Confucius on a fourteen-year journey, first to Wei, the state just west of Lu, then south to the state of Song, and finally to the states of Chen and Cai before he circled back to Wei. Confucius spent much of that time looking for rulers who might be willing to come under his influence and be guided by his vision of a virtuous government. His search was in vain but he never gave up, because he was anxious "to be put to use." He said to those who found his ambitions suspect: "How can I be like a bitter gourd that hangs from the end of a string and not be eaten?" How could he let his knowledge and ingenuity and all his inborn potential go to waste just because the going had been rough?—this, I believe, is what he meant.

Confucius was emboldened to think he could set things right for the world because he was born at a time when such aspirations were within the reach of men living in circumstances similar to his. The Zhou dynasty by the mid-sixth century BC was approaching its five-hundredth year. The political framework the dynastic founders had put in place, an enfeoffment system held together by family ties, was still standing, but the joints had been giving out since the beginning of the Spring and Autumn period, and so the structure could collapse if not shored up. The regional rulers, who were relatives of the Zhou king, should have been the king's strongest supporters, but they preferred pursuing their own ambitions. By Confucius' time, none of the regional rulers was interested in the security of the empire or the idea of the greater good. The same could be said of the members of the aristocratic class, who had once aided their ruler in government—now they were openly competing with him for wealth and women. Their apathy and ineptitude allowed the common gentlemen—men like Confucius who had once been in their service—to step in and take charge of the administrative functions of the government.

The common gentlemen still could not displace the aristocrats as the society's elite, yet if they worked hard enough and were smart, they could be influential in most political contests. But the more discerning ones set their goals higher: They saw an opportunity to introduce a few new ideas about worth (*xian*) and nobleness (*shang*)—which, they felt, could challenge the set of assumptions that had been supporting the existing social hierarchy. They asked whether proof of ability and strength of character should be the measures of a person's worth, and whether men of noble rank should be stripped of their titles and privileges for their incompetence and moral indiscretion. Men who posed such questions were not just seeking a chance to compete in the political world; they wanted to rewrite the rules so that the outcome would benefit the virtuous and the competent. This, in part, explains what Confucius was trying to teach. He believed that the moral resolve of a few could favorably affect the fate of many. But integrity alone, in his view, was not enough. Good men had to be tested in politics.

The man whom Confucius looked back to for inspiration and guidance was the Duke of Zhou, brother of the founder of the Zhou dynasty and regent to the king's young son. Despite the temporal distance between them, Confucius believed that he and the Duke of Zhou wanted the same thing for the dynasty—social harmony and political stability grounded in trust and mutual obligations, with minimal use of legal rules. But the Duke of Zhou was royalty, and Confucius was a professional bureaucrat, which meant that if Confucius did not have a government job he could not have any influence in society and would have few resources to live on. Men who knew him on his travels wondered whether his eagerness for a political position might have led him to overplay his hand and whether he had compromised his principles by letting disreputable men and women act as intermediaries. Confucius' critics included his own disciples—the three or four who accompanied him in his exile.

Confucius' disciples were considerably younger than he was. Young men from a wide range of backgrounds—sons of aristocrats, children of common gentlemen, merchants, farmers, artisans, criminals, and sons of criminals—chose to attach themselves to him in order to learn skills that might get them started on the track to an official career. In the process, they acquired a lot more—a gentleman's refinement and moral acuity, which, in Confucius' mind, were essential to a political career. Confucius was the "master" (*zi*) to these followers, who called themselves his "disciples" or "apprentices" (*tu*). Among his earliest disciples, three stand out in the *Analects*: Zigong, Zilu, and Yan Hui. And it was these three, Zigong, Zilu, and Yan Hui, who accompanied Confucius on his long journey into the unknown.

Confucius was invited to come home to Lu in 484, when he was nearly seventy. It was probably two of his disciples, who had gotten plum jobs in the Lu government the year before, who orchestrated the move. To get Confucius to agree, they thought, the ruler should offer him a nice sum to retire on. The plan worked. Once back, Confucius found himself in a comfortable position. He no longer had financial worries, and the people of Lu treated him with the kind of respect he had not known before. The ruler and his counselors addressed him as the "elder statesman," and they would approach him for advice when natural disasters struck or when they were thinking of raising taxes or raising an army against a state they perceived to be a threat. The number of Confucius' disciples also grew. And even though Confucius says in 2.4, "At seventy, I followed what my heart desired without overstepping the line," he was not free of care. From the dialogues in his later life, it seems he weighed the opposing views of history and of human character with greater precision. He also spoke more frankly about his defeats and about feeling tired. Yet his voice was unstrained. It was the voice of someone who had lived and traveled, who had done all he could to guide the world away from a violent and arbitrary course while knowing that his efforts would have no effect on those who held the reins. Toward the end of his life, he told his disciple Zigong that he intended to remain silent, and when Zigong protested, Confucius replied, "What does Heaven ever say? Yet the four seasons move in order, and the hundred things come to life. What does Heaven ever say?"

Much of Confucius' thought and character can be gleaned from the *Analects*, but without the more formal commentaries and the private ruminations scholars kept in their notebooks or let slip into their essays, we would not have been able to get close to Confucius. Take, for instance, 14.39. Here we learn that Confucius "was playing the stone chimes when a man, carrying a bamboo basket, went past his door" and said, "How squalid this *kengkeng* sound! If no one understands him, then he should just keep what he believes to himself and that's all: 'If the water is deep, just wade across it. If the water is shallow, lift your hem and cross it.'" To this, Confucius replied, "If [this man] is so resolute, he should not have any difficulties." We would not have known how to approach this record if the commentaries did not tell us that the man carrying a bamboo basket was a recluse, someone who had had enough of this world and wanted out, and that the poem he declaimed was a reflection of his feelings and his stance. There are several such men in the *Analects*, but this one is the most inscrutable; equally opaque is Confucius' response, which, as some scholars point out, is not just aimed at the recluse—it also allows us an entry into Confucius' secret self. If this man is resolute, Confucius says, then, unlike himself, "he should not have any difficulties."

Commentaries explain not only who the man "carrying a bamboo basket" was but also the point of his message to Confucius. Collected commentaries, however, do a lot more. They give us a group of exegetical materials on any particular question and point out competing interpretations, when they exist, each with its supporting evidence. We are not told in most cases the choicest reading, but if we are patient and are willing to work at it ourselves, we may learn to sort out the plausible from the suspect, the judicious from the ideological; and in the process we are introduced to scholars we would not have known if not for the editors' erudition and acumen. The collected commentaries, I feel, are a testimony to the moral weight of scholarship—to the all-consuming labor of searching through the knowledge in one's library and in one's head to find a reasonable, and perhaps even an exact, explanation of a word or of a statement attributed to a venerated man or someone in his circle.

The nineteenth-century scholar Liu Baonan was the first to

attempt a collected commentary on the *Analects* with a very broad scope. He gave his work a modest disguise as a subcommentary to the Han dynasty exegesis. This was the convention of his time, to acknowledge Han learning as the foundation of Qing scholarship. But one only needs to open Liu Baonan's *Collected Commentaries of the* Analects (*Lunyu zhengyi*) to realize how generous his vision was and how rigorous were his techniques. There have been other attempts since his, most notably that of Cheng Shude, but I decided to follow Liu because of my respect for the Qing scholars, for their polymathic minds and their trust in evidential research.

It took Liu Baonan twenty-seven years to draw together *Collected Commentaries of the* Analects, and it was not quite finished when he died. I often wondered what spurred him on during those years. What possessed him as he pored over the *Analects*? Was it Confucius? Was it the scholarship? Was it the moral conundrums in this book? Did he know? Could he have singled out one thing? Liu Baonan did not make such distinctions, I decided, and this was the final lesson I learned from him: Scholarship draws you closer to someone from the distant past and to the difficult questions he asked, and, in the end, everything obsesses you—the scholarship, the man, and his questions.

I have known old scholars who had memorized the *Analects* when they were children and had then forgotten about the book as their interests took them to questions in history or geography, philology or cosmology. But then, one day, after they had lived for many years, they found themselves reciting what Confucius says in 14.31: "Not to anticipate deception and not to expect bad faith and yet to be the first to be aware of such behavior—this is proof of one's worthiness." Or what he says in 1.16: "Do not worry that other people do not know you. But be concerned that you do not know them." The words in the *Analects*, having been dormant for so long, suddenly sprang to life for them and became a source for reflection and self-understanding. But, they would add, this knowledge also "bolsters them up" and "gets them on their way."

Suggestions for Further Reading

The Cambridge History of Ancient China: From the Origins of Civilization to 221 B.C. Edited by Michael Loewe and Edward L. Shaughnessy. Cambridge: Cambridge University Press, 1999.

Chin, Annping. *The Authentic Confucius: A Life of Thought and Politics.* New York: Scribner, 2007.

Falkenhausen, Lothar von. *Chinese Society in the Age of Confucius (1000–250 BC).* Los Angeles: Cotsen Institute of Archaeology, UCLA, 2006.

Fingarette, Herbert. *Confucius—the Secular as Sacred.* New York: Harper & Row, 1972.

Graham, A. C. *Disputers of the Tao.* La Salle: Open Court, 1989.

Li, Wai-yee. *The Readability of the Past in Early Chinese Historiography.* Cambridge, MA: Harvard University Asia Center, 2007.

Makeham, John. *Transmitters and Creators: Chinese Commentators and Commentaries on the* Analects. Cambridge, MA: Harvard University Asia Center, 2003.

Mencius. *Mencius.* Translated by D. C. Lau. Harmondsworth: Penguin Books, 1970.

Pines, Yuri. *Foundations of Confucian Thought: Intellectual Life in the Chunqiu Period, 722–453 B.C.E.* Honolulu: University of Hawaii Press, 2002.

Schaberg, David. *A Patterned Past: Form and Thought in Early Chinese Historiography.* Cambridge, MA: Harvard University Asia Center, 2001.

Schwartz, Benjamin. *The World of Thought in Ancient China.* Cambridge, MA: Belknap Press of Harvard University Press, 1985.

Shaughnessy, Edward. *Rewriting Early Chinese Texts.* Albany: State University of New York Press, 2006.

Xunzi. *Xunzi: A Translation and Study of the Complete Works.* Translated by John Knoblock. 3 vols. Stanford: Stanford University Press, 1988–1994.

A Note on the Translation

This translation inherits nearly two thousand years of Chinese scholarship and four hundred years of Western attempts to span the language. In order to produce a version that is both new and true to the original, we must build on the scaffolding erected by scholars and readers of many kinds with a wide range of personal and historical circumstances.

Translations of all the passages cited in the commentaries are my own unless otherwise noted. Translations of titles of Chinese books are in the bibliography, not, for the most part, in the endnotes.

CHINESE CHARACTERS AND ROMANIZATION

Chinese characters in traditional form are provided in the appendices for Chinese terms and Chinese proper names. The more widely adopted *pinyin* romanization is used throughout this work.

Chronology of Chinese Dynasties

There are variants to the dates of early Chinese dynasties and opposing views about whether the Xia dynasty existed at all. I have followed the dates in *The Cambridge History of Ancient China* and K. C. Chang's argument in that volume about the Xia. Chang describes Xia as one among many contemporary states but the dominant polity, which explains why the early Chinese historians refer to it as a dynasty. Archaeological discoveries since 1959 seem to support the broad and sustained influence of a culture centered in northwestern Henan province. This culture could have been that of the Xia.

Legendary Emperors

Yao
Shun
Yu

The Three Dynasties

Xia	c. 1900–c. 1600 BC
Shang	1570–1045 BC
Zhou	1045–221 BC
Western Zhou	1045–771
Eastern Zhou	771–221
Spring and Autumn Period	770–481
Warring States Period	481–221

Qin Dynasty	221–207 BC
Han Dynasty	202 BC–AD 220
Western Han	202–AD 9
(Xin Dynasty, 9–23)	
Eastern Han	9–220
Three Kingdoms	220–280
Six Dynasties	220–589
Wei	220–265
Jin	265–420
Northern and Southern Dynasties	386–589
Sui Dynasty	581–618
Tang Dynasty	618–906
Five Dynasties	907–960
Song Dynasty	960–1279
Northern Song	960–1126
Southern Song	1127–1279
Yuan Dynasty	1279–1368
Ming Dynasty	1368–1644
Qing Dynasty	1644–1911

The Analects
(*Lunyu*)

BOOK ONE

1.1 The Master said, "Is it not a pleasure to learn [*xue*] and, when it is timely, to practice what you have learned? Is it not a joy to have friends coming from afar? Is it not gentlemanly not to become resentful if no one takes notice of your learning?"

An alternative translation of the first sentence might be: "Is it not a pleasure to learn and to repeat often what you have learned?" The differences in reading depend on how one understands the phrase *shixi*. The character *shi* could mean "timely" or "time and time again"; the character *xi* could mean "to practice" or "to repeat [like a bird flapping its wings] what one has learned." The Qing scholar Jiao Xun, for instance, cites the *Analects* 7:8, 6:21, and 11:22 to support his reading of *shi* as "timeliness." He says, "To be able to act in a timely way signifies a higher stage of learning" and so "gives one pleasure." Most scholars from the Six Dynasties and the Song prefer the other interpretation. Huang Kan, for instance, thinks that *shi* here means that "one should review daily what one has learned [each year and throughout his life], not letting a moment go to waste." My decision to side with Jiao Xun has to do with Confucius' fourth-century BC follower Mencius' characterization of Confucius as "a sage whose action was timely." Mencius believes that such a sage is superior to those who are merely "beyond defilement" or "politically responsible," and he regards timeliness in action as the culmination of learning—not just learning as a pile of knowledge but learning, *xue* (學), as Confucius instructed, to fulfill one's humanity both at home and in the broader world and learning to cultivate one's moral and aesthetic sensibilities. A man of this kind of learning will draw even people from afar to his side, but if others "do not take notice of" what he possesses, he will not mind, because he has done it for himself.

1.2 Master You [Youzi] said, "It is rare for a person who is filial to his parents and respectful to his elders to be inclined to transgress against his superiors. And it has never happened that a person who is not inclined to transgress against his superiors is inclined to create chaos. A gentleman looks after the roots. With the roots firmly established, a moral way will grow. Is it not true then that being filial to one's parents and being respectful to one's elders are the roots of one's humanity [ren]?

Master You (Youzi) is You Ruo, one of the younger disciples of Confucius. He, along with Zengzi, Zixia, Zizhang, and Ziyou, was probably responsible for drawing together an early version of the *Analects* to help these disciples transmit the teachings of Confucius. The *Book of Mencius* says that after Confucius died, "Zixia, Zizhang, and Ziyou wanted to serve You Ruo as they had served Confucius because of his resemblance to the sage;" and that "they tried to force Zengzi [Master Zeng] to join them" but Zengzi refused because for him no one could surpass the "immaculate" character of Confucius. Although Mencius' story is about loyalty, it also suggests disagreement among the disciples after Confucius' death as to how to interpret and how to enlarge Confucius' teachings. In fact, a comparison between what Youzi says here and what Zengzi says in 1.4 and 8.7 shows that Youzi sees familial rites as central to attaining social harmony while Zengzi focuses on introspection as the way to self-realization. They seem to be taking Confucius' teachings in two different directions, yet, in the end, both are trying to understand the source of our humanity, *ren* (仁).

There are several ways of reading 1.2, the most obvious of which is to say that Youzi advocates submission to one's superiors as the most expedient way of bringing about peace and harmony, but this simplifies what he is trying to convey about the moral efficacy of the rites. Deeper understanding can be gained from reading the commentaries of the Han, the Six Dynasties, and the Qing, where scholars give more attention to the individual words in this passage. Of the word *hao* (to be inclined to or to have a liking for), for instance, Huang Kan from the Six Dynasties, quoting an earlier scholar, says, "When parents make mistakes now and then, the son must admonish them but in a way that does not violate their self-respect [*bufan*]. And even if he has to repeat this a number of times, how could he have a liking for [*hao*] what he does? . . . A person who is filial to his parents and respectful to his elders [*xiaoti zhi ren*] will speak up for what is right when he has to, but since it is not his intention to transgress against his superiors [*fanshang*], it is certainly not his purpose to throw the existing social hierarchy into chaos." Such a reading is consistent with what Confucius says in 4.18.

1.3 The Master said, "A man of clever words and of a pleasing countenance is bound to be short on humanity."

The Qing scholar Liu Baonan points out that the early classics do not always use *qiao* (clever) and *ling* (pleasing) in a negative sense. But if clever words and a pleasing countenance are all that a man possesses, then he must be lacking in humanity; and, in fact, he could be a glib man, which was what Confucius detested and feared the most, because such a man could manufacture a semblance of humanity without possessing one, and he could be more menacing than those Youzi has in mind, men who have a liking for transgressing against their superiors.

1.4 Master Zeng [Zengzi] said, "Every day I examine myself on three points. When I worked to benefit someone else, did I do my best? In my relationship with my friends, did I fail to be trustworthy? Did I pass on any knowledge I myself had not put into practice?"

Master Zeng (Zengzi) was Zeng Can, the youngest of Confucius' disciples and someone who could not have been under Confucius' tutelage for very long. Of this man Confucius says only that he was "slow," held back, perhaps, by his constant self-examination. Yet it was Zengzi's understanding of Confucius—further refined and expanded by Confucius' third-generation disciple Mencius—that dominated later Confucian thought. Here Zengzi lays the groundwork for Mencius' own teaching on the virtue of introspection, which Wang Yangming in the sixteenth century took to even a deeper level, arguing for introspection regarding not just one's action but also one's intention. The title of Wang's major work, *Chuanxilu (A Record of Knowledge Learned through Practice*), is also a direct reference to the question Zengzi asks himself: "Did I pass on any knowledge I myself had not put into practice?"

1.5 The Master said, "In guiding a state of a thousand chariots, handle all matters with care and respect, and be trustworthy; take a measured approach in your spending, and cherish the people. Employ the common people only at the right time."

Scholars over the centuries could not agree on just how large a state of a thousand chariots was in the Spring and Autumn period. The contemporary scholar Yang Bojun, using the *Zuo Commentary* (the most reliable source of this period) and *Analects* 11:26 as his support, argues that in the early Spring and Autumn this would refer to a powerful state with considerable land, but by Confucius' time this was no longer true. (The *Zuo Commentary* says that in the thirteenth year of Duke Zhao [529 BC, twenty-two years before Confucius was born], the state of Jin had in its possession four thousand chariots.) Both Han and Qing scholars point out that the word *jing* (敬), "respect," suggests *jing* (警), "vigilance"—that if a person is attentive to the affair put in his charge from beginning to end, he is bound to be successful. To "employ the common people at the right time" means to employ people for state projects or military service only at a time when they can be spared from their own work on the land. The Song thinker Cheng Yi observes that the guidelines Confucius sketched out may seem "elementary," but "even the rule of the sage emperors Yao and Shun was no more than a fulfillment of these principles."

1.6 The Master said, "A youngster should be filial to his parents when he is at home and respectful to his elders when he is away from his home. He should be prudent in action and trustworthy in words. He should cherish all people but should stay close to the most humane. And if he has energy left to do more, he should devote himself to the arts."

According to the *Book of Rites*, a child from an elite family would spend nearly all his time with his parents in the first ten years of his life. After that, he would have to "leave home and seek instruction elsewhere." Learning the appropriate way of expressing his affection toward his parents while he is home, will, therefore, prepare him to be respectful to his elders when he is outside the home. What Confucius stresses in this passage and throughout the *Analects* is the importance of grasping the fundamentals of human relationships in early life, before one sets out into the world. Thus, he feels, the cultivation of correct conduct and character should come before a literary education and an education in the arts, *wen* (文). This poses a problem for later scholars like Zhu Xi, who says, "If a person focuses his effort on perfecting his conduct and does not learn from the written words [*wen*], then there is no way for him to study the accomplishments of the former sages and worthies and no way for him to know what things ought to be, and so his action might be the result of selfish intent."

1.7 Zixia said, "If a person is able to appreciate moral worth as much as he appreciates physical beauty, is able to serve his parents with the utmost effort and his lord with no self-interest, and in his relationship with friends is trustworthy in words, though he may say that he lacks learning, I would surely call him learned."

There has been much discussion about the first clause and the word *yi* (易) in the sentence. Many scholars say that the first clause refers to the relationship of husband and wife; that since this relationship is "the beginning of all relationships," Confucius' disciple Zixia "speaks about it first, before the relationship of parents and children, of rulers and ministers," and the relationship between friends. But just what Zixia is trying to say about this man as a husband is a subject of intense debate, because the word *yi* (易) here could mean "to be just like something" or "to regard something lightly." Thus the man could be someone who is able to appreciate his wife's moral worth as much as he appreciates her physical beauty, or he could be someone who appreciates her moral worth but regards her physical beauty lightly. The first reading, I feel, is subtler and seems consistent with how Zixia feels about the bond between the moral and the aesthetic. In 3:8, for instance, he suggests that a woman looking after her appearance can be used as a trope for moral improvement. What is also interesting about Zixia here is that he does not quite fit Confucius' description of him—that "he is good in literary learning"—because in 1:7 his words seem to reinforce what Confucius says in 1:6—that lessons in human relationships have more weight than literary education.

1.8 The Master said, "If a man of position [*junzi*] does not have integrity, he will not inspire awe. And when he tries to learn, he will not persevere to the end. Such a man should stay close to those who do their best and are trustworthy. He should not befriend those who are not his equals. And when he makes a mistake, he should not be afraid to correct it."

This is one of those rare occasions in the *Analects* where the term *junzi* (君子) does not refer to "a man of noble character" or "a gentleman" but rather to "a man of noble birth" or "a man of position," which was the more common designation for *junzi* in early China before Confucius was born. Yet most scholars still understand *junzi* to mean "gentleman" here, which, as one commentary points out, does not make sense because a gentleman, in the context of the *Analects*, is already "someone of integrity" and so would not need a lecture from Confucius about how to reform his character. Besides the term *junzi*, the words *gu* and *zhu* have also generated some debate: whether *gu* means "steadfast" or "inflexible," and whether *zhu* means "to stay close to" or "to be guided by." If *gu* means "inflexible" and *zhu* means "to be guided by," the second and third sentences would read: "If he devotes himself to learning, he will not be inflexible. Let yourself be guided by the principles of doing your best and being trustworthy." I, however, feel that if Confucius is speaking about a man who lacks gravity, he thinks that such a man will not be steadfast in his learning. And if he asks this man "to stay close to those who do their best and are trustworthy," he would want to tell him also "not to befriend those who are not his equals." Of this last remark, nearly all the scholars agree that this does not refer to men who are not your social equals but rather refers to men whose character is not as good as yours. For, other than "to aggrandize yourself," what reasons could there be for you to make friends with those you have nothing to learn from?

1.9 Master Zeng [Zengzi] said, "Tend to the death rites of the recently deceased with utmost care and respect, and do not forget to offer sacrifices to the long-departed; then people will have much to gain in the cultivation of their virtue."

Zengzi says in 19:17 that he has heard his teacher say that only on the occasion of mourning for one's parents is a man able to realize himself to the full. Here he must be urging the ruler to perfect himself in this way, because, as Confucius observes in 12:19, a ruler with a cultivated self will have a moral influence on his people.

The *Jitong* chapter of the *Book of Rites* says, "There are three ways of caring for one's parents: when they are alive, look after them; when they are deceased, tend to the death rites; when the death rites have been completed, offer them sacrifice." It also says, "To conduct sacrifice is to keep on caring for one's parents; it is to continue the act of filiality."

1.10 Ziqin asked Zigong, "When the Master goes to another state, he invariably learns about its government. Does he get his information by asking or is it offered to him?"

Zigong said, "The Master acquires his information by being affable, kind, and respectful, and by showing restraint in his action and a willingness to yield. The way the Master asks for information is different from that of other people."

Ziqin and Zigong were both disciples of Confucius, with Ziqin being the much younger of the two. And unlike Zigong, who was at Confucius' side throughout most of the latter's fourteen-year journey, Ziqin could not have known how Confucius conducted himself when he was in a foreign state, and so he asked this question.

Liu Baonan, citing a commentary by his contemporary Wu Jiabin, says that most rulers would keep a tight lid on what they knew about the affairs of their government, especially when they were around outsiders. But when they met Confucius, it seemed natural for them to share their knowledge with him. Such was the force of his presence, which, as Zigong explains, had nothing to do with skills of entreaty or persuasion.

1.11 The Master said, "When your father is alive, observe what he would like to do. After your father is dead, reflect on what he has done. If for three years you refrained from altering your father's ways, you can be called filial [*xiao*]."

The Song scholar Fan Zuyu says that when the father is alive, a filial son is someone who will look to see what might be his father's wishes. (Zengzi's relationship with his father as described in the *Mencius* is an example.) This reading is different from that of the Han scholars Kong Anguo and Zheng Xuan, which says, "When the father is alive, you can only observe what the son intends to do," not what he does, if you want to gauge his character, because, out of respect for his father, the son is not yet able to act independently. The Qing scholar Qian Daxin professes that he prefers Fan's reading because "what Confucius says here is about filial behavior," "not about how to observe a man's [the son's] character," which is the understanding of the Han scholars. Many commentaries try to explain why Confucius thought that a filial son would try not to change his father's ways in the three years after the father's death. What if the father's conduct was far from being perfect? The Qing scholar Wang Zhong feels that this is simply "the hard truth of being filial [*xiao* 孝]": "If this principle does not exist, then the son upon his father's death in the morning could very well change the father's ways by evening time." Kong Anguo and Liu Baonan say, "When a filial son is in mourning and is still yearning for his departed parent, he feels as if his parent is still alive and so he simply cannot bring himself to alter his father's ways." I find it interesting that Confucius asks the son "to observe" and "to reflect" (*guan*) rather than "to carry out" his father's intent or "to carry forward" his action. Thus in the case where the father's character is wanting, it is up to the son to amend the father's mistakes and to carry out what the father cannot accomplish, but only after he has spent three years in mourning and in quiet reflection on his father's conduct; in the meantime he should "refrain from altering his father's ways."

1.12 Master You [Youzi] said, "Harmony is what is most prized in the practice of the rites [li]. It is what makes the way of the former kings beautiful, and this [principle] applies to matters big and small. Yet it does not always work: if you aim only at achieving harmony [in everything] because you know that it is the ideal and do not let the rules of the rites guide your action, it will not work."

The late Tang–early Song scholar Xing Bing offers a different interpretation of the second half of this passage. He believes that Youzi was addressing the ruler, asking him not just to follow the ritual rules, li (禮), rigidly "in matters big and small" or to "aim only at achieving harmony [he 和]." What Youzi meant, Xing Bing writes, is that a ruler should "use music to harmonize the heart [and emotions] of the people and the rites to check their conduct." Many translations follow the gist of this explanation, though scores of traditional scholars disagree with it. These scholars feel that in his comments Youzi had only the rites in mind and his concern was about how to achieve harmony every step of the way and "in matters big and small." "Harmony here refers only to the rites," Liu Baonan writes, "not to music."

1.13 Master You [Youzi] said, "Trustworthiness comes close to rightness because your words can be counted on. Respectfulness comes close to ritual propriety because it allows you to stay clear of shame and disgrace. If you do not lose the affection of those who are your relatives by marriage, then you could have the respect of your clan."

Youzi stresses that trustworthiness, xin (信), only "comes close to rightness [yi 義]" and respectfulness, gong (恭), only "comes close to ritual propriety [li 禮]," thus suggesting that rightness and ritual propriety are harder to attain. Huang Kan gives an example of

Weisheng of Lu, who lived up to his word but was so inflexible that his action could not have been right. This man waited under a bridge for a woman at an appointed time and day. A sudden downpour caused the stream to flood, and the man, unwilling to go back on his word, held on to the pillar of the bridge as the water rose and was drowned. The Tang scholar Li Ao uses the example of a well-known figure in the history of the Spring and Autumn period to illustrate how a person might be respectful but act contrary to the idea of propriety and the spirit of the rites. The man, Shen Sheng, was an heir apparent in the state of Jin. His father was infatuated with a consort, who coveted Shen Sheng's position for her own son. And when this woman falsely accused him of intending treachery against his own father, Shen Sheng refused to clear his name because, he said, he did not want to castigate her, the only person who could bring comfort to his father in his old age. Finally, Shen Sheng took his own life. Of this man, Li Ao says that he "died out of his respect for his father" and his action was "contrary to the spirit of the rites": "He would have understood the rites if he was able to be respectful to his father without having to die for it."

1.14 The Master said, "A gentleman does not try to stuff himself when he eats and is not worried about the comfort of his dwelling. He is anxious about getting things done and careful about what he says. He gravitates toward those who possess moral integrity because he wants to put himself right. One could say that he is someone who loves learning."

Confucius' disciple Yan Hui exemplified the gentleman in this description. According to his teacher, Yan Hui was "the most eager to learn" and was content to be "living in a shabby neighborhood on a bowlful of millet and a ladleful of water." Neither poverty nor any circumstances of life could have vexed him, because he was driven by a love for the good and a desire for learning.

1.15 Zigong said, "'Poor but not ingratiating, rich but not arrogant'—what do you think of this saying?"

The Master said, "That is all right, but better still is 'poor but joyful, rich but loving the rites.'"

Zigong said, "The *Odes* says:

> 'Like bone filed, like tusk smoothed,
> Like jade carved, like stone polished.'

Is this what you mean?"

The Master said, "Si [Zigong], only with you can one discuss the *Odes*. Someone tells you something and you can see its relevance to what is not said."

The conversation here is about refinement. Confucius takes what Zigong has said and makes it sharper and subtler. Men who are "poor but joyful" or "rich but loving the rites" are larger in mind and spirit than those who are merely holding on to their integrity by not being ingratiating when poor or arrogant when rich. Zigong grasps his teacher's point right away, and in response he declaims a poem that compares the refinement of a gentleman (*junzi*) to "jade carved and stone polished." Confucius must have been pleased with what he heard because Zigong not only could "see the relevance to what is not said" but also spoke his thought in the voice of the *Odes*. Confucius therefore remarks, "only with you can one discuss the *Odes*."

1.16 The Master said, "Do not worry that other people do not know you. But be concerned that you do not know them."

Most commentaries since the Song understand the second sentence to mean that because it is important to stay close to the worthy and to keep a distance from the unworthy it would be to a person's disadvantage if he did not know how to judge others. Earlier commentaries, however, approach Confucius' remark from the perspective of human nature. Huang Kan says, "Human beings have a tendency to make little effort to understand others but to blame others for not understanding them. This is the point Confucius was trying to make."

BOOK TWO

2.1 The Master said, "To rule by virtue is like the way the North Star rules, standing in its place with all the other stars revolving around it and paying court to it."

"To rule," *zheng* (政), is "to correct oneself," *zheng* (正), which means "to rule by virtue." Confucius says in 12:17, "When you set an example by correcting your mistakes, who will dare not to correct his mistakes?" The Qing scholar Song Xiangfeng writes that a true king "takes as his example the working of heaven," whose authority lies in its integrity or virtue, *de* (德). But a king, unlike heaven, is human. And even someone who is born with a large measure of humanity has to make an effort to acquire his virtue "by correcting his own action." Most scholars, following the explanation of the Han scholar Bao Xian, say that this way of governing is the same as to govern "by doing nothing." Some scholars, however, argue that "to govern by virtue" is "doing something," only that "the doing has a semblance of doing nothing"; therefore, even the sage emperor Shun, who, as Confucius says, "ruled by doing nothing," did something—"by holding himself in a reverent position and facing south."

2.2 The Master said, "The three hundred poems from the *Book of Poetry* could be summed up in a single phrase: "They never swerve from the path [*siwuxie*].""

The phrase *siwuxie* (思無邪), which Confucius plucked from *Ode 297*, describes the act of driving a team of horses in the wild—the horses are "spurred on and reined in" but "never swerve from the path."

Scholars who understand *siwuxie* as "having no depravity in intention," I feel, miss not only the resonance in the original poem but also an important aspect of Confucius' teachings, which assumes that our nature is sinewy and that we, too, need to be spurred on and reined in as we race down the path of human life. Confucius in 3.20 illustrates the idea of never swerving from the path through his reading of a love poem, the *guanju*. The Confucian thinker Xunzi, from the third century BC, makes a similar point when he says, "there is sensuality in the *guofeng* section of the *Book of Odes*": "These poems satisfy the yearnings [of the poet] but do not err by going too far."

2.3 The Master said, "If you guide the people with ordinances and statutes and keep them in line with [threats of] punishment, they will try to stay out of trouble but will have no sense of shame. If you guide them with exemplary virtue [*de*] and keep them in line with the practice of the rites [*li*], they will have a sense of shame and will know to reform themselves."

2.3 is an extension of 2.1, but here the ruler does more than just stand in one place, like the North Star, and conduct his government by way of his virtue: he also keeps the people "in line with the practice of the rites." To Confucius, the *fengjian* enfeoffment system of the early Zhou dynasty came very close to being an ideal government because it was grounded in the integrity of the ruler and in the trust between the ruler and the relatives he sent elsewhere with vested power to create new colonies for the young empire. This government was further reinforced with the civilizing power of rites and music, and so it did not need complex laws and regulations to "keep [the people] in line."

2.4 The Master said, "At fifteen, I set my heart on learning. At thirty, I found my balance through the rites. At forty, I was free from doubts [about myself]. At fifty, I understood what Heaven intended me to do. At sixty, I was attuned to what I heard. At seventy, I followed what my heart desired without overstepping the line."

This is Confucius' description of his spiritual journey, which began with him setting his heart on learning and concluded with him letting his heart follow what it desired. In between, though, he found his balance through the rites and was able to relinquish whatever doubts he might have had about himself and to come to understand what Heaven intended him to do. Thus, at the end, when he simply followed his heart's desire, he did not "swerve from the path." And just as effortlessness is proof of a perfect rule, it suggests the culmination of a moral life.

2.5 Meng Yizi asked about being filial. The Master responded, "Do not abandon [the rites] [*wuwei*]."

When Fan Chi was driving the chariot, the Master told him about this conversation, saying, "Mengsun asked me about filiality, and I replied, 'Do not abandon [the rites].'"

Fan Chi asked, "What did you mean by that?"

The Master said, "When your parents are alive, observe the rites in serving them; when they die, observe the rites in burying them; observe the rites in sacrificing to them."

Meng Yizi was a member of the Mengsun family, one of the three hereditary families in the state of Lu. Meng Yizi's early ancestor, Qingfu, was a brother of the Lu ruler Duke Zhuang. Just what was Meng Yizi's relationship to Confucius was a subject of much debate. Some scholars believe that he was a disciple; others, that he was an adversary, the man who managed to thwart Confucius' plan to have the Three Families destroyed and who was therefore, in part, responsible for sending Confucius into exile. Fan Chi was a younger disciple of Confucius and a warrior known for his courage. According to the *Zuo Commentary*, in 484 BC, shortly before Confucius returned home from his exile, Fan Chi and another disciple, Ran Qiu, led the Lu army to victory in a battle against the Qi army.

The term *wuwei* (無違) is problematic because as a command it has no object, and in the context of Meng Yizi's question it could mean "Do not disobey your parents," which, of course, is not what Confucius had in mind. What Confucius means by "filiality," as he tells Fan Chi, is not to abandon the rites when you serve your parents, when you mourn their death, and when you sacrifice to them. One can get a clearer and more tangible idea of the relationship of rites to filiality in the next three passages, 2.6, 2.7, and 2.8.

2.6 Meng Wubo asked about being filial. The Master said, "Give your parents no cause for worry other than your illness."

Meng Wubo was the son of the Meng Yizi in 2.5. My reading follows that of the first-century scholar Ma Rong, who explains, "A filial son will not act thoughtlessly and unduly to bring grief to his parents; he allows his illness to be the only cause for their worry." Two other Han scholars propose a different reading, saying that a filial son "is someone who is always worried that his parents might fall ill." Both readings are possible, but the idea of filiality in Ma Rong's reading is more difficult to realize and is, therefore, more compelling.

2.7 Ziyou asked about being filial. The Master said, "Nowadays this is taken to mean being able to feed your parents. But dogs and horses can do as much. If you are not respectful, how are you different?"

Ziyou was one of Confucius' younger disciples. His appearance in Book Nineteen suggests that he was probably a compiler or an editor of the *Analects*. Confucius says that both "Ziyou and Zixia were good in the cultural arts and literary learning [*wen*]," yet 19.12 shows that the two did not get on after their teacher's death. Ziyou describes Zixia's teaching as one that ignores the roots and gives attention only to the tips. Zixia thinks that it is Ziyou who is confused about what should be taught first and what should be approached last.

The Han exegete Bao Xian points out that the third sentence here could mean either that dogs and horses are doing the providing (for humans or for their own parents) or that they are being provided for. Both readings make sense, but most Chinese commentaries follow the first (which is also my reading), while Zhu Xi's commentary and most English translations follow the second. Of this sentence and the last sentence, Burton Watson's rendering is "But we do as much for dogs and horses as well. If there is no reverence, how is it any different?"

2.8 Zixia asked about being filial. The Master said, "The difficult part is the facial expression. As for the youngsters taking on the burden when there is work to be done and the older ones being served first when there is food and wine, can this be called filial conduct?"

Bao Xian thinks that "the facial expression" refers to the expression on the parents' faces—that it is difficult for a son to be constantly watchful of his parents' expressions, looking for signs of pleasure and displeasure and of wishes waiting to be fulfilled. Another Han scholar, Zheng Xuan, however, feels that "the facial expression" refers to the son's expression—that it is difficult for a son to always maintain a gentle and affectionate demeanor when he is serving his parents, and that only a truly filial son could achieve this.

2.9 The Master said, "I can speak to Hui [Yan Hui] all day, and he does not disagree with me or question what I said. Thus it seems as though he were stupid. But afterward, when I observe what he does on his own, I realize that he is able to give full play to what he has learned. Hui is not stupid at all."

Hui, or Yan Hui, was Confucius' favorite disciple. He was so silent and diffident that even Confucius suspected at first that he might be slow and so could not think for himself. But when he looked further into it, Confucius discovered that Yan Hui preferred "to absorb quietly the knowledge that was presented to him" and then practice what he had learned when he was on his own. Yan Hui describes in 9.11 just how difficult his private quest for knowledge has been even with his teacher's guidance and encouragement.

2.10 The Master said, "Observe [shi] what a person does. Look into [guan] what he has done [you]. Consider [cha] where he feels at home. How then can he hide his character?"

Even though Confucius was rarely categorical in his judgment of others, he believed that it was possible, and, in fact, instructive, to try to understand the truth of a given person. He also encouraged his own disciples to look into themselves (as he had into himself) and to compare their strengths against those of people they knew well.

Traditional commentaries point out the difference between *shi* (視), "to observe," and *guan* (觀), "to look into," and Liu Baonan notes that *cha* (察), according to the Han dictionary, means "to mull over or to consider something." These commentaries also agree that *you* (由) refers to "experiences of the past" or "what one has done."

2.11 The Master said, "A person is worthy of being a teacher if he is able to gain new insights from chewing over what he already knew."

Wengu (溫故) means literally to "keep warm what one already knew." And the "person [who] is worthy of being a teacher" refers either to a person who keeps in mind what he has learned while trying to learn something new or a person who gains new insights by "chewing over what he already knew."

2.12 The Master said, "The gentleman [*junzi*] is not a vessel [*qi*]."

A gentleman, *junzi* (君子), is broad of spirit and intellectually agile; he can take on different problems and apply himself to many situations and so is not a vessel, a *qi* (器), for a specific use. This is the explanation offered by most commentaries. The eighteenth-century intellectual historian Zhang Xuecheng, however, proposes another way of considering the idea of *qi*. Each of Confucius' disciples, Zhang says, took something from their teacher and put it in a vessel, a *qi*, and what the disciple wanted to pass on to his own students was the stuff in the vessel. But this was only a specific understanding of what Confucius had taught, and if other disciples did not agree with it, it could become a source of feuding, which could last for generations. Zhang Xuecheng cites the disagreement between Zizhang and the disciples of Zixia in 19.3 as an early example and the animosity between the Zhu Xi school and the Lu Xiangshan school in the twelfth century as a later example. A gentleman, a *junzi*, however, would not have behaved this way: he would have welcomed a spirited debate, and he would not have perceived himself as a vessel—a receptacle of limited knowledge—in the first place.

2.13 Zigong asked about the gentleman [*junzi*]. The Master said, "He first puts his words into action. He then lets his words follow his action."

Some scholars suggest an alternative reading based on a different punctuation: "He acts first. Whatever he says will follow his action." In either case, the point of Confucius' remark is nicely summed up in the *Book of Rites*: "Because the gentleman is sparing of words and lets his action substantiate his trustworthiness, people will neither exaggerate his strengths nor downplay his weaknesses."

2.14 Confucius said, "The gentleman [*junzi*] is fair-minded and generous; he is not partisan or divisive. A petty man [*xiaoren*] is partisan and divisive; he is not fair-minded or generous."

This is the first time that the term *xiaoren* (小人) is used to refer to someone who is the opposite of a *junzi* (君子). Liu Baonan points out that *xiaoren* could refer either to "a lowly person" or to "a person without any integrity," and that here Confucius has the latter in mind. Most commentaries say that the gentleman, the *junzi*, is able "to glue people together" because he conducts affairs "by way of fairness [*yi*]" and "is trustworthy," while the petty man, the *xiaoren*, "looks after his own benefit" and "likes to enlist you in his clique and separate his interest" from the public interest. 2.14, together with 2.12 and 2.13, gives us a description of some of the basic traits of a gentleman: he is broad-minded and fair; he is responsible and trustworthy; and he is not a "vessel."

2.15 The Master said, "If you learn but do not think, you will be dazed. If you think but do not learn, you will be in danger."

Liu Baonan explains the first sentence by way of the two early Confucian thinkers, Mencius and Xunzi. Mencius says, in 6A:15, "The function of the heart-and-mind [*xin*]" is to reflect and think. "If you reflect [on what you've learned], then you are getting something. But if you don't think, then you won't get anything." Xunzi says, in "Encouraging Learning," "The learning of the gentleman enters his ear, clings to his mind, spreads through his four limbs, and manifests itself through his body. His smallest word, his slightest movement can serve as a model. The learning of the petty man enters his ear and comes out his mouth. With only four inches between ear and mouth, how can he have possessed it long enough to ennoble a whole body?"

Of the second sentence, Liu Baonan lets Confucius offer his own gloss: "Once I spent a whole day without eating and a whole night without sleeping, in order to think. It was no use. It would have been better to use that time to learn."

2.16 The Master said, "To pursue strange theories or to get sidetracked in your studies can only bring harm."

What Confucius says here is difficult to interpret because the term *yiduan* from the fourth century BC onward refers to "heterodox teachings." Mencius speaks of the teachings of Yang Zhu and Mo Di as *yiduan*, and the Song Confucians regard the teachings of the Buddhists and Daoists as *yiduan*. But it would be anachronistic to read 2.16 in that way. The Wei scholar He Yan says that Confucius did not think that there was only one way of pursuing learning. "The moral way has a unifying force," he explains: "Thus different paths of learning [with the same moral drive] will converge at the same point. *Yiduan* refers to paths that will not converge at that point." Other commentaries point to Zixia's remark in 19.4, saying that *yiduan* could mean "byways of learning [*xiaodao*]" that have their worth but could get a person sidetracked or bogged down in his studies. The word *gong* poses another problem. *Gong* can mean either "to attack" or "to pursue one's studies." Those who understand *gong* to mean "attack" offer this reading: "The Master said, 'To attack those with incorrect disquisitions is to put an end to harm.'" But scholars such as Jiao Xun take it to mean the opposite: "To attack those with a different point of view is to bring harm."

2.17 The Master said, "You [Zilu], do you know what I have been trying to teach you? To say that you know something when you know it and to say that you do not know something when you do not know it—this is true knowing [*zhi*]."

Alternative readings of the first sentence are: "You, shall I tell you what it means to know something?" and "You, pay close attention to what I am going to teach you." You, or Zilu, was a disciple and a political ally of Confucius before the latter was forced to leave Lu. Only nine years younger than his teacher, Zilu was known for his bravery and loyalty. But he was also quick to take offense and quick to act. Thus it seems appropriate that Confucius' instruction here is directed to him. In his essay "On the Way of Sons" (*Zidao*), Xunzi gives a more elaborate version of 2.17. Yet his explanation in "The Accomplishments of the *Ru*" (*Ruxiao*) is more insightful. Speaking about the "cultivated *ru*," men who were educated and with a vast knowledge of ritual practice, Xunzi says, "When they know something, they say that they know it. When they do not know something, they say that they do not know it. Within, they do not delude themselves about what they know or do not know. Without, they do not deceive others about what they know or do not know." What Xunzi understands about Confucius' instruction for Zilu in 2.17 is not just that Zilu should be honest about what he knew but that he had to be certain that what he thought he knew was not a delusion.

2.18 Zizhang was studying with the hope of obtaining an official position. The Master said, "Use your ears well and widely, and leave out what is suspect; speak with caution about the rest, and you will make few mistakes. Use your eyes well and widely, and stay away from potential perils; act with caution even after the perils are kept at bay, and you will have few regrets. To make few mistakes in your speech and to have few regrets in your action—these are the keys to securing a career as a salaried official."

Zizhang was clever and articulate, the quickest among the younger group of disciples. His classmates thought him arrogant, but even they had to admit that he was "difficult to emulate." Zizhang asked shrewd questions. In fact, some of the finest observations Confucius makes about human nature and moral refinement came out of his conversations with Zizhang. Here the subject seems to be something practical: Zizhang wants some advice about how to get a government job, and Confucius offers him a few professional secrets. Yet scholars over the centuries like to give Confucius' response a moral tone. Zheng Xuan, for instance, says, "If a person in his speech and action follows Confucius' advice, even though he might not secure an official position, he will have acquired the way of preparing for an official career." Liu Baonan in his gloss of Zheng Xuan's comment says, "In ancient times, the way of recommending men from the local villages and districts for office was to select those who were excellent in conduct and in learning. Thus 'to make few mistakes in speech and to have few regrets in action' implies that a person has acquired the way of preparing for an official career. But during the Spring and Autumn period [Confucius' time], this way of recommendation was essentially abandoned. Members of the hereditary families had a monopoly over government offices. Worthy men lived in reclusion and most of them did not have an official career. Thus Zheng Xuan felt that 'to make few mistakes and have few regrets' and yet not to have gotten an official position was the same as what the ancients considered as having acquired the way of preparing for an official career."

2.19 Duke Ai asked, "What should I do to make the common people come under my sway?" Confucius replied, "Promote the upright and place them above the crooked, and the people will be in awe of you and come under your sway [*fu*]. The opposite will happen if you promote the crooked and place them above the upright."

Duke Ai was the ruler who invited Confucius to come home to Lu in 484 BC. He reigned from 494 to 466, but for much of that time, the hereditary families were in control of the Lu government and the Lu army, and Duke Ai had no authority, no sway, over his people. And because of this, scholars such as Liu Baonan try to historicize the exchange in 2.19, saying that Duke Ai was asking Confucius for advice about how to wrest power away from the Three Families. In response, Confucius told his ruler about the power of moral conduct: if you place the upright over the crooked, the people will naturally bend toward your way, and you do not have to force them to submit to you. Most translators understand *fu* as "to submit." Traditional commentaries, however, point out that *fu* here implies that the people are "genuinely convinced" (*xinfu*) and that they are "in awe of" the ruler and "want to serve him." Thus I translated *fu* as "to come under the sway of," which is consistent with Confucius' response to the head of the Jisun family in 12.19.

2.20 Ji Kangzi asked, "How can I get the common people to be respectful, to do their best, and to encourage each other to strive forward?" The Master said, "Oversee the people with dignity, and the people will be respectful. Honor the elderly, cherish the young, and the people will do their best. Acknowledge the good, teach the incompetent, and the people will encourage each other to strive forward."

Ji Kangzi was the head of the Jisun family, chief counselor to Duke Ai, and the most powerful political figure in Lu around the time when Confucius returned from his exile. Several of Confucius' disciples, most notably Ran Qiu and Fan Chi, were in his personal service. Even though Confucius sometimes treated Ji Kangzi as an adversary, when Ji Kangzi asked for advice, Confucius did not turn him away. Here Confucius tells Ji Kangzi essentially what he told Duke Ai: If you cultivate yourself and are morally responsible, the people will behave the same way.

2.21 Someone said to Confucius, "Why do you not take part in government?" The Master said, "The *Book of Documents* says, 'Filial, only be filial, and a friend to your older and younger brothers—this has an influence on the way of government.' To do this is to take part in government. Why must I take on a position in order 'to take part in government'?"

The Han text *Summary of the Discussions in the White Tiger Hall* (*Baihutong*) says that "this conversation must have taken place after the eleventh year of Duke Ai [484 BC]," after Confucius had come home from his travels. Liu Baonan agrees, saying that after his return to Lu Confucius still "wanted to know about the goings-on in his government but he refused to pursue any official position," which was the reason why someone asked him this question. According to the history in the *Zuo Commentary*, Confucius was welcomed back to Lu as the "elder statesman" (*guolao*). The ruler, Duke Ai, and the chief counselor, Ji Kangzi, went to him for advice, but he was no longer interested in taking up a government office. Liu Baonan also argues that it was not a coincidence that the conversation in 2.21 followed Confucius' talk with Duke Ai in 2.19 and with Ji Kangzi in 2.20.

2.22 The Master said, "If a person does not have the trust of others, I don't see how he can get anywhere. A large cart without a linchpin in its yoke bar and a small cart without a linchpin in its collar bar—how can you get them to go anywhere?"

Either a large cart drawn by oxen or a small cart drawn by horses, without a linchpin in its yoke or collar bar, simply could not perform its function. It is the same with words that no one trusts, Gu Menglin says, "they have no vehicle to put them into motion."

2.23 Zizhang asked, "Can we know what things will be like ten generations from now?"

The Master said, "The Yin followed the rites of the Xia, and what was added and subtracted can be known. The Zhou followed the rites of the Yin, and what was added and subtracted can be known. Whoever succeeds the Zhou, even a hundred generations from now, will be able to know [what was added and subtracted from the rites of the Zhou]."

An alternative translation of the last sentence is: "Whoever succeeds the Zhou, we are able to know what things will be like even a hundred generations from now." The two readings reflect the two sides of a debate: Is Confucius stressing the importance of studying the past?

Or is he saying that it is possible to predict the future? The Song scholar Hu Anguo and the Qing scholar Chen Feng prefer the first reading, and most of the Han scholars prefer the second. Hu Anguo says that Confucius did not really answer Zizhang's question about whether it was possible to know the future because he was more interested in the past. This, I feel, agrees with the Confucius we find in the *Analects*—someone who used history to elucidate his teachings. It also concurs with Sima Qian's understanding of this passage in his biography of Confucius, which says, "Confucius pursued the study of the rites of the Three Dynasties. He compiled and edited all the events related to this subject, noting what was added and subtracted from the rites after the Yin succeeded the Xia so that these things can be known even a hundred generations from now." This, of course, represents the historian's interpretation and is the one I favor.

Even though traditional scholars cannot agree on how to read the last sentence of 2.23, they all seem to think that Confucius' response to Zizhang is about the relationship of constancy and change. The constants are those principles in human relationship—humaneness and rightness, for instance—that rely on the rites for support and fulfillment. "Change" refers to ritual implements and clothing, standards of weights and measurement, minor rules and regulations—things that could vary because of practical considerations and changing customs. Confucius' point in 9:3 is an example.

2.24 The Master said, "To offer sacrifice to spirits who are not your ancestors is ingratiating. Faced with what is right yet doing nothing about it shows a lack of courage."

Han scholars question the intent of those who sacrifice to spirits that are not their ancestors. "This is flattery," Zheng Xuan writes. "Those who make such sacrifices are bribing the spirits, [any spirits], to seek their blessing." Such conduct is "contrary to the rites," He Xiu says, and so "no blessing could be conferred." Liu Baonan cites 3.6 as an example of the Jisun family behaving obsequiously by performing a sacrifice they were not entitled to and of Ran Qiu behaving in a cowardly way by doing nothing to stop a performance he knew to be contrary to the rites.

3.1 Confucius said of the Ji [Jisun] family: "They have eight rows of dancers to perform in their courtyard. If this can be tolerated, what cannot be tolerated?"

The Han scholar Ma Rong, with the support of the early texts, explains that according to the ritual guidelines of the Zhou, the Son of Heaven was entitled to have eight rows of eight dancers perform in the courtyard of his ancestral temple, the regional rulers six rows of eight, the chief counselors four rows of eight, the salaried officials two rows of eight. The head of the Ji family was only a chief counselor in the service of the regional ruler, yet he had eight rows of dancers. One could say that his extravagant display showed only a lack of restraint, but Confucius regarded the ritual violation as a sign of the decline of the Zhou and of the collapse of her *fengjian* political system. Records in the *Zuo Commentary* suggest that Confucius was right: in 562 BC, eleven years before Confucius was born, the Jisuns appropriated the state army for the private use of their family and two other families with hereditary status; and by the time Confucius returned home from his journey in 484, the Jisuns were collecting more land taxes than the ruler of Lu.

3.2 The Three Families had the *yong* ode performed when the sacrificial vessels were being cleared away. The Master said,

> "'Assisting are the great lords,
>   The Son of Heaven, solemn and dignified.'

What significance could there be when these lines are sung in the halls of the Three Families?"

The *yong* (Ode 282) is found in the *Zhousong* ("Hymns of the Zhou") section of the *Book of Poetry*. Confucius' remark here should be read with that in 3.1, since both refer to the ritual violations of the hereditary families. "The Three Families" refers to the Jisuns, the Shusuns, and the Mengsuns, the three hereditary families in the state of Lu. The families were created about a hundred years before Confucius was born, as a desperate measure to address a succession crisis. Over the course of three years, from 662 to 659 BC, three brothers of a recently deceased ruler, Duke Zhuang, were deadlocked over the question of who should be his heir. In the end, the oldest of the three, also the most powerful, forced the middle brother to commit suicide but offered to make his family hereditary, so that this man "would always have descendants in Lu." This was how the Shusuns came into being. The youngest brother was tougher. After he had eliminated the two young rulers his oldest brother had helped to install, he was driven out of Lu, and, with nowhere to go, he, too, took his own life. After he died, the state of Lu guaranteed a permanent home and hereditary status for his descendants. This was the beginning of the Mengsun family. The winner of this political struggle, Jiyou, after his brothers died, also instituted a hereditary slot for his family, the Jisuns.

3.3 The Master said, "Being human and yet lacking humaneness—what can such a man do with the rites? Being human and yet lacking humaneness—what can such a man do with music?

The sixth-century scholar Huang Kan suggests that 3.3 should be considered together with 3.1 and 3.2 as a critique of the conduct of the Three Families. Yet I prefer to give it a broader reading, seeing it as the foundation of Confucius' teaching of the rites (*li*)—that the rites have no relation to a person who lacks moral impulse. The *Book of Rites* offers another way of looking at this relationship. It says, "The rites embody the countenance—and are the manifestation—of humanity. Music represents its harmony."

3.4 Lin Fang asked about the working principle of the rites. The Master said, "An admirable question indeed! With regard to the rites as a whole, it is better to err on the side of being frugal than on that of being extravagant. With regard to the mourning rites, it is better to err on the side of showing too much emotion than on that of fussing over every detail."

Most scholars feel that the conversation between Confucius and Lin Fang, a ritual expert from Lu, is about the relationship of *wen* and *zhi*: refinement and natural proclivities, cultural form and innate character. Liu Baonan refers to Xunzi and the *Book of Rites* on this subject. Xunzi says, in "A Discussion of Heaven," that the rites are meant to help a person "find balance" "in the tug between the call for refinement and his natural proclivities." The *Book of Rites* says, "The rites in practice do not remain the same [they change with the circumstances]. By aiming to find the point where there is neither too much nor too little, they allow a person to hold on to his feelings and yet to be safe from the perils of excess." But here Confucius tells Lin Fang, if the balance is difficult to achieve, it is better to err on the side of "being frugal" and "showing too much emotion." This, too, is "the working principle of the rites."

3.5 The Master said, "The Yi and Di tribes with their rulers are not like the Chinese states, which have none."

An alternative reading is: "The Yi and Di tribes with their rulers are still inferior to the Chinese states, which have none." This is also the reading found in most of the English translations. Chinese scholars, however, are divided on the question of whether Confucius was belittling the Yi and Di or the Chinese states. The Tang–Song scholar Xing Bing, for instance, understands Confucius as saying: "Even though the Yi and Di tribes have their rulers, their conduct is not guided by the rites and they have no sense of rightness; even though the Chinese states, at times, are without their rulers, they have not abandoned the practice of the rites and they have a sense of rightness." The Song thinker Cheng Yi, however, feels differently. He believes that Confucius' utterance is a critique of the behavior of the Chinese—that "even the Yi and Di people have their elders and rulers, which is unlike the Chinese, who, in a state of disorder, are no longer making distinctions between above and below, superior and inferior." Two eminent Ming-Qing thinkers, Gu Yanwu and Wang Fuzhi, seem to agree with Cheng Yi's interpretation, and because these two men lived through a foreign conquest, it is possible, I feel, to understand their reading as a critique of the Ming, of the Chinese dynasty that was toppled in 1644.

3.6 The head of the Jisun family was getting prepared to make a sacrifice to Mount Tai. The Master said to Ran Qiu, "Can you stop him from going ahead with it?"

Ran Qiu said, "I cannot."

The Master said, "Alas! Who would have thought that the spirit of Mount Tai would know less about the rites than Lin Fang?"

Ran Qiu was a disciple of Confucius and a war hero; he was also a chief retainer in the Jisun family. He was probably the person who persuaded the ruler of Lu, Duke Ai, to invite Confucius to come home. Yet Confucius was not kind in his judgment of this disciple because Ran Qiu lacked moral courage. 3.6 is an example. Here Confucius asks Ran Qiu to stop the head of the Jisuns from performing a ritual that is the prerogative of his ruler. Ran Qiu responds: There is nothing I can do. To which Confucius says: In that case, the spirit of the mountain, being even more perceptive than a ritual expert like Lin Fang, would know the performance to be fraudulent and would not accept the sacrificial offering. Liu Baonan in his commentary suggests that we use 3.6 as a gloss of 2.24.

3.7 The Master said, "Gentlemen have no reason to contend. But, of course, there is the archery contest. Yet on such occasions, they bow and yield to each other as they ascend the steps to the hall; afterward, they descend the steps and drink together. Even when they compete, they are gentlemanly."

Chinese moral philosophers like to use archery as a trope for their teachings because the archer aims for the bull's-eye, a point that suggests the right balance in conduct and an upright character. The contest to be the best archer is also a gentlemanly activity because it is a test of one's own skill that does not involve any aggressive move in the game. The early ritual texts also gave the archery contest a political context, saying that when the king was about to make a sacrifice, the feudal lords were asked to recommend their own officials to take part in the occasion, and that the king would then stage an archery contest for the selection process. Here Confucius first says, "Gentlemen have no reason to contend." But then he remembers that they do compete in archery contests. Even so, he stresses, the rituals that guide them through the process can never lead them astray. Mencius, in the fourth century BC, takes the idea of archery to another level, seeing it as a pedagogical device and as a metaphor for moral cultivation.

3.8 Zixia asked, "What is the meaning of these lines: 'Her entrancing smile, dimpling, / Her beautiful eyes so animated and clear. / White renders the colors vibrant and distinct'?"

The Master said, "White is applied after the colors are put in."

"Does the practice of the rites, in a like manner, come afterward?"

The Master said, "It's you who have drawn my attention to such a reading. Only with you do I feel I can discuss the *Odes*."

Of those three lines Zixia quotes from Ode 57, only the first two survived in the received version of the *Book of Poetry*. Yet the third line is most important, for it is the subject of Zixia's conversation with Confucius and a topic of much debate among the later scholars. My reading follows that of the Han and of such Qing scholars as Dai Zhen, Ling Tingkan, and Liu Baonan. Yang Guishan and Zhu Xi of the Song, however, propose another reading of the poem and of Confucius' response to Zixia. First we have Zixia's question: "What is the meaning of these lines, 'Her entrancing smile, dimpling, / Her beautiful eyes so animated and clear. / Distinct colors upon a white background'?" To which Confucius replies, "Painting the colors comes after the white background." The difference between these two interpretations, as several Qing scholars point out, lies in how one perceives a person's natural state—whether it is rich and variegated or plain and innocent. If one's natural state is rich and variegated, as the Han scholars argue, then "the white" in the poem refers to a technique described in an early work on artisans, the *Kaogongji*, which says that white paint is applied with a thin brush "in between the colors to create a pattern." This technique could be compared to the practice of the rites because the rites are able to bring out the brilliance in what is inborn by giving it a distinction and a measure of integrity. And "in the case of a woman endowed with natural charm and beauty," one Han scholar says, "she would need the practice of the rites to perfect them."

Scholars in the West tend to follow the Song reading, seeing "the white" as the plain and immaculate background (and Confucius' idea of human nature), and "colors" as the richness and refinement that ritual practice can bring to a life that is pure at the beginning. I find this interpretation to be more a reflection of the moral agendas of the Song Confucians than what Confucius taught about the rites. And why does Confucius say to Zixia, "Only with you do I feel I can discuss the *Odes*"? This is because in Confucius' response to the question he had asked about a poem, Zixia saw for himself the relevance this answer had in relation to the practice of the rites. It was, therefore, Zixia who drew his teacher's attention to such a reading. Confucius says the same about Zigong in 1.15, where Zigong is able to use a poem to gloss an idea the two have been discussing regarding the rites.

3.9 The Master said, "I am able to speak about the rites of the Xia, but the state of Qii is not able to provide the evidence to illuminate what I say. I am able to speak about the rites of the Shang, but the state of Song is not able to provide the evidence to illuminate what I say. This is because both the records and worthy men of erudition are insufficient in these two states. If they were [more plentiful], I could support my words with evidence."

The state of Qii was where descendants of the Xia were enfeoffed after the people of the Shang overthrew their dynasty. The state of Song was where the descendants of the Shang were enfeoffed after the people of the Zhou overthrew the Shang. Here Confucius makes a forceful statement about the importance of keeping records and having men of integrity be in charge of them, without which someone like himself, with a vast knowledge of the rites, simply cannot support what he says with evidence. Some scholars say that Confucius' remark was probably directed at the Lu rulers, who, being the descendants of one of the principal founders of the Zhou (the Duke of Zhou), should learn from this lesson and become responsible guardians of the Zhou culture.

3.10 The Master said, "As for the *di* sacrifice, after the libation, I have no wish to observe the rest of the ceremony."

According to Liu Baonan, the pouring of libationary wine to entice the spirit of the first progenitor to descend to the ancestral hall "should have occurred at the start of the *di* sacrifice." And for Confucius to say that he wished to leave when the ceremony had just begun must have meant that he disapproved of the way the *di* sacrifice was conducted in the state of Lu—that in his view "the performance was against the spirit of the rites." But what is the *di* sacrifice? Most of the knowledge that we have about this ritual comes from three chapters of the *Book of Rites*: "Record of Minor Points Concerning the Mourning Dress," "The Great Treatise," and "A Summary Account of Sacrifices." All three point out that the *di* was "a grand sacrifice"—that "only a king could perform the *di*" for "the first progenitor of his ancestral line." Yet this ceremony was allowed in Lu, and in no other regional state, because the Duke of Zhou, whose son was enfeoffed in Lu, had accomplished so much for the Zhou dynasty as the regent to his young nephew King Cheng that after he died King Cheng decided to bestow on the state of Lu "the right to perform the *di* sacrifice" in order to honor this man.

3.11 Someone asked for an explanation of [the basis of] the *di* sacrifice. The Master said, "This is not something that I know. The person who knows it will be able to handle all the affairs in the world as easily as having them placed right here," and he pointed to his palm.

Most commentaries follow the Han scholar Kong Anguo, who explains that by responding that he did not know the *di* sacrifice Confucius was avoiding saying outright that he disapproved of the way it was practiced in Lu. But Confucius' answer also supports what the *Book of Rites* taught about the *di* sacrifice—that "only a king could perform the *di*." And if we add to this what he tells Zilu in 2.17 about knowledge and knowing, then Confucius could also be saying: Only a king is granted the right to perform the *di* sacrifice, and if he truly knows the underlying principles of this ritual, his knowledge will be evident in his action; such a ruler has the respect and trust of his people, and so it will be easy for him to manage the affairs in his empire.

3.12 "Sacrifice as if they were present" means sacrifice to the spirits as if the spirits were present. The Master said, "If I do not take part in the sacrifice, it is as if I did not sacrifice at all."

The description in the *Jiyi* chapter of the *Book of Rites* of a gentleman conducting a sacrifice to his deceased parent could serve as a gloss of the first sentence: "On the day of the sacrifice, he enters the room [of the ancestral temple where the rites will take place], and it seems to him that he sees the deceased. After the ceremony is over and he is ready to leave, he is still absorbed in what he thought was the voice of the deceased. And after he has exited the door, he can still hear faintly the sound of the deceased sighing. Thus the filiality taught by the former kings requires that the eyes of the son should never forget his parents' looks, nor his ears their voices; and that his heart should never forget what they were inclined toward and what they liked. Because he loves them completely, they continue to exist. And because he is true in his devotion, they could still appear to him." Thus it is the person who takes part in the sacrifice that makes the spirits present, and this, I believe, is Confucius' point.

3.13 Wangsun Jia asked, "What do you think of the adage 'Better to flatter the god of the kitchen hearth than the god of the southwest corner'?"

The Master replied, "The saying has got it wrong. When you have offended Heaven, there is no spirit you can pray to."

Early sources, including the records in the *Analects*, are able to provide some background to this exchange. When Confucius was in the state of Wei, he had trouble finding employment in the government of Duke Ling. Some people at the time suspected Confucius of being willing to get the ruler's attention through those who were closest to him—through either Duke Ling's wife Nanzi or the court doctor Yong Ju. And this, according to most of the commentaries, is what Wangsun Jia meant by the "southwest corner," which was the darkest spot in a room and, by analogy, Duke Ling's inner circle. Wangsun Jia himself was a chief counselor and a commander in the Wei army, and, like the god of the "kitchen hearth," which was an open space, he had influence in the public arena, in both the political world and the military world. Thus some scholars think that Wangsun Jia was telling Confucius, by way of an adage, Better to ask me for help instead of the ruler's personal attendants. And Confucius' response was a rebuke to such a suggestion or any suggestion that he would stoop so low as trying to get a job through private influence. Mencius, in his defense of Confucius' conduct in the state of Wei, says that if Confucius had been willing to find employment through improper means he would have approached Mi Zixia, who was Duke Ling's favorite courtier and Confucius' disciple Zilu's brother-in-law. In Mencius' view, the fact that Confucius did not ask for Mi Zixia's help shows that "he advanced in a manner that was appropriate and withdrew in a way that was morally right."

3.14 The Master said, "Zhou took stock of the two previous dynasties. Splendid is her culture! I follow the Zhou."

Zhou culture was built on that of the two earlier dynasties, the Xia and the Shang. The Zhou kings looked back on the ritual practices of the Xia and Shang and "made adjustments according to the changing times" and "the changing sentiments of their people." Since the Zhou had the advantage of retrospection and introspection, using the past as a mirror, her culture, in Confucius' view, was grander and more elegant. Moreover, Confucius himself had the benefit of being a native of the state of Lu, which, because of its association with the Duke of Zhou, served as the depository and the center of Zhou culture.

3.15 When the Master entered the Temple of the Great Ancestor, he asked questions about everything. Someone remarked, "Who said that the son of the man from Zou knew the practice of the rites? When he entered the grand temple, he asked questions about everything." When the Master heard this, he said, "Asking questions is the correct practice of the rites."

"The Temple of the Great Ancestor" refers to the temple of the Duke of Zhou. "The man from Zou" refers to Confucius' father, Shuliang He, who, according to Kong Anguo, had once been an administrator in the district of Zou. There are at least three ways of explaining why Confucius "asked questions about everything." Some scholars believe that Confucius "was extremely cautious" even though "he knew the rites well." Others say that because in performing the rites the rulers of Lu had used ritual utensils and robes and sacrificial animals that were the prerogatives of the Zhou king, Confucius asked questions in order to force the ruler and his counselors to defend their practice. I, however, feel that Confucius asked questions even though he knew the ritual rules well because for him each occasion was different and so he would approach the rites as if he were performing them for the first time. Asking questions heightens awareness and enlivens the ritual experience. Thus he said, "Asking questions is the correct practice of the rites."

3.16 The Master said, "It is stated, 'In ritualistic archery, the object is not hitting the hide [of the target] [zhupi] because men do not have equal strength.' This was the way of ancients."

The archery Confucius refers to was archery in a ritual context (lishe), which was performed to music and meant to enforce the idea of "the middle" (zhong), of finding a center in one's conduct and demeanor. This, according to the early ritual texts, was different from archery in a military exercise, where strength and accuracy were important. "To shoot an arrow means to let go—letting go one's intention and purpose," the *Book of Rites* says. "Thus with a composed mind and an upright posture, one is able to hold the bow and arrow steady. In this way, the arrow [like the mind's intention] will have a chance of reaching the center [*zhong*]." Most English translations, following the reading of the Song scholars, render *zhupi* as "piercing the hide." But Cheng Shude, citing the Han commentaries, says that *zhupi* simply meant "hitting the target," which "already implies a test of strength because one must be strong in order to send an arrow to the target."

3.17 Zigong wanted to do away with the practice of sacrificing a lamb in the ceremony of announcing the beginning of a month [*su*]. The Master said, "Si [Zigong], you don't want to waste a lamb, whereas I don't want to see the rite disappear."

It was the practice of the Zhou emperor in the first half of the dynasty to assemble the regional rulers in his capital sometime between late autumn and early winter to hand out the calendar for the next year that would indicate, for instance, whether there was to be a leap month. This was one way for him to assert his authority over his empire. Each of the regional rulers would take the calendar back to his ancestral temple, and he would mark the beginning of each month with an announcement and a sacrificial offering in the temple before holding court with his counselors. The ritual, called *su*, was related to the idea of "renewal" (*su*) and was meant to demonstrate that each month the ruler was ready to revitalize his government. But the practice stopped at the imperial level by the second half of the Zhou dynasty, and, by around 611 BC, about a hundred years before Confucius was born, most of the *su* ritual had disappeared in the state of Lu, save the sacrifice of the lamb. Thus Zigong says to his teacher, Why waste a lamb on a ceremony that no one cares about anymore? Even so, Confucius replies, he cannot let it go. The attachment he expresses is not just a reaction of his heart, because it could also mean that he is still hoping for a revival of the *su*. This is wishful thinking, perhaps, but it is understandable, given his belief in the political efficacy of the Zhou rites.

3.18 The Master said, "If in serving your ruler you try to do everything correctly by the rites, others will look upon you as being obsequious."

This is Confucius' observation on how others might perceive a person who, in serving his ruler, is attentive to the rites. Transgressions against correct behavior, in his view, had been going on for so long and had become so prevalent that the world was confused about right and wrong, and so people would regard a man who was vigilant about rules of propriety as "being obsequious."

3.19 Duke Ding asked, "How should a ruler treat his ministers, and how should the ministers serve their ruler?"

Confucius replied, "The ruler should treat his ministers in accordance with the rites. The ministers should serve their ruler by doing their best."

Duke Ding was the last ruler Confucius served in Lu, and someone who was partly responsible for Confucius' exile. The conversation must have taken place when Confucius was still the minister of crime in his government. It was around this time that Confucius was hoping to find some way to help Duke Ding take back the authority inherent in his position as the ruler of Lu, and here he suggests that the ruler should "treat his ministers in accordance with the rites." Scholars from the Han and Song understand these words to mean that if the ruler did not veer from the rules of propriety, his ministers would follow his example, and they would serve him by doing their best. But the Ming scholar Jiao Hong and the Qing scholar Yu Zhengxie propose another reading. Jiao Hong, quoting an early text, says, "'Only by way of the rites can one govern a state.' The system of the rites was the apparatus the former kings used to create titles and social distinctions and to weed out any shoots of disorder." Yu Zhengxie thinks that the rites (*li*) were different from etiquette (*yi*)— that Confucius could not be telling Duke Ding "to be even more respectful and yielding" to the counselors who had made him look like a minion. "The authority of the rites," Yu writes, "was the way by which a ruler could safeguard his country, implement his decrees, and hold on to his people."

3.20 The Master said, "In the *guanju* poem, there is joy but no immodest thoughts; sorrow but no self-injury."

Confucius told his son to learn the *Odes*, to let the poems teach him to speak, because the voices in them were always appropriate: they "never swerve from the path." And for him, the *guanju* ("Fishhawk"), the first poem from the *guofeng* section of the *Odes*, best illustrates this point. The voice in the poem is that of a young man, probably a prince, yearning for the woman he desires: "Wanting, sought her, had her not, / Waking, sleeping, thought of her." Yet the yearning does not leave the young man wretched, and his thoughts never stray. He does not make an obvious display of his feelings but instead enlists the help of the men and women in his community. "With harps we bring her company," the poem reads. "With bells and drums do her delight."

3.21 Duke Ai asked Zai Wo about the altar to the god of the soil [*she*].

Zai Wo replied, "The Xia used pine. The Shang used cypress. The Zhou used chestnut [*li*], in order, they say, to make the people tremble [*li*]."

When the Master heard about this, he said, "Don't try to explain what is already done. Don't attempt to remonstrate about what is finished. Don't decry what is already past."

Zai Wo became a disciple before Confucius was forced out of Lu in 497 BC. So, like Zigong, Yan Hui, and Zilu, Zai Wo was at Confucius' side when the latter was in exile.

The character *she* could refer either to the altar to the god of the soil or to this god's spirit tablet, and the wood—pine, cypress, or chestnut—could refer either to the material of the spirit tablet or to the trees planted around the altar. One simple explanation of Confucius' rebuke of Zai Wo for his remark is that Zai Wo, who had a reputation for being too clever for his own good, did not know what he was talking about. The trees planted around the altar of this god were those that suited the condition of the soil, which meant that the trees used could be different from region to region, state to state. Thus, Confucius thought, what Zai Wo said about the practice of the Xia and the Shang had no historical basis and his advice for Duke Ai—to plant chestnuts (*li*) "in order to make the people tremble [*li*]"—sounded pathetic. Most commentaries favor this explanation even though Confucius' response does not bear any direct relation to Zai Wo's conversation with Duke Ai. The Qing scholar Liu Baonan offers another theory. Liu believes that Zai Wo's reply to Duke Ai was a coded message, urging the ruler to act aggressively against the Three Families. And when Confucius heard about this, he realized what Zai Wo was trying to convey and advised against it, saying, "Don't decry what is past," meaning the action and deeds from the past that brought the ducal house to its decline.

3.22 The Master said, "Guan Zhong was a man of small capacity."

Someone said, "Does this mean that Guan Zhong was frugal?"

The Master said, "Mr. Guan had three residences, yet every officer on his staff had no separate duty other than the one he was assigned. How could this be considered frugal?"

"In that case, did he understand the rites?"

"Rulers of states put up gate screens [in front of their palaces]. Mr. Guan also put up a gate screen. Rulers of states, when entertaining another ruler, had an earthen stand to be used for wine cups after the guests had drained their cups. Mr. Guan also had such a stand. If Mr. Guan understood the rites, who does not understand the rites?"

Guan Zhong was closely associated with Duke Huan of Qi from the seventh century BC. Duke Huan was the most powerful and the most distinguished regional ruler of the Spring and Autumn period and the first to be given the title of lord protector (*ba*). And in the view of most historians, it was his counselor, Guan Zhong, who catapulted him to that position. Yet Confucius says that Guan Zhong was a man of small capacity. And when asked what he means by that, he goes about answering in an indirect way, by rejecting the suggestion that he said so because Guan Zhong either was frugal or had knowledge of the rites. This, of course, leaves the reader ample room for interpretation. Some scholars say that Guan Zhong showed his limitation as a counselor—and so was a man of small capacity—because under his guidance Duke Huan became only a lord protector and not a true king. The eighteen-century scholar Cheng Yaotian, however, offers a more elegant explanation. He says that a man of large capacity is someone who is able to "hold his accomplishment" without letting it overflow. Emperor Yao was such a man because "his integrity was like that of heaven and so he took heaven as the measure of his capacity." But Guan Zhong was not like Yao: "As his wealth became apparent, his excesses multiplied. By letting his three residences fill with officers and himself indulge in extravagances so that he could show off his riches, Guan Zhong was someone who could not contain his wealth." Confucius, however, was not stuck with his view of Guan Zhong as "a man of small capacity." In 14.16 and 14.17, he offers a powerful defense of this man when he considers Guan Zhong from a different perspective, which shows his flexibility as a judge of human character. And in this as in nearly all such cases, he tries to support every step of his evaluation with detailed knowledge of the person's conduct.

3.23 The Master, speaking about music with the Grand Musician [Zhi] of Lu, said, "This much can be known about music. It begins with vigorous playing [xiru]. And when it goes into full swing, [the sound] is pure and harmonious, [the notes are] bright and distinct, and [the passages] fluent and continuous until the music reaches the end."

Xiru could also mean "playing in unison," but my reading follows that of Zheng Xuan, who says that ceremonial music always begins with the playing of "metal instruments" because this has the power "to arouse an audience and stir their hearts." To this, Liu Baonan adds that after hearing the playing of bells, a person "would be happy to step into the music." Some commentaries say that the music being in "full swing" refers to the sound of the eight types of instruments (metal, stone, string, bamboo, gourd, earthen, hide, and wooden) coming together in a symphony. And "fluency" (yi) is the defining moment. It transcends the effort of playing in harmony, Liu Baonan notes, and allows the music to acquire a life of its own, which is "like the living impulse of plants and trees."

Mencius thinks that one could look at Confucius in light of what the latter said about music: Confucius could advance or retreat, take office or not take office, "all according to the circumstances," in a timely fashion; so, as with a symphony perfectly executed, "from the ringing of the bells at the beginning to the trembling of the jade chimes at the end," there was an "internal order" to his action. Confucius himself felt that music was the culmination of culture, and he had deep respect for the court musicians. These musicians were chosen for the profession because they were blind: "Because they could not see, their mind could not be distracted from sound."

3.24 A border official from the district of Yi asked to have an interview with Confucius, saying, "I have never been denied an interview with a gentleman who has come to this place." Followers of Confucius arranged a meeting for him, and when he came out, he said, "Why should you worry about [your teacher] not having an official position? The world has been without the Way for a long time now. Heaven is about to use your master as the wooden tongue of a bronze bell."

Here a lowly official from a place near the border of Wei and Jin makes a prophetic statement about Confucius. He tells those disciples who followed Confucius into exile not to despair about their teacher's not being able to find a government post because it is Heaven's intent that he should exercise more influence and achieve greater things than what he could accomplish as an official. But exactly what sort of work did Heaven have in mind for him? How was Confucius going to discharge his duty as "the wooden tongue of a bronze bell"? Liu Baonan says that emperors in the past, "when they wished to give a command," would have their officials ring such a bell "to arouse the people and get their attention." A bronze bell with a bronze tongue was used to announce a military order; a bronze bell with a wooden tongue was used "to announce a decree for the purpose of moral instruction." But Confucius did not have an official position and so did not have the political purchase to proclaim his teachings. Still, his later followers said, he was able "to revise the *Odes* and the *Documents*, reform the rites and music, and edit the

Spring and Autumn Annals." In this way, he, too, was like the wooden tongue of a bronze bell, but his utterances were far more consequential than the decrees of even the most powerful emperor.

3.25 Of the *shao* music, the Master said, it was perfectly beautiful and perfectly good. Of the *wu* music, he said, it was perfectly beautiful but not perfectly good.

Shao was the music of the sage emperor Shun. It tells the story of Emperor Yao's decision not to cede his throne to his own son but to Shun, an uncultivated man "from the depths of the mountains," because the emperor had learned from others that Shun's love for virtue was unsurpassed. When this music was played in the court of Emperor Shun, the *Book of Documents* says, even gods and spirits, birds and beasts were drawn to it—they all came under its spell. Confucius first heard this music in the court of Qi, and "for the next three months, he did not notice the taste of meat." "I never dreamt that the joys of music could reach such heights," he says.

    Wu was associated with King Wu, the founder of the Zhou. The music reflected the heroic feat of King Wu, of his conquest of the Shang, and so it was "perfectly beautiful." But unlike Emperor Shun, whose ascension to power was entirely due to the force of his character, King Wu took the world by violent means even though his intention was to set it in order. Thus the *wu* music was not perfectly good.

3.26 The Master said, "To be without tolerance when in a high position, without respect when performing the rites, without sorrow when in mourning—what is the point of witnessing such things?'

The Han thinker Dong Zhongshu offers this reading: "A gentleman is critical of his own faults but not the faults of others. . . . Thus if he uses the measures he applies to himself to check the conduct of other people, then he is someone who is 'without tolerance when in a high position.' If he uses the measures he applies to others to check his own conduct [which means that he would be lax about his transgressions], then he is someone who is 'without respect when performing the rites.' A person who is 'without respect when performing the rites' is wanting in personal conduct, and he will not have the esteem of his people. A person who is 'without tolerance when in a high position' is lacking in generosity, and he will not have the affection of his people."

BOOK FOUR

4.1 The Master said, "A neighborhood suffused with a humane spirit [*liren*] is beautiful. How can a man be considered wise when he has a choice and does not settle on humaneness?"

There are many ways of rendering the idea of *ren* (仁)—"humaneness," "humanity," "benevolence," "moral goodness"—and, when paired with *li* (里), it could mean a neighborhood where humane people live or a neighborhood suffused with a humane spirit, "an air of moral goodness" (*renfeng*). And *li*, "neighborhood," could refer literally to the place where a person lives in or to the wider sphere he travels in, including his profession and his circle of friends. Mencius understands *liren* to mean the latter when he compares the work of an arrow maker against that of an armor maker: one is in the occupation of harming people and the other is in the occupation of protecting people. "Thus," he says, citing Confucius' remark in 4.1, "one cannot be too careful when choosing a profession." I, however, feel that the rhetorical question Confucius asks here is worth exploring. It suggests that most people know that a benevolent neighborhood is morally beautiful, and yet they choose not to reside in it. 4.1, together with 4.6, is Confucius' observation about the human lot regarding men's relationship with the idea of the good: they resist choosing it even when they are drawn to it and know that it is good for them.

4.2 The Master said, "A person who is not humane cannot remain for long either in hard or in easy circumstances. A humane person feels at home in humaneness. A wise person [practices it because he] sees benefits in humaneness."

A humane person, Confucius says in 1.15, is someone who "is poor but joyful, rich but loving the rites." Because he "feels at home in humaneness," he is content and keeps his integrity intact whether in privation or in comfort. But of such persons and of those who "love humaneness without selfish intent and despise the lack of humaneness without fear," the *Book of Rites* says, "there are only a few." And among Confucius' disciples, only Yan Hui fits the description. Yet there are ways of encouraging those who have a lesser quotient of humanity to achieve the same end. The *Book of Rites* says, "The humane person feels at home in humaneness; the wise person [practices it because he] sees benefit in humaneness; the wise person forces himself to be humane because he is afraid of being punished [for doing something wrong]": "The results are the same but the circumstances are different." Liu Baonan believes that this expresses Confucius' view: "He was looking for success, and so was not too demanding" of how one should reach that end.

4.3 The Master said, "Only a humane person is able to like and dislike others."

Liu Baonan says that most people "are not able to like and dislike others" because "when feelings [of like and dislike] are involved, they rely solely on their private sense of love and hate, and so their assessment of good and bad leaves something to be desired." A humane person is different, Liu explains. "[In judging others,] his feelings get it right. When he likes the goodness in men and dislikes the badness in them, his likes and dislikes tally with reason. Thus only a humane person is able to like and dislike others."

4.4 The Master said, "If you truly set your mind on being humane, you are not morally culpable [*e*]."

The word *e* (惡) could also mean "vile," "villainous," "unseemly," "offensive," "despicable," "malicious," or "malevolent." It often appears as "evil" in English translation, which is problematic, because the concept of original sin and of a blemished inborn nature did not exist in early China. My translation here follows the explanation of the Han Confucian Dong Zhongshu, whose understanding of Confucius is a reflection of his work and his combined interests in history, moral philosophy, and legal theory. Dong believes that what Confucius says here is instructive for all, but even more so for the legal officers who are in the business of judging human character, since their decisions in a court of law often have grave consequences for a man's fate. For Dong, the voice that asks us to give consideration to the intent of an action is a voice that speaks for fairness and compassion. This, Dong points out, was also the way that the historian of the *Spring and Autumn Annals* assigned praise and blame. Otherwise, he asks, how could a ruler like Duke Xuan of Song, who had created disorder in his state by letting his brother instead of his son succeed him, escape the judgment of this historian? He was spared because the historian recognized the intent of the ruler to be correct: Duke Xuan thought that his brother would make a better, a more responsible ruler, Dong explains, even though "the action he took to carry out his good intent did not fit the model of the established practice."

4.5 The Master said, "Wealth and eminence are what people desire. If you cannot acquire them by proper means, you should not accept them. Poverty and lowly position are what people despise. If you cannot avoid them by proper means, you should not reject them. If the gentleman forsakes humaneness, how can he be worthy of the name of gentleman? The gentleman does not abandon humaneness, not even for the duration of a meal. He holds on to it whether he is in a hurry or in a crisis."

One could read the first half of Confucius' comment with 4.2. Because the gentleman feels at home in humaneness, he finds contentment in it, so he is able to reject wealth and high position if he cannot have them by proper means and he is willing to accept poverty and a lowly position if he cannot avoid them by proper means. And once a person is at home in humaneness, he will never abandon it, not for the amount of time it takes to eat a meal and not even when he is in a rush or in distress. The Tang–Song scholar Xing Bing says that "eating a meal" refers to "ordinary situations" while "in a hurry or in a crisis" refers to "unusual circumstances."

4.6 The Master said, "I have never seen a person who truly loved humaneness or a person who was truly repelled by the lack of humaneness. A person who truly loved humaneness would think that nothing could surpass humaneness. A person who was truly repelled by the lack of humaneness, while putting humaneness into practice, would not allow any inhumane person to influence his conduct.

"Is it possible for a person, in the space of a day, to devote all his effort to the practice of humaneness? I have never seen a person who lacks the strength to do so. There may be one, but I have not seen such a person."

One could read these words as the conclusion of an interior dialogue Confucius has with himself on the subject of humaneness. The dialogue begins with 4.1, where he asks, Why not settle in a neighborhood imbued with humaneness—why not choose to be humane—when there is a choice? A humane man has acumen and is beyond reproach, Confucius says in 4.3 and 4.4. But such a person's character carries a heavy burden, and while everyone else finds it impossible to bear, he is unaware of the weight because he "feels at home in humaneness" (4.2, 4.5). The fact that such a humane man is uncommon explains why Confucius says that he has "never seen a person who truly loved humaneness or a person who was truly repelled by the lack of humaneness." Can it be that neither of them exists? he asks, But that cannot be so, he tells himself, because he has "never seen a person who lacks the strength" "to devote all his effort to the practice of benevolence." Such is the paradox in the human quest for the good: a person can choose to live a moral life if he wants it, and he has the capacity to do so, yet he resists putting effort into it. The paradox is reinforced in 6.12, 7.30, and 8.7.

The second sentence in most of the English translations reads: "A person who truly loved humaneness could not be surpassed." Yet according to the Han, the Song, and the Qing commentaries, what Confucius is trying to say is that humaneness is unsurpassable for the person who loves humaneness and so he devotes all his effort to its practice. Liu Baonan suggests using what Confucius describes in 4.2 as the difference between a humane man and a wise man to help us understand the difference between a man "who truly loved humaneness" and a man "who was truly repelled by the lack of humaneness."

4.7 The Master said, "The mistakes people make reflect the type [*dang*] of person each one is. Observe their mistakes, and you will know their character [*ren*]."

The Han scholar Kong Anguo believes that Confucius' remark was directed toward the ruler, asking him to be "more understanding" toward those who lacked cultivation and not to judge them against the standard that a gentleman was expected to meet. Kong's reading of the first sentence is, therefore: "The mistakes people make should be looked on separately, each according to the category [*dang*] he belongs to." The Six Dynasties scholar Huang Kan offers this example: "If a farmer does not know how to till the field, then it is his fault, but if he does not know how to write, then it cannot be any fault of his." My translation, however, follows the reading of the Song Confucian Cheng Yi, who says, "The mistakes people make reflect their propensities—the gentleman tends to err on the side of being overly generous, and the petty man tends to err on the side of being overly mean." The Qing scholar Liu Baonan offers yet another way of considering 4.7. He thinks that Confucius' comment here could be a further disquisition on the subject of humaneness (*ren*). In the earlier entries of Book Four, he explains, we learn that there are different kinds of humane men, "those who feel at home in humaneness, those who see benefits in humaneness, and those who are forced to be humane because they are afraid of being punished [for doing something wrong]." Thus from observing the mistakes people make, we are able to see the various degrees of their humaneness. Liu feels that this reading, which is found in the *Biaoji* ("Records of Exemplary Conduct") chapter of the *Book of Rites*, "expresses most fully the meaning of this entry."

4.8 The Master said, "If I should hear the Way in the morning, I would feel all right to die in the evening."

To hear the Way—the way of the sage kings from ancient times—is only the beginning of a person's quest for the morally good. And should that person be "so unfortunate as to die in the evening," "it would be all right," Liu Baonan writes, "even though his journey is far from being complete," because "his worth is far greater than that of those who have never heard of the Way."

4.9 The Master said, "There is no point in talking to a man with professional aspirations [*shi*] who sets his heart on the Way but who is ashamed of poor clothing and poor food."

Most *shi* (士) study with an eye to an official career because their livelihood and their social station are dependent on it. But here, Confucius is referring to a person who "sets his heart on the Way," someone who wishes to serve in government because he aspires to a higher goal. To such a man, poor clothing or poor food should not matter, Confucius says, unless, of course, he is a fake.

Liu Baonan says that most of the young men who studied with Confucius would not have had any experience in government, and so they were aspiring professionals (*shi*) with the hope of having a political career. For this reason, Confucius "spoke repeatedly" about the life and goal "of a *shi*." "It was his way of rectifying names"—his attempt to tell his disciples that "it is important for a *shi* to know what he intends to do with his career before he sets out."

4.10 The Master said, "A gentleman, in his dealings with the world, is not predisposed to what he is for or against. He sides only with what is right."

Scholars from the Qing and the Republican period agree that it is possible to understand "dealings with the world" as referring to either human affairs or human relationships. Still, their commentaries offer us several ways of considering the remark Confucius makes here. The examples Liu Baonan cites from the Han sources are particularly illuminating. One says: "There are cases where the person who swims against the current gets it right while the person who swims with the current is far from being right. There are also cases where what one likes turns out to be harmful and what one despises turns out to be beautiful. How do we explain this? The difference between getting it right and missing it altogether is the difference between seeing something with clear eyes and seeing something with an opaque mind. Thus in his handling of any thing, any matter, the gentleman 'is not predisposed to what he is for or against.' He looks into it by way of what is right."

4.11 The Master said, "The gentleman [*junzi*] worries about the condition of his moral character, while the common man [*xiaoren*] worries about [whether he can hold on to] his land. The gentleman is conscious of [not breaking] the law, while the common man is conscious of what benefits he might reap [from the state]."

Xiaoren here has a broader meaning—not just the small-minded, the petty, man, but the common man, the man whose livelihood depends on the land and whose circumstances do not allow him to brood for any extended period about the condition of his moral life. Of such a man, Confucius seems to say that it is natural for him to worry about the possibility of losing his land because having to move to somewhere else is not an easy matter. Yet this does not stop Confucius from reflecting further on the difference between such a man and a gentleman, whose aspirations are higher and nobler. The gentleman, Liu Baonan explains, "aims at putting himself in order so that he can put other people in order," while the common people "await being governed": they do not brood about the greater good but put the safety of their abode and any extra benefit they might collect from the state above the public interest.

Several scholars point out that *junzi* could also refer to the ruler. If that is the case, then Confucius is making a different statement. Which says: "If the ruler worries about the condition of his moral character, then the common people will need to worry only about their land. But if the ruler thinks endlessly about how to govern his people by means of penal law, then the common people will think constantly about how to reap benefits [from a governing system based on reward and punishment]."

4.12 The Master said, "If in your action you think only of profit, then you will incur much unhappiness [with yourself and with the world]."

Qian Mu says that the object of *duoyuan*, "to incur much blame or unhappiness," could be the self or other people; I feel that it could be both if profit becomes the point of a man's action. Liu Baonan, however, believes that the subject of Confucius' remark is the ruler, and, for support, he cites chapter 27 of the *Book of Xunzi*, which says, "Thus the person who lets the love for rightness overtake the drive for profit will bring order to the world, whereas the person who lets the drive for profit overpower the love for rightness will create disorder in the world." Following Liu's interpretation, the translation thus reads: "If your approach [in government] is driven by the idea of profit, this will create a lot of hostility [among your people]."

4.13 The Master said, "If a person is able to govern a state by means of the rites and with fostering a deferential attitude [among his people] as his goal, what difficulty will he have? If he is unable to govern the state in this way, what good are the rites to him?"

Liu Baonan thinks that we should look upon "deference" (*rang*) as "the tenor and the point of ritual practice [*li*]" and the rites as "the vehicle for cultivating a deferential attitude." He says that "the former kings were concerned about the frequent occurrences of conflict in the world and so established the rites" in order to foster a sense of respect in their subjects. Understanding the ritual institution in this way, Qian Mu says, is quite different from regarding it as purely a means to enforce the distinction between the superior and the inferior in a hierarchy. But here Confucius could also be asking the ruler to be the example of ritual propriety: If the ruler behaves in such a way and is deferential to others, what trouble will he have in governing his people?

4.14 The Master said, "Do not worry that you have no official position. Worry about not having the qualifications to deserve a position. Do not worry that others do not know you. Seek to be worthy of being known."

"Worry about how to get yourself qualified for the position" is a closer rendering of the second sentence, but in my reading I follow Liu Baonan, who thinks that a slight modification of the text— "Worry about not having the qualifications to deserve a position"— is what Confucius intended to say and that the minute change in wording would "convey a greater sense of urgency" about learning. Liu notes that Xunzi, in his essay "Contra Twelve Philosophers," expressed a similar idea when he wrote, "A gentleman is able to strive to become respected, but he cannot make others necessarily respect him. He is able to strive to become trustworthy, but he cannot make others necessarily trust him. He is able to strive to become a person of use, but he cannot make others necessarily use his talents. Thus a gentleman is ashamed about not having cultivated himself, but he is not ashamed about being humiliated by others. He would be ashamed of not being trustworthy, but he is not ashamed if others do not perceive him as trustworthy. He would be ashamed if he has no abilities, but he is not ashamed if his talents are not seen as useful."

4.15 The Master said, "Can [Zeng Can], my way has a thread running through it." Master Zeng replied, "Yes."

After the Master left, the disciples asked, "What did he mean?"

Master Zeng said, "The Master's way consists of doing one's best to fulfill one's humanity [*zhong*] and treating others with an awareness that they, too, are alive with humanity [*shu*]."

Here, Zeng Can, Master Zeng, explains to other disciples what Confucius meant when he said, "my way has a thread running through it." *Zhong* and *shu*, in the view of most traditional scholars, represent an accurate summary of Confucius' teaching—a position that the *Analects* could easily support. Thus Zeng Can was probably right in this regard, but whether his idea of *zhong* and *shu* concurs with that of Confucius is another question. Zeng Can's teaching gravitates toward self-cultivation, while Confucius' covers more ground and is inseparable from government and politics. Thus the Qing scholar Jiao Xun was right to associate Confucius' idea of *zhong* and *shu* to the latter's perception of the sage ruler Shun. He writes,

What is *zhong* and *shu*? To fulfill oneself and others. Confucius said [in the *Doctrine of the Mean*, section 6], "Shun indeed possessed great knowledge. He liked to ask questions and to look into ordinary and accessible words. He tried to conceal what was bad in others and disclose what was good in them. He had a grasp of the two ends [of a question] and aimed to achieve a balanced and measured approach [in governing] his people. It was in this way that he was [the great] Shun!"

Jiao Xun goes on to quote Mencius, saying, "Shun was ready to fall into line with others, giving up his ways for theirs and glad to learn from others that by which he could do good." This, Jiao suggests, is the single thread, the *zhong* and *shu* that characterize Shun's conduct. But since "being unequal is the nature of things," a great man like Shun "would not gauge the nature of everyone in the world by what he understands about his nature," and he would not "dictate that the whole world should learn and know what he has learned and known." Instead, this man "would give full realization to his potential and thereby help others realize their potential" because he is aware of the fact that every person has his own desires and capabilities. Jiao Xun's reading of *zhong* and *shu* is not the same as that of most scholars, which regards the act of empathy or reciprocity as the moral outcome of using oneself as a measure for gauging other people's likes and dislikes because it assumes that everyone has similar propensities. Jiao Xun's idea of *shu* is larger, and he believes that this is how large Confucius wanted it to be, so he employs Shun as an example of someone who had truly embraced it. And, he says, a great man like Shun was "ready to fall into line with others, giving up his ways for theirs" because he knew that his cultivation and his learning would be "incomplete" if he "could not connect with others" and let "a single thread run through their humanity." Jiao Xun refers the reader to 15.3 for further clarification on this point.

An account in a recently excavated text, dated to around 300 BC, seems to agree with Jiao Xun's argument regarding Shun's greatness. It says, "Formerly when Shun was just an ordinary man, as he personally plowed the field at the foot of the Li Mountain, he was already trying to find the middle [*zhong*], a balanced approach [to all kinds of human predicament]. He examined his own intentions and tried not to be at odds with the many wishes and desires of the multitude, and he carried out this principle in matters high and low, far and near."

4.16 The Master said, "The gentleman [*junzi*] understands what is morally right. The petty man [*xiaoren*] understands what is profitable."

Early Confucian scholars, such as Dong Zhongshu and Zheng Xuan of the Han, think that *junzi* and *xiaoren* refer to the social positions of these men. Dong writes, "It is the intention of the ruling elite—the *junzi*—to pursue the idea of what is right because they are afraid of not being able to bring about a moral transformation of the common people. It is the business of the common people to find ways to make a profit because they are afraid of being destitute." Most of the later scholars, however, regard *junzi* and *xiaoren* as moral distinctions, because they think that it was not unusual to find "petty men" among the ruling elite and "gentlemen" among commoners and that in Confucius' view a man's worth had to do with whether this man was alert to what was right. Jiao Xun in such an argument quotes the Warring States thinker Xunzi, who says, in the essay "On the Regulations of a King," "In ancient times, even though a person might be a descendant of a king, a duke, a knight, or a grand officer, if he was not observant of ritual propriety and moral rightness, he would have been demoted to the position of a commoner. On the other hand, even though a person might be a descendent of a commoner, if he was able to accumulate his cultural capital and his learning, rectify his character and conduct, and be observant of ritual propriety and moral rightness, he would have been elevated to the position of a king, a duke, a knight, or a grand officer." To distinguish a *junzi* from a *xiaoren* on the basis of moral worth is more in accord with Confucius' teachings in the *Analects*, though the earlier reading is also possible.

4.17 The Master said, "When you meet a worthy person, think how you could become his equal. When you meet an unworthy person, turn inward and examine your own conduct."

Liu Baonan thinks that the first two sentences of Xunzi's essay on self-cultivation explain perfectly what Confucius means here. Xunzi says, "When you see good, collect yourself and make sure that you absorb what you have witnessed. When you see what is not good, let yourself feel distraught and make sure you look into yourself."

4.18 The Master said, "In serving your parents, be gentle when trying to dissuade them from wrongdoing [*jijian*]. If you see that they are not inclined to heed your advice, remain reverent. Do not openly challenge them [*buwei*]. Do not be resentful even when they wear you out and make you anxious [*lao*]."

A person of integrity would want to dissuade his parents "from wrongdoing," and he would be worried (*lao*) if his parents were resistant to his effort. In such a situation, it would be easy for him to lose his temper and confront his parents with blunt words. This was what Confucius realized, and his advice for the son is "be gentle" when speaking to your parents, remain respectful, do not flout them, but also do not give up and let them have their way.

Scholars in their commentaries focus on the reading of *ji*, *buwei*, and *lao*. Most agree on the meaning of *ji*, "to be gentle," and *lao*, "to feel worried or distressed," or "to be worn out," but this is not so with their understanding of *buwei*. Some say that *buwei* means "not to dare to go against the wishes of your parents and press for your own point." Others think differently, saying that *buwei* here refers to a person's demeanor, of not behaving offensively toward his parents even when they refuse to heed his advice. Those who argue for the second and the more persuasive reading rely heavily on three chapters of the *Book of Rites*—"Tan Gong"; "The Meaning of Sacrifice" (*Jiyi*); and "Regulations in the Home" (*Neize*)—for support. "Tan Gong" says, "In serving your parents, [if they made a misstep,] approach them indirectly and patiently; do not hurt their pride [with angry protest]. . . . In serving your ruler, [if he made a misstep,] approach him directly even at the risk of hurting his pride; do not hide anything." "The Meaning of Sacrifice" says, "If the parents committed wrongdoing, the child should remonstrate with them, but he must not decry them openly [*buni*]." This prompted the Han scholar Zheng Xuan to offer this comment: "Not to decry someone openly means *buwei*, which is the same as saying that in the case of a son he is 'gentle when trying to dissuade his parents from wrongdoing [*jijian*].' This, however, does not mean that the son dare not disobey his parents' wishes, because to do so is to give up altogether his effort of remonstrance."

4.19 The Master said, "While your parents are alive, do not travel to distant places. And if you have to travel, you must tell them exactly where you are going to be."

Again Confucius asks the son to be sensitive to his parents' feelings and not to cause them to fret. But compared with that in 4.18, the advice here is much simpler to follow. Just don't travel too far when your parents are alive, he says, and tell them where you are going to reside when you are away from home in case they need to find you.

4.20 The Master said, "If for three years you refrained from altering your father's ways [after your father died], you can be called filial."

The same statement appears in the second half of 1.11. Refer to the commentary there.

4.21 The Master said, "You must always be mindful of your parents' age. It should give you cause to rejoice and reason for anxiety."

Feelings of joy and anxiety should be inseparable for a child who loves his parents and knows that a good thing—either his parents' health or their long life—cannot last forever. The Qing scholar Liu Kai writes, "Fear is rooted in happiness, and so [for as long as the parents are alive] the child lives constantly in happiness and in fear."

4.22 The Master said, "People in ancient times did not speak carelessly, for they knew to feel ashamed if their action did not measure up to their words."

Liu Baonan in his commentary refers to a statement attributed to Confucius in the "Black Robe" (*Ziyi*) chapter of the *Book of Rites*, which says, "If a person puts what he has said immediately into action, then he cannot exaggerate his words. If he explains immediately what he has done, then he cannot exaggerate what he has accomplished. Thus the gentleman achieves trust by putting action ahead of his words, which makes it difficult for people to play up his good points and play down his bad ones." A passage from the "Records of Exemplary Conduct" (*Biaoji*) chapter of the *Book of Rites*, however, puts it even more forcefully. Again the statement is attributed to Confucius, who says, "A gentleman will not use what a man says to gauge his character. When the moral way prevails in the world, there is more doing than words. When the moral way does not prevail in the world, there are more words than doing. When a gentleman is by the side of a mourner, if he is unable to assist this man with the funeral expense, he will not ask him how much it is; when he is by the side of someone who is ill, if he is unable to offer him the kind of food this man might want, he will not ask what he would like; if he has a guest and cannot put him up, he will not ask this man where he will be staying. The gentleman's relationship with others is like water, while the petty man's relationship with others is like wine. Yet the gentleman can let a relationship characterized by blandness attain its fulfillment while the petty man can let a relationship characterized by sweetness turn sour."

4.23 The Master said, "Few are those who make mistakes by knowing to hold back."

The Han scholar Kong Anguo says, "Neither extreme hits the mark. But excessive behavior suggests arrogance and depravity, which is the same as courting disaster. At least when a person knows to hold back, it is less likely for him to be in trouble." The "Records of Exemplary Conduct" (*Biaoji*) chapter of the *Book of Rites* says, "Being modest closely embodies the idea of propriety; knowing to hold back closely embodies the idea of humaneness; being trustworthy means that one understands human feelings. Although a person could still err if he is respectful and yielding in his conduct, his mistakes would not be so serious. . . . And few are those who make mistakes by being modest and trustworthy, and by knowing to hold back."

4.24 The Master said, "The gentleman tends to be hesitant about speaking but quick to act."

This reinforces what Confucius says in 4.22, 12.3, and 14.27.

4.25 The Master said, "Virtue does not stand alone. It is bound to have neighbors."

"The world is drawn to men of virtue"—this is how most scholars understand what Confucius was trying to say here. But Qian Mu feels that it is also possible to consider this statement in the context of someone who is trying to perfect his virtue: such a person would need friends and teachers—people close to him—in his quest for self-knowledge, and so "virtue also cannot be achieved in isolation."

4.26 Ziyou said, "In serving your ruler, if your reproof is unrelenting and tiresome [*cu*], you will end up being humiliated. If you are that way with your friends, they will drift away from you."

The word *cu* (数) means "tedious, oppressive, unrelenting." But when the same word is pronounced as *shu*, it means "numerous, repetitive." Hence the Han scholar Zheng Xuan suggests another reading: "[In serving your ruler,] if you talk about your own merits and accomplishments repeatedly [, you will end up being humiliated]."

BOOK FIVE

5.1 The Master said of Gongye Chang: "He is fit to marry. Even though he spent time in prison, he did not commit any crime." And he gave him his daughter for a wife.

Gongye Chang was a disciple of Confucius, and, according to different accounts, he was a native of either Lu or Qi. Confucius does not mention why this man had been put in irons, but a few early sources mention that Gongye Chang understood the language of birds, and so, from this inexact information, several stories emerged that tried to explain how his affinity with birds got him into trouble with the law. The most gripping of such stories says that while on his way from Wei to Lu, Gongye Chang "heard birds telling one another to go to Qingxi, where they could feast on a dead body." Shortly after, Gongye Chang met on the road an old woman who had been searching for her son after he did not come home from a trip. The woman believed that her son had died on the road, and after Gongye Chang revealed to her what he had understood from the birds' chatter, the two went to Qingxi and found the woman's son, who "was indeed dead." When the authorities learned about how the body was discovered, they suspected Gongye Chang. How could he have known the body's whereabouts, they asked, if he was not responsible for this man's death? After Gongye Chang was apprehended, he told the jailer one day that the birds outside his window were spreading the news that a cart carrying a large load of grain down the road had just overturned, and when the information was proven right, he was able to gain his release. Scholars all regard such accounts as suspect, yet they like to refer to them in their commentaries because they make good stories.

It is probably not important to know just what Gongye Chang did that landed him in prison, because Confucius did not think that he committed any crime. Xunzi in his essay "Rectifying Theses" makes a forceful argument about the difference between disgrace due to one's own moral failing and disgrace incurred through the force of circumstances, which, he says, even a man of unimpeachable integrity could find himself in. This, I believe, is what Confucius was trying to say about Gongye Cheng: that he did not find any fault with his character.

5.2 The Master said of Nan Rong: "When the moral way prevails in the state, he is not overlooked. When the moral way no longer exists in the state, he manages to avoid punishment and execution." He gave him the daughter of his older brother for a wife.

Confucius had only one brother, Mengpi, who, according to several Han dynasty sources, did not share a mother with Confucius. Mengpi was the son of Confucius' father's concubine from a previous marriage. Born with a clubfoot and to a woman who was driven out of the family after her husband remarried, he was likely a marginalized figure, yet Confucius referred to him as his "older brother." And by the time his daughter was of a marriageable age, Mengpi was probably dead, and so Confucius assumed the responsibility of finding her a husband of worthy qualities.

Nan Rong also appears in 11.6. There we learn that he kept reciting the poem about the white jade tablet: "A blemish in a white jade tablet / can be polished away; / a mistake in these words / can never be mended." Nan Rong must have been vigilant with speech because he realized the trouble a slip of the tongue could cause, which explains why he "manages to avoid punishment and execution" even when the moral way is absent in the state. There has been much debate in the commentary tradition about the identity of Nan Rong: whether he was Confucius' disciple Nangong Tao; whether Nangong Tao was Nangong, a scion of the head of the Mengsun family; and whether Nan Rong also went by the name of Nangong Kuo. Confucius describes Nangong Kuo in 14.5 as "a gentleman" and "an example of the highest virtue."

5.3 The Master said of Zijian: "A gentleman, this one! If there were no gentlemen in Lu, how could he have acquired [his strengths and character]?"

Zijian was Confucius' disciple Fu Buqi. Accounts about him from the late Warring States period and the Western Han suggest two ways of understanding what Confucius meant when he declared that Zijian was a gentleman. One account in the *World of Stories* (*Shuoyuan*) emphasizes Zijian's moral character. It says that while most people in office complained about not having enough time to learn and to be with friends and family when they were ill or in mourning, Zijian felt differently: he said that being in office gave him a chance to put his learning into practice; that the pressure of an official life forced him to find time to be with his friends and family, thereby helping him to reinforce those bonds. This, according to the *World of Stories*, was the reason why Confucius thought Zijian was a *junzi*, a gentleman. And what about the second half of his remark? Confucius says in 4.25 that virtue "is bound to have neighbors," and so Zijian could not have acquired his virtue alone—he must have had help from others. Other sources say that Zijian was a gentleman because when he was an official he knew how to search for talent and delegate responsibilities. *Mr. Lü's Spring and Autumn Annals*, for instance, describes Fu Zijian as someone who "played the lute all day" when he was put in charge of the district of Shanfu, yet "Shanfu was well governed." And when asked why this was so, Zijian responded that he knew how "to employ the skills and the strengths of others." If this story is true, then the second half of Confucius' remark should read: "If there were no gentlemen in Lu, how could [Zijian] have found [the people to help him govern]?"

5.4 Zigong asked, "What do you think of me?"
  "You are a vessel [*qi*]."
  "What kind of a vessel?"
  "A *hu* or a *lian*, a vessel that holds offerings of sorghum and millet in the ancestral temple."

Some scholars think that by characterizing Zigong as "a vessel," Confucius was putting his disciple down, because he also says, in

2.12, "A gentleman is not a vessel"—the gentleman is unafraid to take on different problems and is able to adapt his skills to many circumstances, and so he is not like a vessel, which has only a specific use. They also say that after realizing that his comment might have wounded Zigong, Confucius, to make him feel slightly better, told Zigong that he was like a sacred vessel holding offerings of grain in the ancestral temple. But Zigong in the *Analects* is not someone who possesses only a fixed utility, and so 5.4, as Qian Mu points out, should not have any relationship to 2.12. In fact, Confucius says, in 11.19, "Si [Zigong] does not accept his lot. He is good at moneymaking, and is given to assessing a situation and weighing the favorable against the unfavorable, and is often right in his speculation." This does fit not the description of a man who is good at only one thing. So what could Confucius have meant when he compared Zigong to an implement in the state temple? Perhaps he felt that given his skills in speech and money matters, and his talent in assessing people and gauging a situation, Zigong could have a career in government service.

5.5 Someone said, "Yong [Zhonggong] is humane [*ren* 仁] but is not skillful in speech [*ning* 佞]."

The Master said, "Why does he need to be skillful in speech? A man who responds with a clever tongue often ends up being detested by others. I don't know about Yong's benevolence, but why does he need to be skillful in speech?"

Confucius' characterization of his disciple Zhonggong in 11.3 as someone who is "virtuous in conduct" seems to fit the description of Zhonggong here, that he "is humane" but "not skillful in speech," and Confucius' reply to the interlocutor concurs with what he says in 4.22 and 4.24. Yet the more compelling issue in this exchange is not Zhonggong's character or Confucius' teaching about words and action. It is the question of *ren* (仁) and *ning* (佞). In the early Zhou, *ren* and *ning* were interchangeable and were pronounced the same way, with *ni* as the initial consonant. These two words, even by Confucius' time, remained closely related, which explains why someone was puzzled by the fact that Zhonggong was *ren* (仁) (pronounced as *ning* then) but not *ning* (佞). Confucius' reply, therefore, is an attempt to differentiate the two: that *ren* pertains to human character and *ning* to rhetorical skills; that if a person becomes overly clever with words and seems glib, others will call his character into question. Yet even in the *Analects*, where *ning* nearly always suggests the ruin of virtue because a glib man could skillfully assume the semblance of humaneness, *ren*, one is still able to find instances where it is used without any moral implication, as in the case of Confucius' description of Priest Tuo, who, he says in 6.16, is skillful in speech (*ning*).

5.6 The Master encouraged Qidiao Kai to take office. Qidiao Kai replied, "I am not confident I am ready to take this step." The Master was pleased.

Qidiao Kai was a disciple of Confucius. Confucius "was pleased" with him because Qidiao Kai had self-awareness, so that even when he urged this disciple to consider an official career, Qidiao Kai held back, saying that he was not yet ready. Whether or not Qidiao Kai entered government service at a later time is unknown. The *Analects* mentions his name only once, and even though sources from the Han dynasty have more to say about him, most of these stories are not reliable. One, the *Kongzi jiayu* (*Recorded Conversations from the Private Collection of the Kong Family*), claims that Qidiao Kai "did not want to take up office." But "being unwilling to serve could not have been the teaching of Confucius," the Qing scholar Liu Baonan writes, because Zilu, speaking on behalf of Confucius, had said that "there is no way of knowing what is appropriate and what is right if one does not enter public life," and that "a person will bring confusion to an important relationship if he tries to keep himself unsullied."

5.7 The Master said, "If I cannot practice a proper way here in this world, then I shall take to the open sea and drift around on a bamboo raft. The person who will follow me would be You [Zilu]."

Zilu was overjoyed when he heard these words.

The Master said, "You [Zilu] loves courage more than I, but where can I find the timber [*cai* 材] [to build my raft]?"

It was the Han scholar Zheng Xuan who suggested that *cai* here refers to "the material for the bamboo raft." He writes: "Zilu actually believed that his teacher was going to set off to sea, and so Confucius said, 'You love courage more than I, but I could not find the material'—the timber for the raft—anywhere. Confucius was teasing Zilu because Zilu could not grasp the subtlety of his words." By "subtlety," Zheng Xuan means that Confucius never intended to drift around in the open sea but made the remark for rhetorical effect. Of the last sentence, two other readings are possible: "Zilu loves courage more than I, but there is nothing [no knowledge or moral benefit] I can gain from this disciple" and "Zilu loves courage more than I, but he lacks the ability to make correct judgment." These readings are possible because, in early China, the character *cai* (材), meaning "material," was interchangeable with the particle *zai* (哉) and the character *cai* (裁), meaning "judgment." Yet Cheng Shude points out that "there is much more to be savored if one understands *cai* to mean 'timber,'" which is what Zheng Xuan proposes.

5.8 Meng Wubo asked, "Is Zilu humane [*ren*]?"

The Master replied, "I really don't know."

Meng Wubo asked again.

The Master replied, "You [Zilu] could be put in charge of military levies in a state of a thousand chariots, but I don't know if he is humane."

"What about Qiu [Ran Qiu]?"

The Master replied, "Qiu could be made to assume the stewardship of a town with a thousand households or of a hereditary family with a hundred chariots, but I don't know if he is humane."

"And what about Chih [Gongxi Hua]?"

The Master replied, "Chih, standing in court with his sash fastened high and tight, could be asked to converse with the visitors and guests, but I don't know if he is humane."

Confucius has already sketched out his idea of a humane man and spoken about the paradox inherent in the quest to become one in the first six passages of Book Four. Here the idea becomes more palpable as the discussion moves closer to home—to the question of whether Zilu, Ran Qiu, and Gongxi Hua, men he knows well, are humane. And the approach Confucius takes is to comment on the strengths of these disciples and then to state that he cannot say if they are humane. He is reluctant to speak categorically about what is humaneness and who is a humane man, preferring, instead, to answer the question indirectly: Zilu, Ran Qiu, and Gongxi Hua have these talents, he says, but that is not the same as being humane. Hearing Confucius' response, the listener or the reader may not know what humaneness is, but at least he is able to distinguish the genuine article from its semblance. We can find more examples of this type of approach in 5.19, 7.34, and 14.1. The self-descriptions of these three disciples in 11.26—that Zilu could be put in charge of military affairs, Ran Qiu in charge of civil administration, and Gongxi Hua in charge of diplomacy and court rituals—seem to support what Confucius observes here about their skills and capabilities.

5.9 The Master said to Zigong, "Who is the better man, you or Hui [Yan Hui]?"

Zigong replied, "How dare I compare myself with Hui? Having learned one thing, he gives play to ten, while I go only as far as two."

The Master said, "You are not as good as he is. Neither of us is as good as he is."

Confucius knew that Zigong was good at grading people, but here he asks Zigong to go further, to assess himself against Yan Hui. And when Zigong replies, How dare I compare myself with Hui? he is not being falsely modest, for he gives a precise measure of himself against his classmate, which prompts their teacher to say, Even I am not as good as Hui. Although Confucius considered Yan Hui a better man—better than everyone else he knew and better than himself because Yan Hui was the most eager to learn and someone who would push himself to gain an extra ten steps after he had learned about one—he, I believe, seemed to prefer spending time with Zigong, sharing an idea or talking about poetry; he liked the to-and-fro of their conversations.

The distinction Xunzi makes between a "refined Confucian" and a "great Confucian" in "The Teachings of Confucians" (*Xiaoru*) may help to explain the difference Zigong saw between Yan Hui and himself. A "refined Confucian," Xunzi writes, is someone whose "speech and conduct have the great model" of the past as their standard but who lacks the intellectual acumen to solve problems that lie outside his learning and experience; a "great Confucian" is someone who is able to take his learning and experience to new heights, "from the shallow to the deep," "from past to present," and "from the one to the many."

5.10 Zai Yu [Zai Wo] was sleeping in broad daylight. The Master said, "Rotten wood cannot be carved; a wall of mud and dung is beyond plastering. What is the point of scolding Yu?"

The Master then said, "Formerly, in my relationship with people, after I'd heard what they said, I trusted what they did. Now, in my relationship with people, after hearing what they said, I would go and observe what they do. It was on account of Yu that I made this change."

Zai Yu is the disciple Zai Wo. Although Confucius' remark here suggests that he was more about talk than action, Zai Yu was a good talker—he "excelled in speech." He makes just five appearances in the records of the *Analects*, yet we have a firm impression of this man: he was smart and perceptive but a bit lazy; he asked tough questions with difficult follow-ups, all of which were reasons for irritation. And if the early sources are right, Zai Yu seems to have had a notable career in politics. And so he might have been like rotten wood and a wall of mud and dung, but he was not beyond improvement.

5.11 The Master said, "I have never met a person who is unwavering in his integrity [*gang*]." Someone mentioned Shen Cheng.

The Master said, "Cheng has excessive desires. How could he have reached the point where he is unwavering in his integrity?"

Qian Mu understands *gang* to mean *gangde*, "unwavering in one's integrity." Confucius stresses this idea, Qian Mu says, "because only a person who is unwavering in his integrity is able to apply himself to any situation while remaining upright and unperturbed" by either pressure or temptation. Having excessive desires "weakens a person's resolve," because he is unable to let go his attachments. But what Confucius says here about his disciple Shen Cheng does not imply that Confucius advocates "having no desires" but only not letting desires get out of control.

5.12 Zigong said, "I do not wish others to impose what is unreasonable [jia] on me, and I also do not wish to impose what is unreasonable on others."

The Master said, "Si [Zigong], this is not something that is within your power."

The first sentence in most English translations reads: "What I do not wish others to do unto me, I also wish not to do unto others." Chinese scholars, however, stress that jia means ling, "to bully, to browbeat, to throw one's weight around, to force something unreasonable on another, usually from a position of power." And given this understanding of jia, Qian Mu points out that there are two ways of interpreting Confucius' remark: either Confucius was telling Zigong that he had not gotten to the stage where he was able to refrain from intruding upon others, or he was saying to Zigong that he might be able to avoid intruding upon others but he could not expect others to do the same for him. Qian Mu, following the Han scholar Kong Anguo, prefers the second reading because, he explains, in the first reading Confucius merely berates Zigong for exaggerating his own moral attainment while in the second he conveys an insight about human behavior—that even when a person has acted correctly in his relationship with others, this does not mean that his conduct will be reciprocated. The act of realizing one's humaneness depends on the self, Qian Mu says; you cannot wish it on anyone else.

5.13 Zigong said, "One can get to learn about the Master's accomplishments in literature and the cultural tradition [wenzhang] but not his views on human nature and the way of Heaven [tiandao]."

"Literature and the cultural tradition" (*wenzhang* 文章) refers to history, poetry, rites, and music, areas of knowledge where, in the view of most scholars, Confucius made his most important contributions. But Confucius himself dismissed suggestions that he had something original to add to them. He was a teacher and an editor—a transmitter—he said. Yan Hui put it this way: "He expands me with literature and culture and pulls me in with the rites. I cannot quit even if I want to." These words seem to imply that, for this disciple, the knowledge his teacher imparted to him through literature and cultural practice was enough to get him going and spur him on in his quest for self-understanding. So was this the reason why Confucius was silent on the subjects of human nature and the way of Heaven? Because he felt that these were difficult subjects, too profound and subtle for anyone to pass on? But what a teacher could do was to prepare his students for the journey of discovering their meaning for themselves, and so he instructed them on history and poetry, and he showed them how rites and music could take them to the appropriate measure.

Traditional scholars give considerable attention to the term *tiandao*, "the way of Heaven." They ask: Was Zigong referring to the inexplicable force that gave rise to fortune and misfortune? Or was he referring to the workings of nature, the source of life and change, and its ever-producing power? These scholars also point out that followers of Confucius in the next two centuries did not hesitate to let others know about their views on human nature and the way of Heaven. And so they wonder whether Confucius' silence on these topics was just a matter of personal choice, or whether the world of the Spring and Autumn period was not ready and had no need for such disquisitions. But if the latter was true, why was Zigong so interested to know? Was he ahead of his time?

5.14 Before Zilu was able to put into practice what he had heard, he only feared that he might hear something else.

Zilu's predicament was understandable. He was loyal to those he loved and those he served, and if something needed to be done, he was the first to act and the person who would risk everything to get it done. And so even though Confucius thought that this disciple "had the fire of two," Zilu himself was worried that he could not keep up with everything that called for his attention and, therefore, was afraid to hear "something else."

5.15 Zigong asked, "Why was Kong Wenzi given the posthumous name *wen* [cultured]?"

The Master replied, "He was quick and eager to learn and was not ashamed to seek advice from those who were inferior to him. Therefore, he was given the posthumous name *wen*."

Kong Wenzi was Kong Yu, a powerful counselor in the state of Wei. He and Confucius knew each other well when Confucius was living in Wei, but their friendship ended abruptly after Kong Yu informed Confucius that he was thinking of using force to punish a son-in-law who had been unfaithful to his daughter. According to the history in the *Zuo Commentary*, Confucius was so upset about what he had heard that he told his carriage driver "to hitch up and take him out of Wei without delay." And why was Confucius so enraged? Possibly because he felt Kong Yu was using the power inherent in his political position to settle a personal grudge. This, I believe, was the background to Zigong's question, Why was such a man awarded the posthumous name *wen* (文), "cultured"? To which Confucius responded that *wen*, in fact, tallied with a side of Kong Yu's character that was "quick and eager to learn and not ashamed to seek advice from those who were inferior to him." Several commentaries stress that "inferior" here does not necessarily refer to age or position—that it could also refer to wealth, intelligence, or ability. Song and Ming scholars point to Confucius' judgment of Kong Wenzi as an example of his fairness and generosity—that he was able to see the good in a man whose character was flawed.

5.16 The Master said of Zichan: "He was respectful in the manner in which he conducted himself, reverent in the service of his lord, generous in caring for the common people, and just in the way he employed them."

Zichan, prime minister of the state of Zheng from 543 until his death in 522 BC, was a prominent figure in the history of the Spring and Autumn period. Confucius admired this counselor for all the reasons he mentions here but also for Zichan's political skills and shrewd judgment. And when he heard the news of Zichan's death, he wept and said, "This man possessed the benevolent air of the ancients." Zichan's given name is Qiao, meaning "tall," and his courtesy name is Mei, meaning "beautiful." Scholars feel that *qiao* and *mei* together give a perfect description of his disposition and character.

Zhu Xi explains in his gloss why Zichan was "just in the way he employed [the common people]." Quoting the records in the *Zuo Commentary*, he says, "Within Zichan's administration, distinctions were observed between urban and agrarian societies. People above and people below had separate responsibilities. The farmlands had proper boundaries and irrigation ditches, and every five families were organized into a unit."

5.17 The Master said, "Yan Pingzhong is good at handling social relationships. Even after he has known a person for a long time, he remains respectful."

Some scholars offer an alternative reading of what Confucius says here about Yan Pingzhong, or Yan Ying, who was his contemporary and a counselor from the state of Qi: "Yan Pingzhong is good at handling social relationships. Even when people have known him for a long time, they continue to respect him." But most scholars prefer the reading I have given here. Qian Mu writes, "It is usually the case that the longer you know a person the less respect you will have for him. But this was not true with Master Yan. Though he could have known a person for a long time, his respect for him was like that in the beginning. This was the reason why Confucius spoke approvingly of Master Yan's character."

5.18 The Master said, "Zang Wenzhong housed the great tortoise in a hall where the capitals of the pillars were carved in the shape of mountains and the rafters' posts were decorated with duckweed design. What can we say, then, about his wisdom [zhi]?"

Zang Wenzhong was counselor and chief advisor to Duke Zhuang of Lu in the sixth century BC. People at the time thought that he had an uncanny ability to foretell the future from what he knew and what he observed, and they called him "wise" (zhi), but Confucius disagreed, and his opinion was recorded in several early sources, not just the *Analects*. The *Zuo Commentary* quotes Confucius as having said: "Zang Wenzhong was not humane on three counts. He lacked wisdom (zhi) on three counts. He refused to promote [the worthy counselor] Liuxia Hui; he established six customs barriers; he encouraged the women in his family to weave rush mats [and sell them for a profit]. In these three ways he was not humane. He emplaced a meaningless ritual object; he put no stop to violations related to ancestral sacrifice; he [told the people in the capital of Lu] to make offerings to a large seabird called Yuanju. In these three ways he showed a lack of wisdom." The Han scholars say that the "meaningless ritual object" in the *Zuo Commentary* must have been the "great tortoise" Zang Wenzhong housed. But how could it have been meaningless when its shell was used for divination? Zang Wenzhong must have robbed it of its meaning, they argue, by putting the tortoise in his own private hall when its proper place would have been in the ancestral hall of the ruler of Lu. And in so doing, he was also trying to usurp the ruler's authority; therefore, Confucius said Zang Wenzhong lacked wisdom. Song scholars, however, do not agree with this interpretation. Zang never made the great tortoise his private possession, they say, and if he did, his transgression would have been much more serious than lacking wisdom. The tortoise was placed in his charge because he was the chief counselor, and he "housed" it in the ruler's temple, but to impress the gods and to entice them to come to the temple, he had "the capitals of the pillars carved in the shape of mountains and the rafters' posts decorated with duckweed design." This he should not have done because such adornments were the prerogatives of the Zhou king and not of a regional ruler. It was for this reason, these Song scholars say, that Confucius thought Zang Wenzhong lacked wisdom.

5.19 Zizhang asked, "Ziwen was appointed to the position of prime minister [of Chu] three times, yet he did not appear to be pleased. He had to resign from this position three times, yet he did not appear to be resentful. And as the outgoing prime minister, he invariably gave the incoming prime minister a full account of the affairs of the state. What do you think of this?"

The Master said, "He certainly did his best in fulfilling his duty [as a public official]."

"Was he humane [ren]?"

"That I don't know [buzhi], but then how could he [or anyone] have fulfilled his potential to be humane?"

Scholars over the centuries focus on three questions in their comments: whether it was Ziwen who was given the position of prime minister three times and was forced to give it up three times, because several early sources told a similar story about another prime minister of Chu, Shu Ao; whether when Confucius said "three times" he meant literally three times, because this could not be corroborated with the historical accounts in the Zuo Commentary; and whether to understand buzhi to mean "I don't know" or "he lacked wisdom," because both readings are possible. Most scholars agree that Shu Ao could not have been the prime minister in question because according to early history he was prime minister of Chu for less than seven years and so could not have been appointed three times and been forced to resign three times during that period. They also believe that "three times" means "more than once," because examples from early writings show that it was common to use "three" to denote "more than once." They are, however, divided on the reading of buzhi. Some scholars argue that Confucius was criticizing Ziwen, saying that he "was not wise" because the man Ziwen recommended as his successor later led the Chu army to a crushing defeat in a campaign against the Song. And if Ziwen was not wise, how could he have been humane, which was much more difficult to attain? Other scholars, however, feel that such a reading is too tortuous; they prefer to understand buzhi simply as "I don't know," which, they say, is also consistent with Confucius' answer to Zizhang's next question.

Ziwen is a fascinating figure in the accounts of early history. He was born out of wedlock to a young woman who was the daughter of the ruler of Yun. His father was from the Dou family of Chu. Soon after his birth, his maternal grandmother abandoned him in the marshes. Tigers suckled him and kept him alive until his grandfather, the ruler of Yun, found him and brought him home. Consequently his given name was Gouyutu, which in the language of the Chu meant "suckled by the tiger." Ziwen was first appointed to the position of chief counselor in 664 BC, at a time when the ruler of Chu had just died and the ruler's younger brother was assassinated for his untoward conduct against the ruler's widow. Ziwen did everything he could "to extricate the state of Chu from the crisis it was in" even "at the expense of his own family," upon which effort he built a reputation as someone who was dedicated to serving the state. And it was in this context that Confucius gave his assessment of Ziwen: that he knew Ziwen was responsible and constant in carrying out his public duty, but that he did not know about this man's moral interior, which, like everyone else's, could not possibly have been perfect.

[Zizhang again asked,] "Cuizi had the ruler of Qi killed. Chen Wenzi left the state, thus leaving behind [everything he possessed in Qi, including] the ten teams of horses [which his position entitled him to have]. After he arrived at another state, he said, 'The officials here are not different from our counselor Cuizi,' and so he left and went to yet another state, whereupon he said yet again, 'The officials here are just like our counselor Cuizi.' And so he left that state, too. What do you think of this?"

The Master said, "He wanted nothing to defile him."

"Was he humane?"

"That I don't know, but then how could he [or anyone] have fulfilled his potential to be humane?"

Cuizi was the chief counselor of Qi. Cuizi and his ruler, Duke Zhuang, had once been partners in crime—it was Cuizi who put Duke Zhuang on the throne in 554 BC after helping Duke Zhuang to get rid of his rivals—but the relationship turned hostile when Duke Zhuang imposed his presence in Cuizi's house and became Cuizi's wife's lover. The murder Cuizi committed was, therefore, an act of revenge. The history in the Zuo Commentary, however, does not mention that Chen Wenzi left Qi after Duke Zhuang was assassinated, but speculations abound as to why he left. One says that since Chen Wenzi was an official entitled to only ten teams of horses, with four horses in each team, he could not have had the authority to rectify the violent death of his ruler; therefore, he left, but he was disappointed at every state in which he considered taking up residence. And so Confucius described him as someone who "wanted nothing to defile him." Chen Wenzi makes an interesting contrast to Ning Wuzi in 5.21, who feigned stupidity when the moral way was not practiced in the state.

Traditional historians like to hark back to this chapter in the history of the Spring and Autumn period because the accounts in it say something important about historians and their responsibilities. After Cuizi had done away with his ruler, we are told, the historian of Qi recorded in the official chronicle that "Cui Zhu [Cuizi] assassinated his ruler." Cuizi had this man killed, and when the historian's two younger brothers persisted in making the charge stick, he had them killed as well. But he had to relent after yet another brother refused to have it erased from the record.

5.20 Ji Wenzi always thought three times before taking action. When the Master learned about this, he said, "Twice would have been enough."

Ji Wenzi was the name given posthumously to Jisun Xingfu, chief counselor to three rulers of Lu from 601 to 568 BC. Some scholars consider Confucius' remark about him to be flattering, but others see it as critical. This is because accounts of Ji Wenzi during his long political career could support either interpretation. Records in the *Zuo Commentary* say that Ji Wenzi devoted his life to the service of his state and never considered reaping any personal gain—"his wives were not dressed in silk; his horses were not fed on chestnuts; and he had no gold or jade stored away." Encomiums like these might have prompted scholars such as Zheng Xuan to understand Confucius' remark to mean, "Wenzi always did his best, was worthy in his conduct, and rarely made mistakes, and so there was no need for him to think three times [before taking action]." But early histories also show Ji Wenzi to have been overly cautious, and, as a result, to have often missed his chance to act, as in the case of the political crisis in

609 BC when the heir apparent of Lu, who was the son of the deceased ruler's principal wife, was murdered, and the son of a concubine was put in his place. The aberration in the pattern of succession had devastating consequences for the future of the state, and it happened under Ji Wenji's watch as the chief counselor at the time. He, it seems, did nothing to either avert or correct the situation. Thus it is possible that when Confucius said "Twice is enough," he was actually blaming Ji Wenzi for being ponderous and indecisive.

5.21 The Master said, "Ning Wuzi was wise when the moral way prevailed in his state and acted like a fool when the moral way did not prevail in his state. He could be equaled in being wise but unequalled in being a fool."

Ning Wuzi, whose given name was Yu, was a counselor from the state of Wei. He served only one ruler, Duke Cheng of Wei, and so it must have been under this ruler that the moral way prevailed and did not prevail. Yet early history suggests that Duke Cheng was not incompetent and did not make many serious mistakes, and so the reference to whether the moral way prevailed or not must have to do with whether Wei was in order or not, and with the possibility that if there was disorder, it could have been brought about by outside factors, not necessarily by Duke Cheng himself. And so if Ning Wuzi behaved like a fool during such times, just what was he like to merit Confucius' comment that his acting like a fool was much harder to match than his being wise? Some scholars believe that Ning Wuzi hid his talents when the going got rough and pretended to be a fool to protect himself because he hoped to stay alive and accomplish greater things. Others think that Ning Wuzi always did his best to get his ruler out of a crisis, with no concern for his own safety, and that people around him saw him as a fool. Although Ning Wuzi could have acted like a fool in either case, it would have taken the subtler kind of behavior—to pretend one is a fool when one is not—to earn such high marks from Confucius.

5.22 When the Master was in the state of Chen, he said, "Let's go home. Let's go home! Our young men back home are wildly spirited [*kuang*] and unhewn [*jian*]. They are made of brilliant fabric but they don't know how to shape their material."

Kuang (狂) is a grand word. A person who is *kuang* could be wildly spirited and extravagantly ambitious or sublimely wild and wise. A sublimely wild man is a close relative of a man who, like Ning Wuzi, wears the disguise of a fool. Jie Yu in 18.5 is such a man. But here Confucius is referring to the wildly spirited young men of Lu, who possessed the material but needed shaping. Once a disciple of Mencius asked his teacher, "Why did Confucius miss the wildly spirited young men of Lu when he was in Chen?" Mencius replied, "Confucius himself remarked, 'Not being able to be in the company of those who do not swerve from the appropriate path, one must, then, turn to the wildly spirited [*kuang*] and the overly cautious [*juan* 簡].'" And of the two, Mencius said, Confucius felt that the wildly spirited were the next best, and so "his thoughts turned to them." And when asked why these men were called "wildly spirited," Mencius explained, "Their ambitions were big, and they liked to declaim, 'The ancients, the ancients!' But if you examine their action, it does not quite cover what their words proclaimed."

5.23 The Master said, "Bo Yi and Shu Qi did not dwell on old wrongs [*jiu'e*], and so they were rarely blameful."

An alternative reading of Confucius' remark—and one found in most translations—is: "Bo Yi and Shu Qi did not remember old scores, and for this reason they incurred little resentment." The point there is to explain why other people did not resent Bo Yi and Shu Qi, but the story of these two men does not support such an interpretation. Bo Yi and Shu Qi, who lived during the dynastic transition from Shang to Zhou, were princes from the state called Guzhu. They did not like the fact that the Zhou conquered the Shang by force, and so they refused to eat the grain of the Zhou and, according to some, died of starvation on Mount Shouyang. Mencius gives this description of Bo Yi: "He refused to be present in the court of a reprehensible man, and he also refused to speak to anyone who was reprehensible." Thus the most distinct character of the two brothers in these sources is that they avoided at all cost any chance of being defiled, which is also consistent with the circumstances of their death if the story is true. And since none of the sources suggests that others incurred injuries, what were they meant to forget? For this reason, I prefer the reading suggested by Qian Mu. Qian Mu stresses that Bo Yi and Shu Qi did not remember other people's "old wrongs" (*jiu'e*), which is not the same as saying that they did not remember the wrongs done to them. "Not to dwell on old wrongs," he says, resonates with what Confucius says about himself in 14.35—"I blame neither Heaven nor man [for my not being understood]."

Sima Qian in his biography of Bo Yi and Shu Qi gives Confucius the credit for letting the world and letting posterity know about the conduct and the deeds of these two men. Yet he questions Confucius' characterization of Bo Yi and Shu Qi as "being rarely blameful." "When they were on the point of starvation," Sima Qian writes, "they composed a song, 'We ascended the western hills / And plucked its ferns. / He replaces violence with violence, / And sees not his own fault. / Shen Nong, Yu, and Xia, / How long ago these great men vanished! / Whom now should we follow? / Alas, let us depart, / For our fate has run out.' . . . When we examine this song, do we find rancor or not?"

5.24 The Master said, "Who said that Weisheng Gao was upright? When someone asked him for vinegar, he begged it from a neighbor and gave it to that person."

Here Confucius, as in 5.18 and 5.20, seeks to correct the favorable impression his contemporaries had of Weisheng Gao. If this Weisheng Gao was Weisheng of Lu, then he was the person mentioned in my commentary on 1.13, who was so trustworthy that when a woman failed to show up for a date under a bridge and the water began to rise, instead of leaving, he wrapped his arms around the pillar of the bridge and was drowned. Confucius, however, had doubts about him, yet from his description here, Weisheng Gao seems to have done a nice thing. For it would have been much simpler for this man to tell the person who came to borrow vinegar that he did not have any and send him away than to go to the trouble of asking for it from a neighbor and then giving it to that person. So what was Confucius' problem with Weisheng Gao? Several scholars point out that

Confucius was weighing the question of whether Weisheng Gao was upright because he had a reputation for being "upright." By not telling the person who asked him for vinegar that the vinegar came from a neighbor, Confucius says, he was being dishonest. And why did Confucius stress the seriousness of an incident that seems like a trifle? Because he believed that a person's conduct in ordinary life was a reflection of his character.

5.25 The Master said, "Clever words, a pleasing countenance, nervous shuffling [zugong]—Zuoqiu Ming regarded such things as shameful, and I, too, regard them as shameful. To act like a friend to a person while concealing your displeasure—Zuoqiu Ming regarded such behavior as shameful, and I, too, regard it as shameful."

The textual discussion in most commentaries is about the meaning of zugong (足恭) because the word zu (足) could mean either "more than enough" or "feet." If zu is understood as "more than enough," then zugong becomes "overly courteous," which is the Song scholar Zhu Xi's reading. Most other scholars think that zu refers to "feet." Zugong, therefore, means "shuffling one's feet," "moving backward and forward," "bobbing up and down"—either out of nervous servility or because one is anxious to please. This reading can be corroborated with the Book of Documents and the Book of Rites, where references to how one speaks, looks, and moves one's feet are often grouped together in discussions about a person's conduct. The Book of Rites says, "A gentleman, in his relationship to others, does not overstep as he moves his feet [zu 足] and holds his facial expression [se 色] and his words [yan 言] to the proper measure." Descriptions of Confucius in 10.2, 10.3, 10.4, and 10.5 could serve as examples.

The other topic that scholars raise in their commentaries has to do with the identity of Zuoqiu Ming, whether he was Zuo Qiuming, the historian considered to be the author of the Zuo Commentary. This is a difficult question, but they were probably not the same person, for one had the double-barreled surname Zuoqiu and the other did not, and the Zuoqiu Ming that Confucius referred to was either an older contemporary or someone who lived earlier—certainly someone Confucius admired—and Mr. Zuo of the *Zuo Commentary*, according to most scholars, was either someone much younger than Confucius or someone from an even later generation.

5.26 Yan Yuan [Yan Hui] and Jilu [Zilu] were in attendance. Confucius said, "Why don't you each tell me what you would like to see yourself accomplish [*erzhi*]?"

Zilu said, "I would like to share my carriages and horses, my clothes and furs with my friends, and, even if these things became worn, to have no regrets."

Yan Yuan said, "I would like never to boast of any good points I might have and never to claim credit for work I might have done for others [*wushilao*]."

Zilu said, "We would like to hear what you would like to see yourself accomplish."

The Master said, "To give comfort to the old, to have the trust of my friends, and to have the young seeking to be near me [*huaizhi*]."

Confucius in 11.26 asks his disciples a similar question, but there his question elicits a different kind of response, one that has to do with personal ambitions. Here Zilu and Yan Hui are talking about a deeper sense of attainment—characteristics they hope to find in themselves. And Confucius responds to Zilu in the same vein about what he would like to see himself accomplish, but what he says shows that he is worried not just about the state of his personal virtue. The old, the young, and his equals are all in his thoughts, and each has a place in his private moral universe.

The Song scholar Zhu Xi disagrees with the Han reading of *wushilao* (無施勞), which Kong Anguo explains as "not to make great demands on others." Zhu Xi argues that *shi* could also mean "to exaggerate," "to claim credit," and that *wushilao*, "not to claim credit for the work you have done for others," resonates with *wufashan*, "not to exaggerate your good points." Commentaries also dwell on the meaning of *huai* (懷). They ask just what sort of relationship Confucius wanted with the young. Kong Anguo says *huai* is *gui*, "to return to," "to feel a sense of belonging to a person or a place." Which, Liu Baonan explains, "means that, having received the benefits of his instruction, the young were drawn to [Confucius] as if he were their father or teacher."

5.27 Confucius said, "It's hopeless! I have yet to see anyone who could recognize his mistakes and take himself to task privately."

Liu Baonan writes, "Confucius expressed regret that he 'had not seen a person who truly loved humaneness or a person who was truly repelled by the lack of humaneness.' Here he again expressed regret that he 'had not seen anyone who [could recognize his mistakes and] take himself to task privately.' Thus most important for a person who is committed to learning is to know to correct his mistakes, which is also most difficult to carry out." To do this, this person has to be "utterly sincere in his intention," which, Liu stresses, "is not the same as expressing regret about his mistake or even blaming himself for it." And only "when he is alone," Liu says, will he be able "to see himself honestly" and "grasp the urgency of self-reform."

5.28 The Master said, "In a village of ten households, surely there are those who are as willing to do their best and are as trustworthy as I am. But there is no one who loves learning as much as I do."

Most scholars turn Confucius' remark into a lesson on the importance of learning: that it is not enough just to do one's best and be trustworthy, though "they are fine human qualities," but that "in order to reach higher," "to become a sage," one needs to learn. I, however, believe that Confucius loved learning not just to ennoble his character. He loved learning the correct pronunciation of a poem, and he loved learning a new song he had just heard and liked. Learning gave him pleasure, in fact, so much so that he thought, "there is no one who loves learning as much as I do."

BOOK SIX

6.1 The Master said, "Yong [Zhonggong] could be given a seat facing south."

Confucius, in 11.3, describes his disciple Zhonggong as someone who is "virtuous in conduct." Here, he says that Zhonggong has the integrity fit to be a ruler—fit to be given a seat facing south—should such a position be offered to him. But just who was Zhonggong? What hidden power and what gift of talents did he possess to merit such high praise from his teacher? The *Analects* offers little help, but from the few recorded conversations he had with Confucius and the high standing Xunzi accorded him in his own writing, calling him the true heir of Confucius, it is clear that Zhonggong was someone to be reckoned with, even though the evidence either was lost or was deliberately suppressed. A text bearing Zhonggong's name surfaced recently from among the excavated materials of the Warring States period. After the initial excitement about the discovery, scholars have found that the text does not add much to what is in the *Analects* and the *Recorded Conversations from the Private Collection of the Kong Family (Kongzi jiayu)*, a Han dynasty text in which Zhonggong makes a few appearances.

6.2 Zhonggong asked about Zisang Bozi. The Master said, "He is all right in his simple approach."

Zhonggong said, "To preside over the people with a reverent attitude and simple measures—is this not all right? But if a person who takes simple measures is also uninhibitedly simple [in the way he carries himself], is this not taking simplicity to an extreme?"

Here Zhonggong gives his insight about who would make a good ruler: the person's governing style should be simple, not complicated or convoluted, but he must have gravity, which he cannot hope to possess if he carries himself with uninhibited simplicity. From this conversation, it seems that Zisang Bozi cannot have been such a ruler. And who was this man? Some said that he was Sang Hu, a man from the recluse tradition, who appears in the *Zhuangzi* and the *Songs of Chu*; others thought that he was a counselor from the state of Qin. These are all conjectures. A later construct of this man is found in the Han source *World of Stories* (*Shuoyuan*), where Zisang appears without a stitch on when Confucius comes to pay him a visit and the conversation between them is built on the *Analects* but with a shift in emphasis, from the problem of "taking simplicity to an extreme" to the importance of applying the right amount of refinement so that "the beauty of one's native substance is not lost."

6.3 Duke Ai asked, "Who among your disciples love learning?"

Confucius responded, saying, "There was Yan Hui, who loved learning. He did not transfer his anger elsewhere, and he did not repeat a mistake. But unfortunately he had a short life and is dead now. Since his death, there is no one left who loves learning—at least I haven't heard of anyone."

Yan Hui's love of learning is attested to by what Confucius says about him in 2.9 and 6.11, what Zigong says in 5.9, and what he says about himself in 9.11. But how could the fact that Yan Hui did not shift the focus of his anger and the fact that he did not make the same mistake twice be related to his love for learning? These virtues were a testament to Yan Hui's love of learning, Liu Baonan says, and to the fact that Yan Hui regarded the cultivation of his character as the point of learning.

Yan Hui was about thirty years younger than Confucius. He was one of Confucius' traveling companions during the latter's years of exile. He died probably around 482 BC, at the age of forty-one, just two years after Duke Ai invited Confucius to come home to Lu and a year after the death of Confucius' own son, Boyu.

6.4 Zihua [Gongxi Hua] was sent on a mission to the state of Qi. Ran Qiu asked [their employer], on behalf of Zihua's mother, for an allowance of grain. [He checked first with Confucius about what might be an appropriate amount, and] the Master said, "Give her a *fu*." Ran Qiu asked for more. The Master said, "Add another *yu*." Ran Qiu in the end gave her five *bing*.

Confucius said, "Chi [Gongxi Hua] went off to Qi, drawn by firm-fleshed horses and sporting a light fur gown. I have heard it said, 'A gentleman is busy finding ways to help the poor and desperate—he does not try to top up the supply [in the storehouse] of the rich.'"

Confucius was perhaps most critical of Ran Qiu, of all his disciples, and most unforgiving of his behavior, for reasons I have explained in my commentary on 3.6. Here is one more example of why Ran Qiu may have enraged him. Gongxi Hua was flush, and so his mother did not really need the five *bing* Ran Qiu was able to procure for her. Scholars cannot quite agree as to just how much a *fu*, a *yu*, or a *bing* was. According to Qian Mu's calculation, a *fu* was enough for a person to live on for a month, while a *bing* was a hundredfold more than a *fu*. And so what could have been Ran Qiu's intent in asking for so much grain for Gongxi Hua's family? To ingratiate himself with Gongxi Hua or to make him even richer? Gongxi Hua was also a disciple of Confucius. Like Ran Qiu, he worked with the Jisun family and with the ruler of Lu, and he was often sent on diplomatic missions because of his impressive knowledge of the rituals. Confucius does not have kind words for him here, but from the other accounts in the *Analects*, Gongxi Hua seems to have been affable and unassuming. The *Book of Rites* says that he was put in charge of Confucius' funeral.

6.5 Yuan Si, upon becoming a district steward, was offered a salary of nine hundred measures of grain. He declined.

The Master said, "Don't refuse it. Can you not share it with the people in your village and in the neighboring communities?"

Yuan Si is Confucius' disciple Yuan Xian. Scholars like to contrast his behavior here with Ran Qiu's in the entry above. While Ran Qiu was overly generous with the public funds and was eager to use them to benefit friends who were already living in comfortable circumstances, Yuan Si was overly cautious about what was offered to him even in the case of a well-deserved salary. Yuan Si's fear was that the sum was too large (grain harvested from 450 *mu*, or about seventy acres, according to some calculations) and so might be perceived as improper. To the two disciples, Confucius says: Why not think about the people in need? And to help them, Ran Qiu should stop enriching the already wealthy and Yuan Si should accept what is rightfully his and share it with "the people in [his] village and in the neighboring communities."

6.6 The Master, speaking about Zhonggong, said, "If the offspring of a plough ox has a reddish coat and perfectly formed horns, even if we won't use it in a sacrifice, would the spirit of mountains and rivers refuse to accept it?"

Zhonggong was like the offspring of a plough ox—his father worked in the field—but he was born with a beautiful character, like the calf born with "a reddish coat and perfectly formed horns." And so, even if humans were to rebuff him, the divine spirits would have accepted him as one of them. Thus, Confucius says in 6.1, Zhonggong could be given the seat of the Son of Heaven. He, of course, is speaking not just about Zhonggong but about any person like Zhonggong: his provenance would not matter if he had the making of someone great.

6.7 Confucius said, "Hui [Yan Hui] lets his heart abide in humaneness for three months at a time without straying from it. Others can do it only now and then."

"Yan Hui," Qian Mu writes, "is able to find a home in humaneness," and so is able to stay with it for three months at a time, which is "the duration of a season." "And when the season changes, he might go away from it for a bit," but he always returns to humaneness, and so "it is as if he has never left it." Others, Qian Mu says, "may desire humaneness and be drawn to it time and again," but they will wander off because "they are unable to make humaneness their home."

6.8 Ji Kangzi asked, "Is Zhongyou [Zilu] qualified to hold government office?"

The Master said, "Zhongyou is decisive. What difficulty would he have in handling government affairs?"

"What about Si [Zigong]? Will he do?"

"Si is perceptive—he has a piercing mind. What difficulty would he have in handling government affairs?"

"What about Qiu [Ran Qiu]? Is he qualified to hold office?"

"Qiu has many skills. What difficulty would he have in handling government affairs?"

Confucius, at this stage in his life, had given up altogether his own political ambitions. He had just come home from his exile. The people of Lu regarded him as their "elder statesman," the *Zuo Commentary* says, which explains why their ruler, Duke Ai, and his chief counselor, Ji Kangzi, would consult him about official appointments and their own policies. Here three of Confucius' disciples are being discussed for government jobs. Confucius sums up their strengths, all of which, he thinks, would be a good fit for the demands of office. And since Zilu, Zigong, and Ran Qiu all spent time with him during his years of travel, it must have been Confucius who helped to prepare them for their careers in politics.

6.9 The Ji family wanted to make Min Ziqian the steward of Bi. Min Ziqian said [to the messenger], "Please decline it nicely for me. If they summon me again, I shall be north of the River Wen."

The town of Bi had been in the possession of the Jisuns since 659 BC, when the ruler of Lu gave it to the head of the family as a reward for having successfully defeated an army from a neighboring state. During Confucius' lifetime, several stewards of this city, who were also the family's private retainers, using Bi as their base, took up arms against their employer. Perhaps because this town was associated with rebellions and troublemaking, the gentle and affable Min Ziqian, whom Confucius described elsewhere as "virtuous in conduct," decided to refuse the offer of becoming the town's steward. Confucius himself was different from Min Ziqian. At one time he even contemplated working with a retainer in the Jisun family whom he knew to be planning an insurrection. Confucius was not afraid to get into murky water because he was confident that he would come out clean. Min Ziqian, however, would rather run to the other side of Wen, the river that marked the boundary of Lu and Qi.

6.10 Boniu was ill. The Master went to ask how he was. Holding his hand through the window, the Master said, "We are going to lose him! Such is the force of destiny, that this man should have this illness, that this man should have this illness."

Confucius also considered Boniu (Ran Geng) "virtuous in conduct," and he put him in the same category with Yan Hui, Zhonggong, and Min Ziqian, three disciples who also appear in this chapter. The Han scholars believe that Boniu contracted some unsightly disease, and so Confucius' visit was limited to holding his hand through the window. Others, however, think that because Boniu was seriously ill, "Confucius, out of politeness, decided not to go into his room and, instead, to hold his hand through the window." These details might have been important to some, but it is Confucius' utterance that carries the weight of this occasion. Confucius rarely spoke of death and did not seem at all vexed by the fact that we all have to die. But he lost his composure when Yan Hui died and he also does so here, when he realizes that Boniu is dying. His lament is that of a teacher and of a father, and his indignation has an obscure object, which the Chinese called "destiny," "the inevitable," *ming*: Why take a life, he asks, while it is young and full of promise?

6.11 The Master said, "What an extraordinary man was Hui [Yan Hui]! Living in a shabby neighborhood on a bowlful of millet and a ladleful of water—most people could not have endured such misery, but Hui did not let it take anything away from his joy. What an extraordinary man was Hui!"

Yan Hui was that rare being who was content with any circumstances of life. Deprivation could not have troubled him because he could not take his mind off those things that were of greater importance to him.

He was born with a proclivity toward the good and a love for learning that was unstoppable no matter how trying it was for him to grasp what he was meant to understand.

6.12 Ran Qiu said, "It is not that I am not pleased with my teacher's way. It's just that my strength fails me."

The Master said, "Those whose strength fails them collapse along the way. You draw a line first [to tell yourself how far you are willing to go]."

Descriptions of Ran Qiu's behavior in 3.6 and 11.17 could give support to Confucius' perception of him as someone who drew a line about what he could or could not accomplish in matters that tested his moral courage. Ran Qiu was a contrast to Yan Hui, who loved his teacher's way and who also found it hard to put it into practice. But Yan Hui says in 9.11, "I cannot stop even if I want to," and his quest came to an end only because he died. Liu Baonan believes that death was what Confucius meant by having one's strength give out. Confucius' disciple Zengzi explains it in this way: "The gentleman takes the fulfillment of his humaneness as his burden. Is it not heavy? Only with death does his road come to an end. Is it not long?"

6.13 The Master said to Zixia, "Be a gentlemanly *ru*. Don't be a petty *ru*."

Scholars propose two different ways of understanding Confucius' advice for Zixia. Liu Baonan says that *ru* refers to "village teachers" and also officials in the Zhou court who were responsible for "instructing the people with their knowledge of the six arts," and that since Zixia was thinking about establishing a school, Confucius urged him to be "a gentlemanly *ru*," someone who sought "to understand and transmit bigger things," not minutiae, which was the sort of learning associated with Zixia.

Other scholars, however, feel that what Confucius says here is not about two styles of learning but about two types of human character—the gentlemanly, the authentic *ru*; and the petty, the fake *ru*. This was the question he was most concerned with, these scholars argue, because Confucius realized that it could be difficult to distinguish the two and that, without a clear distinction, right and wrong would be in a muddle. In the context of this reading, *ru* refers not merely to teachers but to ritual specialists, professional men with textual knowledge, the class from which Confucius emerged and which was later associated with his followers.

6.14 Ziyou was the steward of Wucheng. Confucius said, "Have you found any good man?"

"There is Tantai Mieming. He doesn't take shortcuts, and he never comes to my room unless it is on official business."

Ziyou was one of Confucius' younger disciples, someone Confucius characterizes as having shown strength in "the cultural arts and literary learning." There were two districts called Wucheng during Confucius' time, one to the southwest of the capital of Lu, and the other to the southeast. Scholars believe that this was the Wucheng that was located to the southeast of the capital because Tantai Mieming was from that district. According to the Han sources, Tantai Mieming, or Ziyu, was also a disciple of Confucius. From Ziyou's description, Tantai Mieming appears to have been a man of integrity—he neither took shortcuts in fulfilling his public duties nor did he mix personal affairs with official matters. To most people, Mieming's approach as a public official could seem impractical and even a little clumsy, but to the Song thinker Yang Shi, "to hold oneself up using Mieming as the model means that you will never know the shame of having acted in an improper and low-down way."

6.15 The Master said, "Meng Zifan does not like to boast. When his army fled [in the battle against the Qi], he guarded the rear. Yet upon entering the city gates, he whipped up his horses and said, 'I was not so brave as to stay behind [to guard the rear]. It was just that my horses refused to move forward.'"

Meng Zifan was a counselor from the state of Lu. When a war broke out in 484 BC between Lu and Qi, he was the head of a division within the Right Army. A similar account of his conduct and words is found in the history in the *Zuo Commentary*. That same account also tells us that the leaders of the Lu were reluctant at first to fight the Qi army, and that it was Confucius' disciple Ran Qiu who spurred them into action before putting himself in charge of the Left Army. Even though the Right Army was routed by the Qi army in this conflict, the Left Army won a major battle, and thereby the war, under Ran Qiu's command.

6.16 The Master said, "If you have only Song Zhao's good looks and not Priest Tuo's rhetorical skills [*ning*], it will still be hard for you to escape unscathed in the present world."

Song Zhao was the stud, the lothario, of the late Spring and Autumn period. Women found him irresistible, but he, too, had a roving eye and was a transgressor. The wives of both Duke Xiang and Duke Ling of Wei had relationships with him while he served as counselor in their husbands' court.

Priest Tuo was also an official of Wei, but of a much lower rank than Song Zhao. When Confucius is asked, in 14.19, why a morally depraved ruler like Duke Ling of Wei did not lose his state, he explains that this was because Wei had talented men—Zhongshu Yu was in charge of foreign guests, Priest Tuo looked after the ancestral temple, and Wangsun Jia was responsible for military affairs. From this comment, it does not appear that Confucius could have had a negative view of Priest Tuo even though he described him as *ning*. I have pointed out in 5.5 that although *ning* nearly always suggests "glibness" in the *Analects*, it is still possible to find it to mean "skillful in speech," which is the case here. Not only *ning* is used here without any moral judgment; the same can be said about Confucius' description of Song Zhao as having "good looks." In Qian Mu's view, Confucius was making an observation about "the air, the manner, that characterized his times," "he was not reproaching Song Zhao and Priest Tuo about their behavior."

6.17 The Master said, "Who can leave a room without using the door? How is it, then, that no one uses this way [when conducting his life]?"

The Han thinker Dong Zhongshu says that "this way" (*sidao*) refers to the way by which "Heaven, earth, and the sages move" and "transform" things—the *dao* that would remain constant despite the changes in circumstances. Other scholars disagree—they do not think that "this way" refers to anything lofty and beyond reach. "Door" (*hu*) and "the way" (*dao*) are a pair, they argue: "If everyone knows to use the door to leave a room, why is it that they do not use the way [to live a proper life]?" They say that when Confucius mentioned "this way" he was speaking of the rites—ritual rules and practices that could help a person find his balance in conduct and in judgment.

6.18 Confucius said, "If the native material outweighs refinement, you have a rustic [*ye*]. If refinement outweighs the native material, you have a scribe [*shi*]. When there is a right balance of native material and refinement, you have a gentleman [*junzi*]."

What Confucius tries to do here, Liu Baonan explains, is "to rectify the name *junzi*"—to restore the integrity of the name *junzi*. And so he says that when there is a right balance of native material and refinement, you have a *junzi*, a gentleman. A person with too much native material is called *ye*, a rustic. He is not a *junzi*. A person with too much refinement is called *shi*, a scribe. He, too, is not a *junzi*. But why call this man a scribe? Because the duty that a scribe performs is perfunctory—he writes and writes, not knowing what he is writing.

6.19 The Master said, "One is able to live out his life by being upright. If a person is able to survive while living a crooked life, it is due to luck that he is spared."

The first sentence is the most difficult to understand. For why should life be sustained by "being upright"? Liu Baonan uses the ideas in the *Book of Changes* and the *Doctrine of the Mean* to give this explanation: "Being upright [*zhi*] means doing one's best [*cheng*]—not deceiving oneself nor deceiving others. . . . Heaven and earth give life to things by doing all they can. . . . If they do not do their best, nothing can be brought forth—nothing will exist. Doing one's best is fundamental to giving life and sustaining life."

6.20 The Master said, "To know something is not as good as to have a love for it. To have a love for something is not as good as to find joy in it."

Most scholars agree that the pronoun *zhi* (之) , translated as "something" here, refers to learning, and Liu Baonan says that 6.11 and 7.19 best express what Confucius means by finding joy in learning. We read in 6.11 that Yan Hui would not let anything, not his meager diet or poor dwelling, take away his joy in learning, and, in 7.19, that Confucius was so full of joy that he forgot his worries. Learning must give pleasure is Confucius' point here, and pleasure is the proof of one's love for learning.

6.21 The Master said, "You can speak about higher matters to those who are above the middle in intelligence but not to those who are below the middle in intelligence."

Confucius' advice is practical and is applicable to anyone, but especially to teachers and officials charged with the responsibility of instructing the masses. To try to explain abstruse concepts or complex policies to people who simply cannot grasp what you say is not only a waste of your time and effort; your words may also confuse them or mislead them. This is the reason why Confucius "rarely spoke about human nature and Heaven's way," even to his own disciples, Liu Baonan says; and this is also why, when instructing his disciples, he "would do it a step at a time" while "coaxing them to move forward," and he would adjust his teachings to fit the predisposition and temperament of each disciple.

6.22 Fan Chi asked about wisdom. The Master said, "Work for what is appropriate and right in human relationships; show respect to the gods and spirits while keeping them at a distance—this can be called wisdom."

Fan Chi asked about humaneness. The Master said, "The humane man takes on the difficult first and will not attend to any benefits [until he has completed his tasks]."

Fan Chi was a warrior when he was younger. Now it seems that he was considering an administrative position in the Lu government, and so he asked Confucius several times about ways to serve the people of Lu wisely and humanely. Here Confucius gives a crisp response: stay close to the people and make sure that they do what is right in their familial relationships and in their relationship to the larger world; be in awe of the gods and spirits (because they are not something we can understand), and show them respect through the rites but keep them apart from the human world.

Confucius' response to Fan Chi's question about humaneness may seem overly exact and limiting, but it is understandable, given the background of this conversation. The Song statesman and general Fan Zhongyan, many centuries later, rephrased what Confucius says here in a declaration of his own commitment to public service. He said, "To be first in worrying about the world's worries and last to enjoy its pleasures."

6.23 The Master said, "The wise delight in water; the humane delight in mountains. The wise are in motion; the humane are still. The wise are joyful; the humane are long-lived."

What Confucius says here is abstruse. Why do the wise delight in water, and why do the humane delight in mountains? And even more perplexing is the statement that the wise are joyful while the humane are long-lived. What did Confucius mean by "long-lived"? These questions gave rise to many theories and conjectures, some very smart and insightful and others simply outlandish. Qian Mu suggests that we break the statement down into three parts: what the wise and humane delight in; what they are like; and the effects that being in motion and being still have on the wise and on the humane. Liu Baonan in his commentary has a lengthy discussion about what the wise and the humane delight in. Quoting an early Han source, he says that not just the wise but all virtuous men are drawn to rivers or streams because they bring to mind wonderful things—the source, the living impulse, a forward motion, unfathomable depths, clearness and purity. Yet only the humane have a deep connection with mountains: mountains are still and stable; they do not move but they are home to grass and trees, birds and animals, and all living things. The humane find a home in mountains, and they are still, like the mountains, because they are contemplative and their lives are reflective lives. None of the commentaries, I feel, gives a satisfying explanation of why "the wise are joyful," but Cheng Shude proposes an interesting way of considering the statement "the humane are long-lived." He feels that "a long or short life is not measured by the number of years one has lived" but by how one has lived. "A person lived a long life," he explains, if "he was able to realize fully his inborn nature in the time alloted to him." Thus even though Yan Hui died young, he lived a long life. Cheng's interpretation bears Mencius' influence, and so one cannot say for sure that this was what Confucius meant when he said, "the humane are long-lived."

6.24 The Master said, "With one great change the state of Qi could resemble the state of Lu. With one great change, [the government of] Lu could embody the moral way."

Here Confucius expresses his bias: he believed that Qi was inferior to Lu because the founder of Qi, though a capable man, was inferior to the founder of Lu, who was the son of the supreme counselor, the Duke of Zhou. An early Han source says that this was evident from the beginning, just a few years after these two men were enfeoffed to create their separate states in the east. Even then, this source continues, the Duke of Zhou noticed traces of a hegemon in the words and policies of the founder of the Qi and evidence of a true king in his own son's conduct. But by Confucius' time, Qi and Lu had become indistinguishable: the rulers of both places lacked talent and probity. Yet Confucius still believed that with one great change things could turn around in Lu because of her history and also because of his faith in what good counselors like himself could do even in an age of moral depravity.

6.25 The Master said, "A *gu* is not a *gu*. How could it be a *gu*? How could it be a *gu*?

This is another enigmatic comment, even more elusive than that in 6.23. The discussions in the commentaries are primarily about the identity of *gu*, whether it was a drinking vessel used in rituals or a wooden writing tablet. Most scholars feel that it is easier to gauge what Confucius was trying to say if we think of a *gu* as a drinking vessel, and they feel that Confucius' lament was about what his contemporaries had done to a *gu*: either the ritual object was now poorly made and was of inferior quality, or its size and shape had been altered to hold more wine. And so he said, "A *gu* is not a *gu*." But lacking a context, this reading remains speculative.

6.26 Zai Wo asked, "If a humane man, a *renren*, is told that someone is stuck in a well, would he go down the well himself to see what he could do?"

The Master said, "Why would he do that? A gentleman, a *junzi*, can go and take a look but he is not going to hurl himself into a trap. He can be deceived but not ensnared."

A humane man, a *renren*, is someone who is able to feel the fear and anxiety of another more sharply than other people, and also someone who will always act on his empathy. Thus if he is told about a man trapped in a well, he will for sure try to lower himself into the well before attempting to find ways to get that person out. This is an alarming thought for Zai Wo, and so he asks his teacher whether this is indeed what a humane man might do should such a situation arise. Confucius, however, does not wish to talk about the humane man in his response to Zai Wo. He says that "a gentleman, a *junzi*, can go and take a look": a gentleman would try to do the right thing, and he might be deceived but he will not be entrapped. A century later, Confucius' follower Mencius enlarged on this idea to say that a gentleman may be fooled into believing what others tell him if their words seem reasonable, but he cannot be tricked into thinking that a fraudulent way is the correct way.

6.27 The Master said, "The gentleman broadens his learning in literature and holds himself back with the practice of the rites. And so he is able not to go beyond the bounds of the moral way."

Scholars cannot agree as to what Confucius meant here: whether literature and the rites together should be the foundation of one's cultivation or whether one should rely on the practice of the rites to rein in one's knowledge so that one does not swerve from the moral way. Liu Baonan offers a solution. He begins his explanation with a long quotation from the eighteenth-century scholar Cheng Yaotian's elegant essay on why literature matters. Cheng writes:

> What should we learn? Literature. The sages and worthies realized the moral way long before us, and so they are surely our teachers. But they are no longer here, and what is kept is found in the literary tradition. If literature is kept alive, then the *dao*, the moral way, is kept alive; and if the *dao* is kept alive, then teachings of the sages and worthies are kept alive. Thus we have much to gain from studying literature. Moreover, its influence can be more inspiring [than being in the presence of a great man] because it calls upon us to articulate our ideas and beckons us to draw analogies. Thus what literature offers us is more than something to rely on: it takes us by the hand and bolsters us up; it holds us by the arm to get us on our way.

But why learn so widely from literature? Cheng explains that we would know, for instance, that the cultural vestiges of both Emperor Yao and Confucius are rich and beautiful, but without broad knowledge we would not be able to perceive the nuances of their richness and beauty or the differences that lie [in the shades and tones] of their richness and beauty. Building on Cheng's ideas, Liu Baonan says that if we consider literature as "the vehicle for transmitting the *dao*," then "the rites are the means to make it evident." "To learn widely and observe widely allows a person to store up his knowledge of the moral, but he must put it to the test through the practice of the rites."

6.28 The Master went to see Nanzi. Zilu was not happy. The Master swore an oath to him: "If I have done anything wrong, may Heaven forsake me, may Heaven forsake me."

Nanzi, a highly sexed woman known for her indiscretions, was the wife of Duke Ling of Wei. Confucius paid her a visit when he was living in Wei. Sima Qian, in his biography of Confucius, turns these two lines in the *Analects* into a scene that seems slightly risqué. He writes, "The lady was sitting behind a *ge*-hemp curtain. Confucius entered the room. Facing north, he got down on his knees and placed his hands on the ground. He bowed with his head touching his hands. The lady returned the formality from within the curtain—the jade pendants on her girdle tinkled as she bowed."

While Sima Qian found the references to Zilu's displeasure and Confucius' sworn oath a perfect launch for storytelling, Confucian scholars scramble to come up with a reasonable explanation for Confucius' visit. Some say that it was the ritual rules at the time that dictated his decision—that as a distinguished guest in the state of Wei, he had to pay the ruler's wife a visit. Qian Mu, however, offers a more plausible answer: when Confucius was in Wei, he was desperate for a job in Duke Ling's government, and so when no offer came, he went to see Nanzi and also Wangsun Jia.

6.29 The Master said, "Attaining a balance all the time in practical matters and in everyday life [*zhongyong*]—is this virtue not the best? For so long now, it has been rare to find it among the common people."

Most of the discussions in the commentaries circle around the concept of *zhongyong* ((中庸). *Zhong* means "balance" or "equilibrium." *Yong* is more problematic: it means "ordinary" and is often associated with *yong*, meaning "use" or "usable." Something that can be used again and again is a thing that lasts (*chang*), and so *yong* could also mean "constant" or "all the time." Qian Mu sees a difference between what Confucius says about *zhongyong* and the ideas expressed in the *Zhongyong* chapter of the *Book of Rites*—a work that had become one of the four most important texts in the Confucian canon in the last thousand years. The idea of *zhongyong* in the *Book of Rites* is subtle, Qian says, and it is ascribed to sages and sage rulers, but *zhongyong* here refers to the ordinary, to ordinary people and the way of ordinary people. This way was easy to follow, and, in fact, people in antiquity were able to attain a balance in their everyday life all the time, not knowing that this was what they were doing. But since then they had lost that power, Qian Mu writes, and so Confucius' lament was about "the decline of people's customs" in the later generations.

6.30 Zigong said, "If there is someone who is generous to his people and works to give relief to all those in need, what do you think of him? Can he be called humane?"

The Master said, "This is no longer a matter of humaneness. You must be referring to a sage. Even Yao and Shun found it difficult to accomplish what you've just described. A humane person wishes to steady himself, and so he helps others to steady themselves. Because he wishes to reach his goal, he helps others to reach theirs. The ability to make an analogy from what is close at hand is the method and the way of realizing humaneness."

The seventeenth-century thinker Wang Fuzhi gives a shrewd reading of the above exchange. He says that Zigong made the work of "being generous to all and bringing relief to everyone in need sound too easy," and so Confucius knew that Zigong had no idea about what it meant to be "generous to all" or the amount of effort involved in "giving relief to everyone in need." Thus, Confucius says, what Zigong described was "no longer a matter of humaneness," for even sage rulers like Yao and Shun had trouble doing as much. When Confucius speaks about humaneness, he focuses on the method (*fang*). This method does not sound grandiose because it relies on what every human already possesses, which is "the ability to make an analogy from what is close at hand."

BOOK SEVEN

7.1 The Master said, "I transmit but do not innovate. I love antiquity and have faith in it. Perhaps I can compare myself with Old Peng [Lao Peng]."

Most of the discussion in the commentaries concerns the identity of Lao Peng, whether the name refers to a worthy man from the Shang dynasty, or to Peng Zu, who, according to the *Zhuangzi*, lived a long life—hundreds of years—because he knew how to cultivate his body. Some even claim that "Lao Peng" refers to two persons, Laozi and Peng Zu. Yet what is more intriguing is Confucius' self-description—that he transmits but does not create; that he loves antiquity and has faith in it; that he would like to compare himself to Old Peng. To make sense of what he says here, one could begin with Cheng Yaotian's explanation, quoted in the commentary on 6.27, regarding what Confucius understood about the literary tradition— that "its influence could be more inspiring [than being in the presence of a great man]" because, Cheng writes, literature "calls upon us to articulate our ideas and beckons us to draw analogies." This might be the reason why Confucius preferred to transmit rather than to create. And he loved and trusted antiquity because he believed that sages lived in antiquity and that accounts of their conduct were preserved in literature. He ventured to compare himself with Old Peng because, though he knew he could not have a long life like Old Peng, records of the past allowed him to imagine and to reflect on human history for tens and hundreds of years at a time, which in his mind was no different from having been given those years in real life.

7.2 The Master said, "To retain knowledge quietly in my mind, to learn without ever feeling sated, not to weary of teaching [*hui*]—these things are not a problem for me."

Several scholars say that "quietly" (*mo*) is the most important word here. *Mo* does not refer to the absence of sound, they say, because a person can retain something in his mind quietly even when he is in a crowd. Which was what Confucius was able to do: he absorbed and internalized what he'd learned, and so he never felt sated and always wanted more. The word *hui* (誨), "to teach," also needs an explanation. Confucius always used *hui* when he referred to himself as the one doing the teaching. There were other words he could have used, *xun* and *jiao*, for instance, but *xun* meant "to teach by way of giving a lesson or a lecture" and *jiao* meant "to instruct from a superior position," and neither word fit Confucius' idea of teaching, which was to teach by way of imparting light. And "to teach by way of imparting light" was how a first-century dictionary defined *hui*.

7.3 The Master said, "To fail to cultivate virtue, to fail to practice what I have learned, not to direct my steps toward what is right when I know what that is, and to make mistakes and not be able to correct them—these are the things that worry me."

Things that were not difficult for Confucius—learning and teaching—were things he liked to do. They were different from things that worried him, which were all related to the business of self-reform and self-cultivation. What this suggests is that Confucius is just like everyone else: he, too, resists directing himself to what he knows to be right. But the difference between him and everyone else is that he is clear-eyed about what is happening and is, therefore, deeply worried.

7.4 When the Master was at leisure, he was collected and upright [*shenshenru*], and yet at ease [*yaoyaoru*]."

This is a description of Confucius' demeanor when he was at leisure, with no official business to attend to, and it resonates with the descriptions we find in Book Ten. Qian Mu suggests that we understand the modifiers *shenshen*, "collected and upright," and *yaoyao*, "at ease," by way of a tree: the trunk of the tree is "tall and straight"; it sends out "its tender branches effortlessly."

7.5 The Master said, "I must have been slipping fast! It has been so long since I dreamt of the Duke of Zhou."

The Duke of Zhou was the son of King Wen, the man who began the war against the Shang, and a half brother of King Wu. King Wu completed the conquest for his father but died only two years after the founding of the Zhou dynasty, and he left behind an heir, who was only a child. The dynasty could have ended in its infancy had it not been for the Duke of Zhou. He appointed himself regent and acted as the young king's protector. And while the king was still at a tender age, the Duke of Zhou strengthened the new dynasty's claim for legitimacy, and he sketched out a political framework—a *fengjian* enfeoffment system—that helped the Zhou to consolidate its rule and vastly expand its territory. This enfeoffment system had family loyalty and personal integrity as its working principles; it also relied on rites and music for their civilizing effect. In Confucius' mind, the Duke of Zhou was a political genius; he was also the supreme counselor, the person that all other counselors should emulate. But what was Confucius saying here? What did he mean when he said that he was "slipping fast"? What was he slipping from? A moral height he had once attained? Or the hope of becoming a counselor like the Duke of Zhou, someone who could "realize a Zhou dynasty in the east"? The absence of the Duke of Zhou as a specter in his dreams seems to suggest the latter.

7.6 The Master said, "Set your aim for the Way, hold on to your integrity, rely on your humaneness, and get your share of play in the arts."

Confucius tells his disciples that they should set their sights (*zhi*) on the highest idea; that they should aim to live a moral life. And to get there, they should guard (*ju*) their integrity, lean on (*yi*) their humane impulses, and roam freely (*you*) in the six arts. Scholars in their commentaries focus on the verbs Confucius used in his instruction. My translation reflects their reading.

7.7 The Master said, "I have never refused to teach anyone who, on his own, has brought me a bundle of dried meat [on his first visit]."

A bundle was made up of ten strips, and, in this case, ten strips of meat that had been "pounded and rubbed with ginger and cassia bark" and hung out to dry. It was the most modest gift that a person of a junior position could offer to someone of a superior position on their first meeting. Yet Confucius thought that it was quite adequate as a fee for his instruction. There are some scholars who think that Confucius is not talking about "a bundle of dried meat" (*shuxiu*) but about "boys with their hair tied" (also the same characters, *shuxiu*), which, in the context of his remark, would mean that Confucius "never refused to teach anyone who came to him to seek instruction at the age of fifteen or older." Although such an interpretation is possible, the first reading is richer.

7.8 The Master said, "I will not give a person a boost or a start if he does not know the frustration [of trying to solve a difficult problem] or the frenzy one would get into when trying [to put an idea] into words. After I have shown a student one corner of a square, if he does not come back with the other three, I will not repeat what I have done."

Confucius asked very little as payment—or as a gesture of gratitude—from those who came to him for instruction, but once a student was accepted, he would lay out his conditions. If the student is stuck with a problem, he says, he will draw light into a corner of that problem, but it will be up to the student to seek to understand for himself whatever was impenetrable. And for a student who does not suffer the anxiety of learning and the frustration of not being able to articulate an idea, Confucius says, he will not give him "a boost or a start."

7.9 When the Master was eating at the side of someone who was in mourning, he never ate his fill.

7.10 On a day when the Master had wept, he never sang.

Some scholars put 7.9 and 7.10 together as one entry, since both are descriptions of Confucius when he was in the presence of mourners or when he himself was mourning someone's death. And most commentaries point out that these were descriptions of genuine feelings even though they fit what the ritual texts prescribed.

7.11 The Master said to Yan Hui, "Only the two of us are able to act when we are employed and to live in reclusion when we are not wanted."

Zilu said, "But if you were to lead the Three Armies [of Lu], whom would you take with you?"

The Master responded, "I wouldn't take anyone who would try to wrestle a tiger with his bare hands or walk across the Yellow River—not someone who goes to his death without regrets. If I were to take anyone, it would have to be someone who faces the task ahead with some trepidation and who is good at planning and good at bringing the mission to a successful end."

Yan Hui was the person Confucius preferred to have at his side because this disciple would move at the same pace and choose the same path as he, and it is his comment in this regard that makes Zilu anxious. And so Zilu wants to know: If Confucius were asked to command an army, surely he would take a person like Zilu himself, who is unafraid to die, wouldn't he? Confucius' response is not what Zilu expects, but it is a statement most Chinese thinkers and strategists would have endorsed.

7.12 The Master said, "If it is possible to seek wealth, I would be willing to be a guard holding a whip at the marketplace. If it is not, I will pursue something that I like."

Many scholars circle around the question of what Confucius meant by "if it is possible to seek wealth": whether he had in mind "a proper way" to seek wealth or he was referring to the opportunity to seek wealth. I, however, prefer the Qing scholar Song Xiangfeng's more straightforward explanation. In the Zhou dynasty, he says, the only way an educated professional like Confucius would be able "to seek wealth" was to have a government position, and so "to seek wealth" was the same as "to serve in government." Put in this context, Confucius' remark seems to resonate with what he says about Yan Hui and himself in 7.11, and it also supports what he says in 7.16. And what sort of man was "a guard holding a whip at the marketplace"? He was considered the lowliest of officials. And since Confucius was willing to work as a "keeper of granary," Mr. Song says, "being a guard at the marketplace" would not be at all inferior, and so if it was the right time to be employed, Confucius would not be too proud to accept the job.

7.13 The Master always exercised great caution over matters such as the purification rituals, war, and illness.

"The purification rituals" refers to the physical and mental cleansing of the son and the daughter-in-law in preparation for the ancestral sacrifice. The cleansing, the *Book of Rites* says, allows their minds to be totally occupied with thoughts of the deceased, so that when they communicate their intention and wish, the spirits of the deceased might accept their offering. These rituals, as well as war and illness, are all matters that straddle life and death, and so Confucius "exercised great caution" over them.

7.14 The Master heard the *shao* music when he was in Qi. For the next three months, he did not notice the taste of meat. He said, "I never imagined that music could be this beautiful."

The *shao* was the music associated with the sage emperor Shun. Confucius describes it in 3.25 as "perfectly beautiful and perfectly good" because it embodied the peace of a political order. Some said that Confucius first heard it performed in the court of the state of Qi. The Han scholar Liu Xiang offers another version. He writes:

> When Confucius had just arrived at the outer gate of the capital of Qi, he met a boy. The boy tapped on a *hu*-flask [and sang]. For a while the two traveled side by side. The boy had sharp eyes, infallible heart, and proper demeanor. Confucius said to his driver, "Hurry [, don't lose sight of this child]! Just now he was playing the *shao*."

7.15 Ran You [Ran Qiu] asked, "Does the Master give his support to the ruler of Wei?"

Zigong said, "Very well, I will go and ask him."

Zigong went into the Master's room and asked, "What sort of men were Bo Yi and Shu Qi?"

The Master replied, "They were worthy men of antiquity."

"Did they harbor rancor?"

"They sought humaneness and got it. And so why should they have held any rancor?"

Zigong left the room and said, "The Master does not support the ruler of Wei."

This conversation took place around 492 BC, at a time when a succession crisis in the state of Wei pitted the son of a recently deceased ruler, Duke Ling, against a grandson. But the trouble started earlier, in 496 BC. Duke Ling's son Kuai Kui was forced into exile that year after he botched a plan to have his father's favorite consort, Nanzi, killed. With Kuai Kui's departure, Duke Ling wanted another son to succeed him, but this son thought that the proper heir should be Kuai Kui's own son, Zhe, and so, after Duke Ling died, Zhe became the ruler of Wei. Meanwhile Kuai Kui, who had been sequestered in the state of Jin, decided to come home and assume the position that had once been promised to him. His son, however, refused to yield, and so the two were locked in a conflict heading toward a violent resolution. Since Confucius had been in the state of Wei at the time, his disciples wondered about his stand on this issue—whether their teacher was on the side of the Wei ruler Zhe. So Zigong asked him this question, but he phrased it in an indirect way, probably out of consideration for

Confucius' safety because it appeared that Confucius was still under the patronage of the young ruler. But why did Zigong want to talk about Bo Yi and Shu Qi? What analogy could one draw between their story and the predicament confronting the state of Wei?

In both situations, the problem at hand was that of succession. Bo Yi and Shu Qi's father was the ruler of a Shang state. He wanted the youngest son, Shu Qi, to succeed him, but after he died, Shu Qi yielded the position to his oldest brother, Bo Yi. Bo Yi declined, saying that he could not disobey their father's command, and in the end they both ran away, leaving the control of the state to their middle brother. Confucius thought that the two brothers understood the virtue of yielding. And he believed that they chose this path not because they wanted to avoid a confrontation but because they had true affection for one another, and so they held no rancor, not toward each other or toward the world. "They sought humaneness and got it," he says. Implicit in his praise for these two brothers is Confucius' criticism of the father and son Kuai Kui and Zhe, who decided on a violent struggle for the top. Throughout the *Analects*, Confucius seems to be consistent in his belief that power ceded to a person because of his worth has more integrity than power earned through a fight. And we learn in 3.25 that his judgment in this regard was reflected even in his preferences in music.

7.16 The Master said, "Eating coarse grain, drinking water, and a bended arm for a pillow—joy could be found in these things, too. Wealth and power unrightfully gained mean as much to me as drifting clouds."

Qian Mu notes the aesthetic balance of these two statements. One without the other, he says, may seem either too light or too solemn.

7.17 The Master said, "Grant me a few years so that when I reach the age of fifty, I may try to understand the principles of change [*yi*] and be able to steer clear of making serious mistakes."

An alternative translation of the above is: "Grant me a few more years. Let me learn until I am fifty so that I may be able to steer clear of making serious mistakes." The difference in the two readings is due to a slight discrepancy in the two Han dynasty versions of the *Analects*. In place of the character *yi* (易), meaning "change" or the *Book of Changes*, which appears in the Gu version, we find in the Lu version the particle *yi* (亦), which serves to emphasize the last part of the sentence. This, of course, changes the tone of Confucius' remark. Instead of saying *what* he would like to understand if he were allowed to reach the age of fifty, Confucius restates his love for learning: it is not, he says, a longer life he is hoping for but more years to learn so that he may "be able to steer clear of making serious mistakes." I chose to translate the Gu version, which is what Zheng Xuan, He Yan, and Liu Baonan prefer. These scholars seem to suggest that the principles of change or the *Book of Changes* was difficult to comprehend, and so Confucius wanted to wait until he was older and had more experience and knowledge before he would approach this higher level of learning. Liu Baonan writes: "The *Book of Changes* is not just about how to secure fortune and avoid misfortune. There is heaven and earth, and so there is change. When one studies change, one can have a grasp of the way of heaven and earth, and the principles that govern the human world. One is able to know why a sage is a sage if he seeks to understand change."

7.18 The Master always used the correct pronunciation [*yayan*] when reciting the *Odes* and the *Book of Documents* and when presiding over the rites. On all these occasions, he used the correct pronunciation.

"Correct pronunciation" (*yayan*) refers to how words sounded in the royal court of the capital of the Western Zhou. The *Odes* and the *Book of Documents* are "the textual authority on the rules and regulations and the governing principles of the early Zhou kings," the Han scholar Zheng Xuan says. And Confucius believed that mistakes could be made and nuances could be lost if he recited these poems and documents in contemporary pronunciation or in his native Lu dialect, and that only with "correct pronunciation" would he be able to delve into the depths of their meaning. The same, he felt, would be true if he did not use "correct pronunciation" when speaking in a ritual performance. The word *ya*, here translated as "correct," could also mean "classical" or "elegant," and it is often paired with *su*, meaning "colloquial" or "vulgar." It is also used to distinguish itself, which represents the royal center, from what is local or regional, as in the *ya* and the *feng* sections of the *Book of Poetry*.

7.19 The Governor of She asked Zilu about Confucius, and Zilu gave no answer. The Master later said to Zilu, "Why didn't you simply say that he is the sort of person who forgets to eat when pursuing a question, who forgets to worry when suffused with joy, and who does not note that old age is coming?"

According to the Han scholar Kong Anguo, the reason why Zilu "gave no answer" was that he did not know how to characterize Confucius. And the person who asked him the question, the Governor of She, had been a counselor in the court of Chu. He became the administrator of She in 491 BC, after Chu annexed this district from the state of Cai. Confucius traveled to She in around 489 or 488, thinking that a position might be waiting for him there. From the records in the *Analects* (13.16 and 13.18), it appears that the Governor of She took Confucius seriously: he sought his advice on questions concerning government and criminal justice. But the conversation here seems to have taken place before the two met, because the Governor of She wanted to find out from Zilu what his teacher was like. The response Confucius gave in absentia, however, was a bit of surprise—he gave a simple description of what he was really like and said nothing about his professional credentials.

7.20 The Master said, "I was not born with knowledge, but I love antiquity, and I work hard in pursuing it."

My commentary on 6.27 and 7.1 may help explain why Confucius feels that a love for antiquity and a drive to understand it can take him to knowledge, which, he says, he was not born with. Studying the past and having a love for it inspires a person "to articulate [his] own ideas" and "beckons [him] to draw analogies," and so the knowledge he gains belongs to him.

7.21 The Master did not speak about prodigies, extraordinary shows of strength, chaos, and spirits.

The third-century thinker Wang Bi writes, "'Prodigies' [*guai* 怪] refers to strange and inexplicable phenomena; 'extraordinary shows of strength' [*li* 力] refers to such feats as Ao making the boat sway and Wu Huo lifting an object of one thousand *jun* [thirty thousand pounds]; 'chaos' [*luan* 亂] refers to ministers killing their rulers and sons murdering their fathers; and 'spirits' [*shen* 神] refers to ghosts and spirits. Either such things do not add anything to moral instructions or Confucius simply could not bear to talk about them."

What Confucius could not bear to talk about, Huang Kan says, were matters related to chaos, and as for "prodigies," "extraordinary shows of strength," and "spirits," Confucius did not believe that they had anything to do with what he was trying to teach.

7.22 The Master said, "When the three of us are walking [*xing*], I am bound to find my teachers there. I would single out the good points in others and try to follow them, and I would notice their bad points and try to correct them in myself."

Liu Baonan writes: "When Confucius speaks about *xing* [行] [walking], it seems that he is talking about the *xing* in *xingwei* [行為] [action] and the *xing* in *yanxing* [言行] [speech and conduct]. And when three persons are walking, there is really no one among them who is worthy or stupid. Their good points and bad points will become apparent, depending on how they handle each matter as it arises, and so one would choose to follow the good points and correct the bad points in oneself. Confucius, therefore, is not saying that [when someone is walking in the company of two] one person is good and the other person is bad."

7.23 The Master said, "Heaven has given me this power—this virtue [*de*]. What can Huan Tui do to me!"

Huan Tui, according to the history in the *Zuo Commentary*, had been a favorite of the ruler of Song since he was a young man, and by the time he and Confucius crossed paths, he had risen to the position of minister of military affairs in that state. From Confucius' utterance here, it seems that Huan Tui was behind a scheme to have him killed, but it is not clear whether the plot had not yet unfolded when he said these words and Huan Tui was still waiting for him in Song, or the incident was already over and Confucius had managed to escape unharmed. Mencius thought that the first was the likely scenario. He says that Huan Tui "tried to waylay Confucius, and as a result, he had to travel in disguise." Sima Qian imagined a scene based on the second theory, and, to make it stick, he incorporated Confucius' words into his story. He writes, "Confucius came to Song from Cao, and while he was practicing the rites with his disciples under a tree, the military commander of Song, Huan Tui, with the intent to see Confucius killed, uprooted the tree. Confucius stepped aside. His disciples said to him, 'Let's get out of here!' Confucius replied, 'Heaven has given me this power—this virtue. What can Huan Tui do to me!'"

Although it is difficult to know exactly what were the circumstances of Confucius' statement, the first version (with Mencius' interpretation) seems more plausible only because Sima Qian's elaboration of the second is somewhat outlandish. And in the end, neither Mencius nor Sima Qian nor any of the early writers explains why Huan Tui wanted Confucius dead.

7.24 The Master said, "My young friends, do you think I am hiding something? I am not hiding anything from you. There is nothing I do that I do not share with you. That's Qiu for you."

Qiu is Confucius' personal name. By calling himself Qiu, Confucius puts himself on a level with his disciples, and he says, "There is nothing I do that I do not share with you." But what has driven him to make such a declaration? It is possible that his disciples have been complaining about his teaching—that they feel they need more verbal instruction than what their teacher has offered, and so they suspect that he is holding something back. In response, Confucius suggests that they look for instruction elsewhere, in what he does and how he carries himself, and since everything he does he does in plain sight, he says, he is not hiding anything from them.

7.25 The Master taught these four things: culture, conduct, doing one's best, and trustworthiness.

Liu Baonan gives a succinct explanation of the four categories named here. He writes, "'Culture' (*wen*) includes the *Odes*, the *Book of Documents*, the ritual texts, and music, and the teaching of culture means that the instructor [takes these sources and] shows the students how to broaden their learning and how to ask questions, to think for themselves, and to make clear analyses. 'Conduct' (*xing*) refers to correct deportment. 'Doing one's best' (*zhong*) means trying to get it right—trying to find the point of balance—as one gives full realization to one's heart and mind. And 'trustworthiness' (*xin*) stands for constancy—that the self has embodied it as part of its character."

7.26 The Master said, "Since I have no hope of meeting a sage, it would be enough if I could meet a gentleman."
　　The Master said, "Since I have no hope of meeting a truly good man, it would be enough to meet a person of constancy. As for those who claim to have something when they have nothing, to be full when they are empty, to be comfortable when they are tight, it is hard to expect them to be constant."

Some scholars treat Confucius' statement as a critique of the rulers and counselors of his time. Others feel that it is more important to understand how Confucius distinguished, say, the sage (*shengren*) from the gentleman (*junzi*) or the truly good man (*shanren*), and why he thought that it would be hard for those who were dishonest or deluded about themselves to remain constant. Liu Baonan uses the conversation Zizhang has with Confucius in 11.20 to explain the difference between a truly good man and a sage: "A truly good man does not need to tread in the footsteps of the examples from the past [in order to become good], but by not doing this, he cannot enter the inner chamber." "To enter the chamber," Liu explains, means "to enter the sage's chamber"—to reach the inner recesses of knowledge. And as for the difference between a sage and a gentleman, a Han commentary on the *Odes* says this about the gentleman: "His conduct and speech are, on the whole, appropriate, but he has not yet found inner peace and joy. His knowledge and ideas are, on the whole, on the mark, but they still lack rigor and precision. . . . And so he is not yet up to the level of a sage." Sages, gentlemen, and truly good men all have constancy as the basis of their character. And Liu Baonan suggests that it is helpful to think of a man of constancy as someone who never has enough of learning: even when he has gained something substantial, he feels empty because he knows that there is more to absorb. Which is the opposite of those who consider a small accomplishment as total fulfillment and so will stop making any more effort. This the reason why "it is hard to expect them to be constant."

7.27 The Master would fish with a line and a hook but not with a cable with multiple lines and hooks attached to it. He would shoot at birds with a stringed arrow but not if they were roosting.

A cable with multiple lines and hooks was called a *gang*. Several early texts give precise descriptions of such an instrument. A stringed arrow was an arrow attached to a silk cord. A bird shot with such an instrument would not be able to fly away and die elsewhere. In both fishing and hunting, the text says, Confucius liked to practice fair play. This was a sentiment shared by other early thinkers, which means that even in the fifth, fourth, and third centuries BC, some Chinese felt that it was wrong to rob nature of its resources by unprincipled means, and they believed that in the end both nature and humans would suffer if people did so.

7.28 The Master said, "I suppose there are those who try to innovate without having acquired knowledge first. I am not one of those. I use my ears well and widely, and I choose what is good and follow it. I use my eyes well and widely and I retain what I observe. This is the next-best kind of knowledge."

The best kind of knowledge is the knowledge one is born with, which, according to what Confucius says in 7.20, was not the kind

that he possessed. However, from his remark here and also those in
7.1 and 7.20, it seems that he was not sorry that his knowledge was
not inborn, because this gave him a chance to listen well and observe
well and to pursue knowledge the hard way. The quest fulfilled his
life.

7.29 The people of Hu village [being boorish and obstinate]
were difficult to talk to. A young man [from this village] came
to see the Master [and the Master received him]. The disciples
were puzzled. The Master said, "I accepted him when he was
here, but that does not mean I will accept whatever he will be
doing when he is not here. So why should there be a problem?
In coming here, he made his heart pure, and so I accepted him
[as he was,] a purified man. This does not mean, however, that
I approved of what he had done in the past."

Although no one can say for sure why the people of Hu village were
"difficult to talk to," it seems reasonable to assume that they were
"boorish and obstinate," as Zheng Xuan and Liu Baonan suggest.
And Confucius' decision to speak to this young man from Hu reveals
much about what he was like as a teacher: he accepted anyone who
came to him with pureness of heart even though, he said, he could
not vouch for the person's past or future behavior.

7.30 The Master said, "Is humaneness far away? As soon as I
desire humaneness, it is here."

Humaneness is immediately accessible—as soon as I desire it, it is
here; and a person can choose to live a moral life if he wants to, and
he has the strength to do so. But he resists putting effort into it, or,
worse, he finds the other life—a life stripped of its moral impulses—
to be more alluring. This is the paradox Confucius gave a lot of
thought to, much of which is found in Book Four.

7.31 The minister of crime from the state of Chen asked, "Did
Duke Zhao understand the rites?"

Confucius replied, "He understood the rites."

After Confucius had left, the minister of crime bowed to Wuma Qi. He asked him to come forth and said, "I have heard that a gentleman does not behave like a partisan, but, I suppose, some gentlemen do. Duke Zhao took a wife from the state of Wu, which meant that she had the same surname as he. And for this reason, he called her Wu Mengzi [and not Wu Ji]. If Duke Zhao understood the rites, who doesn't?"

Wuma Qi reported this to the Master. The Master said, "I have been fortunate. If I make a mistake, others will be sure to let me know."

When he took a woman with same surname as his, Duke Zhao violated a serious rule in the Zhou ritual institution, which specifically referred to such a practice as incestuous and improper. This ruler must have known that he had done so, because he tried to hide his intention to marry Wu Ji from the Zhou king and after the marriage he referred to his wife as Wu Mengzi and not Wu Ji. But the conversation was about Confucius' behavior. Did he behave like a partisan, and, therefore, not a gentleman, as the minister of crime from Chen implied in his comment, because Confucius knowingly glossed over the ritual transgressions of his ruler? There are different ways of interpreting Confucius' response. His defenders explain that by saying that he was fortunate to have others tell him about his mistakes, Confucius was mocking the minister of crime of Chen for being too slow to realize that it would have been an even more serious ritual violation for him to criticize a former ruler from his state in front of a political counselor from another state. I find this argument rather forced and prefer to understand what Confucius said as a statement about himself. Besides, it is more gentlemanly to admit your mistakes and to feel genuinely grateful when others point them out to you.

7.32 When the Master was singing with others and liked a particular song, he would invariably ask that the song be repeated before he would join in.

Confucius loved singing, and he enjoyed singing with others. And whenever he heard an unfamiliar song that he liked, he asked for it to be repeated so that he could catch some of the nuances before he joined in.

7.33 The Master said, "I am able to work as hard as anyone. But as for being a gentleman in practice and conduct, I have not gotten there yet."

An alternative translation is: "Perhaps I can say that my knowledge of the cultural tradition can match anyone's. But as for being a gentleman in practice and conduct, I have not gotten there yet." Both readings are possible, depending on whether one puts the first two characters, *wen* (文) and *mo* (莫), together as phonetic loans for *wenmo* (忞慔), meaning "making efforts," or treats them separately, with *wen* meaning "cultural tradition" and *mo* as a rhetorical word. In the first reading, Confucius says he may have made a lot of effort but still does not possess the adroitness of a gentleman; in the second, he says his knowledge of the cultural tradition can measure up to anyone's, but he has not yet been able to realize it fully in practice.

7.34 The Master said, "I dare not call myself a sage or a humane man. What could be said of me is that I work toward it without ever feeling sated and I am never tired of teaching."

Gongxi Hua remarked, "It is precisely in this that we, your disciples, are unable to emulate you."

Here Confucius, returning to what he has said in 7.2, 7.19, and 7.33, makes a final argument about why he does not see himself as a sage or a humane man. Gongxi Hua, speaking for all the disciples, says that even if this is true, they, the disciples, still find it difficult to emulate their teacher in his hunger for knowledge and self-improvement.

7.35 The Master was gravely ill. Zilu asked if he could offer a prayer for him. The Master said, "Was there such a practice?"

Zilu replied, "There was. The *Prayers* [*lei*] reads, "We pray to the spirits above and below for you."

The Master said, "In that case, I have been offering prayers for a long time now."

The character *lei* (誄) in the text actually means "eulogy." Most commentaries point out that this *lei* must have been written in error for another *lei* (讄), meaning "prayers": prayers that enumerate the virtues and accomplishments of a living person to help him secure the blessings of the spirits—which was what Zilu was trying to do for Confucius. And "the spirits above and below" refers to the spirit of heaven and the spirit of earth. Scholars say that there are two ways of understanding Confucius' question for Zilu. "Was there such a practice?" could mean either "Was there such a thing as praying to the spirits to ask for recovery?" or "Was there such a thing as asking someone else to pray for me?" And Confucius' remark could be a response to both questions. On the one hand, he tells Zilu that he has been offering his prayers for a long time, so he does not need Zilu's help; on the other hand, he says that his prayers are not about asking the spirits for protection at a time of crisis but about showing them respect by living a responsible life with the aim of "steering clear of making serious mistakes."

7.36 The Master said, "Being extravagant often means that you lack humility. Being frugal often means that you are shabby. I would rather be shabby than lacking in humility."

Liu Baonan thinks that what Confucius says here applies only to the rites. Qian Mu, however, feels that it is relevant to human character. He says, "an extravagant person wants to be at the top of the heap," and so the person is a show-off, and he would be "unwilling to yield to anyone." A frugal person, because "he tries to be abstemious in everything he does, may in the end cut himself off from other people," but "the problem lies within him"—"he will not treat anyone high-handedly."

7.37 The Master said, "The gentleman is large of spirit and mind, while the petty man is always nervous about something."

The gentleman does all he can, and so he is at ease and is not afraid to face the unknown. A petty man has no anchor, and so he frets about everything.

7.38 The Master is gentle but serious and principled, dignified but not fierce, respectful but relaxed.

Only by chiseling and filing could one come upon the paradoxical nature in a gentleman's character, thus seeing him more sharply and more accurately. This is what Confucius shows Zigong in 1.15, and it is reflected here in what other people observed about Confucius.

BOOK EIGHT

8.1 The Master said, "Tai Bo may be said to embody the highest virtue. Three times he yielded his right to the empire. And the people did not know that this was what he had done, and so they did not accord him the recognition he deserved."

Tai Bo was King Wen's uncle and King Wu's granduncle—therefore, an ancestor of the Zhou royal family. He was the oldest son of the Zhou chieftain Tai Wang and was heir to his father's position. But he realized that his younger brother, Ji Li, was a worthy man, and that Ji Li's own son, the future King Wen, possessed the disposition of a sage, and so he relinquished his right to become the head of the Zhou tribe to Ji Li. This gave Ji Li's son and grandson a chance to realize their potential, which they did as founders of a new dynasty. But why did Tai Wang yield his right "three times"? One can find several explanations in the early sources, but Zheng Xuan's is the most compelling and the one that makes the most sense, in Liu Baonan's view. "Tai Bo wished to have his brother established as heir but lacked the authority," Zheng Xuan says, "and so when his father, Tai Wang, fell ill, he used this opportunity to go to the regions of Wu and Yue [in the east] to gather herbal medicine for him. After Tai Wang died, he did not return home, thus letting his brother Ji Li be the presiding mourner. This was the first time he relinquished his right. After Ji Li informed him of the date of the funeral for their father, Tai Wang did not hasten home for it. This was the second time he relinquished his right. After he declined to attend the funeral, he cut his hair and tattooed his body [thus following the customs of his adopted land]. This was the third time he relinquished his right. The most remarkable thing about his yielding his right three times was the fact that he kept his deed hidden, and so 'the people did not know what he had done and did not accord him the recognition he deserved.'" What distinguished Tai Wang from the rest was not that he yielded his right three times, but that he kept what he did out of sight, and this, Zheng Xuan thinks, was the reason why Confucius thought that he exemplified "the highest virtue."

8.2 The Master said, "Unless a man acts according to the spirit of the rites, in being respectful, he will tire himself out; in being cautious, he will become timid; in being brave, he will become unruly; in being forthright, he will become derisive.

"If a person in a ruling position [*junzi*] is generous toward his family and kin, the common people will be inspired to act humanely. If he does not forget old friends and acquaintances, the common people will not be uncharitable."

Most of the discussions in the commentaries are about whether the two sections should be treated as separate entries because there is no obvious connection between them. Yet the ideas in either section give one much to chew over. Confucius in the first section tells us about the subtle power of the rites. It can give a person balance, Confucius says, especially when he thinks that he is behaving correctly and, therefore, does not need anything to hold him back: what this person does not see is the unseemly, the offensive, side of his behavior if he does not rely on the rites to restrain him from going too far. The advice in the second section, inspired perhaps by what the Duke of Zhou says to his son in 18.10, was intended for men in the ruling position, also called *junzi*. These men were different from the *junzi*, the gentleman, who is distinguished by the integrity of his words and conduct.

8.3 When Master Zeng [Zengzi] was seriously ill, he summoned his disciples and said, "Look at my feet. Look at my hands. The *Ode* says,

> 'In fear and trembling,
> As if standing on the edge of an abyss,
> As if treading on thin ice.'

Only now do I know I have been spared from harm, my young friends."

Confucius' youngest disciple, Zeng Can, has a prominent presence in this chapter—five statements are attributed to him. He is called Master Zeng probably because his disciples, along with the disciples of You Ruo, Zixia, Zizhang, and Ziyou, were responsible for drafting an early version of the *Analects*. An overwhelming sense of filial duty distinguished Master Zeng from others, which is what we find here: he asks his disciples to examine his hands and feet before he dies; he wants them to realize that he has kept the body given to him by his parents unharmed, which, he says, was not an easy feat. According to a Han ritual text, *Dai De's Book of Rites*, Master Zeng claimed that he had heard Confucius say, "A child receives from his parents a body that is intact when he is born, and if he keeps it intact when he dies, this is called filiality."

8.4 Master Zeng [Zengzi] was seriously ill. Meng Jingzi came to ask how he was. Master Zeng said, "When a bird is about to die, its cries are sorrowful. When a man is about to die, his words carry weight. A gentleman prizes three things in his pursuit of the Way: he gravely deports himself, and so his temperament is far from being violent and surly; he keeps a dignified expression, and so his character is close to being trustworthy; he uses a proper choice of words and a clear tone of voice, and so he avoids being vulgar and unruly. And as for the sacrificial vessels, there are professionals to look after such matters."

Meng Jingzi was a scion of the Mengsun family, the son of Meng Wubo and grandson of Meng Yizi, and a counselor in Lu in the early Warring States period. Confucius had conversations with both his father and grandfather, but Meng Jingzi was a younger contemporary of Confucius' disciple Zeng Can (Master Zeng). According to the Han scholar Bao Xian, Meng Jingzi paid too much attention to details when conducting the rites, and so when Master Zeng saw him on his deathbed, he pointed out to him the more important matters in ritual practice—those that pertain to one's deportment, countenance, and speech and are essential to the cultivation of one's character.

8.5 Master Zeng [Zengzi] said, "To be able yet to seek the advice of those who are less able; to know a great deal yet to seek the advice of those who know little; to have something [*you*] yet seemingly to have nothing [*wu*]; to be full [*shi*] yet seemingly to be empty [*xu*]; to be trespassed against yet to be content to lay aside any need for reprisal—in the past, a friend of mine devoted his effort to realizing this."

What Master Zeng says here about his friend resonates with the teachings shared by many early thinkers: Mencius, Xunzi, Zhuangzi—and, most prominently, the author(s) of the *Laozi*, because the main arguments in that book are built on the relationships of such concepts as "to have" (*you*) and "not to have" (*wu*), "full" (*shi*) and "empty" (*xu*), and the *Laozi*'s point is that once you have worked out these relationships, you can use your knowledge to survive in the world, to advance yourself, or to cultivate virtue. Master Zeng, of course, has only the moral self in mind when he applies these ideas to what he remembers about his friend, whom most scholars believe to be Yan Hui. In Liu Baonan's mind, an essay called "The Way of Humility" (*Xudao*), by the late Han thinker Xu Gan, best illustrates Master Zeng's point here. Xu says:

> In acting virtuously, can one be likened to an empty vessel? If a vessel is empty, then things will flow into it, ceasing when it is full. Thus the gentleman constantly empties his heart's ambitions and makes his demeanor respectful. He does not use his superior talents to be condescending toward the multitude of people; rather he looks upon others as though they were worthy, and upon himself as though he was wanting. Thus others are willing to tell him what they know and are never tired of doing it. The *Book of Changes* says: "The superior person receives others with emptiness." The *Book of Poetry* says, "That admirable gentleman / What do I have that I could tell him?" In his approach to the way of goodness, the gentleman remembers the big and the small for what they are. Irrespective of their relative importance, he bears them in

mind, and then, at the right time, he will draw upon them and put them into practice. What I know cannot be taken away from me; what I don't know, I will learn it from others—it is by this means that the gentleman is always ahead of others in his achievement while others lag behind.

Xu Gan was an eclectic thinker, even though in the formal histories he is treated as a Confucian. He lived in the last fifty years of the Han dynasty, at a time when the teachings of the *Laozi* were on the rise and when thought and practice tended to defy rigid classifications. Thus Liu Baonan is right to use Xu Gan's writing to illustrate early Chinese teachings, before bibliographers and ideologues tried to separate the two into distinct categories.

8.6 Master Zeng [Zengzi] said, "A man who can be entrusted with the care of an orphan six *chi* tall and charged with the command of a state of one hundred square *li* in size, someone who will not waver when faced with a serious crisis—is he not a gentleman? He is a gentleman."

In Master Zeng's time, six *chi*, according to some calculations, would have been somewhere between three and four feet. So the orphan mentioned here must be a very young child, and traditional scholars say that this orphan was not just any orphan but a child who became a ruler at a young age and so needed a counselor—or a regent—who could take on the responsibility of governing a state of a relatively large size. If this counselor could stand firm in his charge, Master Zeng says, "Is he not a gentleman?"

8.7 Master Zeng [Zengzi] said, "A man of education and aspiration [*shi*] must be big and strong [in spirit and mind], and he must be resolute. His burden is heavy, and his road is long. He takes [the fulfillment of] humaneness as his burden. Is it not heavy? And his road ends only with death. Is it not long?"

A *shi* was not an aristocrat: he was not entitled to any income or privileges he had not earned himself. He was a common gentleman, and his education and aspirations were what put him in a class above the ordinary folk. Confucius was a *shi*, and there were many *shi* among his disciples. Here Master Zeng tells the common gentleman that his principal purpose is not making a living but perfecting his humaneness, which is a burden so heavy that it demands a large spirit and a strong mind, as well as a willfulness that will keep him on that track until he dies.

8.8 The Master said, "The *Odes* are to stimulate [our mind and spirit]. The rites are to steady us. Music is the final lesson."

Poetry, the rites, and music take up a large part of Confucius' remarks in the *Analects*, but rarely do they appear together and in a sequence. This passage has led some scholars to believe that this was how Confucius organized his teachings: poetry comes first, to give our spirit and mind a lift; the rites follow poetry, to hold us back lest we become heady; and only after we have learned to steady ourselves are we prepared to gather up the distinct pieces to create music. Another way of understanding Confucius' comment is to consider the order he proposes here as an analogy for the steps to take to perfect our inborn nature—from inspiring it to reach higher, to teaching it to find balance, to drawing together a life that is as fluent as perfect music.

8.9 The Master said, "The common people can be made to follow a course of action, but they cannot be made to understand the reasons for doing it."

Liu Baonan observes that just as Confucius separated out disciples who could be instructed to follow a particular course of action from disciples who could actually understand why such a course of action was morally superior, he made the same distinction among humans as a whole. Qian Mu feels that Confucius was not trying to belittle the common people but that he was merely telling the ruler that it would be more effective simply to point out the right course of action to his people rather than to rely on "words and argument first to make them understand why they should pursue such a course." Explanations can give rise to misunderstanding and doubt in minds that are not ready to follow what is said, Qian Mu writes, and consequently there will be more obstacles for the ruler to overcome.

8.10 The Master said, "If the people love bravery and at the same time are angry about their poverty, this is a formula for chaos. If the people are infuriated with men who are inhumane, this, too, will lead to chaos."

Since the subject of the second sentence could also be the ruler, it is possible to understand the sentence to say: "If you detest men who are inhumane to an extreme, this may provoke them to instigate incidents of disorder." Nearly all the commentaries follow this interpretation. Still, I prefer mine because it lets the subject of the two sentences stay the same, and, even more important, Confucius in this reading gives the people a more prominent voice. He explains why they might be driven to create social upheaval, and why the ruler should hear them out and try to alleviate their troubles.

8.11 The Master said, "Although a person may have talents as outstanding as those of the Duke of Zhou, if he is arrogant and ungenerous, none of his other qualities are worth admiring."

An arrogant person thinks highly of his own talents, Liu Baonan writes, and an ungenerous person guards what he knows and what he possesses jealously. The two are often the same man. Such a person, in Mencius' words, keeps others "miles away." He may have "beautiful talents," Qian Mu observes, but he lacks "beautiful virtue."

8.12 The Master said, "It is hard to find a person who, after three years of studying, has not yet turned his thoughts to earning a salary."

Confucius was unusually frank about the predicament of a *shi*, a man who got an education because he had higher aspirations. Most of such men wanted respectable jobs, and, in early China, this meant positions in government. And it was Confucius who encouraged them to set their sights on something even higher: Let learning take you to self-reform, he said. Yet he also realized just how hard it was not to think about earning a living while you were studying; he was, therefore, more realistic and more reasonable than his disciple Master Zeng, who seems to suggest in 8.7 that a *shi* should take the fulfillment of humaneness as his sole purpose—and his burden—in life. Perhaps Confucius' remark was informed by his own experience as a man of education and learning: from the time that he was a young man, he was always looking for work, either at home in Lu or during his travels, because he needed a livelihood.

8.13 The Master said, "Have unshakable trust in [the moral path you pursue]. Love learning. Hold on to the way of the good until you die. Do not enter a state threatened with danger. Do not reside in a state embroiled in conflict. Show yourself when the moral way is evident. Seek reclusion when it is not. When the moral way prevails in a state, being poor and lowly is a cause for shame. When the moral way does not prevail in the world, having wealth and position is a cause for shame."

Liu Baonan puts the first two ideas together in this way: When a person knows beyond any doubt that what he wants most is to pursue the moral way, he will love learning for as long as his life permits. But what did Confucius mean by "hold on to the way of the good until you die," and why did he advise staying away from a state that was "threatened with danger" or "embroiled in conflict"? One would imagine that a person who is committed to the way of the good is likely to be drawn to such a place, in order to put his faith to the test. Mencius, however, thought differently. He says, "Though nothing happens that is not due to destiny, one should accept only what is one's proper destiny. This is the reason why he who understands destiny does not stand under a wall on the verge of collapse. He who dies having done his best in following the Way dies according to his proper destiny." To do "[one's] best in following the Way" does not mean that one should seek to be in a perilous place, to right some wrongs and undo the injustice that might have been the source of the trouble. To do one's best, in Mencius' teachings, is to perfect the self. Which, some scholars claim, is also what Confucius means by saying, "Hold on to the way of the good." This seems to make sense in the context of what Confucius says here but becomes problematic when we consider some of his political decisions—his willingness to step into hazardous terrain and spar with men known for their bad behavior.

8.14 The Master said, "If you don't have a particular position, then don't meddle with any of its business."

Confucius' message is simple: Carry out the responsibilities of your office, but don't stick your nose into other people's business. To do so is an act of intrusion or, worse, an act of encroachment, which, Confucius believed, could have unwanted consequences in the political world. Mencius gives several examples of men who would rather risk punishment than overstep the boundaries of their office. And he says this about Confucius: "Confucius was once a minor official in charge of stores. He said, 'All I have to do is to keep correct records.' He was once a minor official in charge of sheep and cattle. He said, 'All I have to do is to see to it that the sheep and cattle grow up to be strong and healthy.' To talk about lofty matters when in a low position is a crime." Given his skills and knowledge, Confucius could have talked about "lofty matters," but he did not, not from his lowly position.

8.15 The Master said, "From the opening song of the Grand Musician Zhi to the closing strain of the *guanju* ode, how the superabundant music fills our ears!"

Music had always been a part of ritual pageant in the Zhou court and in the courts of the regional rulers. Such a concert would start with a song—the grand musician would sing, accompanied by an ensemble of wind instruments called the *sheng*—and it would conclude with six poems from the *Book of Odes*, beginning with the *guanju* and performed with a full chorus and an orchestra of pipes and strings, bamboo and brass. Thus Confucius describes music as *yangyang*, "superabundant and beautiful."

Confucius probably knew the Grand Musician Zhi well. He mentions him in 3.23, and, in 18.9, he says that this man "left for Qi." Zhi was one of the many musicians who exited Lu around the time of Confucius' death. Early histories give no explanation for their exodus.

8.16 The Master said, "Wildly spirited but not forthright, naïve but not honest, simple and tactless but not trustworthy—such men I do not understand."

Confucius' comment is, first, about human nature, that it is often not perfect: some people have a wild spirit, some are naïve, and some are just dull. He seems to accept this fact, but what surprises and piques him is that there are men who will not draw on what Arthur Waley calls "the merits of their faults" and turn those strengths into virtues. Xunzi believes that this is a difference between a gentleman and a petty man. They "are opposites," he says. "When a gentleman lacks in intelligence, he is attentive and earnest, and he follows the proper models from the past. . . . When a petty man lacks in intelligence, he is thievish and likes to cause trouble."

8.17 The Master said, "Learn as if you will never catch up, as though you are afraid of losing whatever you have already understood."

Liu Baonan, quoting Huang Kan, says, "When you think that you will never catch up, you have already gotten there. If you are afraid of losing what you have learned, you will not lose it."

8.18 The Master said, "Sublime was the way Shun and Yu held possession of the empire—they got it without seeking it, and once they had it, they took no part in it, and they thought nothing of it."

Confucius describes the way in which Shun and Yu held possession of the empire simply as *buyu* (不与). But *buyu* could have one of several meanings: that Shun and Yu did not seek to possess the empire (the empire was handed to them); that they knew how to use the right men to help them govern and so it was as if they did not govern at all; or that they thought nothing of what they possessed and never claimed to have owned the empire even though they were its rulers. My translation tries to take all of these readings into account because, as Liu Baonan and Qian Mu suggest, together they give more depth to the idea of Shun and Yu and the idea of their sublimity.

8.19 The Master said, "Great was Yao as a ruler! Sublime was he! Heaven alone was great, and only Yao took it as his model. So vast and boundless was his virtue that the people could not give it a name. Yet sublime were his achievements, brilliant his cultural vestiges."

The idea that the great kings modeled themselves after heaven and earth can be found in many early sources. Chapter 25 of the *Book of Laozi* says:

> Hence the way is great; heaven is great; earth is great; and the king is also great. Within the realm there are four things that are great, and the king counts as one.
> Man models himself on earth,
> Earth on heaven,
> Heaven on the way,
> And the way on that which is naturally so.

The *Book of Xunzi* explains the virtues of Heaven and earth and why they would be the inspiration of a true king. Xunzi says, "Heaven does not speak, yet men know that it is high. Earth does not speak, yet men know that it is substantial. The four seasons do not speak, yet the people know that they will arrive in time. When a ruler has perfected his virtue, though he is silent, others understand him; though he bestows not favor, others gravitate toward him; though he is not angry, he possesses an awe-inspiring dignity."

8.20 Shun had five ministers, and the empire was well governed. King Wu said, "I have ten able ministers."

Confucius commented, "Talent [*cai*] is hard to find—is it not true? Talent flourished in the time of Yao and Shun and at the beginning of Zhou, [yet Shun had only five good men, and as for Wu,] with a woman among them there were only nine such men."

[Confucius said,] "When Zhou already possessed two-thirds of the empire, it continued to serve the Yin dynasty. The virtue of the Zhou could be described as the highest virtue."

When the early Chinese talked about talent, *cai* (材), they had in mind someone who had moral integrity and could, at the same time, handle affairs in the world with skill and vision. Very few could measure up to such standards, Liu Baonan observes, and for this reason Confucius said "Talent is hard to find." This is one question scholars try to address in their commentaries. There are, however, many more. Who, for instance, were the five good men who worked with Yao and Shun and the nine good men who worked with King Wen and King Wu, and who was the woman—did she hold high office? Should the last paragraph be a separate entry, and what did Confucius mean when he said, "When Zhou already possessed two-third of the empire, it continued to serve the Yin dynasty"? Most scholars agree on the identity of the good counselors, and they believe that the woman was either King Wen's or King Wu's wife, and that because she was not allowed a position in government she did not have the political status of a minister. The last paragraph could have been a loose strip of bamboo text that the editors put there because it was also about the history of the early Zhou; and when speaking about "the supreme virtue" of the Zhou, Confucius had in mind King Wen, who, like his uncle Tai Bo, possessed the virtue of yielding. King Wen could have completed his conquest of the Shang, but a sense of humility, perhaps, held him back, and he left the final assault on Shang to his son King Wu. Confucius says in 8.1 that Tai Bo embodied the highest virtue, because Tai Bo "yielded his right to the empire three times," and here, in 8.20, he uses the same characters, *zhide* (至德), "the highest virtue," to describe King Wen.

8.21 The Master said, "I can find no fault with [Emperor] Yu. His food and drink were simple, but for the gods and spirits, he provided lavish offerings to show his filial devotion. His everyday clothes were plain, but his ceremonial robes and caps were of the utmost elegance and beauty. His dwelling was shabby, but he put all his energy into constructing ditches and irrigation channels. I can find no fault with Yu."

Yu was Yu the Great, who, according to early stories, controlled the flood that ravaged the central plains during the time of Yao and Shun. Mencius says, "Yu was entrusted with the task of controlling the flood. He led the floodwater into the sea by cutting channels for it in the ground." And during the eight years when Yu was on the job, "he passed the door of his own house three times without entering." He, in the eyes of the Confucians and their rivals, the Mohists, represented the perfect example of someone who devoted his life to working for the public good without any thought for himself and his family. And even after Shun ceded the throne to him, Yu saw himself as the empire's caretaker, not its master, which explains the comment Confucius makes in 8.18.

BOOK NINE

9.1 The Master seldom spoke about suitability [*li*], destiny [*ming*], and humaneness [*ren*].

The third-century scholar He Yan takes *li* to mean "appropriateness" or "suitability." He says, "*Li* [suitability] goes together with *yi* [rightness]." But most of the later scholars think differently: they say that *li* means "profit." The eleventh-century thinker Cheng Yi writes, "The drive to make a profit [*li*] is detrimental to the drive to do the right thing [*yi*]," and this is the reason why "Confucius avoided talking about it." But how did this happen? How did *li* become disassociated from "rightness" and reemerge as its opposite? Liu Baonan gives much consideration to this question in his commentary. In his view, He Yan's reading of *li* comes from the *Book of Changes* and other early sources, as in such expressions as "it is fitting [*li*] to see the great man," "it is suitable [*li*] to invade and conquer," and "it is fitting [*li*] to cross the wide river." "The gentleman understands the meaning of *li* and *yi*," says Liu Baonan, so that even though it may seem unsuitable for him, say, "to leap into fire or water," because he is trying to save the life of his lord or father, what he does is right and is, therefore, suitable. "The gentleman knows that the question of suitability cannot stand outside the idea of rightness," Liu explains, but "the petty man knows only about suitability [what suits him and what is profitable to him] and not rightness." And as more people talked about *li* apart from rightness as their single objective, it lost its moral significance. But why did Confucius avoid speaking about *li*? The topic, for him, was "too subtle to go into," Liu writes, and Confucius was afraid that people might "misunderstand what he thought about it." And why did he seldom speak about destiny—the force behind life and death, fortune and misfortune?

Perhaps because it was inexplicable, and Confucius was reluctant to talk about anything that he could not explain. And as for humaneness (*ren*), many scholars point out that from the records in the *Analects*, it seems that Confucius spoke often about the subject, which would contradict what is said here. Liu Baonan, following another Qing scholar, Ran Yuan, tells us that Confucius was indeed reluctant to talk about humaneness because he felt he had not achieved it himself and so did not want to speak to others about it, but his disciples, realizing that this was an important subject, recorded everything he said about it and so "it seemed that he spoke much about humaneness."

9.2 A villager from Daxiang said, "How great is Confucius! He is vastly learned, and so has not made a name for himself in any particular area."

The Master, having heard this, said to his disciples, "What should I specialize in? Charioteering? Or archery? I think I will specialize in charioteering."

There are two ways of understanding this exchange: one has the two men trading barbs and the other has the same men being courteous to each other. The two ways contradict each other, yet both are sound. In the first scenario, the villager says of Confucius that he is learned in a broad sense but is not accomplished in any field, and Confucius returns the gibe by saying, Maybe I should try to perfect one particular set of skills—should I specialize in charioteering? Or archery? I think I'll choose charioteering (the most humble of the six arts). In the second scenario, the villager speaks like a man of knowledge: he knows that it would be impossible to associate a man of wide learning with any single profession, and that this was true for Yao and Shun and is true for Confucius; and Confucius responds by saying that he cannot accept such an accolade and that he is considering specializing in charioteering.

9.3 The Master said, "Linen for ceremonial caps is what the rites prescribed. Nowadays, black silk is used, which is frugal. I follow the current practice. To bow at the foot of the dais, before ascending the stairs, is what the rites prescribed. Nowadays people bow at the top of the stairs, after they have reached the dais, which is presumptuous. Though it is against current practice, I still bow at the foot of the dais."

To weave fibers of hemp into linen was more labor intensive than weaving silk, and so Confucius was ready to go along with the contemporary practice of wearing a ceremonial cap made of silk even though it was not what the rites called for. But he refused to follow the practice of bowing after one had climbed the stairs because this would mean that he would stand on the same level as his lord, which was disrespectful, and so he always observed the prescribed rule. Confucius knew that many factors could have contributed to a modification in ritual practice, and he was willing to consider the change if there was a good reason to do so and if it did not encourage laxity or transgressive behavior in human relationships.

9.4 The Master stayed away from four things: he did not put forth theories or conjectures; he did not think that he must be right; he was not obdurate; he was not self-centered.

My reading of the "four things" Confucius avoided follows that of Zhu Xi, who feels that the four are related sequentially. Once you have created a theory, he explains, you think that things must perform according to what your theory dictates; you will refuse to change your mind even when evidence shows that things are otherwise, and this is why the world is only as large as yourself. One could also say that Confucius stayed away from these four things because he saw them as a form of entrapment—what Zheng Xuan calls "an invitation to living a life of ignorance."

9.5 The Master found his life under threat when he was in Kuang. He said, "With King Wen dead, is it not so that his cultural vestiges are invested in me? If Heaven intended this culture to be destroyed, it would not have let the descendants [of King Wen] take part in it. Since Heaven has not destroyed this culture, what can the people of Kuang do to me?"

Traditional scholars first try to explain just what sort of danger Confucius encountered in Kuang and why this should have come about. They all seem to agree that the crisis was a case of mistaken identity. The men of Kuang thought that Confucius was Yang Hu because of their physical likeness, and Yang Hu, though only a family retainer, had at one time been the most powerful figure in the state of Lu—someone everybody feared, from the ruler to the hereditary counselors and even Confucius himself. This Yang Hu, according to the history in the *Zuo Commentary*, had the army of Lu seize the town of Kuang from the state of Zheng in 504 BC, and to curry favor with the ruler of another state, he presented a group of captives to that man. For this reason the people of Kuang held a great grudge against him. Thus when Confucius showed up in Kuang, the men of Kuang, believing that he was Yang Hu, had him surrounded and were ready to take their revenge.

Confucius' response to the crisis in Kuang was a mixture of bravado and confidence: he was certain that he had inherited King Wen's work to keep the Zhou culture alive; and believing that this was also Heaven's intent, he thought that no harm could come to him. But just how did he manage to extract himself from this tight situation? The *Analects* does not say, but the Han dynasty writers pitched in, offering several possible resolutions. One memorable one had Confucius sing a melody, and "after three rounds, the men of Kuang dispersed, and the siege was over."

9.6 The chief counselor asked Zigong, "Your Master is a sage, is he not? But then why does he have so many skills?"

Zigong said, "Indeed, Heaven intended him to become a sage and to acquire many skills."

When he heard this, the Master said, "The chief counselor understood me well. When I was young, I was from a humble station, which is the reason why I am skilled in many menial things. Should a gentleman be proficient in many menial tasks? No, definitely not."

A "sage" (*sheng*), in the minds of the early Chinese, referred to someone who was born with foreknowledge, with an uncanny ability to know the future, which was quite different from skills acquired through learning and practice. Thus the chief counselor (probably of the state of Wu) was puzzled: If Confucius was destined to become a sage, why did he have to acquire so many skills? Zigong, in his attempt to defend his teacher, said that his teacher was endowed with two sets of gifts—the potential to become a sage and the ability to acquire many skills. Confucius, however, felt that it was the chief counselor who understood him better than his disciple. To make his point, he said that it is not necessary even for a gentleman to be "proficient in menial skills"—and how much less so for a sage. And why was he "skilled in many menial things"? This was because he was "from a humble station" and was forced by circumstances to be adept in many things to make a living.

9.7 Lao added that he had heard the Master say, "I could not prove myself in office [*bushi*]. That is why I acquired many skills."

Many scholars say that 9.7 and 9.6 should be considered together— that when Lao (probably a disciple) heard what Confucius said in 9.6, he reminded his teacher of what he had heard him say on another occasion. And what Confucius said in 9.7 could mean either "I could not enter government service as easily as young men of prominent families because of my poor and humble background, and so I acquired many skills" or "The world could not put me to use, and so I acquired many skills in order to put myself to use." The first reading supports Confucius' comment in 9.6, while the second reading offers another reason why Confucius was skilled in many things.

9.8 The Master said, "Do I possess an all-knowing cognizance? I do not. If a simple fellow asks me a question, my mind at first is a complete blank, and I have to knock at both sides [of the question] until everything has been considered [and some clarity begins to emerge]."

An alternative reading is: "Do I possess the ability to know the intent of others? I do not. If a simple fellow asks me a question with openness and sincerity, I will try to take him through the two sides of his question, and I will keep on doing it until he understands it himself." Many scholars prefer the second reading. This, they say, is consistent with Confucius' character and his teaching style—that he would never approach anyone who came to him with a question with ready answers or preconceived ideas even when the person was a simple fellow; that, instead, he would encourage the person to think through the problem himself by taking him through the pros and cons of the matter in question. Some scholars, however, argue that since in 9.2, 9.3, 9.6, and 9.7 Confucius is essentially talking about himself—his early life, his social background, his attempts to make a living—here he must also be referring to himself, to his, and not anyone else's, struggle to understand something; and that knowledge, in his case, came from the struggle, from "knocking at both sides" of the question. My translation follows this reading.

9.9 The Master said, "The phoenix has not been seen. No chart has emerged from the river. It is the end of me, is it not?"

The appearance of the phoenix and the issuance of a mysterious chart from the Yellow River were thought to auger the rise of a sage and the dawning of a world governed by the kingly way. Confucius' lament refers either to the fact that he would not be able to live in such a world or to the fact that he was born in the wrong age and so would never be able to realize his potential.

9.10 Whenever the Master saw a person dressed in mourning clothes, or wearing a mourning headdress [*mian*] with gown and skirt, or a blind man, even if such a person was younger in age, he would invariably rise to his feet, and if he had to pass by such a person, he would always quicken his steps.

Mian could mean "ceremonial cap," and references to those who wore ceremonial caps with gowns and skirts often meant officials. Thus some scholars understand this passage to say that Confucius always showed respect to those in mourning, those who were officials, and those who were blind. But scholars such as Qian Daxin and Qian Mu point out that *mian* could also mean *wen* (綄), a mourning headdress, which seems to make more sense in this context. Many commentaries suggest that we read this entry together with Book Ten to get a sense of how Confucius in his own practice let ritual decorum become an expression of respect and empathy.

9.11 Yan Hui said with a deep sigh, "The more I look up at it, the higher it appears. The more I bore into it, the harder it becomes. I see it before me, yet suddenly it is behind me. But my teacher knows how to coax me to move forward, and he does it a step at a time. He expands me with literature and culture and pulls me in with the rites. I cannot stop even if I want to, but having done all I can, it still seems to stand way above me. I don't know where to start, however much I wish to pursue it."

In Confucius' estimation, Yan Hui was one who loved learning more than anyone else; and, in Zigong's words, he was the one who, "having learned one thing," could "give play to ten." But here Yan Hui himself is speaking about the burden of possessing the urgency to learn and about the labor of learning, which he thinks is inseparable from the love for it. And it seems it was his decision to go at it on his own and his unwillingness to give up no matter how difficult the journey that made him stand out. Yet despite his drive and his gift of perspicuity and understanding, Yan Hui needed instruction from someone who knew how to urge him on and rein him in, and he found it in Confucius, in his words and presence.

9.12 The Master was gravely ill. Zilu instructed the disciples [who were present] to prepare [for the funeral] in the manner of retainers.

When the Master's condition had improved somewhat, he upbraided Zilu, saying, "You have been practicing chicanery for much too long! By pretending I had retainers when I had none, whom were we trying to deceive? Heaven? Besides, would I not rather die in the arms of a few good friends than

in the arms of retainers? And even if I could not have a minister's burial, it was not as if I was dying by the wayside."

The event described here must have happened during Confucius'
fourteen-year exile, after his resignation as minister of crime of Lu
(because, he said, he could not have a minister's burial) and before
his return to Lu (because Zilu remained in Wei and died in Wei, and
was not with Confucius when Confucius came home).

Confucius could not have a minister's burial because after he gave
up his job in Lu he was not appointed to another position of ministe-
rial rank, and a former minister was not the same as a minister—he
was not entitled to have retainers and to have his funeral prepared by
men "in the manner of retainers." Thus it was wrong for Zilu to
think that he could have the disciples pretend to be retainers. "Whom
are we trying to deceive?" Confucius asks. "Heaven?" He scoffs at
Zilu for "practicing chicanery" even though he knows that Zilu
meant well.

9.13 Zigong asked, "If there were a beautiful piece of jade
right here, would you put it in a box and hide it or try to find
someone with a good offer and sell it?"
    The Master said, "Sell it! Sell it! I am waiting for a person
with the right offer."

An alternative translation of Zigong's question is: "Would you put it
in a box and hide it or look to sell it for a good price?" And in
response, Confucius could have said: "Sell it! Sell it! I am waiting for
the right offer." The difference between the two readings hinges on
the word *jia* (also pronounced as *gu*). *Jia* could refer either to the
price of an object or to the broker who offers a price. Liu Baonan
says that since the point of Zigong's question is about whether Confucius is willing to put his talent to use in politics, *jia* must refer to
the person who could give him the right offer for the precious jade
that was his talent; and the person with the offer had to be a perceptive ruler who saw the potential in Confucius and sought his service.
Most scholars stress that Confucius did not hawk his "beautiful
jade" about and that, in his own words, he was "waiting" for the
person with the right offer to come along. And, they claim, when he

said "Sell it! Sell it!" Confucius was merely mimicking Zigong, who had once been a merchant and would, from time to time, still think and talk like a merchant.

9.14 The Master wanted to live among the Nine Yi barbarian tribes. Someone said, "But they are uncouth. How could you put up with their ways?"

The Master said, "A gentleman has lived among them, so how could they be uncouth?"

The two issues here are: Who were the Nine Yi barbarian tribes? And who was the "gentleman" with the transformative power? Most scholars think that "the Nine Yi barbarian tribes" refers to the non-Chinese who lived on the east coast of the Zhou empire, people who were "gentle by nature and could be easily guided to the moral way." These scholars also put Confucius' present remark with what he declaims in 5.7—"If I cannot practice a proper way here in this world, then I shall take to the open sea and drift around on a bamboo raft." The sea route could take him to a better place, away from the Chinese states to the home of the Nine Yi tribes of the east, where, according to the early writings on foreign places, the people were "simple and humane and had a love for life." These scholars, therefore, disagree with those who associate the Nine Yi tribes with another group of barbarians living in the south, around the state of Chu, men whose way of life was "fierce and violent." And when Confucius mentions the "gentleman," is he talking about himself? Is he saying that he could have had a refining influence on the Yi barbarians? While most scholars think so, some feel otherwise, saying that Confucius would never have called himself a "gentleman." The gentleman he had in mind, these scholars say, was probably Jizi, the older brother of the last king of Shang. According to the early sources, Jizi was as virtuous as his brother was depraved—Confucius describes him in 18.1 as a humane man—and after his dynasty fell, he refused to serve the new dynasty and was, therefore, enfeoffed in the eastern region, where the Yi barbarians dwelled. Thus Confucius, in this interpretation, seems to imply that because the gentleman, Jizi, had long ago settled among tribes of the Nine Yi barbarians, the people there could not be "uncouth."

9.15 The Master said, "It was only after my return to Lu from Wei that music was correctly restored, with the *ya* and the *song* each finding its proper place."

Ya and *song* are names usually associated with the "Major" and Minor" sections and the "Hymns" section of the *Book of Poetry*, but, here, as some commentaries point out, they probably refer to the music that accompanied the odes from the *ya* and *song*. And as for *ya* and *song* each "finding its proper place," the early Qing scholar Mao Qiling writes, this must have meant that the music of, say, "The Deer Cry" [from the "Minor" section of the *Odes*] was played only at such celebrations as "the community drinking festival" and "the archery contest and the community feast," which, according to the early Zhou rites, were the right occasions. To give music back its integrity was, in Confucius' view, essential to the restoration of political order, something he was able to realize in Lu after his return in the winter of 484 BC.

9.16 The Master said, "Serving the duke and his high counselors in public life; my father and older brother at home; not daring to let myself be remiss in funerary duties; not to get addled by wine—I have no trouble with these things."

Most scholars agree that the weight of this remark lies in the last part of the sentence, which could mean that these four things are so fundamental to human conduct that either "I have no trouble with them [*heyou yu wo*]" or most people could do these things and so "what need would there be for me [*heyou yu wo*]?"

9.17 Standing by the river, the Master declaimed, "How it flows on like this, never ceasing day and night!"

Commentaries give different explanations of Confucius' remark here. Some understand it as Confucius' lament about the passing of time, which, like the river moving forward, can never turn back. Others, such as the Han thinker Dong Zhongshu, try to force a moral reading on it, seeing the potential of water as the perfect metaphor for the strength, the equanimity, the perceptiveness, the wisdom, the pureness of character, and the courage of a virtuous man. The Song thinker Zhu Xi feels that the statement is about learning. To transform "without ceasing" is a "fundamental characteristic of the Way," Zhu Xi writes, and "it is most evident in the flowing of water. Thus Confucius used this to bring home the message that all those who wished to learn should be vigilant [of their thought and action] constantly, not letting their effort slacken even for an instant." The most cogent explanation of this passage, however, comes from Mencius, a much earlier follower of Confucius. Someone once asked Mencius, "Confucius more than once expressed his admiration for water, saying, 'Water! Water!' But what good did Confucius see in water?" Mencius replied, "Water from a source rushes forward, never ceasing day and night, filling all the cracks and hollows as it advances, before it drains into the sea. Everything with a source is like that, and this is the good Confucius saw in water." The source explains the integrity of a river—that it is always moving, always alive, and that, unlike water "collected in the gutters," it will never dry up.

9.18 The Master said, "I have never met a person who loved virtue as much as he loved physical beauty."

The Han historian Sima Qian tries to fit this utterance into a particular moment of Confucius' life, using it to explain why Confucius was disappointed with the ruler he was hoping to serve. "Duke Ling of Wei was out and about, riding in the same carriage with his consort," Sima Qian writes, "and he made Confucius travel in a separate one behind him. Confucius said, 'I have never met a person who loved virtue as much as he loved physical beauty.'" The historicized version seems affected. It lacks the elegance of the Song scholar Xie Liangzuo's explanation, which says, "To like physical beauty and to dislike nasty odors are true expressions of one's feelings. Thus if a person can love virtue as much as he loves physical beauty, this means that he truly loves virtue. Very few people can do this." If we follow Xie Liangzuo's reading, then what Confucius says here resonates with Zixia's statement in 1.7.

9.19 The Master said, "I could use the example of building a mountain. If with just one more basketful of dirt to go I stopped, then I was the one who stopped [and left the work incomplete]. I could also use the example of leveling ground. If I heaped just one basketful of dirt, then progress was made and I was the one who moved the work forward."

Nearly all the scholars say that the subject of Confucius' statement is learning and cultivation. Entries 7.8, 7.19, 8.7, 9.11, and 9.21 are just a few of those in the *Analects* that could support such a reading. But what Confucius says here is also relevant to almost everything one sets out to accomplish. Mencius makes a similar point when he says, "To try to achieve anything is like digging a well. You can dig a hole nine fathoms deep, but if you fail to reach the source of water, it is just an abandoned well."

9.20 The Master said, "The person I could talk to and never get tired—that was Hui [Yan Hui], wasn't it?"

An alternative translation is: "The person I could talk to without seeing him ever growing tired—that was Hui, wasn't it?" Both readings suggest that Yan Hui was pleased with what his teacher said and was able to absorb what he heard, and so in the first reading Confucius was never tired of speaking to him, and in the second reading Yan Hui was never tired of listening to Confucius speak.

9.21 The Master, referring to Yan Hui, said, "It is a pity! I saw him moving forward but did not see him complete his journey."

Confucius' regret was about Yan Hui's untimely death, not about his not having the will to realize his potential.

9.22 The Master said, "There are seedlings that never grow to flower. And there are plants that have grown to flower but never bear fruit."

Many scholars feel that it is reasonable to assume that Confucius' comment here, like the previous one, is also about Yan Hui, about how early death had ended his chance for self-perfection. But this remains a conjecture. From a different perspective, one could say that the subject discussed here is the same as the one in 9.19.

9.23 The Master said, "The young should have our respect. How do we know that the coming generation may not prove to be the equal of the present one? If a man is forty or fifty and has not done anything to distinguish himself [*buwen*], then he is not worthy of our respect."

Confucius thinks that the young deserve our respect because they are in their prime and are quick to learn. It is their youthful energy that gives them an edge over those who are already in midlife. Thus, he says, if you are forty or fifty and have not accomplished anything of distinction, this means that you have wasted your youth and so do not merit respect. A man of fifty in Confucius' time was considered an old man, an *ai*, someone for whom "learning would no longer be easy." Yet Confucius himself says, in 7.17, "Grant me a few more years so that when I reach the age of fifty, I may try to understand the principles of change and be able to steer clear of making mistakes."

Some of the discussion in the commentaries is about the meaning of *buwen*—which, most scholars agree, has nothing to do with making a name. Confucius, in his conversation with Zizhang in 12.20, objects to the idea that the point of learning, and of cultivation, is "getting oneself known [*wen*]." Instead, he believes that if a person has applied himself to learning in his youth, it will be natural for him "to accomplish something of distinction [*wen*]" by the time he is forty or fifty. Thus one scholar suggests an alternative reading of the second sentence: "How do we know that what the future holds will not come up to our expectations now?"

9.24 The Master said, "How can one not agree with exemplary words? But what is important is that they will lead you to self-reform. How can one not be pleased with gentle and tactful words of advice? The important thing is to try to understand the point of such words. To be pleased [with someone's advice] but not to try to understand [the point of his advice]; to agree with [someone's words] but not [to let his words] bring about self-reform—there is nothing I can do with those who behave like this."

Two words *xun* and *yi* occasioned some discussion in the commentaries. *Xun*, translated here as "gentle and tactful," suggests that the words of advice are phrased in a way that does not violate the self-respect of the person who is being advised. *Yi*, translated here as "to try to understand the point," literally means "to reel off the silk from cocoons," but it also has a larger import, including the idea of "searching for the source, the beginning, or the principles of things."

Liu Baonan, quoting the Han dynasty text the *Huainanzi*, says, "When listening to words that describe what is supreme virtue and what is noble action, even the base and the reprehensible would know to admire them. . . . Yet one would always find lots of people doing the admiring and very few trying to put these ideas into action. Why is that so? It is because people simply are unable to turn back their nature."

9.25 The Master said, "A person should stay close to those who do their best and are trustworthy. He should not befriend those who are not his equals. And when he makes a mistake, he should not be afraid to correct it."

This statement is identical to the last three sentences of 1.8. See my commentary on that passage.

9.26 The Master said, "One can strip the Three Armies of their commander, but no one can deprive even a commoner of his purpose."

The Three Armies represented the entire military force of the state of Lu. They had been at the disposal of the ruler of Lu, but by the time of Confucius' birth, they were in the hands of the three hereditary families. The Han scholar Zheng Xuan writes that even though the commander of the Three Armies is powerful, "his position still relies on the support of other people and so, when faced with a tough adversary, he can be ousted and replaced," but "once a man, even a commoner, is set on his purpose, no one can take it away from him."

9.27 The Master said, "Not to feel ashamed standing next to a man wearing fox or badger fur while himself dressed in a tattered gown padded with silk floss—this could only be You [Zilu]!"

> "Not mean, not grasping,
> How could this not be good?"

Zilu recited these lines all the time. The Master said, "Is this enough to be called good?"

We have already watched the unfolding of Zilu's character in the *Analects* by following what Confucius says about him in 5.7, 5.8, 5.14, 6.28, 7.11, 7.35, and 9.12. In these remarks, Confucius seems dismissive of Zilu, yet this is not because Zilu came from rustic roots. Confucius' opinion of Zilu was formed from his observation of this man: Zilu was quick-tempered; he lacked awareness and judgment; and he was a bit of a bungler. On this occasion, Confucius pointed out a noble side of Zilu, but Zilu was too clumsy to savor the moment for himself. He thought that the first of the two lines from an ode, which includes the phrases, "not mean" (out of envy) and "not grasping," perfectly summed up Confucius' description of him; and he wanted to drive home the point that having these traits was enough for one to be deemed "good," so he "recited [them] all the time." His behavior, once again, tested Confucius' patience.

9.28 The Master said, "Only in the deepest winter do we realize that the pine and cypress are the last to shed their leaves."

Zheng Xuan from the second century and He Yan a generation later both feel that Confucius had in mind "the gentleman" or "a man of worth" when he talked about pine and cypress. Only a man of worth "would not alter his conduct when he finds himself in the most difficult—the most desperate—circumstances," Zheng Xuan writes. Liu Baonan thinks that what Confucius told Zilu in 15.2, when they were on the verge of being starved to death somewhere in Chen or Cai, could support such a reading: "A gentleman," he stressed, "would persevere even in a situation [like ours]. It is the petty man who would not be able to withstand it." To show the relationship of 9.28 and 15.2, Liu also quotes a passage from the *Zhuangzi*, where the author has Confucius say to his disciples: "I face the difficulties ahead and try not to lose my integrity. When the cold winter has arrived and snow and frost have fallen, only then do I realize how the pine and cypress flourish. The perils here in Chen and Cai are a blessing to me!"

9.29 The Master said, "The wise are never perplexed. The humane never suffer from vexation. The brave are never afraid."

"The wise," Liu Baonan writes, "examine all things with clear eyes and so they are not perplexed." The humane, Confucius said, "feel at home in humaneness"; they are at peace "in hard or easy circumstances," and so they do not "suffer from vexation." The brave, in Mencius' view, were not all the same. Some "never showed submission," he says, others always acted "without fear," but it was Confucius who understood "supreme courage." And, according to Mencius' account, Confucius described "supreme courage" in this way: "If, on looking within, one finds oneself to be in the wrong, then even though one's adversary be only a common fellow coarsely clad, one is bound to tremble with fear. But if one finds oneself to be in the right, one goes forward even against men in the thousands."

9.30 The Master said, "A partner in learning may not be good enough as a partner if you are on a quest for moral meaning. A partner on a quest for moral meaning may not be good enough as a partner if you intend to use the rites to help you find a steady frame and an equitable position. A partner who, like you, intends to use the rites to find a steady frame and an equitable position may not be good enough as a partner if you are in the act of exercising moral discretion."

What Confucius is trying to say here is that no human endeavor could be as tough and lonely as the act of exercising moral discretion. And he takes us to this conclusion by the long way, beginning with learning. To find a partner in learning is probably not that difficult, the statement implies, not as hard as finding a partner who, like you, hopes to let learning take him to some moral end. And this, in turn, is not as hard as searching for a partner who, again like you, relies on the practice of the rites to help him "find a steady frame and an equitable position." And even if you have found such a partner, he still cannot help you in matters where you have to decide what is right and what is fair.

9.31 "The flowers of the wild cherry,

> how they flutter this way and that.
> It's not that I don't think of you,
> but your home is so far away."

The Master said, "He did not think of her. If he did, how could distance have been a problem?"

The flowers fluttering mirror the speaker's heart in this lost poem from the *Book of Odes*. His feelings waver: he cares for her and yet he does not. Traditional scholars insist that Confucius used the sentiment expressed in this poem—"but your home is so far away"—to talk about one's relationship with humaneness. "Is humaneness far away?" he asks in 7.30. "As soon as I desire humaneness, it is here." Still, it is possible to read Confucius' response to the poem as a comment on the poet's vacillating heart.

BOOK TEN

Book Ten is essentially a record of what other people observed about Confucius—what he was like at home or at a village gathering, at mealtime or when he took repose, in front of his superiors or around his equals, when he was ill or when friends were ill, when he was in mourning or when friends were in mourning—and also what he ate and what he wore and the guidelines he followed in food and clothes. The appellation Master Kong (Confucius) appears only in the first entry.

10.1 In his own community, Master Kong [Confucius] was agreeable and modest, and he gave the appearance of being too clumsy to speak. In the ancestral temple and at court, though fluent and forceful in his disquisitions, he was also cautious and did not say more than was necessary.

Here we find a description of Confucius when he was in his home village and when he was at the ancestral temple and at the court of his ruler. His neighborhood would be the place where his elders lived, and so he would conduct himself in a "modest" and "agreeable" manner and would defer to them as if he were "too clumsy to speak." But the ancestral temple or the ruler's court presented a different situation, where Confucius had to speak up either in his capacity as a ritual specialist or as a political counselor. And, the text says, Confucius was "fluent and forceful" (*bianbian*), but also "cautious," and he "did not say more than necessary."

10.2 When speaking at court with counselors of the lower rank, he was relaxed and affable. When speaking with counselors of high rank, he was frank but respectful. And in the ruler's presence, though he was filled with reverence and awe, he was perfectly composed.

The first half of 10.2 refers to the gathering of the junior and the senior counselors to discuss state affairs before their audience with the ruler. Confucius is described as "relaxed and affable" with those who were of "the lower rank," which means his equals, since he never attained high office, and as "frank but respectful" with those who were his superiors. The counselors' gathering was followed by the arrival of the ruler, and in this man's presence, though Confucius was "filled with reverence and awe," he was not petrified, for "he was perfectly composed."

It is helpful, I feel, to consider 10.1, 10.2, and 10.3 sequentially. Toward the end of 10.1, we are told about Confucius' demeanor at the court of his ruler. In 10.2, we learn how he behaved at court, and in 10.3, we see how he conducted himself when he was summoned to assist the chief counselor in receiving a guest of the state.

10.3 When the ruler summoned him [to assist the chief counselor] in receiving a guest of the state, his face took on a solemn expression and his steps a brisk pace. When he bowed to those standing around him, raising his cupped hands to the right and to the left, his robed skirt swayed front and back, without being ruffled. When going forward with quickened steps, he was like a bird about to take flight [*yiru*]. After the guest had left, he always came back to report to the ruler, "The guest is no longer looking back."

Ritual performances in the political realm often seemed unnatural and rigid because missteps could lead to serious consequences, and in the case of Confucius they were no different, but observers also pointed out the fluency with which he carried out these formalized movements: "like a bird about to take flight [*yiru*]." Liu Baonan says that *yiru* could mean either "to float like birds in air" or "to be dignified and composed."

The eighteenth-century scholar Jiang Yong notes that a counselor of Confucius' rank would not have been asked to receive a guest of the state—this was the prerogative of the chief counselor—and so it is possible that the ruler asked Confucius "to assist the chief coun-selor" on such occasions because he "knew the rites well."

10.4 When he entered the gate of his ruler, he drew himself in [in a respectful manner] as if the gate were not wide and tall enough to let him through. He did not stand in the middle of the gate and did not tread on the threshold. When he passed by the seat of the ruler, he looked energized and his pace has-tened, and when he spoke, he appeared as if he could not get all his words out. When he gathered up his robe and ascended the hall of his ruler, again he drew himself in, and he held his breath in as if he was not breathing at all. But as soon as he was leaving the hall, descending even just one step, his whole expression would be relaxed with a touch of lightness and gai-ety. And once he reached the bottom of the steps, he moved forward with quickened steps, like a bird about to take flight. But the next time he passed by the seat of the ruler, he would again assume a cautious and respectful demeanor.

Traditional scholars used their knowledge of early history and the rit-ual texts to try to answer some of the questions raised by this descrip-tion. Why, for instance, did Confucius think that when entering the gate of the ruler it was wrong to "stand in the middle" and to "tread on the threshold"? What was "the middle of the gate"? And when the text says "he passed by the seat of the ruler," what does that mean? The gate of the regional ruler, according to the ritual prescription of the Zhou dynasty, was usually divided in two by a post in the middle. Guests of the state would enter through the left side, or the west gate, while the ruler and his counselors would enter through the right side, or the east gate. Confucius avoided standing at the center of the east gate and treading on the threshold, both of which were the preroga-tives of the ruler. And "the seat" in this passage, according to schol-ars, refers to the throne—where the regional ruler would sit when he was holding audience. Afterward, they say, he would withdraw to the *luqin*, a private hall, where he would discuss political affairs with his counselors, and since he would leave first, the counselors who fol-lowed him to the private hall would be passing by an empty seat. Con-fucius, at that precise moment, the record says, "looked energized and his pace hastened." And as he ascended the hall of the ruler, he would again tighten his posture, holding his breath, but as soon as he was ready to leave, "descending even just one step," his whole body would begin to relax, and when he reached the bottom of the steps he would move forward gracefully, "like a bird about to take flight."

10.5 When he carried the jade tablet [of his ruler in the role of an emissary], he drew himself in as if he could not bear the weight. When he held it high, it seemed as if he was bowing to someone; when he held it low, it seemed as if he was offering an object to someone. He looked alert, as though in fear of making a mistake. And he walked in small steps as though his feet never left the ground [like the wheels of a cart]. But he looked amiable when presenting the official gifts and was even more agreeable in a private audience.

Qian Mu points out that the records in this chapter give three descriptions of "drawing oneself in" (*jugong*) as an act of showing respect. In 10.4, when Confucius entered the gate of his ruler's court, he "drew himself in as if the gate were not wide enough and tall enough to let him through," and when he ascended the hall of his ruler, he also "drew himself in" and "held his breath in as if he was not breathing at all." Here, he draws himself in as if he cannot bear the weight of the jade tablet he carries on behalf of his ruler.

Several commentaries note that when Confucius was an official in Lu, his ruler never sent him on a mission to another state. Thus the description of him holding the jade tablet of his ruler refers to something that could not have taken place, and thus it may imply that not all the records in the *Analects* are accurate. Some scholars, in defense of the text's integrity, offer an explanation. They say that in 10.5 Confucius is merely giving his disciples a demonstration of how to conduct themselves should they be sent to another state as representatives of their own ruler—in other words, that ritual performance was a component of his teaching of the rites.

10.6 The gentleman would not use reddish indigo or iron gray to trim his robe, nor vermillion and red for his casual clothes.

In the heat of the summer, he wore an unlined garment of either fine or coarse hemp, but he always topped it with a jacket when he went out. He wore a black dust-gown over lambskin, a white one over fawnskin, and a yellow one over fox fur. His informal fur coat was longer than his formal ones but with a shorter right sleeve. When sleeping, he always had a coverlet, which was one and half times the length of his body. He used the thick fur of badgers and foxes as cushions to sit on. Other than when he was in mourning, he always wore his big sash with jade ornaments [that were proper to his position]. And except for his ceremonial skirts [which were made from single bolts of fabric with multiple pleats], all others were cut pieces sewn together. He never wore [black] kidskin jackets and black caps when making calls of condolence. And on the day of the new moon, he always went to court in his [black] court attire.

This description may give the impression that "the gentleman"—which, scholars say, can refer only to Confucius—was a smart dresser and that each morning he gave a lot of thought to what he should wear during the day and in the evening. Aesthetic and functional considerations were important to Confucius, but even more critical was ritual correctness. Thus his clothes during mourning were unadorned—without jade pendants attached to the sash. And he did not wear black jackets and black caps to funerals because black was an elegant and auspicious color in the Chinese mind, more appropriate for attending the morning court than for paying condolences. Expense, too, was a factor for him. Skirts made from a single piece of fabric were costly, and so, he says, he would wear them only for state ceremonies. In 3.4, Confucius tells Lin Fang, "With regard to the rites as a whole, it is better to err on the side of being frugal than on that of being extravagant." And so, unless the rites absolutely demanded extravagance, he preferred simpler, less lavish attire.

10.7 During periods of purification [before a sacrifice], he always wore a clean undergarment [*mingyi*] made of linen. During periods of purification, he always altered his diet, and he also changed his dwelling place.

Han scholars disagree on the meaning of *mingyi*. Kong Anguo thinks that the term refers to the robe one would wear after a bath of purification. But Zheng Xuan explains *mingyi* as a "clean undergarment" because the undergarment is the most intimate piece of clothing on the person who is performing the purification and it is up to him "to keep it clean." The diet Confucius followed during the period of purification would have consisted of dishes prepared without meat but with fresh ingredients and a clean taste. And he would have changed his dwelling place from his private bedchamber to the front room in the house, to avoid contact with women. Purification before a sacrifice, the *Book of Rites* says, is meant to get a person ready to meet his ancestors with keen perception.

10.8 He did not overeat if the rice was polished or if the meat was finely cut. He did not eat rice that had gone off, nor fish or meat that had spoiled. He did not eat food with a sickly color or a foul odor, nor anything that was overcooked or undercooked. He did not eat food that was not in season, nor did he eat except at mealtimes. He did not eat meat that was not properly cut off or meat paired with the wrong sauce. Even when there was plenty of meat, he would not eat more meat than grain. Only in the case of wine was no limit laid down, but he never drank to the point of being addled. He would not touch wine that had been sitting overnight nor dried meat bought from a shop. And even when he kept a plate of ginger on the table [after the meal was over], he did not eat too much of it.

Another reading of the first sentence is: "He did not mind if the rice was polished [or not] or if the meat was finely cut [or not]." This means that Confucius was able to find joy in fine or coarse food. The reading reflected in my translation, however, gives more weight to the question of balance, which is what this passage is intended to teach us: not to eat in excess even when the food is of the highest grade; not to eat more meat than rice even when meat is plentiful; and not to overeat even ginger, a condiment that could clear the head and tame one's breath.

Here we also learn that Confucius rejected food that "had gone off" or was incorrectly prepared. Scholars who are eager to distinguish Confucius from an epicure claim that the reference to meat "not properly cut off" has a ritual overtone. In Confucius' time and throughout the Zhou, they say, a gentleman, even when he was eating at home, would follow the rules prescribed for a formal sacrifice. Meat was served in a large chunk on these occasions, and each portion was "cut off" from it. Confucius would refuse his share if the meat was not "properly cut off" (*gebuzheng*). This, as these scholars point out, is not the same as saying that Confucius would refuse the meat if it was not "properly cut up" (*qiebuzheng*). The latter would mean that Confucius was spurning the cook for his skills, but it was not until the Han dynasty, they say, that cooks began to cut meat up and serve it in slivers or slices.

Cooking and ritual practice in early China had a close relationship in other ways. Writings about culinary techniques were often anthologized in ritual texts, perhaps because in practice such techniques were governed by the same principles of fluidity in movement and timeliness in execution. This was something the fourth-century BC thinker Zhuangzi observed. In a story about a cook, he says that looking at this man taking apart an ox is like watching someone perform a ritual dance.

10.9 After he had assisted his lord in a sacrifice, he did not keep his portion of the sacrificial meat overnight. And he did not let the meat from a sacrifice conducted in the family sit for more than three days. After three days he would not eat that meat.

From preparation to completion, sacrifices conducted in the political world usually took three days: the sacrificial animal was slaughtered in the early morning on the first day; the king and the regional rulers would perform the sacrifice on the second day; and the ceremony would last another day, with the first- and second-level officials assisting their regional ruler in this round of sacrifice. Thus by the time the officials and the guests were sent home with a portion of the sacrificial meat, three days would have passed, and, in Confucius' view, this meat might spoil if it was allowed to sit overnight. He applied the three-day rule also to the meat used in a family sacrifice.

10.10 He did not speak [*yu*] during meals and did not converse [*yan*] when he was resting in bed.

Traditional scholars distinguish between *yu* (discussing a serious topic) and *yan* (carrying on a casual conversation).

10.11 Even when the meal was just coarse grain and vegetable broth, he always set aside a portion as an offering, and he did so with solemnity and respect.

An alternative reading is: "Even when all he had was coarse grain, vegetable soup, and melon, he would make the offering with solemnity and respect." In either case, the point is that Confucius always remembered his ancestors at mealtime, and no matter how simple the food might be, he would make his offering in a respectful manner.

10.12 He did not sit unless the mat was properly straightened.

Many scholars believe that the slip of bamboo text with this passage was misplaced—that it should have been bundled together with "He did not eat meat that was not properly cut off" in 10.8. In fact, this was how the passage was found in several early texts: "Confucius did not sit unless the mat was properly straightened and did not eat meat that was not properly cut off."

10.13 When celebrating a drinking festival in the local community, he left as soon as those with walking sticks had left.

Commentaries on the *Book of Rites* mention four types of drinking festivals at the local level, and the one described here seems to fit the *zha* sacrifice, which took place toward the end of the year with the village elder as the host and those over the age of sixty as the honored guests. Scholars say that the respect Confucius showed toward those "with walking sticks" seems to resonate with the point of the occasion and its ritual regulations, which specified just who could sit and who should stand and how many dishes a sixty-year-old, a seventy-year-old, or an eighty-year-old was allowed. Yet despite the orderliness these rules suggest, the *Book of Rites* also records that when Confucius asked his disciple Zigong whether he enjoyed the *zha* festival he had just attended, Zigong said, "People in our entire state seem to have gone crazed. So how could I have enjoyed it?" This, of course, meant that the drinking had gotten out of hand. In response, Confucius told Zigong to loosen up: "To work hard for a whole year and to have just one day of pleasure is not something you are able to understand. To live under pressure all the time without any leisure was something that even King Wen and King Wu could not achieve. To live in leisure and never feel any pressure was something King Wen and Wu would not do. To allow both pressure and leisure in one's life was the way of King Wen and King Wu."

10.14 When the villagers were performing the *nuo* [to drive away the spirits of disease and pestilence], he would put on his court robe and stand on the eastern steps.

The *nuo*, like the *zha* festival, was an occasion with the potential of spinning out of control because it involved the whole community—thus a large crowd—plus exorcism and again drinking. And while this was going on, why did Confucius stand on the eastern steps, dressed in his court robe? Kong Anguo from the Han says that Confucius stood outside the ancestral temple to assure the spirits inside that the *nuo* was meant to drive away harmful spirits but not them. Other scholars think that the gesture showed Confucius' willingness to accept certain popular beliefs and that by putting on a court robe he brought a certain amount of dignity to the occasion, which in turn would discourage others from going too far.

10.15 When he asked after someone in another state, he would bow twice [as if the person were present] before seeing the messenger off.

Bowing twice emphasized the sincerity of one's greeting, and the type of bowing Confucius performed, Liu Baonan says, was not *qishou* (prostrating with both hands and head on the ground) but *kongshou* (prostrating with hands on the ground and head lowered but not all the way to the ground). Liu also says that since Confucius was not acting in any official capacity, the person being asked after was probably a friend; and that he must have included a gift with his message, since that was the custom.

10.16 When Ji Kangzi sent him a gift of medicine, he bowed and accepted it, and he said [to the messenger], "Since I don't know anything about this medicine, I dare not taste it."

Ji Kangzi was the chief counselor of Lu and probably the man responsible for inviting Confucius back to Lu after his long absence. Here ritual etiquette demanded that Confucius accept this man's gift, but since the gift was medicine—something that could be harmful to the body if one ingested it without knowing its properties—he gave the messenger what seemed like a reasonable explanation for not tasting it, and because his decision was based on good sense, Confucius did not think that it violated ritual propriety.

10.17 The stables caught fire. [Having learned about it] upon his return from court, the Master asked, "Was anyone hurt?" He did not ask about the horses.

Scholars believe that the stables referred to here were Confucius', for if the fire had happened on state property, there would have been a record of it in the official chronicle, but the *Spring and Autumn Annals* of the state of Lu does not mention such an incident. Thus the damage done was to his personal property, yet Confucius asked only if anyone got hurt in the course of the fire.

10.18 When the ruler bestowed on him a gift of cooked food, he would taste it right away after he had straightened his sitting mat. When the ruler sent him a gift of uncooked meat, he would cook it and make an offering to his ancestors. When the ruler sent him a live animal, he would raise it at home.

When he was assisting his ruler at a meal, while the ruler was making an offering, he would taste the food first.

Most commentaries refer to the *Yuzao* ("Beads of Jade") chapter of the *Book of Rites* to explain why Confucius would "taste the food first" (*xianfan*) while the ruler was making an offering. According to this source, if an official was a guest of his ruler at a meal, he would make an offering after the ruler had made his. But if the official was merely assisting his ruler, then he could not make an offering, and the correct decorum was for him "to taste the food for his ruler and then to take a drink and wait until the ruler was ready to eat."

10.19 When he was ill and the ruler paid him a visit, he lay with his head to the east, and with his court robe draped over him and his grand sash placed across his waist and hanging down [the side of his bed].

It was in observance of correct decorum that a sick person, upon an impending visit from his ruler, would have his bed placed so that he would be facing his ruler when the latter entered his room. And since the spatial arrangement of a room in early China was such that one would enter the door in an eastward direction, the person lying on the bed with his head to the east would be able to face his visitor. And here we see that Confucius also insisted on greeting the ruler in his court robe and grand sash.

10.20 When the ruler's order came to summon him to court, he would set off on foot, without waiting for the carriage to be harnessed.

When Mencius' disciple Wan Zhang asked whether Confucius acted appropriately in this situation, Mencius said yes, because Confucius was an official at the time and the duties of his office demanded that he respond as fast as he could to the ruler's request. Xunzi says essentially the same: "not to wait for the carriage to be harnessed and to just throw some clothes on and set off on foot" when a counselor is summoned by his lord is "correct rites."

10.21 When he entered the Temple of the Great Ancestor, he asked questions about everything.

This repeats what was recorded in 3.15. See the commentary on 3.15.

10.22 When a friend died, if this person did not have a kinsman who could take his body in [and give him a proper service], he would say, "I will arrange to have his funeral in my house."

Scholars point out that one should put this in the context of a longer passage in the *Book of Rites*, which reads: "When a guest [from afar] could not find a place to stay, Confucius would say to him, 'I have a place for you in my house. [In fact, you are welcome here] when you are living, and should you die while you are staying with me, I can also arrange to have your funeral in my house.'"

10.23 Unless the present from a friend was sacrificial meat, in accepting it he did not bow, even when the present was as sizable as a carriage and horses.

Horses and carriages were heavy gifts, while sacrificial meat seems slight, but one had the weight of commodities while other abounded with ritual significance. And of the two—and, in fact, of all the gifts bestowed on him—Confucius would accept only sacrificial meat with the utmost respect. Such was the way Confucius decided on the importance of things.

10.24 In bed, he did not lie like a corpse. At home, he did not carry himself like a guest.

A corpse is a body, a shell, "without its master," says the Han dictionary: it simply cannot hold itself together. Thus Confucius would not "lie in bed like a corpse," but neither was he so disciplined that he would assume the demeanor of a guest when he was at home.

10.25 Whenever he met a person in mourning clothes, though the person might be a close friend, he always changed his countenance [to assume a grave expression]. Whenever he met a person wearing a ceremonial cap or a person who was blind, though the person might be on familiar terms with him [*xie*], he always greeted the person with the utmost courtesy. When he passed by a person dressed in funeral attire, he always leaned forward with his hands on the crossbar of his carriage [to show his respect]. The same could be observed even when the person was someone carrying official documents [of maps and household registration] [*fubanzhe*].

Some scholars argue that *xie* could also mean "lowly" and that the character *ban* in *fubanzi* could be a misprint for the character *fan*, meaning "a peddler." The alternative reading for the second sentence to the end thus becomes: "Whenever he met a person wearing a ceremonial cap or a person who was blind, though the person might be from a lowly class, he always greeted him with the utmost courtesy. When he passed by a person dressed in funeral attire, he always leaned forward with his hands on the crossbar of his carriage. The same was observed even when the person was a peddler." According to these scholars, the point here is that when the context was mourning, Confucius was consistent in his conduct toward others, irrespective of their social standing.

There is also some disagreement among scholars about the social position of the person carrying documents consisting of maps and household registration. Some say that such a man commanded respect in the Zhou because he held in his hands the official record of all the people living in his state. Others feel that such a man was merely a lowly clerk, an errand boy. I follow the latter because it is consistent with the central idea in this part of the description.

When a sumptuous meal was brought forth [to honor the guest], he would always change his expression and rise to his feet [out of respect for the host].

He would also change his expression when there was a clap of thunder or a fierce wind.

One would change one's expression when something new or unexpected was introduced into the circumstances. The change, in the case of Confucius, often had a ritual overtone, and here we see that he would change his expression when he was in the presence of mourners, of a generous host, or of an unusual natural phenomenon. To the mourners and his host, he showed respect, but he was in awe of nature's prodigies, though he did not speak about them because he did not talk about things he did not understand.

10.26 When climbing into a carriage, he always held his body erect as he clutched the mounting rope in his hand. When inside the carriage, he did not keep looking all around; he did not talk in a loud voice or at rapid speed; and he did not point at this or that.

Since the Han there has been a lot of discussion of the second sentence, about Confucius' gaze while he was in the carriage. Some understand it to mean that Confucius did not look backward so as to block the views of others in the carriage. Others say that he did not look beyond the crossbar in front or either side of the carriage. Both explanations, in Liu Baonan's view, come to the same conclusion: that Confucius "absorbed what he saw and heard" inside the carriage. This was also the reason why he "did not talk in a loud voice or at rapid speed" and why he "did not point at this or that."

10.27 Startled by the signs of an unfriendly presence, it rose up and circled a few times before alighting. [The Master] said, "The female pheasant on the mountain bridge—how timely, how timely!" Zilu saluted it. The bird flapped its wings three times [*sanxiu*] and flew away.

Many scholars find this passage hard to handle. The character *xiu* in *sanxiu*, for instance, means "to sniff," but in the context of the present description, it does not make sense. Was the bird sniffing at something Zilu gave her? If so, why were we not told about it first? This led the Song Confucian Zhu Xi to conclude that there had to be gaps in the record. Other scholars say that *xiu* (嗅) was probably a loan word for *ju* (昃), which could mean either "to stare" or "to flap one's wings." Other questions about this passage made some suspect the record's authenticity. The contemporary scholar Qian Mu, however, simply accepts it as an epiphanic moment in Confucius' life when he observed how the mountain bird responded to his sudden presence in her world. Confucius called it "timely," a word others used to distinguish him from other sagely men of the past. Though he would never have described himself in this way, timeliness was what Confucius sought in his conduct: he loved the moral immediacy of the idea and its aesthetic possibilities.

BOOK ELEVEN

This chapter is about Confucius' disciples. Again dialogues are important because they allow us a close look at Confucius' relationship with the disciples: just how he talked to them and sized them up and what he meant to teach them when he conversed with them.

11.1 The Master said, "Those who studied rites and music before [entering government service] were rustics [*yeren*]. Those who studied rites and music after [they had entered government service] were men from hereditary families [*junzi*]. When it comes to the question of employment, I prefer those who studied rites and music first."

There are many theories about the use of "before" and "after." Some scholars say that it refers either to the rulers before and after the Three Dynasties or to the rulers before and after the founding of the Zhou dynasty. Others think that "before" refers to Confucius' early disciples, those who followed him on his "journey around the states," and "after" refers to the later disciples, those who came to study with him after he had returned to Lu. I, however, am persuaded by Liu Baonan's reading, which is reflected in my translation. "Before," Liu argues, refers to men who were not aristocrats and so had to get an education in rites and music before they were considered for an official position, while "after" refers to men who inherited their position in government and so began to study the rites and music only when they were already in office. And of these two groups, Confucius would recommend the former for office—men, like himself, who had to rely on their knowledge of rites and music and their hard work to gain a footing in government. Confucius also had more trust in these men who were from a simpler background because, unlike those from the hereditary families, they were better men and better prepared in making the right judgment before they stepped into the messy world of politics.

There is also some discussion in the commentaries about *yeren* and *junzi*. *Yeren* could refer to rustics, or "men of the field"—men who lived in the countryside and not in fortified towns. *Junzi* is a more complicated issue, for in the *Analects* the term usually refers to a morally superior man, but here it takes its older meaning of "men born with hereditary status."

11.2 The Master said, "Those who followed me [on my travels] to Chen and Cai are no longer studying with me now."

This chapter of Confucius' travels received a lot of the attention in the early writings, probably because during this stretch of his journey "provisions ran out" and Confucius nearly starved to death. But Confucius was not alone, as he tells us here and in 15.2, and the disciples who followed him to the wilds of Chen and Cai were Zilu, Zigong, and Yan Hui. None of these disciples was with him, however, after he returned to Lu: Zigong had a position in the state of Qi, Zilu had been killed in violent political struggle in the state of Wei, and Yan Hui had died of illness.

The alternative reading—"None of those who followed me [on my travels] to Chen and Cai had an official position then"—is probably influenced by Mencius' remark that Confucius "was in a dire strait somewhere between Chen and Cai because he had no political connections at court."

11.3 Virtuous in conduct: Yan Yuan [Yan Hui], Min Ziqian, Ran Boniu [Boniu], Zhonggong.

Skillful in speech: Zai Wo, Zigong.

Skillful in administrative affairs: Ran You [Ran Qiu], Jilu [Zilu].

Accomplished in cultural pursuits: Ziyou and Zixia.

Here is a summary of what Confucius thought were his disciples' strengths, which, on the whole, can be corroborated with the records of these disciples' speech and conduct in the *Analects*. Since the disciples were referred to by their courtesy names, some scholars feel that this was not a direct quote from Confucius, who always called his disciples by their personal names. They further point out that the entry does not begin with "The Master said."

11.4 The Master said, "Hui [Yan Hui] is of no help to me. He is pleased with everything I say."

Confucius' remark here about Yan Hui should be read together with 2.9, 9.11, and 9.20, and also with my commentary on 2.9.

11.5 The Master said, "How filial is Min Ziqian! No one would disagree with what his parents and brothers said about him."

According to several Han dynasty sources, the story of Min Ziqian involved the familiar narrative of a nasty stepmother who thought only of the welfare of his half brothers and showed no love for him. Yet, unlike the father in many other stories of the kind, his father was quick to notice the inequity and quick to act. But when the father tried to drive his wife out, Min Ziquan stopped him. He told his father, "With our mother home, only one child is neglected. With her gone, all four children will suffer." These words, as the story goes, managed to move his stepmother and his half brothers so deeply that they changed their ways, and thereafter had only love and affection for him. Some scholars consider this an example of a son who disobeys the command of his father and yet fulfills a larger sense of filiality.

11.6 Nan Rong repeated often the poem about the white jade tablet. Confucius gave him the daughter of his older brother for a wife.

The white jade tablet to which this refers is found in Ode 256: "A blemish in a white jade tablet / Can be polished away; / A mistake in these words / Can never be mended." Nan Rong chanted this poem to remind himself of the troubles that misspoken words could bring. And as I explain in my comments on 5.2, maybe because Nan Rong was vigilant in speech, he managed "to avoid punishment and execution" even when the moral way did not exist in the state. For these reasons, Confucius considered him a suitable husband for his niece.

11.7 Ji Kangzi asked, "Who among your disciples love learning?"

Confucius responded, "There was Yan Hui who loved learning. But unfortunately he had a short life and is dead now."

This is a slightly truncated version of the conversation between Confucius and Duke Ai in 6.3. This record could have come from a different line of transmission, but it also makes sense from an editorial point of view to have Confucius' remark repeated here as a preamble to the next four entries, which are about Yan Hui's death.

11.8 When Yan Yuan [Yan Hui] died, his father, Yan Lu, asked the Master if he would sell his carriage so that he, the father, could use the money to buy his son an outer coffin.

The Master replied, "Whether a son is talented or not, he is still a son to his parents. When my son Li [Boyu] died, he had an inner coffin but no outer coffin. I did not go on foot in order to provide him with an outer coffin. Since once I held the rank just below that of a counselor, it would not be right for me to go on foot."

11.9 When Yan Yuan [Yan Hui] died, the Master cried out, "Oh, Heaven is destroying me! Heaven is destroying me!"

11.10 When Yan Hui died, the Master wept with uncontrollable emotion. His followers said, "Master, you have gone too far."

The Master said, "Have I? If not for this man, for whom should I show so much sorrow?"

11.11 After Yan Yuan [Yan Hui] died, the disciples wanted to give him a lavish burial. The Master said, "That would not be appropriate." The disciples gave him a lavish burial anyway.

The Master said, "Hui looked upon me as a father. But in this matter I could not treat him like a son. This was not my doing—it was on account of you, my young friends."

We learn in 11.9 and 11.10 that Confucius was feeling so bereft after Yan Hui's death that even his disciples asked him to show some restraint. Yet when Yan Hui's father asked him to sell his carriage so that he could buy his son an outer coffin, Confucius refused. And when his disciples acted against his objection and gave Yan Hui a grand sendoff, he was upset. Did he love Yan Hui or not? Many scholars over the years have brooded about this question and offered their explanations, yet it is Confucius himself who can best clear the air. We learn in 9.12 that years before Yan Hui's death, when Confucius looked as if he were on the point of dying, Zilu asked the rest of the disciples to act as Confucius' retainers so that their teacher could go to his grave with the formalities of a minister. As it happened, Confucius' condition improved, and when he realized what Zilu had been prepared to do, he scolded him for "practicing chicanery" because he at the time had no official position. "By pretending I had retainers when I had none, whom were we trying to deceive?" he said. "Besides, would I not rather die in the arms of a few good friends than in the arms of retainers?" This, I believe, was Confucius' point about Yan Hui's burial. Did Yan Hui, who had been poor, need an outer coffin or a lavish burial when he had a few good friends to bid him farewell? Besides, such things bear no relationship to feelings. They simply cannot express the depth of one's loss, which for Confucius was like having lost a son.

11.12 Jilu [Zilu] asked about how to serve the spirits of the dead and the gods. The Master said, "You can't even serve men properly, how can you serve the spirits?"

"May I then ask about death?"

"You can't even understand life, how can you understand death?"

Confucius' response may be a disparagement of Zilu, suggesting that Zilu was not ready to serve the spirits or understand death, or it may suggest his own reluctance to let his mind travel beyond the human world. Scholars such as Liu Baonan, however, offer another way of looking at this conversation. They argue that there was nothing facetious about the questions Zilu asked: serving the spirits was an "all-consuming business" in early China, and everyone was mindful of death, since no one knew when it might come to call. But "only a person who did his best to serve his parents while they were alive is able to let them enjoy his offerings after they are dead," and this, Liu Baonan explains, was what Confucius was trying to say to Zilu. And as for death, "if one reveres life, one has respect for death," Liu writes. Mencius expresses the idea best when he says, "Though destiny determines everything, one accepts willingly only what is proper destiny. That is why he who understands destiny does not stand under a wall on the verge of collapse. He who dies after having done his best in realizing the moral way dies according to proper destiny."

11.13 When Min Ziqian was attending the Master, he looked upright; Zilu looked tough and unbending; Ran You [Ran Qiu] and Zigong looked affable. The Master was pleased. He said, "A man like You [Zilu] will not die a natural death."

Confucius was pleased, the commentaries say, because each disciple seemed distinctly himself, but watching Zilu, he had the foreboding that Zilu would not live out his years because he was "tough and unbending." His hunch, of course, turned out to be correct. The history in the *Zuo Commentary* tells us that Zilu was caught in a succession dispute between a father and a son in the state of Wei, and he died a violent death in the final confrontation of the two sides.

11.14 The people of Lu wanted to rebuild the treasury. Min Ziqian said, "Why can't we just restore it? Why must we rebuild it?"

The Master said, "This man rarely speaks, but when he does, he always gets it right."

Most commentators feel that Min Ziqian was not just talking about a building—whether to pull it down and erect a new one in its place or to renovate the old one. The remark had a political background, they say. Ever since the Three Families drove Duke Zhao out of Lu in his twenty-fifth year of rule, they had wanted to rebuild the treasury, because the structure, being a storehouse of wealth and weapons, stood as a symbol of the ducal authority in their state. (Thus "the people of Lu," here, refers to the Three Families.) Min Ziqian, however, was against the idea. He wanted restoration—not just a restoration of the old building, but a restoration of the old political structure.

The question of whether to have the existing political structure dismantled and to start anew or simply to fix it and reinforce the foundation received a lot of attention in the eleventh-century debate on reform. The historian Sima Guang, who opted for repair and renewal, used a metaphor similar to what we find here.

11.15 The Master said, "Why do I hear You [Zilu] playing the zither inside my door?" The disciples began to treat Zilu with disrespect.

The Master said, "You [Zilu] may not have entered the inner room, but he has ascended the hall."

A long explanation of Confucius' remark about Zilu playing the zither is found in the Han dynasty source *Shuoyuan* (*World of Stories*). The music is described there as "the rustic sound of the north." Confucius characterized such music as "violent and abandoned," and he contrasted it with the "gentle and measured" sound of the south, which added "a liveliness to the air" but "no pangs of pain and sorrow to the heart." But he then pointed out that such ideas were not fixed: the sound of the south had, in fact, originated in the north but was kept alive in the south, he said; it was Shun, a rustic man, who was most closely associated with "gentle and measured" music, and it was the last king of Shang, a royal, who was the maker of "violent and abandoned" music. Several commentaries cite this source in trying to explain why Confucius was displeased with hearing Zilu playing the zither in his home. He did not like the stubborn and unbridled sound, they say, and he was also worried that Zilu's intemperate music, like his "tough and unbending" appearance, could signal that his life might not end well. Yet when other disciples began to shun Zilu because of his remark, Confucius offered a correction, saying that Zilu might not have entered the inner recess of his teaching but he had already stepped inside the gate.

11.16 Zigong asked, "Of Shi [Zizhang] and Shang [Zixia], which one is worthier?"

The Master said, "Shi overshoots the mark, while Shang falls short."

"Does this mean, then, that Shi is the better of the two?"

The Master said, "Overshooting the mark is about as imperfect as falling short."

Liu Baonan cites separate chapters of the *Book of Rites* to point out the two possible ways of understanding "overshooting the mark" and "falling short"—whether Confucius was referring to a lack of ritual propriety or to his disciples' natural propensities. A passage in "Confucius Relaxing at Home" (*Zhongni yanju*) suggests the first scenario, while the *Doctrine of the Mean* (*Zhongyong*) implies the second. Yet we know that the person who is smart and impatient and the person who is slow and methodical are both prone to ritual blunders. This was true with Shi (Zizhang) and Shang (Zixia), as the *Analects* can bear out, especially in 19.12, 19.15, and 19.16.

11.17 The wealth of the Jisun family exceeded that of the Duke of Zhou, yet Ran Qiu had been collecting taxes for them to add further to their wealth. The Master said, "He is no disciple of mine. My young friends, you may beat the drums and attack him."

The history in the *Zuo Commentary* offers a detailed account of the events that led up to the scene here, where Confucius is clearly enraged with Ran Qiu, the disciple he should have felt most indebted to because Ran Qiu had orchestrated his return to Lu and helped him to secure the honorific title of *guolao*, our "elder statesman." Toward the end of 484 BC, right after Confucius came home, the

Zuo Commentary states, the head of the Jisun family sent Ran Qiu, who was their chief steward, to Confucius, to sound out their plan to collect land taxes from their tenants. When Ran Qiu put the question to him, Confucius said, "I don't understand a thing about it." Privately, however, he told Ran Qiu, "The gentleman gauges his action according to the spirit of the rites—when conferring a benefit, he tries to be generous; when performing a service, he aims for what is most appropriate; when imposing a tax, he is sparing." Confucius also said this: "If the Jisuns really want to do the right thing, there is always the standard set by the Duke of Zhou. Now if they want to act as they please, why come to me?" The standard set by the Duke of Zhou is discussed in 12.9. It was called *che*, where "people were taxed one part in ten" and where the tax in kind came only from the public land they worked on. The early commentaries referred to the *che* as the "universal standard"—a standard that made the most sense because "people will have sufficiency" in bountiful or lean years, which meant that the ruler, too, will increase his wealth. (Ran Qiu's role here was further complicated by the fact that Jisuns were not in a position to collect taxes because they were hereditary counselors, not rulers. Thus whatever authority they had wrested from their ruler could not have been legitimate.)

What Confucius said privately to Ran Qiu proved to be useless. By the spring of the next year, "the land tax was administered," according to the chronicle of the Lu; by winter, a locust plague was recorded. Now Confucius was furious with Ran Qiu. And so when he tells the other disciples that they "may beat the drums and attack him," he means that it is all right for them to criticize Ran Qiu publicly for his offense.

11.18 Chai [Zigao] is simpleminded; Can [Zeng Can, or Zengzi] is slow; Shi [Zizhang] is given to excess; You [Zilu] tends to be unruly.

Zigao was a disciple of Confucius, and, according to the history in the *Zuo Commentary*, he was with Zilu shortly before Zilu was killed in an act of bravura in the final chapter of the succession crisis in Wei. And it was Zigao who asked Zilu not to get involved in a conflict whose outcome had already been decided. This Zigao appears in the *Analects* twice: here, where he is described as stupid or simpleminded (*yu*), and in 11.25, where the conversation implies that he lacks learning. Scholars over the years have come to Zigao's defense, pointing to a few stories about this man from the Han dynasty, which suggest that, rather than being simpleminded, Zigao possessed an innocent, an uncomplicated, mind. But why does Confucius say Zeng Can (Zengzi) is "slow"? This, as I indicate in my comments on 1.4, could be because Zeng Can spent too much time reflecting on his own conduct. And as for Zizhang and Zilu, Confucius' characterization of these two disciples here resonates with what we find in the records of the *Analects* about them. Liu Baonan feels that the evaluation of these four men was consistent with what Confucius had always said about his disciples—that some were overly cautious while others were wildly spirited, and none, with the exception of Yan Hui, could hold on to a position of equanimity.

11.19 The Master said, "Hui [Yan Hui] is almost there, yet he frequently lives in poverty. Si [Zigong] does not accept his lot, and so he is good at making money. And [because of it] he is given to assessing a situation and weighing the favorable against the unfavorable, and is often right in his speculation."

Yan Hui had nearly perfected his character—he was "almost there"—even though, for the better part of his life, he lived in deprivation. This means that circumstances made no difference to him because he loved learning and he was on a quest for self-understanding. Zigong was different, their teacher observed: he would not accept his lot, and so he learned to make money; in so doing he acquired the skills of "assessing a situation" and "reading people," and so he was "often right in his speculation." Although Confucius preferred Yan Hui, he also appreciated Zigong, for not bowing to his circumstances and for being able to let the skills he learned as a tradesman sharpen his wit and judgment.

11.20 Zizhang asked about the way of a truly good man [*shanren*].

The Master said, "He does not tread in the footsteps of

those before him, but, then, he is unable to reach the inner recesses [of moral knowledge]."

A *shanren* is a person born with a strong moral impulse. Such a person may have success in "curtailing violence and killing," but he will not be able to reach "the inner recesses"—and possess the moral insight and presence of a sage—if he does not follow the cultural vestiges and learn from the rites and music left behind by the former kings. This is the reading of the traditional commentaries.

11.21 The Master said, "You show approval of him because he seems sincere in what he says. But is he truly a gentleman, or does he simply put on a dignified appearance?"

The Han scholars believe that this is the second part of 11.20—that being "sincere in speech," being "gentlemanly in conduct," and being "dignified in appearance" are the attributes of a "truly good man." The Song scholar Zhu Xi disagrees. He feels that the point Confucius is trying to make here is the difficulty of distinguishing a true gentleman from a fake—that even a person whose words seem genuine could turn out to be an imposter. My reading follows Zhu Xi's because his reading reflects a central concern in Confucius' teachings, not just about what is true but also about the gap between speech and conduct.

11.22 Zilu asked, "When I hear something [that needs to be addressed], should I take action right away?"

The Master said, "When your father and elder brother are still alive, how can you take action as soon as you hear something?"

Ran You [Qiu] asked, "When I hear something [that needs to be addressed], should I take action right away?"

The Master said, "Upon hearing such a thing, you should take action right away."

Gongxi Hua said, "When You [Zilu] asked you whether he should take action as soon as he heard something [that needed to be addressed], you said, as long as his father and elder are still alive [he should not]. But when Qiu [Ran You] asked you the same question, you said, he should take action right away. Now I am confused. May I beseech you for an explanation?"

The Master said, "Qiu [Ran You] tends to hold back, and so I like to urge him on. You [Zilu] has the fire of two, and so I like to restrain him."

Ran You (Qiu) was not afraid to die on the battlefield, and if he was holding back, it was because he had political ambitions and so was cautious about not offending those who could make or break his career. (3.6 and 11.17 offer examples of such behavior.) And this was the reason why Confucius wanted him to take action as soon as there were things to be done, lest he should change his mind. Zilu was just the opposite. He was someone ready "to wrestle a tiger with his bare hands" and ready "to go to his death without regret." Confucius was fearful for Zilu's life, and so he wanted him to think before he acted, and the most effective way to hold him back, he felt, was to ask this disciple to be mindful of the fact that his father and elder brother were still alive. To many scholars, this example clearly illustrates what Confucius was like as a teacher: he guided his disciples each according to his temperament.

11.23 When Confucius found his life under threat in Kuang, Yan Hui fell behind. [Later, when they reunited,] Confucius said, "I thought you were dead."

Yan Hui replied, "With you, Master, still alive, how would I dare to die?"

The crisis at Kuang, first mentioned in the *Analects* (9.5), received a lot of attention from historians and writers of the Warring States period and in the Han. They tried to explain why Confucius was surrounded by an angry mob when he entered the town of Kuang and how he managed to disband the crowd and save his own skin. But here we learn that Yan Hui was not with him when his life was "under threat." This bit of information in the early records, together with the conversation that followed, became, again, fodder for speculation. Scholars ask: Just how did Yan Hui get left behind? Was it chance or did he deliberately stay out of sight? And why did he say that he would not "dare to die" while his teacher was still alive? In addressing these questions, they like to emphasize the love Yan Hui had for Confucius—like that of a filial son for his father, they say. And just as such a son would not act rashly while his father was alive, for fear that his death might leave his father all alone, Yan Hui, who unlike Zilu was cautious and "good at planning," made himself scarce until it was safe to emerge. But how did he know that Confucius would survive the mob in Kuang? Han writers seem to think that Confucius' integrity eventually would have become apparent to the people there and that when the people realized the man that he was they would have let him go. Such arguments are built on hindsight—they let Yan Hui off the hook too easily if his absence in Kuang was unintended.

11.24 Ji Ziran asked, "Could one consider Zhong You [Zilu] and Ran Qiu to be great ministers?"

The Master replied, "I thought you were going to ask me about other things, yet you are only interested in questions about You [Zilu] and Qiu. The term 'great ministers' applies to those who serve their lord in a moral way. If they simply cannot, then they stop. Now You and Qiu are men appointed to fill the ranks of a supervisory staff [in a hereditary family]."

"Does this mean, then, they will always do what they are told to do?"

The Master said, "Not if they are told to kill their father or their ruler."

Ji Ziran was probably a member of the Jisun family, scholars say, and so was interested to learn from Confucius if Zilu and Ran Qiu were fit to be called "great ministers." Confucius, at first, seemed irritated by his question, and when he did respond, it was not with the glowing evaluation one might expect from someone who was devoted to his students and who wanted them to fare well in the world. But this was the kind of teacher Confucius had made himself to be, clear-eyed and exact, and when Ji Ziran pushed him further, when he wanted to know whether Zilu and Ran Qiu were officials of the kind who would simply follow orders since they lacked the scrupulosity and courage of great ministers. Confucius said no, there were still things they would not do—they would not kill their father or their ruler even if ordered to do so.

11.25 Zilu wanted to find a way to let Zigao become a steward of Bi. Confucius said, "You are going to do harm to someone else's son."

Zilu replied, "But there are people for him to govern and the altar of grain and soil for him to look after. Why must one read books to be considered to have learned?"

The Master said, "It is for this reason that I dislike glib men [*ningzhe*]."

Zigao was one of the youngest of Confucius' disciples, and when Zilu wanted to recommend him to the Jisuns, to let him be a steward in this family's stronghold, a town called Bi, Confucius raised strong objection, saying that if Zilu decided to follow through with such a plan he would be doing a disservice to this young man—to "someone else's son." Zigao, in Confucius' view, was not ready to accept an appointment from this powerful political family, which had nearly always gotten their way both with those who were above and those who were below them. Even someone as savvy as Ran Qiu, we learn in 11.17, could only follow orders when he was in their service. This, I believe, was what Confucius was afraid of, that Zigao would be powerless against the Jisuns because he, by nature, was "simpleminded" and had a long way to go in his education. Zilu, in defense, argued that Zigao could learn on the job—that learning should not just be "reading books." This, of course, was how he had learned, which, Confucius would say, accounted for Zilu's rough and stubborn character and for his tendency to act without thought. And as for Confucius' final comment, it could refer to Zilu, that Zilu's retort was glib (*ning* 佞), or it could also refer to those whose education consisted only of worldly experience, without the benefit of history and poetry.

11.26 Zilu, Zeng Xi, Ran You [Ran Qiu], and Gongxi Hua were seated in the Master's company. The Master said, "Just because I am a little older than you are, don't let that stop you [from speaking your mind]. You have often said, 'No one understands me.' If someone did understand you [and appreciate you], what would you do then?"

Zilu quickly offered a response: "If I were to govern a state of a thousand chariots, one that was squeezed between two powerful states, worn out by unwanted warfare, and made even weaker by famine, I would be able, within three years, to give the people courage and let them know the right way to put their lives in order."

Confucius smiled at him.

"And Qiu [Ran Qiu], what about you?"

"If I were put in charge of a place measuring sixty or seventy *li* square, or even fifty to sixty *li* square, I would be able, within three years, to meet the people's needs. As for the practice of rites and music, I will have to leave them to the gentlemen."

"What about you, Chi [Gongxi Hua]?"

"I am not sure if I can do this well, but I am willing to learn. I would like to be a minor official, assuming the role of either an assistant in ritual affairs at the ancestral temple or a junior diplomat, dressed in a black robe and ceremonial cap, at a conference of the regional rulers."

"And you, Dian [Zeng Xi]?"

Zeng Xi had been playing the zither. Now his playing was coming to the end. With the last note still vibrating in the wind, he put down his instrument, stood up, and said, "What I would like to do is different from what we have just heard from these three."

Confucius said, "There is no harm in that. We are all telling each other what's on our mind."

Zeng Xi replied, "In late spring, when the spring clothes have just been made, with five or six young men or six or seven young boys, I would like to go bathing in the River Yi and enjoy the breeze at the rain prayer altar, and then come home singing."

Confucius sighed and said, "I am for Dian."

When others had left, Zeng Xi stayed behind. He asked, "What did you think of what those three said?"

The Master responded, "Each spoke what he had set his mind on."

"And why did you smile at Zilu?"

"One should govern a state by way of ritual propriety, but his words lacked modesty, and so I smiled at him."

"[Despite what he said,] was Qiu [Ran Qiu] not concerned with governing a state?"

"How can an area of sixty or seventy—or even sixty or fifty—square *li* not be considered a state? [And so you are right, he was talking about governing a state.]"

"And what about Chi [Gongxi Hua], was he also talking about governing a state?"

"If performing the ceremonies in ancestral temples and performing them at diplomatic gatherings are not the business of regional rulers, what are they? If Chi thinks that [in assisting the ruler in fulfilling these duties] he plays only a minor role, who, then, has the major role?"

The major portion of the translation of this passage is from my work *The Authentic Confucius*. And since my understanding of the passage and of its relationship to Confucius' life and teachings has remained nearly the same as in that book, I have decided to include my comments here with minor revision:

One can read a lot into this scene. Over the years, followers of Confucius from the right and the left did exactly that. Some claimed that the conversation was fabricated and then appended to the *Analects* by a rival school, most likely the Daoists, either as a tease or as proof that even Confucius in the end had come around to their point of view; that even he had given up the state, the ancestral temple, music, and ceremony, to join them in the immaculate water. Others, such as the sixteenth-century thinker Wang Yangming, insisted that a kin in spirit at "a play-ful moment" drew out in plain sight a Confucius at his truest. Wang said that "the other three disciples had useful talents," but Zeng Xi alone "was self-possessed wherever he might be," whether he was "among the barbarians" or "in the middle of a crisis." Wang's reading tallies with what we learned about Confucius' secret self in 5.26 and 7.19, for instance, about what he wanted most and what gave him satisfaction. Yet if we were to settle on this view, we would not be able to explain why for so long Confucius had been singularly stubborn in his search for political opportunities to fill his ambitions. His resignation—and the calm that ensued—was a late thing in his life, but it was not a form of surrender.

BOOK TWELVE

12.1 Yan Yuan [Yan Hui] asked about humaneness. The Master said, "Restrain the self and return to the rites [*keji fuli*]. This is the way to be humane. If for one day you are able to restrain the self and return to the rites, this means that your capacity to be humane will open up to the world. Humaneness rests with the self. How could it come from others?"

Most of the discussion in the traditional commentaries is about *keji fuli*. Did Confucius say, One should rein in the self so that it does not swerve from the measure of ritual propriety (which is how the Han scholars understand the sentence)? Or did he say, One should suppress one's selfish desires and realize a higher, a universal, set of principles (which is how the Song Confucians explain it)? The second reading is a reflection of Song metaphysics, but it is not what Confucius meant to say, as later scholars point out, because the concept of a universal principle is simply not present in the *Analects*.

The second part of Confucius' response also needs some explanation. Traditional scholars understand the sentence to read: "If for one day you are able to restrain the self and return to the rites, the whole world will gravitate toward humaneness." Qian Mu, however, holds a different view. He says that Confucius' point about making an effort "to restrain the self and return to the rites for one day" is that this will enable a person to have a quicker and more effective start in cultivating his humanity. "The importance of such an effort has to do with tending the self," Qian Mu notes, and "not with effecting a change in other people." My translation reflects Qian Mu's reading.

Yan Yuan [Yan Hui] asked, "May I ask about the specific steps to go about this?"

The Master replied, "Do not look at anything that is contrary to ritual propriety. Do not listen to anything that is contrary to ritual propriety. Do not speak in ways that are contrary to ritual propriety. Do not act in ways that are contrary to ritual propriety."

Yan Yuan said, "Even though I am not that smart, I will do my best to put into practice what you have said."

It is up to the self to make the effort not to look at and listen to anything that is contrary to ritual propriety, and not to speak and act in ways that are contrary to ritual propriety. But who sets the standard of ritual propriety? Again it is the self: each person has to rely on his sense of humaneness to find what is right in his relationship with the world. But he also needs direction—guidelines with a moral orientation—that can point out for him just how much is too much and how much is not enough. On this subject, Confucius says in 3.3, "Being human yet lacking humaneness—what can such a man do with the rites? Being human and yet lacking in humaneness—what can such a man do with music?"

12.2 Zhonggong asked about humaneness. The Master said, "When abroad, conduct yourself as if you were receiving an honored guest. When employing the people in your state, deport yourself as if you have been put in charge of a grand sacrifice. Do not impose on others what you do not desire for yourself. In this way, you will not incur any resentment whether your work is in the state or in a hereditary family."

Here Confucius reinforces what he says in 12.1. But he is more precise about what he considers the correct performance of the rites, and since its operating principle is "do not impose on others what you do not desire yourself," the performance must be an expression of one's humaneness. And in order to become truly humane, a person must always hold his actions to that measure. Confucius tells

Zhonggong: Whether you are abroad or at home, in charge of a mission or administering a state, whether you are dealing with officials or the common people, "conduct yourself as if you were receiving an honored guest" and "deport yourself as if you have been put in charge of a grand sacrifice."

12.3 Sima Niu asked about humaneness. The Master said, "A humane person is reluctant to speak."

"Being reluctant to speak—is that what it means to be humane?"

The Master replied, "When it is difficult to carry it out, how can this person not be reluctant to speak [about it]?"

Most scholars assume that it is the realization of humaneness that is difficult to carry out, and that a humane person would not think to speak about it before he tried to fulfill it in action. This, of course, is consistent with what Confucius says throughout the *Analects* about the relationship of words and action—that a gentleman is "hesitant to speak but quick to act" (4.24); that he would "let words follow action" (2.13) because he "would feel ashamed if [his] action did not measure up to [his] words" (4.22). Liu Baonan, however, thinks that to say that someone is "reluctant to speak" could imply that this person has a "heavy heart"—he is hesitant to speak because he is in a hard place about how to act—and that this is the reason why Sima Niu's question about humaneness ended up being a conversation about words and action. Sima Niu, Liu explains, was the brother of Huan Tui, a minister of military affairs from Song, who at one time tried to waylay Confucius when Confucius traveled through that state. This Huan Tui was a favorite of the ruler of Song, but he let his ambition get ahead of his sense of duty. And so at the height of his career, he decided to challenge the authority of his lord. Sima Niu learned about his brother's plan before it became unraveled, and he did not know what to do: whether to keep the plan a secret and thereby "bring disaster to his state," or to inform on his brother and "let his whole clan be exterminated." The historicist approach suggested by Liu assumes that Confucius knew about the problem Sima Niu faced and so when the latter asked about humaneness, Confucius assured him that it was all right "not being able to bring himself to talk about it"—this, he said, was in fact a sign of one's humaneness. Such a reading may seem forced at first, but it makes sense when we put it in the context of the next two entries, where Sima Niu again is the interlocutor.

12.4 Sima Niu asked about the gentleman [*junzi*]. The Master said, "A gentleman has no vexations and no fears."

"Having no vexations and no fears—is that what it means to be a gentleman?"

The Master said, "When such a person looks into himself and finds that he has done nothing wrong, what vexations and what fears could he have?"

Again, if we accept as true that Sima Niu was in a quandary about his brother Huan Tui, then Confucius' response to his question about the gentleman seems to be directed toward the set of problems that troubled Sima Niu. Confucius says that a gentleman has no vexations and no fears because he finds nothing reproachable about his intention and his action. This, of course, implies that as long as Sima Niu, through introspection, uncovers nothing wanting about himself, he, too, should be free of vexations and fears. But Sima Niu's predicament was especially taxing because he was the younger brother of someone whose mischief making could have violent consequences for his family and state. And according to Liu Baonan and Qian Mu, Confucius could not have been unaware of this, but he also felt that such were the grounds for testing one's moral resolve.

12.5 Sima Niu, in a state of distress, said, "All men have brothers. I alone have none."

Zixia responded, "I have heard it said, 'Life and death are a matter of destiny; wealth and honor rest with Heaven.' The gentleman is respectful and [tries to be] free of errors. He is courteous toward others and conducts himself with ritual propriety. All men within the four seas are his brothers. Why should he be worried about not having brothers?"

We learn from the *Zuo Commentary* that after Sima Niu's brother Huan Tui failed in his attempt to usurp the authority of his lord, the

ruler of Song, he fled to the state of Cao, and members of his clan
also had to take off, which explains why Sima Niu ended up in the
state of Lu. Sima Niu gave up his fief when he left Song, and he had
short stays in Qi and Wu, but none of these places worked out for
him. And since most of his brothers were on Huan Tui's side, he felt
quite alone in the world. But Zixia said to him that he was told that
though men had no control over destiny, they had the potential to
perfect their character; and therefore a gentleman knew that when
he set his mind to act with propriety and to be respectful to others,
he would always have brothers "within the four seas." Most scholars
assume that Zixia was quoting what he had learned from Confucius.

12.6 Zizhang asked about keen perception. The Master said,
"When slanders that seep under your skin and grievances that
cut through the flesh do not drive you to an immediate
response, you may be said to have keen perception. And if
indeed you are this clear-eyed, you may be said to have far-
reaching perception."

The seventeenth-century scholar Lu Longqi says that the key to
understanding Confucius' response is by way of his interlocutor:
Zizhang had large ambitions and a high opinion of his own intellect,
and when he asked about keen perception, he probably expected his
teacher to begin with something grand—something that he alone
could grasp. Confucius, however, surprised him. His description of
keen perception was tactile, beginning with slanders and grievances
that can gnaw at you and pain you. And if they "do not drive you to
an immediate response," he said, then "you may be said to have keen
perception," and keen perception not only of things near at hand but
also of things from a great distance—the subject that had prompted
Zizhang's question in the first place.

12.7 Zigong asked about the way of governing. The Master
said, "Sufficient food, a well-equipped army, and the trust of
the common people."
   Zigong said, "Suppose you are forced to do away with one,
which of the three would you let go first?"

The Master said, "The army."

Zigong continued, "Suppose you are forced to give up one more, which of the two would you let go now?"

The Master said, "Food. Death has been the human lot since the beginning of time, but a state cannot survive if it does not have the trust of the common people."

Liu Baonan gives a most thoughtful reading of this dialogue between Zigong and Confucius. When a state has sufficient food, a well-equipped army, and the trust of the people, he says, it cannot but be strong. But this was not the point of the conversation, he notes. Confucius and Zigong were talking about which of the three bases a government should give up when a state is in distress—when it has been struck by disasters such as drought or plague. Confucius' answer is "army first," which Liu understands to mean military conscription because this would give the people some relief. But if the situation deteriorates and the state is sliding into an even darker place, what might be the next thing to forgo? Confucius says food, because since the beginning of time there has always been death from starvation, but trust is something a ruler should never give up. But this does not mean that Confucius had little regard for the lives of the common people. When a state was on the verge of collapse, Confucius felt, its only hope for survival was having the trust of the people. In Liu Baonan's words, "Even when the people were dying from hunger, they could not find anything to criticize about their ruler's integrity."

12.8 Ji Zicheng said, "What matters about a gentleman is the stuff he is made of. What need is there for cultural refinement?"

Zigong said, "I am sorry to hear what you have just said about the gentleman. Even a team of horses cannot catch up with [misspoken words] from a tongue. The stuff of a gentleman is not different from his refinement, and his refinement is not different from the stuff he is made of. The skin of a tiger or a leopard, shorn of hair, is not different from the skin of dog or a sheep."

It is telling that Zigong should have had this conversation with Ji Zicheng, who, according to some early sources, was a counselor from the state of Wei. As I point out in my comments on 11.19, it was Confucius who made the observation that because Zigong refused to accept his lot, he learned to make money, and in so doing he acquired the skills of "assessing a situation" and "reading people." This means that Zigong was able to let his experience in moneymaking hone his mind and wits, and so, one could say, what became of him through refinement was indistinguishable from the stuff he was made of. To support his argument here, Zigong could have pointed to himself.

12.9 Duke Ai said to You Ruo [Youzi], "This is a lean year. I don't have enough to keep things going. What should I do?"

You Ruo replied, "Why not apply the [Zhou] system of *che*, under which the people were taxed one part in ten?"

"If I don't seem to have enough if I tax them two parts in ten, how will I manage if I tax them one part in ten?"

You Ruo replied, "If the people have enough, how can their ruler be left without enough? When the people do not have enough, how can their ruler hope to have enough?"

There are three separate questions that need to be addressed: the time of this conversation, the nature of the two kinds of taxes being discussed, and whether You Ruo was indeed the person Duke Ai approached regarding the state of Lu's financial troubles. Some scholars think that this conversation must have taken place sometime between the years 483 and 482 BC, when the farmers of Lu were left with very little to live on after repeated plagues of locusts, and their ruler was worried about the military buildup in the neighboring state of Qi. It was for this reason, they say, that Duke Ai turned to You Ruo for advice: he needed more revenue for military spending and other expenditures and did not know how to get it. Liu Baonan, however, feels that this happened before 483, before the situation in Lu became desperate but at a time when the ruler was already strapped for money. So in this scene Duke Ai is hoping that You Ruo can help him find a solution to the financial woes of his government.

You Ruo's response—reduce the tax to one part in ten—may have seemed counterintuitive. But, like his teacher, You Ruo believed that if the ruler were to extract even more from his people when they were already living in privation, he in the end would have the most to lose. The third-century BC Confucian Xunzi, in his essay "Enriching the State," says that one could think of the land and fields as the roots of a state's wealth, the granaries and storehouses as the branches of its wealth. "If the land and fields are desolate while the granaries and storehouses are full, if the people are left with nothing while the treasuries and arsenals are overflowing with supplies," Xunzi writes, "this means that the country is on the verge of collapse." And to avoid such a calamity, he writes, the ruler must nurture the roots: he must allow the land and fields to flourish and his people to have enough—which means that he cannot overburden them with taxes, especially during lean years. And a reasonable tax, You Ruo tells Duke Ai here, is one part in ten, the standard set by the Duke of Zhou. The "one part," according to many of the early sources, was not taken from the crop the people harvested each year from the land that belonged to their homesteads; it was the crop grown on a parcel of public land to which every family in a nine-family unit had to contribute their share of work. This was the reason why in 594, about fifty years before Confucius was born, when the ruler of Lu, Duke Huan, introduced a land tax—a tax based on the crop yield from the farmers' own land—his action was thought to be "against the ritual propriety." The author of the *Zuo Commentary* writes, "To increase his wealth, a ruler should not collect more grain from his people than what he receives through the labor he borrows from them."

Finally there is the question of You Ruo. He was the Youzi (Master You) who appears in 1.2, 1.12, and 1.13. He was forty-three years younger than Confucius, and by 484 or 483 he was still in his twenties, and so could not have been in a position that would have allowed him access to the ruler of Lu. Thus there may have been some confusion in the transmission of this account—an error on the part of a scribe, perhaps. If that is so, we still do not know who the person in this conversation with Duke Ai was.

12.10 Zizhang asked, "How does one take virtue to a higher level, and how does one know that one's judgment is clouded?"

The Master said, "If you hold on to doing your best and being trustworthy [in words] as your principle and try always to direct your intent and action to what is right, you will be taking virtue to a higher level. When you like a person, you want him to live. When you dislike a person, you want him to die. To wish him to live at one moment and to wish him to die at the next, this is clouded judgment. [The Ode says,]

> 'Not for her wealth, oh, no!
> But merely for the novelty.'"

The Song scholar Cheng Yi says that the two lines from Ode 188, "I Ventured into the Wild," are "misplaced bamboo strips," which, he believes, should come at the beginning of 16.12. But given the context of the poem—a woman decrying the fickleness of her husband, saying that it was not the wealth of the other woman but the novelty of a fling that made him unfaithful—these two lines seem to fit well with what Confucius says here about "clouded judgment." In his view, feelings are what clouds judgment, and feelings of like and dislike can weigh so heavily upon one's thoughts about another that they metamorphose from a wish of life to a wish of death.

12.11 Duke Jing of Qi asked Confucius about the way of governing.

Confucius replied, "Let the ruler be a ruler, the subject be a subject, a father be a father, a son be a son."

The Duke said, "Right! If indeed the ruler is not a ruler, a subject is not a subject, a father is not a father, a son is not a son, even though there is plenty of grain, will I be able to eat it?"

Scholars like to give a historicist reading of this conversation. Confucius' response, they argue, was directed toward Duke Jing's private troubles: this man was losing the authority of his position and the respect of his subjects, and he was also having difficulty deciding which of his sons should be the heir apparent, so, in the eyes of his people, he lacked the integrity of a ruler and of a father. Yet what Confucius said also expressed a fundamental concept in his political teachings. One later historian explains: When rulers and subjects, fathers and sons give considerable thought to the question of what it means to be ruler or subject, father or son, then "they will come to realize the weight [and enormous responsibility] inherent in these names." Confucius himself refers to the concept as "rectifying names" (*zhengming*) in 13.3 when Zigong asks him about "the way of government."

Scholars also try to establish when the meeting may have taken place. Most believe that it happened in 517 BC, the year the ruler of Lu was forced into exile by the hereditary families. They say that Confucius left Lu for Qi, to avert the turmoil back home and to find a job. They also point out that a year later, in 516, Duke Jing's chief counselor, Master Yan, gave this ruler very similar advice about how to put his state and family in order, which, these scholars say, could suggest that Master Yan, following Confucius' lead, was putting more pressure on Duke Jing to act responsibly. I, however, feel that Confucius did not visit the state of Qi until much later, perhaps around 505, when the retainers in the hereditary families of Lu were edging toward staging an uprising. Knowing that an upheaval was imminent, Confucius left for a safer place. And by this time it was probably not that hard for him to secure a government position elsewhere because he was already known outside of Lu as a wise counselor and a capable administrator. Did Duke Jing offer him a job after their meeting? We are told in 18.3 that he did consider giving him one, but when the question of position and salary came up, he dithered, saying that he was too old and too tired to find a suitable fit for Confucius' talents in his government. Duke Jing did not die until fifteen years later, and after his death it took less than a decade for his descendants to lose the rulership to a member of the powerful Chen family, which was something that the counselor Master Yan had predicted long before.

12.12 The Master said, "The person who could bring a legal case to a conclusion by speaking from just one side of a dispute is You [Zilu], is it not?" Zilu would never wait for a moment to fulfill his promise.

An alternative reading of Confucius' comment about Zilu is: "The person who could decide on a legal case from hearing just one side of a dispute is You (Zilu), is it not?" This puts Zilu in a negative light—since it suggests that he would make up his mind before hearing the other side of the argument—which is not consistent with the remaining comment about him, that he was trustworthy. My translation reflects the reading of Liu Baonan and Qian Mu. Liu says, "Because Zilu had the trust of others, people did not think that he could deceive them, and so even when he was speaking from one side of a dispute, they believed that it had to be the honest truth."

12.13 The Master said, "In hearing litigation, I am no different from others. Yet what I think is important is to bring it about that litigation no longer exists."

Most scholars focus on the second sentence, but Liu Baonan thinks that we should consider the two sentences together, beginning with Confucius' remark that he was no different from others in hearing litigation—which meant that in deciding a case, he, like any responsible legal officer, would listen closely to the words of the parties involved and observe closely their manners and dispositions—but what was more important than hearing litigation was not letting litigation happen at all. By the latter remark Confucius could have meant either that the adjudicator should try to get the two sides to work out their differences without having to resort to litigation, or that the adjudicator should get the side that has no reason to litigate to stop pursuing the case. Most traditional scholars, however, have yet another view. They feel that Confucius was trying to get to the root of the problem. They say that it was his belief that litigation would not exist if people learned to respect one another and let their conduct be guided by ritual propriety.

12.14 Zizhang asked about the way of governing. The Master said, "Never be weary when you are in the position you occupy. Do your best when you conduct business."

In their commentaries on this passage, scholars like to quote the *Elder Dai's Book of Rites*, which says that in order to carry out a policy effectively, the official in charge has to take the lead and be an example to his people. I, however, prefer to understand it as the way

Confucius told it, which I read to mean: When you are not tired of your job, you will do your best, and that is the most effective way to conduct business in government.

12.15 The Master said, "The gentleman broadens his learning in literature and holds himself back with the practice of the rites. And so he is able not to go beyond the bounds of the moral way."

Since this is a repetition of 6.27, one could refer to the commentary there.

12.16 The Master said, "A gentleman helps others to realize what is good in them. He does not help others to realize what is reprehensible about them. A petty man is just the opposite."

The *Elder Dai's Book of Rites* gives slightly more depth to what Confucius observes here about the gentleman. It says, "The gentleman likes to see other people doing what is good, but he will not pressure them to do so. He does not like to see other people doing what is not good, but he will not show his anxiety. He may be worried about the mistakes other people made, but he will not try to patch things up for them. He will enhance the goodness of others, but he will not cause them to become arrogant. When a person is arrogant, he will not move forward. When a person has his flaws patched up by someone else, he will not know to correct them."

12.17 Ji Kangzi asked about the way of governing [*zheng*]. Confucius replied, "To govern [*zheng*] is to correct [*zheng*]. When you set an example by correcting your mistakes, who will dare not to correct his mistakes?"

Confucius, as I understand him, believed that having the awareness to correct your mistakes was the key to perfecting your character and also the way to realizing a strong and moral government. His teaching about "rectifying names" in 12.11 and 13.3 follows this idea, for to rectify names is to reform one's ways in a continuing effort to give integrity back to such names as "father" and "son," "ruler" and "subject."

12.18 Ji Kangzi was troubled about the problem of thieves, and he asked Confucius for advice.

Confucius said, "When you do not have excessive desires, even if you were to offer rewards for stealing, people would not do it."

Here Ji Kangzi was worried about something specific—the prevalence of thieves in Lu. Confucius' response implies that Ji Kangzi, who was the most powerful man in Lu, more powerful than the ruler he served, was himself no different from a thief: this man stole from the people, even from those who were desperate, because he could not rein in his desires. Confucius' criticism of Ran Qiu in 11.17 had already exposed the greed of this man's family, and in the present exchange, Confucius tells it to Ji Kangzi straight: If you stop stealing from others, the people will also stop, and, in fact, "even if you were to offer rewards for stealing, the people would not do it."

12.19 Ji Kangzi asked Confucius about the way of governing, saying, "In order to realize the moral way, how about if I were to kill those who do not live by it?"

Confucius replied, "As head of the government, why would you need to kill anyone [to bring about moral order]? The character of those at the top [*junzi*] is like that of the wind. The character of those below [*xiaoren*] is like that of grass. When wind blows over the grass, the grass is sure to bend."

Usually when they appear in the *Analects*, *junzi* and *xiaoren* refer to "the gentleman" and "the petty man." But here, as Qian Mu points out, they probably refer to their older meaning of "the ruler" and "the ruled"—which were purely designations of position, without any moral intimation. And the central question in this conversation is how to order society. Ji Kangzi suggests the eradication of the bad. But Confucius says: You are the head of the government—the most powerful man in the state—why would you need to kill anyone? Think about the power you hold—you are like the wind, which can bend whatever is in its path. Moreover, if your power is founded on integrity, surely you can bring all the people under your moral sway.

What Ji Kangzi proposed would have been easier for the ruler to carry out—all he had to do was to get rid of the undesirable elements under his authority. Confucius' idea of a good government, however, puts the responsibility on the ruler, on his cultivation and conduct, and though it has gone through many transformations in the twenty-five hundred years since, the idea remains a principal tenet in Confucian political thought.

12.20 Zizhang asked, "What must an educated professional [*shi*] be like before he can be said to possess a gentleman's adroitness [*da*] in all he does?"

The Master said, "You tell me first what you mean by possessing a gentleman's adroitness."

Zizhang replied, "Being a person that everyone would know, whether he is in the service of the state or in the service of a hereditary family."

The Master said, "You are talking about fame [*wen*], not about possessing a gentleman's adroitness. A person who is gentlemanly and adroit is by nature fair-minded and upright, and he is bent on aiming at what is right. He also listens to what others have to say and is observant of their expressions and moods. He is ever mindful of not being high-handed. Such a man possesses a gentlemanly adroitness whether he is in the service of the state or in the service of a hereditary family. A person who covets fame takes on the appearance of humaneness, which is belied by his deeds, and he is not troubled by his hypocrisy. Surely people would know him or his reputation whether he is in the service of the state or in the service of a hereditary family."

One of the most difficult Chinese words to render into English is *da*, which can mean "to reach," "to have arrived," "to be accomplished," or "to have gotten through." *Da* is often associated with *tong*, "connectibility" or "interchangeability," which is the case here, and when applied to a person's character, it suggests fluency and adroitness, which is my translation. Liu Baonan writes, "*Da* means to connect, to have a thorough understanding of things [*tong*]. A person who has a thorough understanding of the correct way to relate to others will find no obstacle to his action." And this, Liu says, is what Confucius means when he tells Zizhang in 15.6 that "if you impart sincerity and trust in your words, and integrity and respect in your deeds, you will get on even in the lands of the barbarians."

Liu Baonan also points out that Confucius was most suspicious of those who coveted fame because they would do anything to have their name known. Such were the ways of "the village goody men," men he berated as "the ruin of virtue."

12.21 Fan Chi accompanied the Master on an outing to a clearing below the rain altar. He said, "If I may, I would like to ask how one takes virtue to a higher level, how one corrects moral transgressions, and how one knows when one's judgment is clouded."

The Master said, "Excellent questions! To get things done before thinking about the reward—is this not taking virtue to a higher level? To attack what is wrongful and not what is wrongful in a particular person, is this not the way to correct the moral transgressions [of another] [*xiuni*]? To let a sudden fit of anger make you forget the dangers you risk for yourself and for those who are nearest and dearest to you—is this not clouded judgment?"

My translation of the second sentence in Confucius' response follows that of D. C. Lau. But nearly all the other scholars offer a different interpretation. They understand the first part of it to read: "to criticize what is wrongful in yourself and not what is wrongful in other people." This, they say, was what Confucius thought of as the correct and the most effective way "to rectify moral transgressions." I find their reading weaker than what D. C. Lau suggests. To get the other person to reform by first scrutinizing yourself for mistakes represents the thinking of Zengzi and, later, Mencius, which does not fully encompass what Confucius taught about emotions and their relationship to perception and moral rightness. If Confucius did say—as I believe he did—that to correct the moral transgressions of other people, one should criticize "what is wrongful and not what is wrongful in a particular person," he was separating out the wrongful act from the person who committed it. This is smart, because anyone who has erred will have a clearer view of what he has done if you, as the observer, choose to examine his mistake—why it is wrong—and not him.

There has also been some discussion in the commentaries about a possible reason this conversation took place. Some scholars feel that the visit to the rain altar evoked, in Fan Chi's mind, the events of 517 BC. In that year, the Jisun family expelled the ruler, Duke Zhao, from Lu, and when there was a severe drought in the autumn, a major sacrifice was conducted at the rain altar. When the drought persisted, another sacrifice was performed. Early historians say that the second appeal to the gods was a pretext "to assemble a crowd in order to drive out the Jisuns." The present conversation must have taken place more than thirty-five years later, after Confucius had returned to Lu, because Fan Chi belonged to the younger group of disciples. This, again, was a time when Lu was faced with natural disasters and the possibility of usurpation by the Jisun family. Thus, these scholars argue, Fan Chi asked these questions to see if his teacher felt that were sufficient moral grounds to depose the Jisuns. Qian Mu, however, feels that, "without solid evidence," one simply cannot know what Fan Chi was thinking when he was at the rain altar.

12.22 Fan Chi asked about humaneness. The Master said, "Love others."

He asked about wisdom. The Master said, "Know others."

Fan Chi failed to grasp what the Master meant.

The Master explained, "Raise the upright and place them above the crooked—this will cause the crooked to be upright."

After Fan Chi left his teacher, he saw Zixia, and he said, "A while ago, I saw the Master, and when I asked him about wisdom, the Master said, 'Raise the upright and place them above the crooked—this will cause the crooked to be upright.' What did he mean?"

Zixia said, "What a wealth of riches is in these words! After

Shun had gained possession of the empire, he searched from among the multitude [for someone of worth] and raised Gao Yao to a position at the top, and because he did so, those who were without humaneness stayed away. After Tang gained possession of the empire, he searched from the multitude [for someone of worth] and raised Yi Yin to a position at the top, and because he did so, those who were without humaneness stayed away."

I think there are two reasons why Fan Chi had difficulty understanding his teacher's words. First, Confucius did not make clear the relationship of "love others" and "know others." And second, his statement about the upright and the crooked did not seem to be a direct response to Fan Chi's question about "wisdom." Zixia's gloss answered Fan Chi's second question—"know others" means to know how to search from among the multitude for the talented and upright, and when they are raised above others, as in the case of the counselors Gao Yao and Yi Yin, those who lack humanity will "stay away." But what is also implied in Zixia's response is this: A humane ruler needs to be wise. He cannot just say that he loves his people; he has to have insight into human nature—he must "know others"— and he has to select the most worthy to assist him in government. By so doing, he realizes his love and concern. The *Elder Dai's Book of Rites* says, "The mark of a humane man is no more than loving others. The mark of a wise man is no more than being able to know who is a worthy." Yet a ruler cannot be said to be humane unless he is also wise.

12.23 Zigong asked about the way of being a friend. The Master said, "Be honest when there is a reason to reprove a friend, and guide him with a deft hand. But if he is unwilling to listen, you should stop, because you don't want to be humiliated."

One might compare what Confucius says here about the way of being a friend with what he says in 4.18 about the way of being a son. Even though both statements are about how to dissuade another person from wrongdoing, his advice on how to approach the problem varies depending on whether one is dealing with a friend or with a parent.

12.24 The gentleman makes friends by way of his interest and his education in the arts and in culture. He finds support from his friends in the cultivation of his humanity.

Qian Mu feels that it is helpful to read this statement of Confucius with 9.30. "The first sentence is about how to find a partner in learning," Qian writes. "The second sentence is about how to find a partner in the quest for moral meaning, in one's attempt to steady the self through the rites, and in the act of exercising moral discretion."

BOOK THIRTEEN

13.1 Zilu asked about the way of governing. The Master said, "Take the lead, and then put the people to work."

Zilu asked him to elaborate. The Master said, "Do not let up on your effort."

Kong Anguo understands Confucius' first statement to read: "Guide them first with the force of your integrity to gain their trust, and then put them to work." His interpretation resonates with what Zixia says in 19.10: "The gentleman earns the trust of his people first, before he subjects them to arduous labor. If he does not have their trust, they will think that he is trying to abuse them." But most scholars prefer a more straightforward reading of that sentence, which is reflected in my translation and in this statement from the *Elder Dai's Book of Rites*: "If a ruler wants to run his government efficiently, there is no better way than taking the lead himself and getting to work first."

13.2 Zhonggong, after being appointed as a steward in the Ji family, asked about the way of governing. The Master said, "The first thing is [to assemble your staff and] to assign them to the right positions. Try to overlook their minor shortcomings. Promote those of outstanding talent."

"How can I recognize those of outstanding talent in order to promote them?"

The Master said, "Promote those you recognize to be outstanding. As for those that you miss, will other people let them slip by you?"

Once a person has been appointed to a high position in government, the first order of affairs is to assemble a strong team—this, Liu Baonan believes, was Confucius' message for Zhonggong. And Liu observes a similar argument in *Mr. Lü's Spring and Autumn Annals*, a work from the late third century BC, which says, "To do something well, it is harder to do it oneself than to assign the work [to qualified men]. How do I know this? In walking, man cannot compete with a fine horse. But if he gets into a carriage and drives the horse, the horse becomes the lesser of the two. The ruler who likes to get involved in the business of every official in his government is like the man who thinks that he can compete against a fine horse in walking, and in the end he is the one to lose."

If delegating power is important in governing, how does one assemble a strong team, and how does one search for talented men? This is Zhonggong's second question. As a start, Confucius says, he should appoint those he knows to be capable, and then others will for sure put forth names of people who have escaped his attention. The Qing scholar Song Xiangfeng says that these words of Confucius resonate with a line from the eleventh hexagram, *tai* ("Peace"), in the *Book of Changes*: "When one pulls up the rush plant, it pulls up others of the same kind with it."

13.3 Zilu asked, "If the ruler of Wei were to wait for you to take charge of his government, what would you do first?"

The Master said, "It would have to be rectifying names."

Zilu said, "Are you really so out of touch? How does one rectify names?"

The Master replied, "How boorish you are! With things he does not understand, a gentleman would know to keep quiet. If names are not rectified, what is said will not seem reasonable. When what is said does not seem reasonable, nothing will get accomplished. When nothing gets accomplished, rites and music will not flourish. When rites and music do not flourish, punishments and penalties [will take their place, and they] will fail to be just when put into use. And when punishments and penalties fail to be just in practice, people will not know where to put their hands and feet. Thus when a gentleman names something, the name can surely hold up in speech. When he says something, his words can surely be carried out in action. When a gentleman speaks, there is nothing casual or careless about what he says."

When names have lost their integrity, words can no longer be trusted, and when words cannot be trusted, nothing can get done: government will cease to function, and the state will come to its demise. This is the reason why Confucius says that if he were put in charge of an administration, he would rectify names first. And because Zilu mentions specifically the state of Wei, some scholars think that Confucius' response was directed toward its young ruler, Zhe, who did not behave like a son to his father during the succession crisis of 492; when asked indirectly about his view of this man in 7.15, Confucius expressed his disapproval. Given this background, it does seem to make sense that Confucius would want to rectify names first—let the ruler Zhe be a son to his father—and then words and deeds will fall into place: rites and music will flourish, and there probably will be no need for punishments and penalties. But should there be a need to institutionalize punishments and penalties, fairness would prevail. And people would not be confused about what to do because they would not be under the threat of arbitrary rule.

Xunzi gave further consideration to this subject in his essay "Rectifying Names." In antiquity, he says, when there were "clear-eyed and keen-sighted rulers," "it was easy to unify the people." These men simply "presided over their people with authority" and gravity, and "the people were converted to the moral path as though by some divine force." But "the sage kings are gone," Xunzi observes, and no one, not even a gentleman, can wield that kind of magic anymore. All rulers since then have had to rely on words—on disquisitions and argumentation—to conduct business, and the best among them have understood that rectifying names was their first and most important task, for it would inspire trust and keep "crooked theories and deceitful words" at bay.

13.4 Fan Chi wanted to learn [from his teacher] how to grow grain crops. The Master said, "An old farmer would be a better person to ask." He wanted to learn how to grow vegetables.

The Master said, "An old gardener would be a better person to ask."

After Fan Chi had left, the Master said, "What a simple-minded person [*xiaoren*] Fan Xu [Fan Chi] is! If those above love the rites, then none of the common people will dare to be disrespectful. If those above love rightness, then none of the common people will dare to be disobedient. If those above love trustworthiness, then none of the common people will dare not to be forthcoming about the truth of things. When [the governing principle of a place] is like this, then people will flock to it from all directions with their babies strapped to their backs. What need is there to learn about growing grain crops?"

Confucius called Fan Chi a *xiaoren,* which, here, means a commoner, a "simple-minded" fellow, because Fan Chi did not know that, as someone who aspired to have a political career, he did not have to learn the skills of a farmer. Mencius expressed a similar sentiment in reproaching an agriculturalist who urged rulers to work side by side with their people in the field. He said, "There are affairs of great men [*daren*] and affairs of the common people [*xiaoren*]. . . . Hence it is said, 'There are those who use their minds and there are those who use their muscles. The former rule; the latter are ruled. . . .' This is a principle accepted by the whole empire." Mencius also pointed out that sage rulers worried about every aspect of the people's lives, whether they had warm clothes and enough to eat and whether they knew how to conduct themselves in human relationships. With so much on their minds, Mencius said, "how could these rulers have the leisure to plough the fields?" Rulers such as Yao and Shun used their minds, he added, but not on how to plough the fields.

13.5 The Master said, "A person may be able to recite the three hundred poems, but if he is unable to put [this knowledge] to full use when he is given a political assignment, or if he is unable to hold his own in a diplomatic exchange when he is sent abroad on a mission, no matter how many poems he has learned, what good will it do?"

Recitation of the three hundred poems was, for Confucius, a mark of a person's education and moral refinement. He tells his son, in 16.13, "Unless you learn the *Odes*, you won't be able to speak." But this knowledge was also an aid in government and in diplomacy, and its most prominent example is found in the records in the *Zuo Commentary*. The occasion was the visit of Prince Zha (Ji Zha), a royal descendant from the state of Wu, to the state of Lu in the year 544 BC. This prince had shunned political power only to become the supreme arbiter of manners and conduct. According to the *Zuo Commentary*, when he was a guest at the court of Lu, his host, Duke Xiang, asked the musicians to play selections from all four sections of the *Book of Odes*, and Prince Zha's appreciation of the regional differences among these songs, of their aesthetic quality, and of their moral and historical dimensions, which he declaimed in a series of comments, made the visit a diplomatic success. And so even though he wanted no part in politics, his performance as a representative of his own state had a strong political element. Confucius was only seven when this event took place, but examples like that of Prince Zha must have had a profound influence on his deliberations about the function of poetry.

13.6 The Master said, "If he himself is upright, he does not have to give orders and things will get done. If he himself is not upright, even though he gives orders, they will not be obeyed."

Most scholars assume that the subject of the present discussion is the ruler, but Confucius could have been referring to anyone in a superior position. And his point here falls in with what he says in 2.1, 2.3, 12.17, and 13.13. It receives further elaboration in Xunzi's essays "Nothing Indecorous" (*Bugou*) and "Rectifying Names" (*Zhengming*).

13.7 The Master said, "The political institutions of Lu and Wei are like brothers."

It is helpful, I think, to consider 13.7, 13.8, and 13.9 together. The remarks Confucius makes in these records are all concerned with the state of Wei: Why does the state of Lu have a special affinity with the state of Wei? Who from the state of Wei is an exemplary figure? And what should the government do for its people?

What Confucius says here in 13.7 could refer to the historical antecedents of Lu and Wei: The two states are close like brothers because their royal ancestors, the Duke of Zhou and Kangshu, were brothers. The Song dynasty scholars take the statement in a different direction. Zhu Xi says, "The two states were originally like brothers. But during Confucius' time, the situation in both places had declined to the point of being disorderly. Thus the state of their governments resembled one another. This was the reason why Confucius voiced his lament." I, however, feel that there is yet another way of understanding Confucius' remark. The political institutions of Lu and Wei were alike because both states had excellent counselors even though their rulers were morally depraved and politically inept—this, I believe, is what Confucius was trying to say. His statement here is, therefore, an expression of his optimism about these two governments, and this optimism can also be found elsewhere in the *Analects*. He says in 6.24, for instance, "With one great change, [the government] of Lu could embody the moral way." And when he is asked in 14.19 why a ruler like Duke Ling of Wei, a man of no scruples, was able to hold on to his state, Confucius says that this was because Wei had a fine counselor "in charge of foreign guests," an honest priest "looking after the ancestral temple," and a competent general "responsible for military affairs." (And in 13.8 he names another man of merit from the state of Wei, someone of princely descent.) Such views about Lu and Wei seem to have been widespread during Confucius' time. The *Zuo Commentary* tells us that when a family retainer from Qi considered fleeing to either Lu or Wei during a political crisis in his own state, he made sure that he did not commit anything that could be thought of as a transgression, because, he said, "[If I did,] then I wouldn't be able to face the gentlemen of Lu and Wei."

13.8 The Master said of Prince Jing of Wei, "He showed a sensible attitude toward running a household. When he first began to have some possessions, he said, 'That is about right.' When he accumulated some more, he said, 'That is about perfect.' When he had a wealth of assets, he said, 'That is opulent enough.'"

Confucius preferred frugality in most things, even when it came to the rites. But this does not mean that he was suspicious of wealth and looked down on the wealthy or that he believed it was more virtuous to live the life of a poor man. What he says in 1.15, "poor but joyful, rich but loving the rites," is a more accurate reflection of what he thought about this question and whom he felt were the virtuous among the poor and the rich. Prince Jing of Wei fit the idea of the virtuous rich, for he had restraint—he understood ritual propriety—even after his wealth had swelled. A remark attributed to Prince Zha of Wu, a man known for his astute judgment of human character, supports Confucius' appraisal of Prince Jing. Prince Zha called Prince Jing of Wei a "gentleman."

13.9 The Master went to the state of Wei. Ran You [Ran Qiu] drove the carriage for him. The Master said, "What a lot of people here!"

Ran You said, "When you already have a lot of people, what else should you do?"

"Make them rich."

"Once they are rich, what comes next?"

"Instruct them."

Central to the Confucian vision of a good government is one that is able to attract people from far and near. Mencius advised the rulers of his time to stop making war and to start looking after their people's livelihood when they complained that their populations were declining. But here Confucius simply states what he sees when he arrives at Wei—that there are a lot of people living there. Since that is the case, Ran You asks, what should the government of Wei do for them? Make them rich, Confucius says. And after that? Teach them to live a moral life, Confucius replies. But why must a ruler ensure his people a stable livelihood first before instructing them about ritual propriety? Mencius explains that to fail to act in that order would be a form of entrapment, because the common people, unlike the educated men, "would not be able to have a constant heart if they were without a constant means of support." "Lacking a constant heart, they will abandon all sense of measure and do as they please, stopping at nothing. And to punish them after they have committed misdeeds is to entrap them." "Thus," Mencius says, "a clear-sighted ruler will institute for his people a means of support that will allow them to have enough to care for their parents and to look after their wife and children, and a means of support that will allow them to eat their fill in good years, and to be spared from starvation in bad years. Only then will the ruler guide them toward goodness." Xunzi addresses the question more tersely. "If you do not make the people rich," he says, "you will have no means to help them cultivate [an appropriate expression of] their feelings. If you do not instruct them, you will have no means to help them manage their [messy and unruly] inborn nature."

13.10 The Master said, "If someone were to employ me [in government], it would take me only a year to bring things to an acceptable condition. After three years, I would have real accomplishments to show."

The Han historian Sima Qian thinks that Confucius made this remark after he had reached the state of Wei, and that he uttered it with the hope that the ruler of Wei might offer him a job. And to get a clearer sense of what Confucius meant by "an acceptable condition" (*ke*) and "real accomplishments" (*youcheng*), Liu Baonan suggests that we put 13.10 in the context of 13.9. Reading it this way, we can say that "an acceptable condition" refers to a comfortable livelihood for the people, and "real accomplishments" to their moral education.

13.11 The Master said, "How true is the saying that only after good men [*shanren*] have been in government for a hundred years is there the possibility of winning the war against cruelty and doing away with capital punishment."

About these "good men," Confucius observes in 11.20 that they may be good, but if they do not follow the cultural vestiges of the past, they will not be able "to reach the inner recesses" of moral knowledge. And because "they have not reached the inner recesses," the Han scholar Zheng Xuan says, "when they are in government, they are unable to have success in their early tenure." In fact, Confucius thought that it would take them a hundred years just to manage the problem of cruelty and to do away with the worst form of punishment. But things would be different if a true king were in charge. And this, Zheng points out, is the topic in the next entry.

13.12 The Master said, "Even if we were to have a true king, it would have to take a whole generation before humaneness could prevail."

Most of the discussion in the commentaries is about why it would take even a true king a whole generation, or thirty years, to realize his vision of moral rule and of a moral transformation of his people. The Qing dynasty scholar Bao Shenyan writes, "When hunger and cold both arrive at the same time, even if the the sage ruler Yao or Shun were in command, he still would not be able to stop men from becoming robbers and bandits. When wealth and poverty exist side by side, even if the supreme judge Gao Yao were in charge of the law, he still would not be able to stop the strong from bullying the weak." Besides, when a true king has just taken the reins, "he must first look after the people's livelihood, and then proceed to guide them with teachings of rightness and ritual propriety," Bao Shenyan goes on to say, "and the reason why [Confucius thought] 'it would have to take a whole generation' is that the ruler has to gauge the abilities of his people. He must not rush things."

13.13 The Master said, "If you know to correct yourself, what difficulty will you have should you decide to serve in government? If you do not know to correct yourself, how can you hope to correct others?"

This is similar to what Confucius says in 12.17 and 13.6. One could refer to those entries and their commentaries.

13.14 Master Ran [Ran Qiu] returned from court. The Master said, "Why so late?"

Ran Qiu replied, "There were government matters [*zheng*] [to discuss]."

The Master said, "They must have been the private business [*shi*] [of the Jisun family]. If they were government matters, though I am no longer employed, I would have heard about them."

From the history in the *Zuo Commentary*, we know that Ran Qiu was the chief retainer in the Jisun family even before Confucius came home. We know also that Confucius did not have a position in government after his return—he was a retired statesman, the "elder statesman." From the *Analects*, we learn that Ran Qiu's unwillingness to confront the Jisuns about their transgressions had enraged Confucius on several occasions. This is the probable background of the conversation here, an assumption the Han scholar Zheng Xuan made when he decided to focus his reading on two words: *zheng* (政) and *shi* (事). "*Zheng* are the ruler's instructions [for his people]," he says, "and *shi* are [the private] instructions of a counselor." And when the record says "Master Ran returned from court," the word "court" (*chao*), Zheng Xuan explains, refers to "the private court of the Jisun family." Most of the scholars since Zheng Xuan agree with his reading, and therefore much of the discussion in their commentaries is about the term "private court" (*sichao*): whether such a thing existed and, if so, where it took place—on the grounds of the hereditary families, or somewhere else. Several early records say that *sichao* could refer to the offices next to the ruler's official court. A late Warring States source, the *Kaogongji* (*Records for Examining the Artisans*), for instance, informs us that on both sides of the building where the ruler held court there were "nine offices where the nine counselors held their private court." The other question scholars ask is whether Ran Qiu, a family retainer, could have gained entrance to the ruler's court. Here the *Zuo Commentary* says that when Ran Qiu accompanied his employer to an audience with the ruler in the spring of 484, he actually had to wait for the latter somewhere else on the ruler's estate. This meant that Ran Qiu, being in the private service of the Jisuns, was not allowed to be present at the ruler's court and so could not have been in any of the discussions regarding state affairs. This gives support to Confucius' reproof of Ran Qiu for being evasive, if not dishonest, about where he had been and the talks he had been privy to.

13.15 Duke Ding asked, "Is there a saying that can bring prosperity to a state?"

Confucius replied, "No saying can do that, but there is something that comes close to it. People have a saying, 'It's difficult to be a ruler, and it's not easy to be ministers and officials.' But if the ruler knows that it is difficult being a ruler, would it not come close to having a saying that can bring prosperity to a state?"

Duke Ding asked, "Is there a saying that can bring a state to its demise?"

Confucius replied, "No saying can do that, but there is something that comes close to it. People have a saying, 'I get no pleasure from being a ruler except for the fact that no one goes against my words.' If what the ruler says is good and no one goes against him, is this not good? But if what the ruler says is not good and no one goes against him, would it not come close to having a saying that can bring a state to its demise?"

Liu Baonan mentions several early sources that he thinks might throw light on this conversation between Confucius and Duke Ding, the ruler who was partly responsible for forcing Confucius out of Lu in 497 BC. The first one is Ode 236 from the *Book of Poetry*. This poem is about King Wen after he received Heaven's mandate to "assail the great Shang" and to found a new dynasty. Two lines at the beginning of this poem warn the future king, "It's hard to trust heaven, / it is not easy being a king." The sentiments expressed in these words are elaborated elsewhere, in the Duke of Zhou's speech to the Duke of Shao in the *Junshi* chapter of the *Book of Documents*, for instance, where the Duke of Zhou says, "Heaven is not to be trusted. Our course of action is to continue upholding the virtue of our former kings so that Heaven will not abandon the mandate King Wen had received," and also in a Han dynasty commentary to the *Book of Poetry*, where there is an account of three counselors urging the new ruler not to be complacent and not to neglect his work because "he should always take his government as his worry and never consider his position as an entitlement to pleasure."

The second part of this conversation is about remonstrance—whether the ruler is entitled not to have his words contradicted, and if this is the case, why should he bother to have counselors? Liu Baonan uses several examples to illustrate Confucius' point of view, and the finest, I feel, comes from the *Sayings of the State* (*Guoyu*). In this scene, a minister says to a ruler who has turned a deaf ear to any sensible advice: "In the past, our former kings had counselors to help them put an end to mistrust and misconduct, and to avert any serious crisis. But now you have abandoned the old [and wise in your government] and have decided to do your scheming with children. And you say, 'No one is to go against my command.' But [the decree] 'not to go against you' is in itself a transgression. And [to expect your counselors] not to go against you is to descend the steps to destruction."

13.16 The Governor of She asked Confucius about the way of government. The Master replied, "See to it that those who are near are pleased, and those who are far away are drawn to it."

I would put Confucius' remark in the context of the history of She around the time of his visit—a subject I have discussed in *The Authentic Confucius*. In that work, I wrote:

> The district of She had originally been a part of Cai. In 493, the ruler of Cai decided to move his capital east to be nearer to [the state of Wu], which was his ally at the time. The area around She, was, therefore, left to its own devices. Two years later, the government of Chu took control of She, and its representatives encouraged the people of Cai, who had decided not to move east with their ruler, to come and settle in She and to recognize Chu as their new overlord. When Confucius arrived in She, the governor had just been assigned there, his subjects were essentially a foreign people, and he was a long way from his own political base in Chu.

Given these circumstances, it made sense for Confucius to tell the governor to make sure that people who were already under his jurisdiction were pleased with his policies and that people who were far away wanted to come to live in She. The governor remained in his position for twelve years, according to the records in the *Zuo Commentary*. He returned to the capital of Chu in 479 to help deal with a crisis at the Chu court but returned to She as soon as it was resolved. He spent the remaining part of his life in She.

13.17 When Zixia was appointed the steward of Jufu, he asked about the way of government. The Master said, "Don't try to rush things. Don't look to small gains. If you rush things, you won't reach your goal. If you look to small gains, you won't be able to accomplish the important tasks."

Xunzi, in his essay "On Attracting Men of Administrative Talents" (*Zhishi*), says that it would take at least three years for the ruler to put his government in order: one year to establish his character as someone who is flexible, magnanimous, and respectful; another year to find the right balance in his attempt to weigh all matters concerning his people and the state; and a third year to implement a fair system of rewards and punishments. "Do not reverse the order of beginning and end," Xunzi warns the ruler; if you think you can hurry things by establishing a system of rewards and punishments first, "you will have trouble enforcing your policies, and the ruler and the ruled will resent each other." Even though the plan Xunzi lays out here (for those who have just taken charge of administering a state or a district) varies slightly from what Confucius says in 13.10, both stress that to ensure success in governance, the ruler and his stewards need to take the long view and cultivate trust first: quick solutions, such as threats of punishment, will not have any moral effect on the people, and, in fact, they will often breed hostility and set the stage for insurrection.

Mr. Lü's Spring and Autumn Annals gives a wonderful example of the folly of thinking small and worrying about petty advantages. The army of Chu had suffered a major defeat but had to face the enemy once more in a final test. Their commander asked the ruler to hand out some gold from his treasury chest to the remaining troops to boost their morale. The ruler refused, his army lost, and the enemy stormed into the capital and rifled all his gold. This goes to show, the text says, "If you cannot give up small gains, you will not have any big gains."

13.18 The Governor of She said to Confucius, "Right here, in our place, there is a man called Upright Gong. When his father stole a sheep, he bore witness against him."

Confucius responded, "Where I came from, those who are considered upright are different from this man. Fathers cover up for their sons, and sons cover up for their fathers. Being upright lies therein."

Upright Gong, the son of a common thief, has been a problem for the Chinese for at least twenty-five hundred years. It is a most satisfying sort of problem, however, because this man's conduct fueled a debate about family and state, and it raised a most relevant question about the two contending institutions: Which should have our loyalty if we were forced to choose between them? And Confucius' response to the Governor of She drew even more attention from moral philosophers and legal historians in the centuries that followed. The Song dynasty thinkers (whose reading is reflected in most of the English translations) understand Confucius to say that fathers and sons should cover up for each other and that uprightness is found in such behavior. The Qing scholar Cheng Yaotian has a different point of view. This scholar is deeply suspicious of men like Upright Gong, who seemed to have acted solely for the public good. In an essay called "Talking about the Public Spirit," he writes:

> When everyone else acts out of private motives, and one person makes a show that he does not, is this then truly a case where private motives do not exist? If even the sages find it difficult to realize what is called "public spirit," and one person finds it easy, does it mean that this person has made simple what everyone else considers difficult? Has he gotten what he claims to have?

But Cheng also rejects the reading the Song scholars suggest. If they were right, he says, then the tussle between the two opposing loyalties could never be conceived of as a moral problem, because the person faced with this question would always stand on the side of his family. Cheng prefers to understand Confucius in light of the latter's strength as a moral thinker. Thus, he argues, in saying that "uprightness lies therein [zhi zai qizhong]," Confucius meant that in being human a person has to "use the fullness of his private affections to realize what is good for the public."

13.19 Fan Chi asked about humaneness. The Master said, "Remain reverent in your private life; be respectful in handling affairs; do your best in your relationship with others. Do not leave them behind even when you go and live among the Di and Yi [border] tribes."

One can refer to 12.1 and 12.2 for a more precise, a more tactile description of being reverent in private life and being respectful in handling affairs. But in Qian Mu's view, what Confucius wanted to emphasize here was that a person should not let go of these rules even when he had settled among the Di and Yi, among people who lived beyond the reach of culture and refinement, because, though their conduct might have lacked ritual propriety, the Di and Yi were still part of the human race.

13.20 Zigong asked, "What sort of men could be considered good enough to be in government [shi]?"

The Master said, "Men who have a sense of shame in the way they conduct themselves and, when sent abroad, will not bring disgrace to the mission their ruler has entrusted to them."

"What would be the next best?"

"Those who are good sons in the eyes of their kin and fine young men in the eyes of their neighbors and villagers.'

"And the level below that?"

"Men who insist on keeping their word and seeing their actions through to the end. They have little pebbles for brains and are inferior indeed. But I suppose you can say that they come next."

"And what about those who are in public life right now?"

"Unh? They are puny vessels, men with hardly any capacity. They don't even count!"

There were *shi* before Confucius' time—men who received an education in order to have a career in government—but it was Confucius who spelled out the requirements for the job. The most qualified, in his view, were those who had a sense of shame in the way they conducted themselves and were deft players in the political world so that they would not "bring disgrace to their ruler" when sent on a mission abroad. And the next best were those who possessed stellar characters in the eyes of family and neighbors, but whose administrative and diplomatic skills were not necessarily well honed. And on the level below that were men who would keep their word and see their actions through to the end: they were truthful but inflexible; they made *kengkeng* sounds as if they had "little pebbles for brains." And as for the men in office in his own time, Confucius said they were "puny vessels" that could hold only ten pecks of grain or less.

13.21 The Master said, "Not being able to be in the company of those who do not swerve from the right path, I must turn to the wildly spirited [*kuang*] and the overly cautious [*juan*]. The wildly spirited forge ahead [without reservation]. The overly cautious refrain from doing certain things."

Confucius' remark here about the company he sought reflects what he says in 2.2 about "the three hundred poems in the *Book of Poetry*": "They never swerve from the path." But while he was able to find that sudden rightness in a poem, he did not have such luck with people. There was no one, it seemed, who could give him the pleasure that a good poem had in store for him—a pleasure he describes in 2.2 and in 3.20 as the moral and aesthetic idea of balance, a balance in advancing and retreating, spurring on and reining in, letting go and holding back.

To understand how Confucius felt about men who were wildly spirited (*kuang*), one could refer to 5.22 and the commentary there. He had less to say about men who were overly cautious (*juan*). But from his description here, one could infer that he had in mind men who were watchful about not going too far, not overstepping the line of ritual propriety. Mencius, however, is more critical of the overly cautious. He says that such men will always try "to steer clear of the squalid and unclean," thus suggesting that they are overly scrupulous and priggish. And Mencius thinks that the overly cautious were Confucius' last choice for association: he would turn to them only after he had failed to find "the wildly spirited." It is difficult to know if Mencius is right, but from the affinity Confucius had with Zeng Xi in 11.26, it does seem that he was drawn to the wildly spirited.

13.22 The Master said, "People from the south have a saying, 'A man lacking constancy will not make a shaman or a doctor.' Well put, is it not? [The *Book of Changes* says,] 'The person who lacks constancy in upholding his virtue will be met with disgrace.'" [Commenting on this,] the Master said, "It means that there is simply no point for him to have his fortune told."

This passage poses many questions, the most difficult of which is how to integrate the two statements attributed to Confucius. A large number of scholars, beginning with the Han, seem to think that the gap can be narrowed if we understand the first sentence to read: "The people from the south have a saying, 'A shaman or a doctor cannot do a thing for a man who lacks constancy.'" There would then be continuity in what Confucius said, they argue, since both of his statements would have a single target, the fickle man who wanted to have his fortune told. And to support their reading, these scholars refer to a longer but similar passage in the *Ziyi* ("Black Robe") chapter of the *Book of Rites*, which is also ascribed to Confucius. There, Confucius says:

> People from the south have a saying, "A man lacking constancy cannot have his fortune told." These must be words passed down from the ancient time. If tortoise shells and yarrow stalks cannot know your fortune, how much less so [a shaman,] a human being! The *Book of Poetry* [Ode 195] said, "The tortoise shells are tired, / They have no fortunes to divulge. . . ." The *Changes* said, "The person who lacks constancy in upholding his virtue will be met with disgrace."

The problem with the above interpretation is that it was too neatly worked out. Why, one might ask, could Confucius not be talking about the shaman *and* the person who sought his advice? Why could he not be saying that both the soothsayer and the seeker need to have constancy? With the recent discovery of a large number of bamboo texts in central China, we now have a much earlier—a 300 BC—version of the *Ziyi* text, and compared with the passage cited above from the received version, there are two principal differences. The bamboo text begins with "The Master said, 'The people from Song [not the people from the south] had a saying,'" and it ends much earlier, with the two lines from the *Book of Poetry*, which means that the quote from the *Book of Changes* is not in this version, which predates the received text by about 150 years. One possible explanation for the discrepancies is that the early Han editors used the record in the *Analects* to expand the *Ziyi* chapter and so they included the quote from the *Book of Changes*; they also modified the attribution of the saying in the *Ziyi* from "the people from Song" to "the people from the south" to make the passages in these two separate texts more uniform. And then, in later Han, scholars like Zheng Xuan returned to the *Ziyi* chapter to explain Confucius, but by that point, the *Ziyi*, in its amplified version, already had an unmistakable connection to the *Analects*.

13.23 The Master said, "The gentleman harmonizes [*he*] without being an echo. The petty man echoes [*tong*] and does not harmonize."

To illustrate Confucius' point here, most commentaries refer to an analogy the Qi counselor Master Yan used in a conversation with his ruler on the same topic. The account is found in the *Zuo Commentary*, and in it, Master Yan tells his ruler that finding harmony in government is like making soup. "Water, fire, vinegar, meat paste, salt, and plums—these are the ingredients to prepare fish and meat in a soup," he says, "and it is up to the cook to harmonize them and balance the flavors, to add a bit more of this or that when the flavors are too bland and to dilute it a bit more when the flavors are too strong." "The same can be said about the relationship between the ruler and his counselors," Master Yan continues. "In what the ruler considered acceptable, there must be something that is unacceptable. And so it is up to the counselors to put forth to him what is not unacceptable in order to [refine and] improve his idea of what is acceptable. In what the ruler considered unacceptable, there must be something that is acceptable. And so it is up to the counselors to put forth to him what is acceptable in order to [refine and] improve his idea of what is not acceptable. In this way, the ruler will be able to realize a fair government and not commit any transgressions, and the people will no longer have contentious thoughts." Master Yan contrasts this approach toward government, where ruler and counselors work together to adjust the extremes and to find a balance and harmony (*he*) in administrative styles and policies, to another type of approach, where the counselors simply echo (*tong*) whatever the ruler says. "This is like trying to improve the taste of water with more water. Who would want that?"

13.24 Zigong asked, "What would you think of a person if everyone in the village liked him?"

The Master said, "I still would not be able to tell [one way or another about him]."

"What would you think of a person if everyone in the village disliked him?"

"I still would not be able to tell [one way or another about him]. Better if the good people in his village liked him and the bad ones disliked him."

Confucius tends to reserve judgment about those who are known by their reputation. Reputations, good or bad, are built on perception: they are mercurial, and they are hard to support. For this reason, he despises men who take manufacturing perception and manipulating public sentiment as their calling. Only men of integrity can offer a correction. He says in 4.3, "Only a humane person is able to like and dislike others."

13.25 The Master said, "The gentleman is easy to serve but difficult to please. He will not be happy if, in trying to please him, you veer from the proper way; but when he employs others, he does so with respect to their capacity. The petty man is difficult to serve but easy to please. He will be happy even though, in trying to please him, you veer from the proper way; but when he employs others, he expects them to be able to handle everything."

In his remark here and in 13.26, Confucius tries to persuade us of his idea of the gentleman. He first gives him a palpable description, and then he sharpens the idea by contrasting this man against the petty man.

13.26 The Master said, "The gentleman has breadth of character [*tai*] but is not arrogant. The petty man is arrogant but has no breadth of character."

Confucius comes back to this idea in 20.2 and gives a precise explanation of what he means when he states that "the gentleman has breadth of character but is not arrogant"; such a man, he says, "dares not to be disrespectful whether he is dealing with a few or with many, with people big or small." Zhuangzi, from the fourth century BC, takes the idea to another level. Though he has often been thought of as an adversary of Confucius and a competitor in China's early intellectual wars, the two have more in common than Confucius' later defenders care to admit. An example can be found in what Zhuangzi says about the kind of man he admires. Zhuangzi calls him "the great man [*daren*]." He writes in the "Autumn Flood" (*Qiushui*): "[The great man] will not act for the sake of profit, but he does not despise the porter at the gate. He will not wrangle for goods and possessions, but he makes no exaggerated show of yielding these things to others. . . . He does not despise the greedy and base, . . . the glib and sycophantic." The Qing dynasty scholar Jiao Xun equates "breadth of character" (*tai*) with "adroitness" (*tong*). Zhuangzi, in his description of the "great man," magnifies the idea of adroitness: this man, though principled himself, is at home with the greedy and the base, the glib and the sycophantic.

13.27 The Master said, "Unwavering [in integrity] [*gang*], resolute [in one's moral conviction] [*yi*], simple as [a piece of unadorned] wood [*mu*] and hesitant [as if too clumsy] to speak [*ne*]—these qualities come close to being humane [*ren*]."

216 THE ANALECTS

It was the third-century scholar Wang Su who first suggested the reading of *gang*, *yi*, *mu*, and *ne*. Liu Baonan follows Wang Su in his commentary and gives a clearer explanation of these four concepts, using Confucius' own words in the *Analects*. My translation reflects their interpretation, and it also draws from other records in the *Analects*.

13.28 Zilu asked, "How should a person conduct himself in order to be considered good enough to serve in government [*shi*]?"

The Master said, "He must be critical, encouraging, and affable to be considered good enough to serve in government: critical and encouraging to his friends; affable to his brothers."

Confucius already has discussed with Zigong the qualifications of a *shi*, a man who possesses the knowledge, the skills, and the character to be in government service. When Zilu asks him the same question here, Confucius again turns to the subject of character, but now he wants to consider this man's relationship to his friends and family, to those who are closest to him. Confucius makes a distinction, however, between friends and family: Be critical and encouraging to one, he says, and be affable to the other. A distinction must exist, Liu Baonan says in his commentary, because these two sets of relationships are different in nature. "Friends are drawn together by their sense of rightness; brothers stay together because of the love and affection they have for each other." Mencius also stresses this point in his teaching. He says, "Father and son would be at odds if they were to tax each other over a moral issue. It is for friends to demand goodness from each other. For father and son to do so would seriously undermine the love between them."

13.29 The Master said, "A good man will give his people seven years of instruction before he is ready to arm them for military action."

One should consider Confucius' remark here together with what he says in the next entry. Both are about sending troops to war, which, he feels, is a matter of deadly seriousness. Here he says that a good man, a good ruler, "will give his people seven years of instruction" before he is willing to dispatch them to the battlefield. And just what sort of instruction does Confucius have in mind? Most scholars believe that it is a combination of moral education and military training. Just military training alone would not be enough, they argue: a person would need to learn about rightness, propriety, and trust before he felt that he was ready to die for his duties. And seven years, Zheng Xuan says, would be ample time for the ruler to cultivate the love and loyalty he would need from his troops in order to carry out a successful undertaking.

13.30 The Master said, "If you send your troops to war without first instructing them, this is the same as throwing them away."

Here Confucius adds more urgency to what he states above about the importance of giving the people proper instruction before sending them to war. Not to do so, he stresses, would be the same as treating their lives callously. This point can be found in several Warring States and early Han texts, most notably the *Mencius*. On one occasion, Mencius tells a military commander of Lu, "To send the people to war before they are trained is to bring disaster to them." On another occasion, he decries the ruler of Liang for dispatching his people, even his young men, to war, "making pulp of them," because of his own blind ambition.

BOOK FOURTEEN

14.1 Xian [Yuan Si] asked what conduct could be considered shameful.

The Master said, "When the state is governed according to the moral way, one would accept a salary. When the state is not governed according to the moral way, it would be shameful to accept a salary."

"[If a person] does not insist on winning and is not boastful, begrudging, or covetous, can such conduct be called humane?"

The Master said, "One can call that difficult, but I don't know whether it measures up to being humane."

Xian is Yuan Si's given name, and so, scholars say, he must have been the person who recorded the above conversation. If someone else were responsible for it, that person would have used the courtesy name Yuan Si.

Most scholars like to consider this conversation together with 6.5 and 8.13. In 6.5, we learn that Yuan Si was a district steward in Lu, and when he declined an offer of nine hundred measures of grain for his service, Confucius chided him for being uptight and priggish. He said, "Can you not share it with the people in your village and in your neighboring communities?" But here he seems to think that it would be shameful to accept a salary, any amount of salary, from a dysfunctional government, which, in fact, is how one would describe the political practice in Lu around this time. If this was how Confucius felt, why did he scold Yuan Si for not accepting a salary in 6.5? Was his response there—about how to put Yuan Si's salary to use—not more imaginative? Confucius also shows more flexibility in 8.13, where his thoughts about what would be a cause for shame cover more ground than what he says here, and where he surprises us by saying, "When the moral way prevails in a state, being poor and lowly is a cause for shame."

The second half of the present conversation has also received a lot of attention across the centuries. The discussion tends to focus on the difference between difficult feats (*nan*) and humane action (*ren*). And most scholars agree that what Yuan Si describes is difficult to realize but that it pertains only to personal cultivation, to the effort of "making oneself immaculate." "If a man is able to conduct himself in this way," the Qing scholar Ruan Yuan says, "then he cannot bring harm to anyone. But he also cannot benefit others—he cannot help others 'to steady themselves' or 'to reach their goal.' For this reason, Confucius did not consider such conduct as humane." What Ruan Yuan refers to in his comment is what Confucius says in 6.30 about "the method and the way of realizing humaneness." The humane person, Confucius explains there, draws his analogies from what he likes and dislikes, and so because he wishes to steady himself and reach his goal, he helps others to steady themselves and reach their goal.

14.2 The Master said, "An educated professional who longs for [the ease he finds at] home does not live up to the name of an educated professional [*shi*]."

Here Confucius again returns to the subject of *shi* (士): to the question of who is qualified to have a career in government. But instead of talking about character and skills, he is looking at this man's emotions and his attachments: if such a person still yearns for his home—for his wife and children and for the ease he finds in his home—then he is short of being a *shi*. For a man who is truly qualified for government service will "set his mind on realizing humaneness and rightness," Liu Baonan explains. This means that he will be ready to go wherever his responsibilities take him and will be able to resist the tug toward home. The urge to go home has been an important theme in the writings of the Chinese scholar-officials. And that urge gets stronger and becomes harder to resist when the moral way does not prevail in the state. Confucius must have been aware of this fact, and probably for this reason he wanted to be very clear about who was able to fulfill the idea of a *shi*.

14.3 The Master said, "When a state is governed according to the moral way, be exact [*wei*] in speech and action. When the state is not governed according to the moral way, be exact in action but soften your speech."

When the moral way prevails in the state, one can afford to take a chance and be exact (*wei*) in speech and conduct. (*Wei* means, literally, to risk the danger of standing on a high place.) When the moral way does not prevail in the state, one should be exact in conduct but tactful in speech. This was Confucius' advice for those in government service. And to follow it or not could mean the difference between life and death. Here again we find a point of agreement between him and the fourth-century BC thinker Zhuangzi, who, in the voice of Confucius, says, "If you appear before a tyrant and force him to listen to sermons on humaneness and rightness . . . you will be called a pest. He who pesters others will be pestered in return."

14.4 The Master said, "A person who has integrity is sure to have something to say, but a person who has something to say does not necessarily have integrity. A person who is humane is sure to possess courage, but a person who possesses courage is not necessarily humane."

Liu Baonan writes in his commentary, "Integrity [*de*] is not made apparent through words [*yan*]. Humaneness [*ren*] is not made apparent through courage [*yong*]. Yet according to Confucius, there must be people who possess integrity or humaneness. These virtues, therefore, are disclosed and inferred through one's talent and natural propensities." And in Liu's view, Xunzi gives the "fullest and the clearest" explication of Confucius' statements here. But on the question of words and integrity, I think, Xunzi goes further than Confucius. Xunzi feels that if a person "is reluctant to speak and takes no pleasure in speaking," even though his conduct "is modeled after the former kings" and "dictated by ritual propriety and rightness," he "is not the best man to serve in government." A gentleman must engage in moral persuasion, is Xunzi's point, and so he has no choice but to take part in arguments and debates. Xunzi also explains in a separate essay why a humane man is sure to possess courage: "This man likes to share his joys with the world when the world recognizes him, but he will stand alone without fear when the world does not recognize him." Xunzi considers the courage exemplified by a humane man to be the "highest kind" even though it does not dazzle and is not loud and explosive.

14.5 Nangong Kuo said to Confucius, "Yi was a fine archer, and Ao [was strong enough to] overturn the boats [of his enemies], yet neither was able to die a natural death. Yu and Hou Ji personally planted seeds in the field and were able to gain possession of an empire." The Master made no reply.

After Nangong Kuo had left, the Master said, "A gentleman, this man. An example of the highest virtue, this man!"

There have been several conjectures about the identity of Nangong Kuo. The Song scholar Zhu Xi says that he was Nan Rong, who appears in 5.2 and 11.6. The Han scholar Kong Anguo says that he was the Lu counselor Nangong Jingshu. Liu Baonan thinks that they are both wrong, but he does feel that Nangong was an aristocrat, because surnames such as Nangong (South Palace), Beigong (North Palace), Donggong (East Palace), and Xigong (West Palace) were common appellations for scions of hereditary families.

The more interesting question, however, has to do with the story of the archer Yi and the strongman Ao. Both men, according to the history in the *Zuo Commentary*, were figures from the Xia dynasty. Yi was a hunter and a local chieftain. He, by means of his warrior stance, was able to overshadow the authority of the ruler of Xia with his own. But eventually he became complacent, and he let his disciple Hancu handle all his business while he pursued animals in the wild. One day, as Yi was coming home from the hunt, Hancu had him killed. Hancu then had Yi cooked in a stew and served to Yi's son. The House of Yi was China's own House of Atreus. Yi's murderer fathered two sons with Yi's wives. One of the sons was Ao. Ao, like his father, could raise hell of his own. In a battle against another tribe, he singlehandedly capsized the enemy boats. But this warrior also ended his life badly—at the hands of a man whose father he had killed. In the same passage, Nangong Kuo also introduces Yu and Hou Ji. They represent another kind of man. Yu tamed the flood and was the founder of the Xia dynasty; Hou Ji taught farming and was the progenitor of the Zhou people. Both men worked in the field, sowing seeds and tending crops, and they came to possess an empire. By contrasting how the hunter and the agriculturist, the warrior and the driver of civilization, each fared in the end, Nangong Kuo makes his point, and so Confucius feels that he has nothing to add except that he thinks Nangong Kuo is a gentleman.

14.6 The Master said, "A gentleman but not humane, there are such examples. But there has never been a petty man who is humane."

Confucius feels strongly that only a few persons can be called humane (*ren*). Even when a person is "not competitive, boastful, begrudging, or covetous," he resists calling him humane. He says in 4.6 that, in fact, he has "never seen a person who truly loved humaneness or a person who was truly repelled by the lack of humaneness," although he is sure that all humans have the strength to devote themselves "to the practice of humaneness." Such is the paradox in the human pursuit of the good. The gentleman would take his quest seriously, but even he could falter, for, as Confucius' disciple Zengzi observes, "the burden is heavy, and the road is long."

14.7 The Master said, "When you love someone, how can you not encourage him to work hard? When you want to do your best for someone, how can you not try to instruct him [to do the right thing]?"

Some scholars think that the first part of this remark was intended for the ruler and his officials, who were meant to spur the people on and to stop them from slacking. The second part, they say, was addressed to the counselors, who were bound by their duty to remonstrate with the ruler when he faltered. But Liu Baonan feels that there is no need to make such a distinction. What Confucius said here, in Liu's view, could be applied to the local official who was administering a district or a counselor who was advising the ruler at court. In fact, Liu says, a person would want to do both if he genuinely cared for the other person: like "a kindly father toward his child," he would encourage him to work hard (*lao*) and he would guide him to the right path (*hui*).

14.8 The Master said, "In preparing for a diplomatic agreement, Pi Chen would compose a draft in the wild; Shi Shu would discuss it; Ziyu, the master of protocol, would revise it; and Zichan of the Eastern Village would put on the final touches."

We have already learned in 5.16 how Confucius felt about Zichan, the counselor from the state of Zheng, who preceded him by about a hundred years. Here and in the next entry, he talks not only about the admiration he had for this man but also about how Zichan worked with other counselors and the kind of political environment he created in the state of Zheng. One can find a similar description of the above in the history in the *Zuo Commentary*, where it is said, "In administering a government, Zichan selected the capable and gave them responsibilities." And on his staff was one Pi Chen, the record says. This man "was good at strategizing," but ideas would come to him only "when he worked in the wild" because his mind "would draw a blank when he was in the city." This explains why Confucius says that when being put in charge of preparing a diplomatic agreement, Pi Chen would write his draft "in the wild."

14.9 Someone asked about Zichan. The Master said, "He was a generous and a caring man."

He asked about Zixi. The Master said, "That man! That man!"

He asked about Guan Zhong. The Master said, "He was a man [*ren*]. After Guan Zhong seized control of the district of Pian, which had three hundred households, from the head of the Bo family, Bo was reduced to living on coarse rice, yet, to the end of his days, he had nothing resentful to say."

Confucius' admiration for Zichan must have been broadly known, for his accolades were also recorded in the history in the *Zuo Commentary*. Yet not everyone agreed with his assessment of Zichan, not even Mencius, Confucius' staunchest defender. Mencius also thought Zichan "a generous and caring man" but so much so that in the winter if he saw people having a hard time crossing a frozen river, he would take them across in his carriage. Why did he not simply build a bridge for them? Mencius asked. It must have been that "Zichan did not know how to govern." Most scholars think that Mencius' argument was thin and his example trivial. On the question of Guan Zhong, too, Mencius, could be disparaging. He said that Guan Zhong was the kind of counselor not worth emulating. Yet Confucius accorded Guan Zhong the highest praise, defending his conduct as "humane," *ren* (仁), in 14.16 and 14.17, and calling him here "a man," *ren* (人), which, scholars thought, was synonymous with "being humane," *ren*. Just how do we account for the differences of opinion between Confucius and Mencius regarding Zichan and Guan Zhong? This is the kind of question that requires longer study. Still, it is interesting to note the large stock Confucius put in counselors like Zichan and Guan Zhong—men whose conduct at times had been deemed suspect and even wrongful. Zichan, as soon as he took office, bribed the powerful to keep them content so that they would be willing to work with him. And Guan Zhong chose to serve Duke Huan of Qi, a man who had murdered his own brother (and Guan Zhong's lord). Why was Confucius willing to overlook such irregularities? Did he feel that moral questions of a lesser order—questions that could end up being obstructive—should not be asked of men bound for greater things? And as for the head of the Bo family, he was a counselor of Qi. When Guan Zhong decided to shift his loyalty to Duke Huan, the latter offered him Bo's fief. Scholars thought that Bo must have committed some grave misdeed to see all of his property confiscated, and that he must also have recognized something extraordinary in Kuan Zhong and so he held no rancor.

Finally, there is the question of Zixi. He was a counselor from Zheng. Scholars, however, were not interested in who he was but in what Confucius said when his name was mentioned. *Bizai, bizai* ("That man! That man!"), they thought, implied that this person, in Confucius' view, was inconsequential.

14.10 The Master said, "It is difficult to be poor and not resentful, and easier to be rich and not arrogant."

Some scholars believe that this refers to the head of the Bo family in the previous entry—that after he was stripped of his possessions, he was not bitter, which, Confucius thought, was admirable. But Liu Baonan thinks that the comment was directed at the ruler, to let him know how difficult it was for people to live in poverty. Perhaps it was for this reason that Confucius says in 13.9, first "make the people rich" and then "instruct them."

14.11 The Master said, "Meng Gongchuo would be an excellent retainer in the family of Chao or Wei, but he could not possibly be a [good] counselor in the state of Teng or Xue."

Here Confucius acts like a casting director for the political stage. Meng Gongchuo was a hereditary counselor in the state of Lu and so could not possibly be a retainer for the Chaos or the Weis, which were hereditary families in the state of Jin. Nevertheless, Confucius imagined how Meng Gongchuo would fare in such a role, and since he had worked with this man, he knew that being an elderly retainer in either family would suit him well because the Chaos and the Weis greatly appreciated worthy men, of which Meng Gongchuo was one. But being a counselor in a small state like Teng or Xue, even with the formal title of *daifu*, would be disastrous for Meng, who treasured solitude and quiet reflection, for there would be too many tedious affairs to take care of.

14.12 Zilu asked about the complete man. The Master said, "A man with the knowledge of Zang Wuzhong, as devoid of greed as Meng Gongchuo, as courageous as Zhuangzi of Bian, as skilled in the arts as Ran Qiu, and then further refined by rites and music—he could be considered a complete man."

The Master [paused and then] continued, "But why does a complete man of our times need to be like that? If he is mindful of what is right when he sees profit, is ready to lay down his life when faced with danger, and does not forget what he said as a youth about promises made long ago, he can well be a complete man."

One could say that Confucius lowered the standard of a complete man for the people of his times, but as a statement, this is also more tangible and more forceful than the measures he proposed at first. The sentiment that is particularly memorable—"[if he] does not forget what he said as a youth [*pingsheng*] about promises made long ago [*jiuyao*]"—could have a different reading, "[if he] does not forget the words he has repeated all his life even when he is experiencing protracted hardship," if one were to understand *pingsheng* to mean "all one's life" and *jiuyao* to mean "protracted hardship."

As for the four men mentioned above, we have already learned about Meng Gongchuo in 14.11, and Confucius' disciple Ran Qiu should be familiar by now. Zhuangzi of Bian was well known in Confucius' time for his strength and bravery. He could wrestle two tigers at a time, according to one story, but he also had a tendency to go too far even when his intentions were good. In fact, this was how he met his death: in order to prove his loyalty to the ruler, one early source says, he charged the enemy time and again, even after his ruler had told him to stop, and he was finally cut down after he had killed seventy men. Zang Wuzhong had a similar problem, though he was a very different kind of man. Like his grandfather Zang Wenzhong, someone Confucius refers to in 5.18, he was very smart, but in spite of this he managed to offend the powerful Jisun and Mengsun families of Lu and so had to flee to Qi; and just as the ruler of Qi was ready to offer him a fief, he again did something ungracious, and the gift was withdrawn. Confucius is quoted in the *Zuo Commentary* as having said, "It is difficult to handle one's knowledge and intelligence [even when one has them]. It was not without reason that the state of Lu could not put up with a man who had Zang Wuzhong's knowledge and intelligence. [He was driven out] because his behavior was disagreeable and lacking in the principle of reciprocity." Zang Wuzhong, Zhuangzi of Bian, and Ran Qiu all had extraordinary talents, but without the refinement of music and the rites, they remained incomplete.

14.13 The Master asked Gongming Jia about Gongshu Wenzi, saying, "Is it true that your master did not speak, did not laugh, and did not take anything?"

Gongming Jia replied, "Whoever told you that must have

exaggerated. My master spoke only when it was the right time for him to speak, and so others were not tired of him speaking. He laughed when he was happy, and so others were not tired of him laughing. He only took when it was right for him to take, and so others were not upset about his taking."

The Master said, "So it was like this. Or was it like this [and so people thought that he did not speak, did not laugh, and did not take anything]?"

Gongshu Wenzi was Gongsun Ba, a counselor from the state of Wei and a slightly older contemporary of Confucius. After he died, the *Book of Rites* says, the ruler of Wei honored him with the posthumous title of *wenzi* ("the refined one") for the compassion, loyalty, and civility he had displayed in his service to the state. Confucius did not have a chance to meet him, but he heard about him, and here he asks Gongming Jia whether it is true that Gongshu Wenzi "did not speak, did not laugh, and did not take anything." After Gongming Jia tells him why one might have said this about Gongshu Wenzi, Confucius' initial response seems favorable—"So it was like this [*qiran*]." But then he repeats the sentence, this time as a question— "Or was it like this?"—which suggests that he did not believe that this was the reason why Gongshu Wenzi had a reputation for not speaking, not laughing, and not taking anything.

14.14 The Master said, "Zang Wuzhong used his fief, a town called Fang, to bargain [with his ruler] for an heir [to continue the Zang family line] in Lu. Although he claimed that he did not coerce his lord to accept the deal, I do not believe it."

Confucius says in 14.12 that Zang Wuzhong, the head of the Zang family, was a man of exceptional knowledge, but then he also says in the *Zuo Commentary* that in his conduct this man could go too far and be his own worst enemy. In 550 BC, Zang Wuzhong was forced to leave home after he bungled his relationship with the power brokers of Lu. And according to records in the *Zuo Commentary*, before he crossed the border into Qi, he sent a message to his ruler, asking the latter to grant his family an heir so that "the sacrifices to his ancestors could be continued," and in exchange, he said, he would give up Fang, a town that had been in his family's possession for generations. The ruler accepted the deal and allowed Zang Wuzhong's half brother to succeed him as head of the Zangs. Here Confucius seems to question the moral ground of this transaction.

14.15 The Master said, "[As lord protector,] Duke Wen of Jin was politically expedient [*jue*] but not principled [*zheng*]. Duke Huan of Qi was principled but not politically expedient."

The Zhou dynasty was on the brink of collapse around 771 BC, after an invading army executed her king. The king's heir and his supporters, however, managed to avoid an endgame when they decided to move the capital from its base in the west to a city in the east. Still, the dynasty never fully recovered from this blow, and from the start of the Eastern Zhou dynasty, it was evident that the Zhou kings had neither the will nor the power to handle threats of foreign invasion and conflicts among their own kind. This gave rise to a series of lord protectors (*ba*) in the next century. There were five altogether. Duke Huan of Qi was the first of the five, and Duke Wen of Jin was the second. All five lord protectors were regional rulers, and they all had to earn the title of *ba* through military prowess and the force of their character. Duke Huan held on to the title for forty-two years, from 685 to 643, and Duke Jin for eight years, from 636 until his death in 628. Here Confucius gives his assessment of the two men. He says that Duke Jin was *jue* but not *zheng*, and Duke Huan was *zheng* but not *jue*. Nearly all the scholars agree on the meaning of *zheng* as "morally correct" "or principled," but *jue* has proved to be a tougher but also more interesting question. The Han scholar Zheng Xuan said that *jue* meant "deceitful" or "duplicitous" (*zha*), and most commentators and translators followed him. But a handful of scholars had doubts. And so they attempted an exhaustive search for the meaning of *jue* in the early sources, gathering numerous examples of how the word was used in different contexts, and concluded that it conveyed the more neutral meaning of "expediency." They argued that expediency, specifically political expediency, did not always lead to duplicity. The Qing scholar Song Xiangfeng says, "When one carries out the principle of expediency properly, then it becomes [a question of] finding a point of balance [*quan*]. When one does not

carry out the principle of expediency properly, it becomes a duplicitous act [*zha*]." And since Duke Wen always put expediency ahead of
principle, it was more likely that he was duplicitous. Thus, Liu
Baonan points out, when Confucius said that this man was "politically expedient but not always principled," he "was commending
him for being expedient but was regretting the fact that he could not
always be principled." But putting principle ahead of expediency
also has its problems. For one thing, it can make a man inflexible,
which is what the records of history showed about Duke Huan of Qi.
The Ming dynasty scholar Yang Shen puts it this way: "Duke Wen
accomplished more than Duke Huan, but he was also guilty of more
wrongdoing. The state of affairs urged Duke Huan to act faster, but
his concern for the moral principle of things often did him more
harm than good."

14.16 Zilu said, "Duke Huan had [his older brother] Prince Jiu
killed. Shao Hu died on account of what had happened [to his
lord], but Guan Zhong did not." Then he added, "Did his conduct fall short of being humane?"

    The Master said, "It was due to Guan Zhong's strength that
Duke Huan was able to assemble the regional rulers nine times
for their joint meetings without flexing his muscles. Such was
his humaneness. Such was his humaneness."

Here we learn more about Duke Huan—that he had his older brother
killed, which was not exactly what a man of principle would have
done. But the point of this discussion is not about him but about his
chief counselor, Guan Zhong—whether this man was humane. And
to get at this question, one needs to know something about the history of these two men and how they ended up working together.
Duke Huan (Prince Xiaobai before he became the ruler of Qi) and
Prince Jiu were half brothers and sons of Duke Xi. Their older
brother, Duke Xiang, succeeded their father, but his behavior was
abominable—he committed incest with his sister and murdered her
husband, who also happened to be the ruler of Lu. This man also
died violently, at the hands of his own subjects, but before this took
place, his two younger brothers managed to find refuge elsewhere,
Prince Xiaobai (later Duke Huan) in Ju and Prince Jiu in Lu. And as

soon as he died, Prince Xiaobai returned home and declared himself Duke Huan, ruler of Qi, and he sent word to the ruler of Lu, asking him to have his brother Prince Jiu done away with and Prince Jiu's two attendants, Shao Hu and Guan Zhong, sent back to Qi. Lu had just suffered a defeat by the Qi army at this point, and out of the fear of further retaliation, the men of Lu fulfilled Duke Huan's wish. Shao Hu committed suicide right after his lord was killed, but Guan Zhong did not. He was escorted back to Qi, where he accepted Duke Huan's offer of a position as his chief counselor. It was this fact that troubled Zilu, but Confucius gave a different view: It was through Guan Zhong's skills and vision that Duke Huan was able to call together the regional rulers nine times to have a conference without the use of force, thus ensuring peace in the Zhou empire for many years. Was this not an achievement of the highest order? Such was Guan Zhong's humaneness, Confucius said; such was his humaneness.

14.17 Zigong said, "Guan Zhong was not humane. When Duke Huan had Prince Jiu killed, he chose not to die, and instead he decided to serve Duke Huan as his counselor."

The Master said, "When Guan Zhong served as the counselor of Duke Huan, he saw to it that Duke Huan would stand as the lord protector among the regional rulers, drawing all the states together under one empire. To this day, people [of all the Chinese states] still benefit from what he accomplished. If not for Guan Zhong, we would be [like the barbarian tribes,] wearing our hair loose and fastening our robes to the left. How could he have acted on the petty loyalty of a common man or a common woman and committed suicide in a ditch without anyone taking notice?"

The discussion about Guan Zhong continued. Here Zigong voices his objection: Why did Guan Zhong choose to live and then to offer his service to the man who instigated the death of his lord? In response, Confucius again focuses on Guan Zhong's contributions in the larger scheme of things: that he was the one who helped the Chinese states to define a new kind of leader, a *ba*, a lord protector. This leader was not perfect—he was not like the former kings and would not have dreamt of usurping the place of the present king—but through the force of his character and strengths that had been tested, he could hold the empire together in times of peace and war. During the forty years when Duke Huan was the lord protector, with Guan Zhong at his side, the non-Chinese states were effectively checked from further expansion, and the Chinese states were able to coexist and to agree in principle, and often in practice, on the guidelines for trade, irrigation, selection of heirs, and family relationships. But did Guan Zhong know, when he accepted the job from Duke Huan, that he was going to help this ruler accomplish great things? Confucius says that Guan Zhong had bigger ambitions than any common man or woman. But did he feel that Guan Zhong had a plan for the prince from the start? A number of the early writers said that Guan Zhong thought only of Qi when he returned home. He wished only to look after the people of Qi and their altars of soil and grain, and in so doing, he reorganized the government's civil and military structures, introduced social reforms, and bolstered morale. As Qi grew stronger and more confident, it became the state others turned to when they were in a crisis or needed military assistance. And so it was not in Guang Zhong's original design that he was going to help Duke Huan "draw all the states under one empire." But it happened, and it is to Confucius' credit that, in spite of the inimical feelings between Lu and Qi and the objections his disciples raised on moral grounds, he took a nonpartisan position and a position that was difficult to defend when he acknowledged Guan Zhong's achievement, saying that "to this day, people [of all the Chinese states] still benefit from his accomplishments."

14.18 Gongshu Wenzi had his family retainer Zhuan promoted along with him to positions within the court. When he heard about this, the Master said, "He deserved the posthumous name 'the refined one [*wen*].'"

Confucius had never met Gongshu Wenzi, but he was interested in hearing about what he was like from people who had known him. In 14.13, he asks why Gongshu "did not speak, did not laugh, and did not take anything." Here, after he has learned that this man was so generous in spirit that he recommended a retainer on his staff for a position in the court of Wei, thus letting the retainer serve side by side with him, Confucius comments that Gongshu Wenzi deserved the posthumous title of "the refined one."

14.19 When the Master talked about the moral depravity of Duke Ling of Wei, Ji Kangzi said, "If that was the case, how did this ruler not lose his state?"

Confucius replied, "It was because he had Zhongshu Yu in charge of foreign guests, Priest Tuo looking after the ancestral temple, and Wangsun Jia responsible for military affairs. When it was like this, how could he have lost his state?"

I have already made the argument in my commentary on 13.7 that what Confucius expresses here and in 13.8 is optimism for the state of Wei because it had competent counselors. And so even if the rulers were inept and depraved—and Duke Ling was such a ruler—the counselors could hold the state up and keep things running smoothly.

14.20 The Master said, "If a person speaks immodestly [*buzuo*], he will have a difficult time carrying out his words in action."

The Han scholar Ma Rong offers a different perspective. He thinks that when Confucius spoke about the man whose words were *buzuo*, he meant to praise him. Ma Rong writes, "A person who had real integrity would be able to speak without shame [*buzuo*], but then it must have been difficult for him to accumulate the stuff [that made him the genuine article]." Following his reading, one could translate Confucius' remark in this way: "If a person is able to speak without shame, [he is the genuine article, but] it must have been difficult for him to acquire the integrity [he possesses]."

14.21 Chen Chengzi killed Duke Jian [of Qi]. Confucius [fasted for three days and] had a ritual bath, and he went to court. He reported to Duke Ai, saying, "Chen Heng [Chen Chengzi] murdered his ruler. I ask that you take punitive action against him."

Duke Ai said, "Go and tell the three counselors."

Confucius, afterward, said [to someone else], "I take my position after the three counselors [and so should have reported to them], but [since this was a matter of great urgency,] I simply had to speak to my lord [right away]. Yet my lord said to me, 'Go and tell the three counselors.'"

He went to see the three counselors, and they did not approve of his proposal. Confucius said, "I take my position after the three counselors [and so should have reported to them], but [since this was a matter of great urgency,] I simply had to speak to my lord [right away]."

In the spring of 481 BC, Chen Chengzi, the head of a hereditary family in Qi and a counselor to the ruler, in a violent showdown with another counselor at court, managed to have both his rival and his ruler killed. The news of these events must have come as a shock to Confucius because a similar scenario could play out in Lu, and so he took the matter directly to his ruler even though, he said, it was not his place to do this because his position was below the three counselors. Thus he must have been disappointed when, after he had spoken his mind, Duke Ai said to him, "Go and tell the three counselors"—in other words, Go and tell the heads of the Three Families. And, of course, the three families were not interested in what Confucius had proposed. Why should they be if they were pursuing the same ends as their Qi counterparts? The record in the *Zuo Commentary* offers a similar version with some variants. It says:

On the sixth day of the sixth month, Chen Heng from the state of Qi slew his ruler Ren. Confucius fasted for three days [before going to see Duke Ai]. Three times he implored the ruler to initiate a punitive action against the state of Qi. Duke Ai said, "Qi has sapped our strength for so long now. If I were to follow your advice and attack them, what do you think might be the outcome?" Confucius replied, "Chen Heng murdered his ruler. At least half of the people from Qi oppose him. Our men plus at least half of theirs can certainly quash their army." Duke Ai said, "Why don't you tell the Jisuns what you propose to do?" Confucius declined. After he withdrew, he told others, "I take my position after the three counselors [and so should have reported to them], but [since this was a matter of great urgency,] I simply had to speak to my lord [right away]."

Duke Ai is evasive in both versions. But even if he had agreed with Confucius that he should send a punitive expedition against Qi, he still could not have carried it out, because the Lu army was under the authority of the Three Families. And Duke Ai's response to Confucius—"Go and tell the three counselors"—sounds a sad note about the hopelessness of his own situation. But Confucius remained respectful—he gave himself a thorough ritual cleansing before he went to see Duke Ai, the man who remained in his mind the ruler of Lu.

14.22 Zilu asked about how to serve one's ruler. The Master said, "Do not deceive him, and only then will you able to confront him directly [and deliver your admonishment]."

The Han scholar Kong Anguo says, "In serving your ruler, you should never deceive yourself [and him] about what is right. Only then are you able to risk offending his dignity and delivering your admonishment." My translation follows Kong Anguo's gloss.

14.23 The Master said, "The gentleman reaches the higher things. The petty man understands the lower things."

One could put Confucius' comment here together with that in 4.16 and say that the higher things pertain to "what is morally right" and the lower things pertain to "what is profitable." But another reading is also possible. Confucius in 14.35 describes his spiritual journey as a traveling upward that began with learning at a low level. The term "higher things" in that context refers to the integrity that heaven possesses, which is what a gentleman hopes to achieve, and "lower things" refers either to practical learning or to the skills and education that give him his footing. Thus Confucius could be saying: "The gentleman reaches for higher things. The ordinary man is content with understanding things at a low level."

14.24 The Master said, "People of antiquity engaged in learning to cultivate themselves. People today engage in learning with an eye toward others."

Xunzi, in his essay "Encouraging Learning," offers a smart and succinct explanation of what Confucius says here. He writes, "The learning of the gentleman enters his ear and is impressed on his mind; it spreads through his four limbs and is visible whether he is active or still. His smallest word, his slightest movement can serve as a model. The learning of the petty man enters his ear and comes out of his mouth. With only four inches between ear and mouth, how can he have possession of it long enough to refine a seven-foot body? [Confucius put it in this way:] 'People of antiquity engaged in learning to cultivate themselves. People today engage in learning with an eye toward others.'"

14.25 Qu Boyu sent a messenger to Confucius. Confucius sat down with him and asked, "What has your master been doing?"

The messenger replied, "My master wishes to make fewer mistakes but has not been able to do so."

After the messenger left, the Master said, "A fine messenger! A fine messenger!"

Qu Boyu was a highly respected counselor in the state of Wei. The Han historian Sima Qian says that Confucius stayed with Qu when he first arrived in Wei. This is highly unlikely, given the fact that by the time Confucius reached Wei, Qu Boyu was already in his nineties. From the record here, it seems that Confucius would have gotten his news about Qu from a messenger the latter sent. And though this man was only a messenger, Confucius received him as if he were an equal—he "sat down with him." And the comment at the end is also about the messenger. His honest answer clearly impressed Confucius.

The philosopher Zhuangzi had his own ideas about Qu Boyu, which were comparable to the messenger's description of this man, only more radical. He writes, "Qu Boyu has been going along for sixty years and has changed sixty times. There is not a single instance in which what he called right in the beginning he did not in the end reject. So now there is no telling whether what he calls right at the moment is not in fact what he called wrong during the past fifty-nine years." One could say that by questioning everything he knew and believed in, Qu Boyu was trying to make few mistakes, but this Qu

Boyu has nothing to do with the historical Qu Boyu. Like many characters in the *Zhuangzi*, he is merely a vehicle for the author.

14.26 The Master said, "If you don't have a particular position, then don't meddle with any of its business."

Master Zeng [Zengzi] commented, "The gentleman does not allow his thoughts to go beyond what his position calls for."

This is a repeat of 8.14, and so one can refer to the commentary there. Master Zeng is Confucius' disciple Zeng Can (Zengzi).

14.27 The Master said, "The gentleman would be ashamed to let his words run ahead of his action."

Confucius made this point many times. One can refer to 2.13, 4.22, 4.24, 14.20 and their commentaries.

14.28 The Master said, "The way of the gentleman consists of three things, none of which I have been able to realize: the humane never suffer from vexation; the wise are never perplexed; the brave are never afraid."

Zigong said, "The Master has just given a description of himself."

Confucius gave the humane, the wise, and the brave the same descriptions in 9.29. Here, he says that the characteristics of such men make up "the way of a gentleman." But he claims that he is unable to accomplish any one of the three. Most traditional scholars say that Confucius was being modest when he spoke about himself. Qian Mu, however, offers a different perspective. He says that only when a person perceives himself in this way will he keep on going, "keep on making progress," and never become complacent. Zigong's comment is, therefore, important: it relates what the observer sees. And in Zigong's view, Confucius has already arrived at the goal.

14.29 Zigong was given to assessing people [*fangren*]. The Master said, "Si [Zigong] must be a man of worth! I am afraid I haven't got the time for such things."

The Han scholar Kong Anguo understands *fangren* to mean *bifangren*, "to assess people," "to compare one person against another." But most scholars follow another Han scholar, Zheng Xuan, who thinks that *fang* was a phonetic loan word for *bang*, "to criticize others," "to point out the mistakes of others." If Zigong was merely prone to assessing the strengths and weaknesses of others, they argue, Confucius would not have said "I'm afraid I haven't got time for such things," because he had a tendency to do the same. Thus these scholars conclude that *fangren* must have referred to a negative trait, to Zigong's fondness for "passing judgment on others." Qian Mu, however, is on the side of Kong Anguo. He says that even though Confucius himself liked to gauge other people's character, he still could be critical of Zigong for wasting too much time doing it. And I would add that there is no record in the *Analects* that suggests Zigong was quick in forming an opinion or was given to seeing the faults of others, but there is plenty of evidence that shows him to be interested in "assessing others" and also in the process of considering the many sides of a situation and then giving his best guess as to the outcome.

14.30 The Master said, "Do not worry that other people do not know you. Be concerned about your own lack of ability."

This is slightly different from 1.16, but in both comments Confucius emphasizes that what should worry a person is not why others do not take notice of him—of his knowledge or talent—but what is wanting in him.

14.31 The Master said, "Not to anticipate deception and not to expect bad faith and yet to be the first to be aware of such behavior—this is proof of one's worthiness."

Here Confucius describes the workings of subtle intelligence in a man of worth. This man does not anticipate deception or bad faith

in others, but he is the first to know should it occur. This means that
he holds no preconception about anyone but is alert to any attempt
at chicanery. This resonates with what Confucius tells Zai Wo in
6.26 about the gentleman—if he "is told that someone is stuck in a
well," he "can go and take a look but he is not going to hurl himself
into a trap."

14.32 Weisheng Mu said to Confucius, "Qiu, why are you
always hopping around? Could it be that you are practicing
the glibness [of a persuader]?"

Confucius said, "I would not dare to be glib [*ning*]. It is just
that I worry about getting stuck in one place and with just a
single point of view [*gu*]."

This conversation must have taken place during Confucius' peripa-
tetic years, when he was wandering from place to place in search of a
position. Weisheng Mu's question was reasonable because to an out-
sider Confucius could appear to be no different from a traveling per-
suader, someone who relied on his glib tongue to land himself a job.
Weisheng Mu was also older than Confucius, most scholars say, and
so he addressed Confucius by his given name and asked him a question that verged on being disrespectful. Still, Confucius took it seriously. He said that he could not find rest in any one place because he
worried about "getting stuck in one place and with just a single point
of view [*gu*]." *Gu* could also mean *gulou*, "moral decline," some
scholars note, and so it is possible also to understand Confucius to
say that he felt compelled to move around because he wanted to alert
the world about its "moral decline" (*gulou*).

14.33 The Master said, "A fine [chariot] horse is praised for
her inner integrity [*de*], not for her strength."

A fine horse is "gentle and tame," and her integrity reflects that of
the driver, who guides her with deft hands, and so the two are essentially one as they race across the open plains or around the twists of
riverbanks. Thus, Confucius said, she is not praised for her strength.

14.34 Someone said, "What do you think of the expression 'Repay a wrong with kindness'?"

The Master said, "How, then, would you repay kindness? Repay a wrong with uprightness. Repay kindness with kindness."

The ideas here are amplified in the *Book of Rites*, and again they are attributed to Confucius: "Those who repay a wrong with kindness must be men who make excessive demands on themselves to be generous [toward others]. Those who repay others' kindness by doing them wrong are men who should be treated as criminals of a capital offense." The Qing scholar Wu Jiabin offers further insight. He says:

> A person who deals a wrong [*yuan*] with uprightness [*zhi*] simply does not want to put his grievance [*yuan*] under covers. It is human nature to rejoice in seeing justice [*zhi*] being done. . . . In the case of a grievance, one hopes to forget it. In the case of kindness, one hopes never to forget it. Thus he who repays a wrong with uprightness does so with the wish that there will be no trace of grievance left in his mind, and he who repays kindness with kindness does so with the wish that the kindness of others will never disappear from his mind. The mind cannot forget a grievance, but one can use an open and upright response to overcome that feeling. The opposite of openness and uprightness is pretense. To teach people to respond to a wrong with kindness is to teach them to engage in pretense. How could that be right?

14.35 The Master said, "No one understands me." Zigong said, "Why is it that no one understands you?" The Master said, "I blame neither Heaven nor men [for my not being understood]. I begin my learning on the ground and travel up to reach a higher knowledge. It is, I believe, only Heaven that understands me."

"Learning on the ground" (*xiaxue*) could refer either to learning how to handle practical problems in the human world or to learning that gives one a moral footing. In either case, Qian Mu says, if you start from the ground, "the further you reach, the less blameful you will become until you arrive at a point where only heaven understands you." Your virtue will be a match for heaven's. Xunzi describes this state as follows: "Though silent, others understand him; though he bestows not favor, others gravitate toward him; though he is not angry, he possesses an awe-inspiring dignity."

14.36 Gongbo Liao spoke ill of Zilu to the head of the Jisuns. Zifu Jingbo reported to Confucius, saying, "There is no doubt that my master harbors suspicion [about Zilu], but I still have enough sway [with him] to see that Gongbo Liao gets executed and his corpse gets exposed in the marketplace."

The Master said, "It is destiny whether the moral way prevails or whether it is cast aside. What effect could Gongbo Liao have on the course of destiny [*ming*]?"

Just from what Zifu Jingbo says to Confucius, we know that he, Gongbo Liao, and Zilu were in the service of the Jisun family at around the same time. But just what kind of ill words could Gongbo Liao have spoken about Zilu, and why did Zifu Jingbo think that they were so damaging that it was necessary for him to act first, to have Gongbo Liao done away with before any harm could come to Zilu? It was the Song scholar Zhu Xi who placed this conversation at a particular moment in the history of Lu. He thinks that it must have taken place around 498 BC, during the twelfth year of Duke Ding's reign, when Zilu, as the chief retainer of the Jisuns, managed to convince the head of the family, Ji Huanzi, that he should have the family base destroyed and start anew. Zilu's secret plan was "to restore the office of the duke," who was the legitimate ruler of Lu, and "to deal a serious blow to the hereditary families." If Zhu Xi is right about the time and place of this conversation, it is understandable that Zifu Jingbo came to Confucius with an urgent call to action: Zilu's head could roll if Gongbo Liao revealed Zilu's plot to the Jisuns, and Confucius, as Zilu's teacher, would be implicated.

Now comes the question of destiny, *ming* (命). This is a difficult idea to grasp, and much has been written about it, but the one essay that makes a cogent point about what Confucius was trying to say here is found in the works of the seventeenth-century scholar Zhang Erqi. He writes:

Rightness is what it ought to be and cannot be violated, and it refers to the way of being human. Destiny is what is and cannot be contested, and it refers to the way of Heaven. . . . The gentleman knows destiny through [his understanding of] rightness. When rightness is obstructed, he realizes that it does not have a place in destiny. Thus, when he finds himself unable to advance because of destiny, he will not lose his sense of rightness as he retreats. A petty man knows destiny through the use of cleverness and force. If force proves unequal to the challenge, he tries cleverness, and if both should fail, he calls it destiny. The gentleman makes peace with destiny by way of rightness, and so his mind is large and generous. The petty man challenges destiny with cleverness and force, and so his mind is filled with resentment. The common people also have their way of making peace with destiny. They do so when they realize that they are left with no alternatives.

In the context of these words, one could say that Confucius was someone who understood well just how difficult it was to carry out what was right in the world he lived in, and because he had been frustrated in his effort he was able to look at destiny with clear eyes. But as Zhang Erqi says, even when one has to retreat, the negatives destiny deals out can never take away the sense of rightness that is already in one's possession.

14.37 The Master said, "Worthy men steer clear of the world. Next are those who steer clear of a particular place. After them are those who steer clear of [people with] hostile looks. And finally there are those who steer clear of [people with] hostile words." The Master said, "There were seven such men who did exactly that."

Here Confucius states the different reasons for avoidance: when the world has given up any attempt at moral rule; when a place has become dangerous to reside in; when people show animosity toward you in their looks and in their words. There have been conjectures about who were the seven men who shunned the world, or a certain place, or a certain kind of men, and some scholars think this statement should stand on its own as a separate entry.

14.38 Zilu spent the night at the Stone Gate. The gatekeeper asked him, "Where did you come from?" Zilu said, "From the Kong family."

"Is that the person who knows that what he is working toward simply cannot be realized?"

What is revealed here is quite astonishing. Even a gatekeeper, the record says, knew that Confucius was working toward something that could not be fulfilled. Perhaps the gatekeeper was no ordinary gatekeeper. Perhaps he was someone who sought his reclusion in the guise of a gatekeeper, in which case he would have been a kindred spirit of the man "carrying a bamboo basket" in 14.39.

14.39 The Master was playing the stone chimes in Wei when a man, carrying a bamboo basket, went past his door. This man said, "This playing is fraught with a heavy and careworn heart." He continued, "How squalid this *kengkeng* sound! If no one understands him, then he should just keep what he believes to himself and that is all: 'If the water is deep, just wade across it. If the water is shallow, lift your hem and cross it.'"

The Master said in response, "[This man sounds like he knows what he wants.] If he is so resolute, he should not have any difficulties."

The man carrying a bamboo basket was a recluse, "a worthy man," Confucius would say, someone who steered clear of the world. A few like him appear in the *Analects*, and they all seem resolute. Of these men, I wrote in *The Authentic Confucius*: "They all know to adjust the length of their garment to the depth of the water—letting themselves steep in the world when virtue is high and plenty, and lifting themselves up when virtue is shallow and scarce. Confucius sees their point and commends their decision, but he also thinks that if these men are so clear-eyed about what to do and how to act, then they 'should not have any difficulties' at all. He, however, is different. His love for the human race is born out of the squalid, and his relation to the world does not change because of the moral climate."

14.40 Zizhang said, "*The Book of Documents* says, 'Gaozong stayed in his mourning hut, and for three years he did not speak.' What does that mean?"

The Master replied, "It was not just Gaozong; all the ancients followed the same ritual practice. After their ruler died, for three years the hundred officials would attend to their responsibilities, and they would look to the prime minister for guidance."

The *Book of Rites* explains why it was right for a son to observe a three-year mourning period after the death of a parent. It reads: "The greater the wound, the longer it will last. The more unbearable the pain, the more slowly it will heal. The ritual rules were decided in accordance with human feelings, and so the three-year mourning period was intended for those who suffered the deepest pain." It also says that "the mourning of three years would actually come to an end with the close of the twenty-fifth month." "The sorrow and pain have not diminished altogether, and the longing for the deceased has not been forgotten, . . . but it is time to resume the normal rhythm of life." The same source also gives a description of a mourning hut, which was a "slanting shed, unplastered," in which the son would stay before the deceased was buried: "He would sleep on a rush mat with a clod of earth as his pillow, and he would not speak unless it was related to the funeral." "After the burial," the *Rites* says, "the inclined posts were set up on lintels, and the hut was plastered with mud but not anywhere that could be seen." Gaozong stayed in such a hut during the mourning period, the *Book of Documents* says; during that time, "he did not speak," and it is this statement that Zizhang cannot quite understand. For Gaozong was King Wu Ding, the fortieth ruler of the Shang dynasty, and if he sequestered himself in a hut to mourn the death of his father, who, then, would be in charge of his government, and who would be looking after his people? In response, Confucius says that it was not just Gaozong, but that "all the ancients followed the same ritual practice." And during that time, the officials knew to fulfill their responsibilities, he explains, and there was always a prime minister to give them guidance. Moreover, to say that Gaozong did not speak did not mean that he was silent throughout the mourning period: either Gaozong "did not speak about government affairs," the Han scholars say, or "he was reluctant to speak."

The recently discovered bamboo manuscript *Yueming*, also known as *Fuyue zhi ming* ("The Command of Fuyue"), from 300 BC, has sparked an interest among scholars in Gaozong and his chief counselor Fuyue. Accounts of their meeting and of their joint rule are found in several early sources from the received tradition. There are important variants among these records, but the storyline remains essentially the same: Gaozong had been silent for three years, and his officials were worried about the day-to-day governing of his empire; finally a man with a sagely stature appeared to him in a dream; Gaozong had the likeness of this man drawn, and with this in hand, his officals found such a person among the laborers sent to repair the walls on the distant frontier; Gaozong made this man, Fuyue, his prime minister, and from that point on, the empire was well governed. A critical disagreement among these accounts hinges on the question of why Gaozong had been silent for three years. The *Analects*, quoting the *Book of Documents*, says that Gaozong was in mourning, but other sources say that Gaozong "had been reflecting on a moral way" of ruling and on "how to revive the Shang dynasty," which explains why he was looking for a capable man to assist him. The excavated version agrees with the latter—a version that adds more weight to Gaozong's silence.

14.41 The Master said, "If those at the top love the rites, then it will be easy to govern the people."

This follows what Confucius says in 2.3. If a ruler lets his ritual conduct be an example to his people and the ritual rules be the guide to their conduct, then the people "will have a sense of shame and will know to reform themselves." People who know how to reform themselves will be easy to govern.

14.42 Zilu asked about the gentleman [*junzi*]. The Master said, "He cultivates himself in order to acquire a respectful attitude."

"Is that all?"

"He cultivates himself in order to give ease to those around him."

"Is that all?"

"He cultivates himself in order to give ease to the people. To cultivate oneself in order to give ease to the people—even the sage rulers Yao and Shun found it difficult to do."

Both Liu Baonan and Qian Mu believe that *junzi* here refers to the ruler, not to the morally superior man, which means that Zilu's question is about where a ruler should begin if he wants to bring peace to the world. In either case, Confucius' response resonates with the last chapter of the *Doctrine of the Mean*, which says, "When the gentleman [or the ruler] is sincere and respectful, the world is at peace."

14.43 Yuan Rang sat, squatting, while waiting [for Confucius to arrive]. The Master said, "To be neither deferential nor respectful as a youth, to have nothing exceptional to pass on as a grown man, and to keep hanging on to life and not die when old—this is what I call a pest." He then tapped on Yuan Rang's shin with his stick.

The last two entries in this chapter are about Confucius on his own turf, in his home village and with people like Yuan Rang, whom he had known nearly all his life, which might be the reason why he could speak to him so bluntly. Yuan Rang would not have minded, I believe: he knew that Confucius meant no harm even though the words were harsh, and he probably had heard them before. His appearance in other sources, particularly the *Book of Rites*, show him to be unbridled and irreverent—the opposite of Confucius. This led some scholars to believe that Yuan Rang was an early precursor of the Daoist tradition; without historical support, this is likely to have been mere speculation. Still, just from the description here—of how he sat as he greeted Confucius—one could well imagine him to be a man with few inhibitions. And scholars want to know why Confucius tapped him on the shin. Most agree that the gesture was meant to remind Yuan Rang to kneel instead of squatting. Squatting with one's legs spread apart and a slumped back was considered unseemly. It lacked the alertness that the body could project if it was in the kneeling position with legs close together and a straight back, which, in the context of ritual practice, was regarded as the correct way to greet a guest.

14.44 A young boy from Que took on the task of being a messenger [for the people] of this district. Someone asked Confucius, "Do you see him as someone who is eager to make progress in his learning?"

The Master replied, "I have seen this boy sitting down [in a gathering of adults] and walking abreast of his elders. He is not someone who seeks to make progress. He simply wants to grow up fast."

According to several early sources, Que was Confucius' home district. Here someone observes that a boy from Que, in spite of his young age, undertook the huge responsibility of relaying messages for the people in his community. Surely the boy was driven by his eagerness to learn and to make progress, the man says. Confucius, however, saw another aspect of this young boy's character—that he would behave as if he were an adult and his elders' equal. This, in Confucius' view, suggested that the boy was not eager to learn, only eager "to grow up fast."

BOOK FIFTEEN

15.1 Duke Ling of Wei asked Confucius about military formations. Confucius responded, "I know something about the use of ritual vessels but have not learned anything about commanding troops." The next day, Confucius decided to leave Wei.

On his first visit to Wei, Confucius stayed for about five years, and for a long time he could not obtain an audience with Duke Ling. Some of his critics suggested that he even approached two disreputable characters in Duke Ling's inner circle, Duke Ling's wife and his doctor, imploring them for help. Now it seems that Confucius finally got his chance to have a face-to-face meeting with this man, yet just because Duke Ling asked the wrong question, he decided to leave Wei. But how could this be? Given how Confucius felt about sending troops to war—if you do not instruct them first, "this is the same as throwing them away"—it appears, from this conversation, that he realized he had been seeking the wrong man to serve. And just how soon did he leave? The text says "the next day," but preparation for a long journey would have required weeks, if not months, and so it probably makes more sense to say that "the next day, Confucius decided to leave."

15.2 In Chen, when their provisions ran out, [Confucius'] followers had become so weak that none of them could rise to their feet. Zilu, with a resentful look, said, "Does a gentleman find himself in circumstances as bleak as this?"

The Master said, "Of course the gentleman would find himself in circumstances as bleak as this. It is the petty man who would not be able to withstand it."

Confucius and his disciples had many bad moments on their journey. The crisis in Chen or Cai was perhaps the darkest, for, as the *Analects* says, "their provisions ran out," and it looked as if they might starve to death. The possibility of such an end—that is to say, to die without consequence in some forgotten wilderness—was something Zilu could not accept, and so he asked Confucius, Why should such ill luck befall a gentleman? And why should it not? was Confucius' response—but a gentleman would persevere, and he would make peace with destiny should it turn against him, because he has done his best to perfect his character. It would be different in the case of a petty man, however—he would not be able to endure such a test.

These few lines from the *Analects* made an enormous impression on the early Chinese mind. Several historians and thinkers attempted their own versions of the crisis: Zhuangzi added poignancy and philosophical depth to the story through a dialogue he created between Confucius and Yan Hui; Xunzi pursued more closely the ideas in Confucius' original utterance; and Sima Qian let the whole episode evolve into a work of the historical imagination.

15.3 The Master said, "Si [Zigong], do you think I am the sort of person who learns many things and who retains this knowledge in his mind?"

Zigong replied, "Yes. Is it not so?"

"No. I bind it together into a single thread."

Since Confucius had said (in 7.2) that it had never been a problem for him "to retain knowledge quietly in [his] mind" and "to learn without ever feeling sated," Zigong thought that this was an accurate description of his teacher, but Confucius disagreed. Here, he says that he binds knowledge together into a single thread. But just what could the "single thread" refer to? Most scholars point to 4.15, where Confucius says, "My way has a thread running through it," and his disciple Zeng Can (Zengzi) explains that the thread pertains to *zhong* (doing one's best to fulfill one's humanity) and *shu* (treating others with an awareness that they, too, are alive with humanity). Liu Baonan and Qian Mu, however, feel that what Confucius says here has almost no relationship to 4.15. For what Confucius has in mind is not the question of how to live a moral life but the question of knowledge—just how to make sense of the many things that one has learned. Action is inseparable from knowledge in Confucius' teaching, Liu Baonan says, and it is through action that one binds knowledge into a single thread. Confucius illustrates this point in 13.5, where he says, "A person may be able to recite the three hundred poems, but if he is unable to put [this knowledge] to full use when he is given a political assignment, . . . no matter how many poems he has learned, what good will it do?" The single thread, Qian Mu observes, could also refer to the binding principle in any category of knowledge. For example, Confucius thought that the three hundred poems "could be summed up in a single phrase: 'They never swerve from the path.'"

15.4 The Master said, "You [Zilu], there are only a few who understand virtue [*de*]."

Qian Mu says that what Confucius means here is this: To understand virtue—to truly know it—one has to get it in oneself, through one's own realization, something only a few people are able to do.

15.5 The Master said, "The one ruler who was able to order the world without taking any [deliberate] action [*wuwei*] was Shun. So what did he do? He held himself respectfully and faced south—that was all."

What Confucius says here reinforces what he told Zilu about the gentleman in 14.42—that he "cultivates himself in order to acquire a respectful attitude" and "to give ease to the people." From the point of view of the observer, it seems that this person is not doing anything, which is not so because even Yao and Shun found it difficult to realize.

The idea of *wuwei* (無為), doing nothing or not taking action, is usually associated with the teachings in the *Laozi*. Confucian scholars insist that there are fundamental differences between what Confucius says here about Shun and what the author of the *Laozi* says when he states, "The sage acts by doing nothing [*weiwuwei*], and everything is in order." Some differences do exist, but it is also true that both teachings emphasize the ruler's cultivation as key to an ordered world. And, in the words of the Confucian thinker Xunzi, a ruler who has succeeded in his effort possesses a subtle mind, one that is able to discern "the first sign of a crisis and evidence of something profound."

15.6 Zizhang asked about getting on in the world. The Master said, "If you impart sincerity and trust in your words, and integrity and respect in your deeds, you will get on even in the lands of the barbarians. If you do not impart sincerity and trust in your words, and integrity and respect in your deeds, how can you get on even in your own region or in your own neighborhood? When you stand, you see the plumb lines in front of you. When you ride in a carriage, you see them resting on the crossbar. Only then will you be getting on in the world."

Zizhang wrote down these words on his sash.

Zizhang was interested in having a career in government and being successful in that career. Put simply, he wanted to get on in the world. Confucius told him in 2.18 about how to prepare himself for an official career, and the advice there was pragmatic—that Zizhang should use his ears and eyes well and widely in order to make few mistakes in speech and have few regrets in action. Here the advice has a moral tone. To get on in the world, Confucius says, a person has to impart "sincerity and trust" in his words, "integrity and respect" in his deeds. In fact, he cannot depart from these measures for a moment, even when he is just standing or when he is traveling in a carriage. Zizhang must have wanted to remember these words, because he wrote them down on his sash.

15.7 The Master said, "How upright Shi Yu was! He was straight as an arrow when the moral way prevailed in the state, and he was also straight as an arrow when the moral way was absent. How gentlemanly Qu Boyu was! He took office when the moral way prevailed, and he let his knowledge and skills be rolled up and hidden away when the moral way was absent."

Both Shi Yu and Qu Boyu were counselors from the state of Wei. According to *Han Ying's Commentary to the Book of Poetry*, Shi Yu, before he died, instructed his son to have his funeral conducted in the secondary hall and not in the main hall with the full rites. The reason for this, he said, was that he had failed as an advisor to the ruler, on account of which, a worthy man like Qu Boyu was not advanced and an unworthy man like Mi Zixia was not dismissed. The story is probably fictional, but it makes the point that Shi Yu was straight as an arrow even on his deathbed.

As for Qu Boyu, the records in the *Zuo Commentary* say that when the chief counselors of Wei drove their ruler out in 559 BC, one of them said to Qu Boyu, who was a young man at the time, "You know well about the tyranny and the cruelty of our ruler. [We expelled him] for fear that the state's altar of grain and soil might be overturned. So what are your plans?" Qu Boyu said in response, "A ruler has the full authority of his state, and so who among his subjects would dare to oppose him? And even when one opposes him and topples him, how would one know [that the new ruler] is any better [than the old]?" Thereupon, "he got ready to leave, and he exited from the nearest gate." Some twelve years later, on the occasion when the chief counselors were thinking of taking their ruler back, Qu Boyu again decided to get out of Wei. Each time, it seems, he did not stay away for long, and because he lived into his nineties, his tenure in government also had a long stretch. Thus we learn, in 14.25, that some sixty years after his first attempt to hide away his knowledge and skills, he was still alive and well in Wei. Confucius' admiration for him is unmistakable, and, in Li Baonan's view, he seemed to feel that Qu Boyu was worthier than Shi Yu because while "Shi Yu was upright in his conduct," "Qu Boyu tried to keep the Way upright."

15.8 The Master said, "Not to speak to a man who is capable of absorbing what you say is to let the man go to waste. To speak to a man who is incapable of absorbing what you say is to let your words go to waste. A person of wisdom does not let either men or words go to waste."

Most scholars, in explaining the present statement, refer to a passage from the *Balanced Discourses* (*Zhonglun*), a work by the late Han thinker Xu Gan, who writes: "A gentleman must value his words. If he values his words, he respects himself. If he respects himself, he respects the way he follows. By respecting the way he follows, he is able to give his teaching integrity. If he squanders his words, then he belittles himself. If he belittles himself, he discredits the way he follows. And if he discredits the way he follows, then he is letting his teaching go to waste." But just to value your words is not enough, Xu Gan observes, for in speaking to another person, it is important "to phrase your words in a manner that would not go beyond the knowledge and concerns of the person you are speaking to." If you exceed that limit, he will be confused and become suspicious of your intention. "It is like showing someone with poor vision something indistinct or talking to someone hard of hearing in a whisper." This, Xu Gan feels, was what Confucius was trying to get across. But Confucius said more. He felt that it was equally important not to miss an opportunity to speak to a person who can grasp what you are trying to say. This second point must have had extra significance for those who took teaching seriously.

15.9 The Master said, "A man of high purpose and a man with deep humaneness would not seek to stay alive at the expense of humaneness. There are times when they would sacrifice their lives to have humaneness fulfilled."

Most scholars disagree with Kong Anguo's comment that "men of high purpose and men of deep humaneness do not cherish their lives." Qian Mu says, "What Confucian teachings emphasize is how to live. Only when a person knows how to live, will he know how to die." And knowing how to live, the Qing scholar Jiao Xun notes, is about "making the right choices about life and death." In Jiao Xun's view, Mencius, illustrates this point when he says in 6A:10:

> Though life is what I want, there is something I want more than life.
> That is why I do not cling to life at all cost. Though death is what I
> loathe, there is something I loathe more than death. That is why there
> are troubles I do not avoid. In a situation where there is nothing a per-
> son should desire more than life, if there are means to stay alive, why
> not use them! In a situation where there is nothing a person should

loathe more than death, if a person can avoid troubles that could
threaten his life, why not do it!

The situations where, Mencius thought, one should choose life over
death would be "those where there is no rightness to be gotten." The
circumstances Guan Zhong found himself in provide an example.
Confucius, in his defense of this man, says in 14.17, "How could
Guan Zhong have acted out the petty loyalty of a common man or
woman and committed suicide in a ditch?" To die in this way would
have meant that he did not understand about life.

15.10 Zigong asked about the practice of humaneness. The
Master said, "Artisans who wish to excel at their craft must
sharpen their tools. When you live in any given state, you
should serve the worthiest among the counselors and befriend
the most humane among the educated professionals."

As in 1.15, Confucius is again having a conversation with Zigong
about refinement. Just as an artisan must sharpen his tools if he
wants to perfect his craft, a person who wishes to practice humaneness must stay close to the worthy and the humane to come under
their influence as he refines his own character.

15.11 Yan Yuan [Yan Hui] asked about how to govern a state.
The Master said, "Follow the calendar of the Xia dynasty, ride
in the carriages of the Shang, wear the ceremonial cap of the
Zhou, and as for music, embrace the music of *shao* and *wu*.
Ban the tunes of Zheng and keep at a distance from glib men.
The tunes of Zheng are licentious. Glib men are dangerous."

The question has been asked a number of times, and up to this point,
Confucius has been calling for the ruler and the officials to rectify
names and reform themselves. But here he is talking about the standard of rites and music and what calendar to use. This has led the
scholars to believe that here he is considering a different kind of
problem, one having to do with the change in the rules and practice

of government: just what guidelines to follow and how to adapt the model of the true kings to changing circumstances. Confucius does not talk about how to adjust the model to change, but from his response to Yan Hui we know that this is what is on his mind, and from the preferences he specifies, one can work out the principles underlying his choice.

First, there is the matter of calendars. The differences among the three calendars in question had to do with which month a dynasty had designated as the first month, the "correct month" (*zhengyue*), of the civil year—the second new moon after the winter solstice, as in the Xia; the first new moon after the winter solstice, as in the Shang; or the lunar month that contains the winter solstice, as in the Zhou. Confucius thought that the Xia calendar suited the annual rhythm of farming communities, and so, he said, that was the one the government should use. And as for carriages, the Zhou carriages could be lavishly adorned, with jade, gold, ivory, or leather, but the plainest and sturdiest ones were simply made of wood with only a rush mat on the seat. The wooden carriage was also what the ruling elite of the Shang traveled in, and given the fact that Confucius preferred frugality in matters that had a ritual significance and were part of a public performance, this was what he favored. But in the case of ceremonial caps, he opted for the style of the Zhou, which was elegant but not extravagant. The cap also had pendants of jade beads hanging in front to stop the eyes from wandering, and silk bands hanging on the sides to block the ears from hearing any distracting sound. Confucius had already spoken about the glorious effect the music of *shao* had on him: after he heard it, he "did not notice the taste of meat for the next three months." He described this music and the music of *wu* as beautiful, which was not how he felt about the music of Zheng. The music of Zheng is like the voice of a glib man: one is lustful and the other treacherous, and both have the power to lead one's judgment astray.

15.12 The Master said, "A person who does not think ahead about the distant future is sure to be troubled by worries close at hand."

People who do not take preventive measures about potential troubles ahead will find themselves always having to deal with problems after they have arisen—this is the understanding of most scholars. But Qian Mu thinks that another reading is also possible: "Even with people who do not have worries in the far distance, they will surely have troubles right in front of them."

15.13 The Master said, "I should give up hope! I have never met a person who loved virtue as much as he loved physical beauty."

This is what Confucius says in 9.18, but here he adds that he "should give up hope" of finding such a man. See my comments on 9.18.

15.14 The Master said, "Zang Wenzhong betrayed the integrity of his office. He knew Liuxia Hui to be worthy, yet he did not recommend him for a position equal to his."

Confucius says in 5.18 that the chief counselor Zang Wenzhong, who lived a hundred years before him, lacked wisdom because of his transgressions against ritual practices. Here, he accuses him of having betrayed the integrity of his office because he deliberately held Liuxia Hui back when it was his responsibility to help someone as talented as Liuxia Hui to advance in his career. Qian Mu is right to say that Zang Wenzhong made a sharp contrast to Kongshu Wenzi, who, as we read in 14.18, "had his family retainer, Zhuan, promoted along with him to positions within the court."

15.15 The Master said, "Be hard on yourself and be sparing when criticizing others—this way you will keep resentment at bay."

The Han scholar Dong Zhongshu writes, "One should govern others by way of humaneness [ren] and govern oneself by way of what is right [yi], which is what is meant by 'Be hard on yourself and be sparing when criticizing others.'" "This statement," he says, "is found in the *Analects*, but, so far, it seems, people have not given it much thought. . . . To point out the mistakes in yourself is to be good and honest. To point out the mistakes in other people is to be hurtful. To be hard on yourself means that you are generous. To be hard on others means that you are unkind. . . . A person in the ruling position would be regarded as intolerant if he were to govern the people by imposing on them the measures he set for himself in his own cultivation." *Mr. Lü's Spring and Autumn Annals* makes a similar point about the difference between making demands on oneself and making demands on others. It says, "A gentleman would make demands on others based on their abilities, but he would make demands upon himself by the standard of what is right. If you make demands on others based on their abilities, this means that your demands are easily satisfied, and when this is true, you will win their hearts. Moreover, if you make demands on yourself by the standard of what is right, this means that it will be difficult for you to make mistakes, and when this is true, your conduct will likely to be correct."

15.16 The Master said, "I can never do anything for a man who has not been asking himself, 'What should I do? What should I do?'"

Confucius' comment here reinforces what he says 15.12. Both statements emphasize preparedness before trouble descends, but here Confucius seems to say that if a person does not constantly ask himself what is the best thing to do, then when he finds himself in a jam, there is no one—not even Confucius—who can help him. This reading follows the interpretation of the Han scholar Dong Zhongshu and the Song scholar Zhu Xi.

15.17 The Master said, "There is something hopeless about a group of men spending time together all day, not touching on the question of what is right in their conversations and wanting only to show off their cleverness."

To ask oneself constantly the question of what is right is to put heavy demands on the self, because, given the many variables of the human condition, it is difficult to know just what is right. But in the view of Confucius and his followers, this is how a person will learn to make fewer mistakes and perfect his character. Thus Confucius could not understand why a group of men would spend a whole day together without ever mentioning the one subject they should be most concerned with. Discussion of this topic could help them to see more clearly, he thought, but men preferred talking about things that could let them "show off their cleverness."

15.18 The Master said, "The gentleman makes rightness the substance. He works at it through ritual propriety; he expresses it with modesty; he brings it to completion by being trustworthy. Now that is a gentleman!"

Rightness is again the topic. Here Confucius refers to rightness simply as *zhi*, the substance of a gentleman, and to ritual propriety, modesty, and trustworthiness as the virtues the gentleman pursues and the proof of his distinction.

15.19 The Master said, "The gentleman is worried about his own lack of ability and not about the fact that others do not appreciate him."

This is almost exactly what Confucius says in 14.30. One can also refer to 1.1 and 14.24.

15.20 The Master said, "The gentleman is troubled to think that after he is gone from this world, his name will vanish unnoticed."

Passages 15.19 and 15.20, when read together, tell us clearly where Confucius stood on the question of whether a person should have a reputation, a name (*ming*). No, Confucius would say, while the person is alive, and yes, after he is dead. Contemporaries' views of you—even favorable ones—need not mean much (perhaps Confucius is speaking from experience), since many factors are at play while you are alive; but to have no trace of you remain after you are gone would be a tragedy, since this would mean that you did not do anything to make people of later generations acknowledge your existence. On the question of name, therefore, Confucius takes a long view of things, placing his trust in the judgment of history and in reputations that have endured the test of time. Historians in China liked what he said; Sima Qian from the Han was the first to pick this up, and he carried it further, suggesting that it was the historian's responsibility to rescue men of worth from oblivion. He writes, "[Otherwise,] how can folk of the villages who wish to perfect their behavior and establish their names be known to later generations, unless through some gentleman who rises high in the world?" Confucius, in Sima Qian's mind, was such a gentleman.

15.21 The Master said, "The gentleman makes demands on himself. The petty man makes demands on others."

My translation, which is identical to Burton Watson's, is based on He Yan's commentary. The alternative translation, "The gentleman seeks it in himself; the petty man seeks it in others," is literal but not precise, because one cannot be sure just what the "it" is that the gentleman or the petty man seeks. The phrase "making demands," on the other hand, is clearer, and the sense is corroborated by 14.24 and 15.15. A person who makes demands on himself takes his cultivation and his self-reform as the point of his life's pursuit, and he will not blame anyone else for his mistakes; a person who makes demands on others, however, is not interested in self-reform, and so even when he engages in learning, he does it for a name or for social elevation, and such a person never takes the blame for his own mistakes. The Song thinker Yang Shi feels that it is important to put 15.21 together with 15.19 and 15.20 because, in the end, Confucius believed that as long as a person tried to find it in himself, nothing would be lost even if his name disappeared altogether in posterity.

15.22 The Master said, "The gentleman is self-assured but not competitive. He likes to be in a group but does not form any clique."

"A person who is self-assured," Liu Baonan observes, "will tend to be competitive. A person who likes to be in a group will tend to form cliques. But the gentleman is neither competitive nor cliquish." The Ming thinker Liu Zongzhou says, "A person who is self-assured is aware of the fact that he stands apart from others, but because he is not competitive he does not reject things outside [what he holds dear]. A person who likes to be in a group is easily at one with others, but because he is not cliquish, he will not go along with things [he does not believe in]. This is the measure the gentleman observes in his relationship with the world."

15.23 The Master said, "The gentleman does not recommend a person based on what that person said, and he does not disregard what a person said because of what he knows about the person."

When recommending someone for office in ancient times, the *Book of Rites* says, one could point to the person's virtuous character, his accomplishments, or his words; and according to Liu Baonan's understanding, "if the recommendation was based on a person's fine words, then it was also necessary to look into his character and his accomplishments."

The weight of the first half of 15.23 is balanced by that of the second half, where Confucius shows that he is willing to give words their fair share, and so he says that they cannot be dismissed just because the speaker's character is in question.

15.24 Zigong asked, "Is there a single word that can serve as the guide to conduct throughout one's life?"

The Master said, "It is perhaps the word *shu*. Do not impose on others what you yourself do not want [others to impose on you]."

The word *shu* appears in 4.15. There, I translate *shu* as "treating others with an awareness that they, too, are alive with humanity," which agrees in spirit with Confucius' explanation of *shu* here. Scholars also suggest reading 15.24 with what Confucius describes in 6.30 as "the method and the way of realizing humaneness."

15.25 The Master said, "In my judgment of others, whom have I condemned, and whom have I praised? If there is someone I have praised, you can be sure that he has been put to the test. The common people today are like those [in the past] who kept the Three Dynasties on a straight path."

Confucius goes beyond what he states in 15.20 with regard to the question of human character. Here, he places his trust in the judgment of history and of the common people, for it was the common people who kept the Three Dynasties—of Xia, Shang, and Zhou—on a straight path. And that straight path, Qian Mu says, has "its foundation in a public sense of fairness [dagong] that all humans possess. And because all humans possess this sense of fairness, there is no need for me [or you or anyone] to fix blame or praise." In the history of the Three Dynasties, "everyone praised Emperor Yu, King Tang, Wen, Wu, and the Duke of Zhou without exception. Everyone condemned King Jie, Zhou, You, and Li without exception." This, in Qian Mu's view, was what Confucius mean by "whom have I condemned, and whom have I praised?"

15.26 The Master said, "I am old enough to have seen scribes [shi] leave a gap when they are unsure about a word and horse owners leave the driving to those with the right skills. Nowadays there are no such cases."

What Confucius says here about scribes and owners of horses reflects his overall attitude toward those who are presumptuous—men who make false claims to knowledge or skills they do not possess. This was how Zilu behaved in 13.3, and Confucius berated him, saying, "With things he does not understand, a gentleman would know to keep quiet." The Han historian Ban Gu in the bibliography section of the History of the Former Han gives this explanation: "According to the mode of working in ancient times, scribes wrote down exactly what was in the documents, and when they were not familiar with a word, they would leave a blank or they would ask senior scholars [who might have such knowledge]. But in periods of moral decline, right and wrong could no longer be verified, and so people relied on their own speculations."

15.27 The Master said, "Clever words will upset [the idea of] virtue [*de*]. Impatience with small things will upset big plans."

Clever words and a glib tongue could confuse the distinction between right and wrong, and so what they upset is the idea of virtue. In this, I follow the explanations of Kong Anguo and Zhu Xi. The concept of *buren*, "being impatient with something," is also discussed in the commentaries. The Qing scholar Wu Jiabin notes that the rule of the former kings could be characterized as *buren*, "being impatient with," but, he says, what they were impatient with were not small things. Since "only a truly humane person is able to like and dislike others," what the former kings were impatient with—what they could not bear to witness—must have been the suffering of humanity. And what might be an example of impatience with lesser things? The blunt courage of a common man is Zhu Xi's suggestion.

15.28 The Master said, "When a crowd of people dislikes a person, you must look into the matter closely yourself. When a crowd of people likes a person, you must look into the matter closely yourself."

This is essentially a restatement of 13.24, where Confucius asked Zigong to be cautious about the opinions of the crowd when judging a person's character. There, he said it would be better to trust the views of men of integrity, but here he suggests that each person look into the matter himself.

15.29 The Master said, "It is humans who can enlarge the Way [*dao*]. The Way cannot enlarge humans."

Dao here refers to the moral way, and, like nature's life-giving way, it is constant—it never fails to do its best and never fails to be trustworthy. And the Way belongs to us, Confucius says: it waits for us to give it integrity and greatness. The *Doctrine of the Mean* says, "The Way would not have come into shape if there was no one to fulfill it." The Han historian Ban Gu writes, "The Way of the Zhou declined during the reign of King You and King Li, but this did not mean that the Way came to an end, only that these two rulers had cast it aside. When King Xuan came to the throne, he reflected on the virtues of the former kings; he let light break in upon the stagnant and he mended the smashed and broken; he explained the accomplishments of King Wen and King Wu; and the Way of the Zhou was revived in its original splendor."

15.30 The Master said, "To make a mistake and not to correct it—now that is called making a mistake."

Confucius understood that it was natural for humans, including himself, to make mistakes. This did not trouble him. A genuine mistake, he thought, is not to correct a mistake you have made. In *Han Ying's Commentary to the Book of Poetry*, he is quoted as saying, "To make a mistake and to correct it, this is the same as not having made a mistake." Of all his disciples, he felt, there was only one, Yan Hui, who "did not repeat a mistake."

15.31 The Master said, "Once I spent a whole day thinking, not bothering to eat, and a whole night thinking, not bothering to sleep, but I gained nothing from it. It would have been better if I'd spent the time learning something."

This is about thinking in isolation and thinking without the context and the support of learning. This could be either a futile effort, which is what Confucius says here, or a dangerous exercise, which is what he says in 2.15.

15.32 The Master said, "The gentleman makes plans to realize the Way; he does not make plans to secure food. If you decide to till the field [and plant crops], there still will be times when you will go hungry. If you decide to devote yourself to learning, there will be times when you may receive an official stipend [for putting your knowledge to work]. The gentleman worries about the Way. He does not worry about being poor."

Confucius puts two choices before the young men of his time: devote yourself to learning or be a farmer. The object of learning is realizing the Way and the object of farming is putting food on the table. And even if you opt for farming, he says, there will still be times when you will not have enough to eat; yet if you concentrate just on learning, there will be times when you will find yourself being given a stipend—and therefore a livelihood—for applying what you have learned to affairs of the government. Confucius is prodding others to choose learning, most scholars say. Even so, Liu Baonan points out, most of the educated men during the Spring and Autumn period would have had a hard time earning a living from a government job: nearly all of them had to worry about going hungry, and farming, they thought, would allow them self-sufficiency. Thus Fan Chi asked Confucius in 13.4 about how to grow vegetables and grain crops, and even recluses who ran away from the world to keep themselves immaculate—men such as Chang Ju and Jie Ni in 18.6—had to work in the field and plant crops in order to stay alive.

15.33 The Master said, "Your knowledge is sufficient [to govern the people], but if it is beyond the strength of your humaneness to guard it, you will lose it even though you have gotten it. Your knowledge is sufficient to govern the people and it is within the strength of your humaneness to guard it, but if you lack the dignity to rule over your subjects, then they will not respect you. Your knowledge is sufficient to govern the people and it is within the strength of your humaneness to guard it and you possess the dignity to rule over your subjects, but if you do not rally them into action in accordance the rites, it is still not good enough."

This statement, in Qian Mu's words, is about "the way of governing the people," and since it is Confucius who speaks here, "the way" must refer to the way of a moral government, which he describes in four steps: "Knowledge comes first; humaneness is the agent that puts it into play, and there must be a sufficient amount of it to fulfill what knowledge demands, or otherwise that knowledge will be lost; the man who has the requisite knowledge and humaneness as a ruler must also possess the dignity that will gain the respect of his subjects; and finally, to rally his people into action, this man must follow the measures of ritual propriety.

15.34 The Master said, "The gentleman is not able to absorb trivial knowledge but is able to take on large responsibilities. The petty man is able to absorb trivial knowledge but is not able to take on large responsibilities."

An alternative translation is: "You cannot appreciate a gentleman from what he does in trivial matters, but he is someone who is able to take on large responsibilities. A petty man is not able to take on large responsibilities, but you may be able to appreciate what he does in trivial matters." This follows Zhu Xi's commentary, which says that the point of Confucius' statement is about how to know a person, "what to look for when assessing his character." My translation reflects the earlier reading, from the Han and Wei dynasties. This is the reading Liu Baonan prefers. It is more straightforward (and less forced) than Zhu Xi's, he says, because the focus does not shift from the person who is trying to gauge the character of another person to the person being observed.

15.35 The Master said, "The common people rely more on humaneness for living than on water and fire. I have known people who died from treading on water and fire. But I have never known anyone who died from treading on the path of humaneness."

People cannot live without water and fire, yet humaneness is even more vital to them than water and fire—this is Confucius' first point. He then observes that water and fire, but not humane action, can kill. Most people would agree with what he says about water and fire, but his statement about humane action is easy to refute because history never lacks examples of men and women who chose to die in order to fulfill their humaneness. Scholars over the years brooded about this problem and tried to come up with a reasonable explanation, and the best they could offer was that those who gave their life for humaneness did not really die because, though their physical bodies perished, their heart and spirit remained alive.

15.36 The Master said, "When encountering matters that involve the question of humaneness, do not yield even to your teacher."

What this statement implies is that in matters involving the question of humaneness you should not yield to anyone, not your teacher, your parents, your superiors, and not even your ruler. This is a dangerous pronouncement, since many people would understand it to mean that one's own heart has the highest moral authority, but that is not a position Confucius would have supported. Confucius is cautious about letting the heart handle moral questions because it tends to overreact and override sound judgment. This was the advice he gave Zizhang in 12.6 and Zilu in 7.11 and 17.8. Still, he felt, there are occasions when a person should trust only his sense of humaneness to help him see clearly and act correctly. And what might those occasions be? The Han thinker Dong Zhongshu offers a powerful example from a well-known story in the history of the Spring and Autumn period. The army of Chu laid a siege on the capital of Song in the year 594 BC, the early records say. After nearly eight months, the soldiers were exhausted, and as they were running out of provisions, the ruler of Chu sent his commanding general to the capital of Song, to see if the people of Song had the strength to hold on to their city. What the general found out was that the people of Song were so hungry that they were forced to eat the children of strangers, with whom they had exchanged their own children. The sight so horrified him that he told the enemy the truth about the situation back at his camp—that they were coming to the end of their provisions and were ready to abandon the siege. The question people asked over the years was whether the general had betrayed the trust of his ruler when he sided with the enemy, to which Dong Zhongshu responded that the commander simply "could not bear the sight of extreme suffering." He said, "Those who are humane are guided by what is natural. [The commander] Zifan was simply responding to the promptings of his heart when he sympathized with the people of Song, and so he gave no thought to the possibility that other people might perceive his action as a form of usurpation." This, in Dong's view, was what Confucius meant when he said, "When encountering matters that involve the question of humaneness, do not yield even to your teacher."

15.37 The Master said, "The gentleman is true [to what is right] but does not commit himself to the small idea of trust."

Much of the discussion in the commentaries is about the difference between *zhen* (being true to what is right) and *liang* (small idea of trust). Liu Baonan says, "The gentleman carries out things in accordance with what is right. Everything he handles complies with the correct way. His actions are not driven by any small idea of trust." Qian Mu says, "A person who is true [to what is right] is true to himself, and he is constant. A person who is committed to the small idea of trust seeks to be trustworthy to others." The Qing scholar Jiao Xun uses Confucius' statement here to explain why Mencius felt that "those who held on to one point or one extreme were crippling the Way." Finally, Confucius himself characterizes *liang* in 14.17 as "the petty loyalty of a common man or a common woman." This type of loyalty also fits his description in 13.20 of those men who have "little pebbles for brains" because they "insist on keeping their word and seeing their action through to the end."

15.38 The Master said, "In serving your lord, carry out your duties with respect before giving thought to a salary."

Qian Mu says, "To carry out one's duties with respect is to give full attention and complete effort to the task at hand." What this means, the *Book of Rites* says, is that "if you are in the military, you should not dodge difficult assignments, and if you are at the court, you should not avoid menial jobs." If this is how you approach your responsibilities, you will not be brooding about a salary.

15.39 The Master said, "In educating others, [one should] let go all preconceptions of class and categories."

Most scholars say that when Confucius made this remark he was thinking about the way of a teacher—that in teaching, one should let go all distinctions based on class, wealth, and degree of intelligence and accept all who are willing to learn. That is the reason why, when considered together, his disciples seem like a hodgepodge of all sorts: from the rich (Ran Qiu and Zigong) to the poor (Yan Hui and Zhonggong), from the aristocratic (Meng Yizi) to the rustic (Zilu), from the quick (Zizhang) to the slow (Zengzi). And since Confucius thought that everyone could be taught, a few scholars argue that the present statement is really a reflection of his view of human nature. This, I feel, is a stretch, because Confucius was not interested in offering a theory on human nature—he left that to his followers Mencius and Xunzi, several generations later—and he did not really speak about the subject, apart from making this brief comment in 17.2: "People are similar by nature; they become distinct through practice."

15.40 The Master said, "When your paths [*dao*] are different, there is no point in seeking advice from one another."

The Qing scholar Wu Jiabin says, "Several people could all be pursuing the same goal of realizing the good, but there would be differences among them. They all know in their hearts good and bad, gain and loss, but they are not able to seek advice from one another." Mencius' description of Bo Yi, Yi Yin, and Luixia Hui illustrates the point. All three men pursued the good, but their paths were different: Bo Yi had an immaculate character and would keep himself immaculate at all costs; Yi Yin had such a strong sense of responsibility that he felt he was to blame for any man or woman "who could not enjoy the benefits" of a good rule; Liuxia Hui "harbored no grudge," no matter what circumstances he found himself in, and he could inspire others to be generous and tolerant. Yet Liu Baonan observes, toward the end of his commentary, "Followers of Confucius in later times would hold up one idea and trash a hundred others. As soon as similar and different views arise, they herald theirs as the correct one. They rebuke and strike at each other, which shows that they do not possess the hefty spirit of the sages and that they do not at all understand what Confucius meant when he said, 'there is no point in seeking advice from one another.'"

15.41 The Master said, "Get your point across, and that would be enough."

In speech or in argument, as long as you clearly express the point you want to make, that is enough, and there is no need for embellishment. The *Book of Etiquette* gives similar advice to those sent abroad on a mission: "If you say too much, you will seem pedantic. If you say too little, you will not get your point across. If what you say is just enough to convey your point, then you will have hit the mark."

15.42 The Master Musician Mian came to call. As he approached the steps, the Master said, "Here are the steps." As they reached the seating mats, the Master said, "Here are the mats." When everyone was seated, the Master told him, "So-and-so is over here. So-and-so is over there."

After the Master Musician Mian had gone, Zizhang asked, "Is this the way to talk to a music teacher [*shi*]?" Confucius replied, "Yes, this is the way to assist a music teacher."

In his commentary, Liu Baonan puts emphasis on the last statement, "this is the way [*dao*] to assist a music teacher." Court musicians in early China were blind, the assumption being that blind people possessed a sharper sense of hearing and keener cognizance of the nuances in sound and music. And just as there were different ways (*dao*) of living a moral life (15.40), there was a particular way of assisting a master musician, which Confucius showed as he guided Mian down the steps and to his seat and then introduced him to the guests sitting on the mats. Scholars like to stress Confucius' generosity and kindness, which make this episode especially memorable, but the source of his generosity and kindness was not sentimentalism but respect—the respect Confucius had for a master musician.

BOOK SIXTEEN

Book Sixteen is an anomaly—several scholars have raised this point—because Confucius is referred to not as "Master" but by his official title, "Master Kong" (Kongzi or, in Latinization, Confucius), throughout and he speaks in a manner that is unlike the one we have come to associate with him. This is not how he talks, one might say, or how he articulates his ideas. And in a number of the entries, his natural way of expressing himself is replaced by lists of dos and don'ts, and his descriptions of human character have been parsed into categories. This type of deliberation resembles that of the Warring States thinkers, and since the *Analects* is an accrued text, it is possible that the writings in Book Sixteen are interpolations from this later period.

16.1 The Jisun family was about to send an army to attack Zhuanyu. Ran Qiu and Zilu came to see Master Kong [Confucius], and they told him, "The Jisun family is going to take action against Zhuanyu."

Confucius said, "Qiu, [should this happen,] is it not your fault? A former king in the past gave the rulers of Zhuanyu the responsibility of sacrificing to Mount Dongmeng. Moreover, Zhuanyu lies within the boundaries of the territory that was enfeoffed to Lu, and her ruler is a subject of our altars of soil and grain. So what reason could there be to attack Zhuanyu?"

Ran Qiu replied, "This is what our lord wished, not what the two of us wanted."

Confucius said, "Qiu, [the historian] Zhou Ren said: 'Assess your ability and see if you are able to take on the responsibilities of your position. If you are not able, then you should resign. What use would an assistant be [to a blind person] if he did not give him support when the man tottered and did not hold him up when he fell?' Besides, what you've said is wrong. Whose fault is it when the tiger or the rhinoceros escapes from his cage, when the tortoise shell or the jade is smashed in its coffer?"

Ran Qiu said, "But Zhuanyu is well fortified, and it is situated near the Jisun family's stronghold, Bi. If the Jisuns do not take Zhuanyu now, then it will be a source of worries for their descendants later on."

Confucius said, "The gentleman despises those who do not come out and say what they want but instead find some other way to make the same pitch. I have heard that the head of a state and the head of a hereditary family should not worry about poverty but should worry about inequity in the distribution of wealth. They should not worry about a lack of population but should worry about discontentment and unrest. When there is equity in the distribution of wealth, there will not be poverty. When there is concordance [in a society], there will not be a lack of population. When people are content, there will not be any threat of [the state or the family] being toppled. This being the case, when people from a distance are unwilling to yield to your influence and rule, improve your ways and cultivate your virtue in order to attract them. Once they are attracted to you, see to it that they are content. Now the two of you are meant to be assistants to your lord. Yet when people from a distance are unwilling to yield to his influence and rule, you are unable to help him attract them, and when the state is falling apart and is on the verge of collapse, you are unable to help him ensure its survival. Instead, you work with him on getting his men armed [and ready to attack those who live] within the state. I fear that the worries of the Jisun family do not lie in Zhuanyu but lie within the walls of their own home."

This is the longest entry in the *Analects*, and it contains a sustained dialogue between Confucius and Ran Qiu. It is difficult to determine whether this account has any historical credibility. The history in the *Zuo Commentary* makes no mention of a conflict between Zhuanyu and the Jisun family, but what it does say is that in the year 639 BC the ruler of Zhuanyu together with the rulers of three other minor states "presided over the sacrifices to Taihao and the spirit of the Ji River." Thus there is a discrepancy between this record and the *Analects* regarding the ritual responsibility Zhuanyu was assigned—whether its rulers were to sacrifice to Mount Dongmeng or to Taiho and the spirit of the Ji River. Most of the traditional commentaries follow Kong Anguo's gloss regarding the history of Zhuanyu. According to this Han scholar, the rulers of Zhuanyu, with the surname of Feng, were descendants of the legendary figure Fu Xi, who was regarded as the inventor of fire and writing; Zhuanyu was a vassal state of Lu, and so was a subject and a dependent of Lu, and since the beginning of the Zhou dynasty, its rulers were given the prerogative of offering sacrifices to the spirit of Mount Dongmeng, which was situated in the eastern part of Lu, in what is the present-day Yi prefecture in Shandong province.

The gist of the conversation here, like the discussions Confucius has with Ran Qiu in 3.6 and 11.17, is again about the responsibilities of a political advisor. Thus when Ran Qiu tries to place the blame on his employer, the head of the Jisuns, for wishing to attack the people of Zhuanyu, Confucius shoots him down, saying, If you were unable to lead him to the right path, then you should resign. And when Ran Qiu tries to defend the action of his lord, Confucius becomes even more angry, saying, "The gentleman despises those who do not come out and say what they want but instead find some other way to make the same pitch." But he also offers Ran Qiu this advice: Ask your lord to address the extreme unfairness in the distribution of wealth and the discontent people feel toward their government; get him to cultivate his character and not to resort to the use of arms when he is dealing with his own subjects. Song scholars, who like to exaggerate the weight of Confucius' political influence in Lu, say that Confucius, through Ran Qiu, "must have dissuaded" the Jisuns from taking up arms against Zhuanyu, and that this is why we cannot find any record of such a conflict in the early histories. Their argument, for lack of evidence, reads a bit like wishful thinking.

16.2 Confucius said, "When the moral way prevails in the world, it is the Son of Heaven who orchestrates rites and music, and punitive expeditions. When the moral way does not prevail in the world, it is the regional rulers who orchestrate rites and music, and punitive expeditions. When the regional rulers are in charge, it is unlikely for them to hold on to their authority for more than ten generations. When the hereditary counselors are in charge, it is unlikely for them to hold on to their authority for more than five generations. When the family retainers are in charge, it is unlikely for them to hold on to their authority for more than three generations. When the moral way prevails in the world, affairs of government do not rest with the hereditary counselors. When the moral way prevails in the world, the common people do not find themselves joining in the discussion and the planning [of their government's policies]."

Many scholars regard Confucius' statement as a concise outline of the history of the Spring and Autumn period, beginning with the "Son of Heaven," King Ping, after he ceded most of his authority to the regional rulers who had helped him to move his court to the east in the aftermath of a major debacle in the dynasty's western capital. This, in Confucius' mind, marked the start of a political course that was dominated at first by the regional rulers, and then in turn by the hereditary counselors and the family retainers—a course he characterized as one in which the moral way did not prevail because the Zhou king was no longer in charge of rites and music, and punitive expeditions. Most commentators do not dwell on this point. Instead, they are interested in what Confucius said regarding the length of time these political players were able to hold on to power. Scholars such as Kong Anguo and Ma Rong from the Han and Liu Fenglu and Feng Lihua from the Qing enumerate their own lists of ten generations of regional rulers, followed by the five generations of hereditary counselors, and then the three generations of family retainers. Some focus only on the history of the Lu, while others include the histories of many other regional states. What Confucius said at the end also caught the scholars' attention. Just what did he mean, they ask, when he said that "the common people do not find themselves joining in the discussion and the planning" of their government policies "when the moral way prevails in the world"? One scholar puts it this way: "A state has big plans and the right counselors in charge of them. When [the common people, who are like] children begin to voice their views, these plans will get botched."

16.3 Confucius said, "It has been five generations since the ducal house lost the authority to determine ranks and salaries at court. It has been four generations since the [Lu] government has been under the control of the hereditary counselors. This is the reason why the descendents of the Three Families are on the decline."

Ever since the hereditary counselor Xiangzhong of the East Gate had the legitimate heir of Duke Wen, a son by his principal wife, killed and put in his place the son of a secondary wife, "the rulers of Lu no longer had control of their state." This, the *Zuo Commentary* says, marked the rise of the hereditary families with the Jisuns at the forefront. The "five generations" of the ducal house, which Confucius mentions here, refers to the ducal reigns of Xuan, Cheng, Xiang, Zhao, and Ding, while the "four generations" of hereditary counselors refers to the four consecutive heads of the Jisun family, Wenzi, Wuzi, Huanzi, and Pingzi. And since Confucius has already made it known in 16.2 that the hereditary counselors would not be able to hold on to their power for more than five generations, he feels that it is reasonable to say that "the descendents of the Three Families are on the decline." And indeed they were slipping as their family retainers—men like Yang Hu and Gongshan Furao—were becoming more hostile and presumptuous, behaving as if they, too, could become rulers.

16.4 Confucius said, "There are three types of friendship that can benefit you and three types of friendship that can harm you. It would be to your benefit to be friends with those who are upright, those whom you can trust, and those of broad learning. It would do you harm to be friends with those with practiced manners, an affected sweetness, a glib tongue."

The contrast between the two types of friend is clear: it is the distinction between the genuine article and a fake. A true friend is upright

and upfront with you about any misstep you may have made. You
can benefit from his straight talk; you can trust that he is speaking to
you for your good; and you can learn from his broad knowledge.
The person you should stay away from is someone who is a clever
fake. Because he wants something from you, he tries not to offend
you—this explains his "practiced manners" and his "affected sweetness"—but as soon he has gained your favor, he will try to mislead
you with his facile tongue.

16.5 Confucius said, "There are three kinds of pleasure that
can benefit you and three kinds of pleasure that can harm you.
The pleasure of hitting the right measure in your practice of
rites and music, of celebrating the goodness of others, of having many worthy friends—all this will benefit you. The pleasure of being self-important, of being a slacker and a loafer, of
drinking and feasting to excess—all this will do you harm."

It is human nature to seek pleasure, but it is the sudden rightness in
the playing, in the doing, that gives lasting pleasure; it is also this
kind of pleasure that has the potential to transform us. This, I believe,
is Confucius' point about rites and music. But he also talks about the
joy of celebrating other people's achievements and of having true
friends, friends possessing the characteristics he describes in 16.4.
Such pleasure comes from a warmer place—it springs from the heart.

16.6 Confucius said, "There are three kinds of mistake a person is likely to commit when attending a gentleman. To speak
when it is not one's turn to speak is being impetuous. Not to
speak when it is one's turn to speak is being evasive. To speak
without taking notice of the other person's expression is being
blind."

Xunzi cites this passage in his essay "Encouraging Learning," and
then he adds: "A gentleman is neither impetuous, nor evasive, nor
blind. He responds to others in a timely and appropriate manner."
Qian Mu thinks that the mistakes people tend to make when speaking often spring from a lack of respect, but by being close to a

gentleman—to someone who is neither impetuous, nor evasive, nor blind—"they can make progress in cultivating their moral selves."

16.7 Confucius said, "The gentleman guards himself against three things. When he is young and his blood-and-vital force is still unsettled, he guards himself against sensuous temptations. When he is in his prime and his blood-and-vital force is vigorous and unyielding, he guards himself against being combative. After his blood-and-vital force has declined, he guards himself from being grasping."

The "blood-and-vital force" (*xueqi*) did not become a topic of intellectual discussion in China until the Warring States period. Thus we can be fairly certain that the voice in the present statement is not that of the historical Confucius. His later disciples Mencius and Xunzi, however, sparred across the century over the question of how to deal with those problems stemming from the physical and sensual side of our nature. Mencius said that one should "let one's will [*zhi*] be in charge of one's vital force [*qi*]" and nourish one's vital force with just the right amount of attention, which meant that one should "neither forget to tend to it nor help it grow." Xunzi gave a lot more thought to the question. In fact, one could say that the driving force of his moral teaching is an attempt to understand the unstable elements of our nature and to find a reasonable and moral solution to our obsessions with beautiful objects or beautiful women, with wanting to win or wanting to be right, and with wanting to have more of pleasure or more things.

16.8 Confucius said, "The gentleman stands in awe of three things. He is in awe of Heaven's mandate, of great men, and of the words of sages. The petty man is unaware of the presence of Heaven's mandate; he belittles great men; and he regards the words of sages with mockery."

It is difficult to explain "Heaven's mandate" as it was first conceived in early Zhou. The idea unfolded through the teachings of Confucius and of the Warring States thinkers Mencius, Xunzi, Mozi, Zhuangzi, the authors of the *Laozi*, and many more, each with his own take on how it relates to human existence and to the human will. "Heaven's mandate," within the Confucian canon, refers to what is and what must be after one has done one's best. There is no blame and no rancor about what may befall because one stands on destiny's path, knowing that there is no more one could do. Thus, Confucius says, the gentleman is in awe of—is always aware of—that which is beyond his effort. The petty man, however, is remiss with regard to Heaven's mandate because, to him, it is "blurry and indistinct," He Yan says. Such a man cannot see it clearly and so he is not in awe of its power. And the same can be said about the petty man's treatment of the great men and of the words of sages. "The great man is upright but is not arrogant, and so the petty man belittles him," He Yan explains. "The words of sages cannot be understood by means of small knowledge, and so the petty man mocks them."

16.9 Confucius said, "Those who are born with knowledge are at the top. Next are those who acquire knowledge through learning. Behind them are those who have difficulties [absorbing knowledge] but are still determined to learn. And at the bottom are people who have difficulties [absorbing knowledge] and do not even attempt to learn."

Even though Confucius acknowledges the fact that humans are born with different degrees of intelligence, he sticks to his basic premise that, in the end, it is about effort: nearly everyone can possess knowledge as long as he is persistent in his pursuit of learning.

16.10 Confucius said, "There are nine things the gentleman gives thought to: he aims to be clear in vision, keen in hearing, amicable in his expression, courteous in his manners, conscientious in carrying out his words, and respectful in attending to his responsibilities; and when he is in doubt, he asks questions; when he is angry, he reflects on the unwanted consequences this could cause; when he sees a chance for gain, he asks whether it is right."

By giving thought to something, one gives attention to what one is doing and so will have greater success in achieving it—this is how Sun Qifeng explains the passage, citing Mencius, who says, "If your mind gives thought to it, you will get it. If not, you won't get it." But what is more interesting, and indeed surprising, is the list of things the gentleman "gives thought to," which includes not just perception and demeanor but also occasions when he is in doubt or angry, or when he sees a chance for gain. And what Confucius says about the thoughts that go through a gentleman's mind on such occasions is also illuminating.

16.11 Confucius said, "'Seeing goodness, he acts as if [it is running ahead of him and] he is not able to catch up. Seeing what is not good, he acts as if he is recoiling from the touch of hot water.' I have known people like this, and I have heard such an expression. 'He lives in reclusion in order to pursue his purpose. He practices what is right in order to attain the moral way.' I have heard such an expression but have not yet known someone like this."

Yan Hui talks about his pursuit of the good with the same sense of urgency that is described in the first statement here. He says in 9.11, "The more I look up at it, the higher it appears. The more I bore into it, the harder it becomes. I see it before me, yet suddenly it is behind me." Thus it is possible that Confucius has Yan Hui in mind when he says, "I have known people like this." Qian Mu thinks that Confucius' remark regarding the second statement is also about Yan Hui. Because Yan Hui died young and could not fully realize what he had learned, Confucius saw only Yan Hui's "hidden virtue but not how it could be put to use," Qian Mu writes, and if Yan Hui was short of attaining what was morally right, no one else, in Confucius' view, could have achieved such a feat.

16.12 Duke Jing of Qi had four thousand horses. On the day he died, people could not find anything praiseworthy to say about him. Bo Yi and Shu Qi died of hunger at the foot of

Mount Shouyang. Up to this day people still sing praise of them. This is what it means.

Speculations abound about this bit of record for two reasons: no speaker is mentioned, and the remark at the end seems to suggest that the contrast between Duke Jing and the two brothers, Bo Yi and Shu Qi, is meant to illustrate some point, for which there is no reference. Some scholars say that 16.12 is a continuation of 16.11—that Confucius remains the speaker and the discussion, in part, is still about men like Bo Yi and Shu Qi, who cultivated their character in reclusion but did not have a chance to realize their virtue in practice. But if we accept this theory, then how do we account for the comment about Duke Jing of Qi? The Song scholar Cheng Yi suggests another reading: the two lines cited from Ode 188 in 12.10, he says, should be placed at the beginning of this entry, thus allowing the two examples to illustrate the idea that what people praised was "not a person's wealth but the fact that he was different." In my commentary on 12.10, I have already expressed doubt about this interpretation.

16.13 Chen Kang [Ziqin] asked [Confucius' son,] Boyu, "Have you been taught anything special?"

Boyu responded, "I have not. One day my father was standing there by himself, and as I crossed the courtyard with quickened steps, he said, 'Have you learned the *Odes*?' I answered, 'Not yet.' He said, 'Unless you learn the *Odes*, you won't be able to speak.' I then went back and learned the *Odes*. Another day, he was again standing there by himself, and as I crossed the courtyard with quickened steps, he said, 'Have you learned the rites?' I answered, 'Not yet.' He said, 'Unless you learn the rites, you won't be able to find your balance.' I then went back and learned the rites. I have been taught these two things."

Delighted by what he heard, Chen Kang said, "I asked one question and learned three things. I learned about the *Odes*; I learned about the rites; and I learned that the gentleman maintains some distance from his son."

Whether it is other people's children or his own, Confucius offers the same instructions: Learn the *Odes* and let the rites guide your conduct to the proper measure. This is what his son, Boyu, revealed. What it means, of course, is that Boyu received no special treatment from his father and that Confucius did not believe in imparting his teaching through secret transmission.

Quoting the Song historian and ritual scholar Sima Guang, Liu Baonan says, "'Distance' [in the context of Chen Kang's remark] does not refer to emotional distance but to the ritual propriety with which the father receives his son," which means that he would always maintain the "dignity of a father," not becoming overly familiar with his son. Liu also says that according to the ritual regulations of early China, fathers and sons among the governing elite had to live in separate residences in order to avoid suspicion of favoritism, which explains why Boyu met his father while "crossing the courtyard." And even on the rare occasion of seeing his father, the son, "out of respect," quickened his steps.

16.14 The ruler of a state refers to his wife as "lady," and she refers to herself as "little child." The people of the state refer to her as "the lady of the lord," but when they are abroad, they refer to her as "our humble little lord," while the people of other states also refer to her as "the lady of the lord."

Like 16.12, the present entry is, again, an anomaly, which led the Republican period scholar Liang Qichao to conclude that this was a passage from a ritual text that somehow found its way into the *Analects* as a bookend to this chapter. Other scholars feel that there is no reason not to believe that Confucius is the speaker. Confucius, they say, is stating the various ways of addressing the wife of a ruler in a manner that is appropriate to the speaker's relationship to her.

17.1 Yang Huo [Yang Hu] wished to see Confucius, but Confucius did not want to see him. He, therefore, sent Confucius a piglet as a present [so that Confucius would be forced to go to his house to thank him]. Confucius waited until Yang Huo was not at home to pay his respects, but on the way back he bumped into this man. Addressing Confucius, Yang Huo said, "Come here! I want to talk to you." He continued, "Would you call a man humane if he clutches a cherished jewel in his bosom while letting the country go lost and adrift? I would say not. Would you call a man wise if he is eager to take part in government while letting opportunity slip by again and again? I would say not. Days and months are rushing forward. Time is not on our side."

Confucius said, "Right. I shall take up office."

Yang Hu was a dark horse from the late Spring and Autumn period, with an ambition that knew no bounds, and attitude and swagger to match. He dominated the politics of Lu from 507 to 502 BC even though he was only a retainer in the Jisun family. At the height of his power, he took a huge risk in attempting to have his own lord, the head of the Jisuns, eliminated, but his plan went awry: another hereditary family came to the Jisuns' rescue and defeated his army in the capital of Lu. According to the account in the *Zuo Commentary*, when the battle was over, Yang Hu "took off his armor, walked over to the ruler's palace, rifled the precious jades and the great bow"; he then went home "to have a meal and a nap." This episode ended Yang Hu's political career in Lu, but it did not stop him from seeking his fortune elsewhere. Confucius' meeting with Yang Hu must have happened sometime before 502, when Yang Hu was still making preparations for an all-out assault on the governing elites of Lu. Thus it is strange that this man should be the one to give Confucius a lecture for not putting his talent, "his cherished jewel," to use in helping to keep their country from going adrift. Confucius must have been aware of the insincerity of his plea, for Yang Hu cared only for his own interests. His call for Confucius to serve the state was a call for Confucius to serve him, and for this reason Confucius had been dodging his approach until they bumped into each other by chance. Even then—even when Yang Hu was trying to persuade Confucius to join him—he behaved like a bully, but in the end he managed to wring only a vague answer out of Confucius.

17.2 The Master said, "People are similar by nature; they become distinct through practice."

Much of the discussion in the commentaries focuses on the question of whether Confucius' statement here is the precursor of Mencius' more pronounced stance that "human nature is good." Qian Mu's comments, I feel, are the most succinct; they also reflect the more astute observations from the earlier generations of scholars. Qian Mu believed that Confucius was reluctant to talk about human nature—as Zigong tells us in 5.13—and therefore that the point of his assertion in the present passage was not about human nature (*xing*) but about practice (*xi*). By stating that human natures are alike, Qian Mu says, Confucius "is encouraging people to learn," because through learning—and practice—there will emerge differences in skills and intelligence, understanding and perception. Unlike Mencius, who was "interested in contrasting humans with animals"—and thus his theory that humans are of a higher order because their nature is good—Confucius, Qian Mu observes, was only concerned about "how humans might be compared against each other."

17.3 The Master said, "Only the most intelligent and the most stupid are not inclined to change."

Many scholars suggest reading 17.3 together with 17.2. Here, Confucius seems to say that he would like to amend just slightly what he said earlier, and say that most humans, though not all, not the most intelligent or the most stupid, have a malleable nature, and so it is important to put effort into shaping that nature into something of moral worth. Liu Baonan feels that it would be a mistake to understand "the most stupid" as those who are born with a despicable nature, as some scholars from the Han and Tang suggest. He agrees with the Qing scholar Dai Zhen, who says, "When a person is born with low intelligence, it will be difficult to explain to him the teachings of rites and moral rightness. This is the reason why he may give up learning altogether and why [Confucius said] he is 'not inclined to change.'" But Dai Zhen also thinks that it is possible for such a person to meet the right friend or the right teacher—someone who is able to inspire him to learn and help him get out of the rut. He writes, "Confucius said, '[the most stupid] are not inclined to change,' not that 'they are unable to change.'"

17.4 The Master went to Wucheng. While there, he heard the playing of stringed instruments together with the sound of singing. He smiled and said, "Why use an ox knife to kill a chicken?"

Ziyou replied, "In the past, Master, I have heard you say, 'A gentleman, having been instructed in the moral way, will know to love others. The common people, having been instructed in the moral way, will be easy to govern.'"

The Master said, "My young friends, what Yan [Ziyou] just said is right. What I said earlier was meant to be a joke."

The Chinese would use the expression "Why use an ox knife to kill a chicken?" in much the same way as we would describe certain efforts as "much ado about nothing." But how do we understand it in the context of this conversation? Just what brought on the joke? What does the "ox knife" refer to, and which chicken was Ziyou trying to kill? And why did Confucius apologize to Ziyou for a remark he made in jest? Ziyou, we learn, was the steward of Wucheng, a small district in the state of Lu. When Confucius heard music and singing being performed there, he realized that Ziyou, in trying to give the people of Wucheng an education, had taught them to play stringed instruments and to sing in poetic verses, which, Confucius thought, was not something most men in similar positions would do.

And so he smiled, and he compared it to using an ox knife to kill a chicken. This put Ziyou on the defensive. Citing a remark Confucius had made on another occasion, he said that instruction in "the moral way"—by this he meant music—would allow the governing elite to be more caring and the common people to be more amicable and, therefore, easier to manage. Confucius, sensing that Ziyou was not happy about being teased, said Ziyou was right: "What I said earlier was meant to be a joke."

17.5 Gongshan Furao was about to stage a rebellion, using Bi as his base. He summoned the Master, and the Master wanted to go. Zilu was not happy about it, and he said, "We may be at the end of our road, but why must we go to Gongshan?"

The Master said, "This man must have had some purpose in mind when he summoned me. If he can put me to use, can I not, perhaps, create a Zhou dynasty in the east?"

Gongshan Furao—Gongshan Buniu in the records in the *Zuo Commentary*—was a protégé of Yang Hu. He assumed Yang Hu's position as chief retainer of the Jisuns following Yang Hu's failed attempt to topple the hereditary families in 502 BC. Before long, Gongshan also made his ambitions known; the *Analects* clearly states that he wanted "to stage a rebellion." And like Yang Hu, he solicited help from Confucius. But this time, instead of giving Gongshan a vague answer as he had done with Yang Hu, Confucius took the offer seriously, which prompted Zilu to ask, Are we really so desperate? In response, Confucius said he thought that Gongshan had set his sights on bigger things, beyond his own interests. And if such a man could put him to use, Confucius mused, could he not accomplish something truly grand? The goal he had in mind was to realize in the east, in his home state, a Zhou dynasty with the pluck and vision of her founders from the west, men like King Wen and King Wu and the Duke of Zhou. As history shows, Confucius, in the end, decided not to join Gongshan. He was appointed minister of crime in the Lu government soon after, and when Gongshan finally took his band of men to the streets in 498, Confucius was working for the other side: by then it had become his responsibility to suppress the rebel forces and restore order to Lu.

17.6 Zizhang asked Confucius about humaneness. Confucius said, "To be humane is to be able to realize five things when dealing with the world."

"May I ask what are these five?"

"Being respectful, large-minded, trustworthy, quick in response, and generous. If you are respectful, you will not be met with insult. If you are large-minded, you will win the hearts of the people. If you are trustworthy, people will have confidence in you. If you are quick in response, you will get things done. If you are generous to others, this will be enough [storing up of kindly feelings] to ask them to do things for you."

Given the fact that the interlocutor, Zizhang, is someone who is keen on having an official career, many scholars feel that when he asks about "humaneness" (ren), he must be referring to humane government (renzheng). What Confucius says in response seems to confirm this view. Yet the "five things" he mentions also illustrate a basic point in all his teachings on humaneness, which is that humaneness has reciprocity as its working principle. They reinforce what he says in 6.30: "A humane person wishes to steady himself, and so he helps others to steady themselves. Because he wishes to reach his goal, he helps others to reach theirs."

17.7 Bi Xi summoned the Master, and the Master wanted to go. Zilu said, "In the past, I have heard you say, 'A gentleman will not enter the domain of someone who has acted, in person, like a reprobate.' Now Bi Xi is about to use the district of Zhong Mou to stage a rebellion, and you are thinking of joining him. How would you explain this?"

The Master replied, "Yes, I have said that. But have I not also said, 'Some things are so hard that no amount of grinding could wear them thin, and some things are so white that no dye could color them black'? Moreover, how can I be like a bitter gourd that hangs from the end of a string and can not be eaten?"

Bi Xi was a family retainer working for Zhao Jianzi, a hereditary counselor from the state of Jin. We do not know for sure why Bi Xi decided to rebel against Zhao Jianzi, but from the records in the *Zuo Commentary*, we learn that Zhao Jianzi had an inimical relationship with another hereditary family, the Fans, also of Jin, and that he feuded with the state of Wei over territorial issues. This, in turn, drew the Fans and the state of Wei together as close allies. The *Zuo Commentary* says that in the year 490 BC, "Zhao Jianzi sent a punitive expedition against the state of Wei on account of Wei's support for the Fan family. The army laid a siege on the district of Zhong Mou." An earlier record in the same source says that Zhong Mou was once under the jurisdiction of Jin and was in the possession of the Zhao family. What this suggests is that for some reason Zhong Mou was forced out of the hands of the Zhaos, and, by 490, the Zhaos were trying to get it back. The event that led to the Zhaos' losing Zhong Mou could have been the uprising Bi Xi instigated, the Qing scholar Jiang Yong explains; and if that was the case, then Bi Xi must have been on the side of the Fans even though he was Zhao Jianzi's employee. Confucius got himself involved in some version of this political tangle because he was a sojourner in the state of Wei during those years.

The invitation from Bi Xi was the third time that a family retainer asked Confucius to join him as the retainer was preparing to revolt, which makes one wonder just what sort of reputation Confucius had among his contemporaries and what sort of feelers he put out to make men like Gongshan and Bi Xi think that he might accept their offer. Here Confucius gives us his story. He says that he cannot let the stuff he was born with be hollowed out and tossed away like the flesh of a bitter gourd. He simply cannot imagine himself as an empty shell hanging from a string. And because this is how he has chosen to live his life, he is willing to work with all types, even those whose conduct is suspect, and he is confident that no amount of grinding or dye could wear his principles thin or cast a shadow over his character.

17.8 The Master said, "You [Zilu], have you heard about the six words [referring to the six noble tendencies] and the six problems as a result of letting [these noble tendencies] get stuck in a state of benightedness [*liubi*]?"

Zilu replied, "No, I have not."

"Sit down, and I will tell you. To love humaneness without a love for learning leads to foolishness. To love the quickness of intelligence without a love for learning leads to an unmoored life. To love trustworthiness without a love for learning leads to harm [done to others and to oneself]. To love forthrightness without a love for learning leads to derisiveness. To love courage without a love for learning leads to unruliness. To love unwavering strength without a love for learning leads to wild behavior [that could be offensive to others]."

Liu Baonan suggests using Xunzi's writings on obsession and benightedness (*liubi*) to understand what Confucius meant by the six problems attendant on the nobler human tendencies. These problems all have to do with the absence of a love for learning. Without learning, these tendencies would be on their own, in the dark, without light and guidance, and they often produce results that are at odds with what they might have achieved. Confucius in 8.2, 17.23, and 17.24 expresses the same idea in slightly different ways.

17.9 The Master said, "My young friends, why is it that none of you learn the *Odes*? The *Odes* can give the spirit an exhortation [*xing*], the mind keener eyes [*guan*]. They can make us better adjusted in a group [*qun*] and more articulate when voicing a complaint [*yuan*]. They teach you [the humane and the right way] to serve those who are as close to you as your parents and as distant from you as your ruler. They also let you become familiar with the names of birds and beasts, plants and trees."

Confucius has already stated his love for the *Odes* and what they can do to refine our moral and aesthetic sensibilities in 1.15, 2.2, 3.8, 3.20, 8.8, 16.13, and many other places. Here, using just four words, *xing* (興), *guan* (觀), *qun* (羣), and *yuan* (怨), he gives a summary of the transformative power of the *Odes*, for the private self and for its relationship to the larger world, whether the relationship is close or distant. Poetry is also able to bring us closer to the natural world, Confucius observes, as we learn the names of the birds and beasts, the plants and trees.

The Qing scholar Jiao Xun, in his preface to a study of the *Book of Poetry*, points out the difference between learning from poems and learning from lectures about right and wrong. He explains, "Poems do not speak explicitly about something. They say it metaphorically. They do not speak about moral principles but about human feelings. They do not try to harangue us; they simply stir our emotions." The sound of poetry is "gentle and true," Jiao Xun writes, unlike the voice of the self-righteous man, who can easily "exasperate the listener" or, if he is speaking to the ruler, "bring harm to himself."

17.10 The Master said to Boyu, "Have you applied yourself [*wei*] to [what you have learned from] the *Zhounan* and *Shaonan* poems [*wei Zhounan Shaonan*]? Unless a person applies himself to what he has learned from the *Zhounan* and *Shaonan* poems, he will be like someone standing with his face toward the wall."

Most scholars understand *wei* to mean "applying one's effort to the study of," but Liu Baonan thinks that *wei* suggests "practice"—"to take what one has absorbed and put it into practice"—a reading that reflects what Confucius has said about the point of learning poetry. Confucius tells his son, Boyu, in 16.13, "Unless you learn the *Odes*, you won't be able to speak." He says in 13.5 that to be able to recite the three hundred poems would not do a person any good if this person, when given a political assignment, is unable to apply his knowledge to the task at hand. But what is Boyu meant to learn from the *Zhounan* and the *Shaonan*, which are the initial two sections of the first block of the *Book of Poetry* called "Airs of States"? Liu Baonan explains that "since the *guanju* [the first of the *Zhounan* poems] celebrated the courtship of a prince for his fair maiden," Confucius must have wanted his son to learn something about the proper relationship between a man and a woman, a husband and his wife, which is the most fundamental of all human relationships. Liu Baonan may be right, but Confucius may also have favored these poems because he thought that they were the most beautiful and the most morally sound and because they were associated with the Duke of Zhou and the Duke of Shao, the two counselors from the early Zhou he admired above all other historical figures.

17.11 The Master said, "When we say 'the rites, the rites,' can we be talking just about jade and silk? When we say 'music, music,' can we be talking just about bells and drums?"

Most scholars agree that there are two ways of understanding Confucius' remark here. Confucius could be saying this: Gifts of jade and silk and instruments of bells and drum are objects that are meant to bring to life the spirit of the rites or the spirit of music; but whether or not the outcome has integrity has nothing to do with the objects themselves—it depends solely on the person who carries out the rite. Such a reading could find support in 3.3. Or, as the Han scholars suggest, Confucius could be making an observation about the political ramifications of rites and music—that what is cherished in rites and music is not any of the objects used to implement the process but the order and the transformative influence they can bring to society.

17.12 The Master said, "To assume a dignified exterior with only a soft pith for an interior—that kind of person, to take an analogy from the riffraff [of the world], is like a thief that makes his way into a house by boring a hole through the wall."

The type of person Confucius berates here is someone who carries himself like a gentleman but has the heart of a thief. What this man steals is the fine exterior of a true gentleman, but he is a fake because he has "only a soft pith for an interior." This theme appears again in 17.13, 17.17, and 17.18, and what is interesting is that Confucius characterizes such an act as a form of stealing. And when a person steals the reputation of the good and of the virtuous, he brings ruin to the idea of the good and the virtuous—this is the reason Confucius despises such men.

17.13 The Master said, "The village goody man is a thief [and the ruin] of virtue."

Most scholars agree that the most insightful commentary comes from Mencius. It is embedded in a conversation between him and his disciple Wan Zhang. Mencius says:

> [The village goody man says,] "What is the point of having noble ideals? Words and deeds take no notice of each other anyway. . . . So why keep saying 'the ancients, the ancients'? And why must you walk alone? You are born into this world, so try to be a part of it. And you will do fine if you seem friendly to everyone." Thus he fawns on the world with flattery. Such is the village goody man [*xiangyuan* 鄉愿]. . . . [Confucius thought that this man was the ruin of virtue] because if you want to censure him, you cannot find any evidence of his wrongdoing, and if you want to attack him, you cannot find a clear target. He is in tune with the prevalent custom and blends with the sordid world. When in a state of repose, he appears to be conscientious and trustworthy. When actively engaged with the world, he appears to be principled and immaculate. People are all pleased with him, and he thinks he is in the right.

According to Mencius, Confucius had said, "Of those who passed by my gate without entering my house, the only ones that caused me no regret were the village goody men."

17.14 The Master said, "To hear something on the road and then right away to launch into a disquisition—this is to forsake virtue."

Here Confucius is berating the "talking heads" of his time—men who have a theory about, and an angle on, everything, even things they have just heard. What they say, therefore, has no integrity, and as he sees it, they have forsaken virtue. Xunzi describes such men as those who allow themselves no time for learning and reflection and no time to ask questions about what they do not understand. "Whatever enters their ears comes out of their mouths," which is the opposite of what a gentleman does, he writes. "A gentleman would keep quiet when he has doubt, and he would not form any viewpoint before he asked all the questions [he needed to ask]."

Some scholars believe that the object of Confucius' disparagement is the gossip-monger: he hears something on the road and passes it on to others right away. This, one can say, is also an act of forsaking virtue.

17.15 The Master said, "Is it really possible to work side by side with a petty fellow when serving one's lord? Before he gets what he wants, he is already worried about not being able to get it. After he has gotten it, he worries about losing it. And when he worries about losing it, there is nothing he won't do [to try to hold on to it]."

According to Liu Baonan, what a "petty fellow" wants to get is "an official position with a salary." And because this man's worry is about securing a spot and keeping it his, "he is too cowardly to speak candidly to his lord and to give him honest advice." In the *Analects*, entries 17.12, 17.13, and 17.15 all describe aspects of this "petty fellow." The *Book of Rites* also makes this observation: The gentleman and the petty fellow are alike in that they both worry about losing what they have gained, but while the petty fellow is afraid of losing his position, the gentleman is afraid of losing his grip on the responsibilities his position demands.

17.16 The Master said, "People in ancient times had three kinds of shortcomings, but even these [, I regret to say,] seem to have disappeared today. In ancient times, those who were wild dared [to act and speak their mind]. Today, those who are wild are simply out of control. In ancient times, those who were self-regarding had principles. Today, those who are self-regarding are contentious and bad-tempered. In ancient times, those who were stupid were at least straightforward. Today, those who are stupid are deceitful."

Confucius' point is that if a person is born with a flawed streak, he should turn it into a strength. If he is wild, this should give him the courage to pursue his purpose and speak his mind. If he is self-regarding, he should be a man of principle. If he is not smart, he should be respected for his honesty and candor. But as Confucius notes with regret, the people of his time simply threw away the positive potential of their flaws and let themselves slide into hopeless depravity.

17.17 The Master said, "A man of clever words and of a pleasing countenance is bound to be short on humaneness."

Since this is identical to 1.3, one can refer to the commentary there.

17.18 The Master said, "I hate the thought of purple assuming the place of vermillion. I hate the thought of the tunes of Zheng bringing confusion to classical music. I hate the thought of clever talkers overturning states and families."

This again is a restatement of Confucius' feelings toward anything or anyone—the color purple, the tunes of Zheng, or a clever talker—that has only the semblance of the genuine article. Entries 15.11, 15.27, 17.12, 17.13, 17.14, and 17.17 all try to address his problem with either Zheng tunes or glib men. But why did Confucius dislike the color purple? According to the Warring States sources, around the middle of the Spring and Autumn period, beginning with the lord protector Duke Huan of Qi, rulers of the regional states preferred to wear purple rather than vermillion, which was the official color of ceremonial robes in the Zhou court. The reason for Confucius' aversion to purple is twofold: it is a mixed color (and so not authentic like vermillion), and it is proof of how easy it was for a strongman like Duke Huan to alter a tradition that was the prerogative of the Zhou king.

17.19 The Master said, "I wish not to speak anymore." Zigong said, "If you do not speak, what will there be for your disciples to transmit?"

The Master said, "What does Heaven ever say? Yet the four seasons move in order, and the hundred things come to life. What does Heaven ever say?"

Among Confucius' earlier followers, Xunzi was the one who wrote most elegantly about Heaven and its awesome power and about men who modeled themselves after Heaven. Obviously Confucius was a precursor, but Xunzi must have also learned from the *Laozi*. In "A Discussion on Heaven" he says, "The ranks of stars move in progression, the sun and moon shine in turn, the four seasons succeed each other in good order, the yin and yang go through their great transformations, and the wind and rain bestow their broad influence. All things obtain what is congenial to them and come to life, receive what is nourishing to them and grow to completion. One does not see [Heaven's] working but sees only the results. Thus it is called godlike." And a man who perfects his virtue, Xunzi writes in "Nothing Indecorous," is also godlike: "Though silent, others understand him; though he bestows no favor, others gravitate toward him; though he is not angry, he possesses an awe-inspiring dignity." But how does such a person instruct others if he says nothing? This was Zigong's question. "He lets his own character and his own conduct be the measure," Liu Baonan explains. "Like the movement of Heaven's way, you will be able to know it when you see it."

17.20 Ru Bei let Confucius know that he would like to see him. Confucius declined on the grounds that he was ill. But as soon as the man carrying the message went out the door, he took up his zither and began to sing, making sure that this man heard him.

It is common in China as elsewhere to use illness as an excuse to decline an invitation to a meeting. But here Confucius wants the messenger to know that he is really not ill and that there is a reason for his not wanting to meet with the messenger's lord, Ru Bei. But just what is that reason? We cannot know, since there is no reliable source about this man except that he was a native of Lu.

17.21 Zai Wo asked about the three-year mourning period, saying, "A year is already too long. If a gentleman neglects the [nonmourning] rites for three years, those rites will be in ruins. If he does not allow himself to perform music, it will be the undoing of music. [In the course of a year,] as the old grain has been used up, new grain has ripened for harvest, and four types of timber have been drilled in turn to rekindle fire. A year of mourning is quite enough."

The Master said, "And would you be able to eat rice and wear brocade and feel comfortable doing it?"

"I would."

"If you feel comfortable doing it, then go ahead. But the gentleman in mourning finds no relish in tasty food, no pleasure in music, and no ease even in his own home. So he does not eat rice and wear brocade. But if you feel comfortable doing it, then go ahead!"

After Zai Wo had left, the Master [turned to others and] said, "Yu [Zai Wo] lacks humaneness! A child does not leave his parents' arms until he is three. The three-year mourning is the practice observed by all in the world. Did Yu [Zai Wo] not also have three years of love and affection from his parents?"

I wrote in *The Authentic Confucius*: "The *Analects* rarely records what happens after a conversation is over. Rarer still is the above scenario, where the reader is allowed to hear what Confucius said in the absence of his principal interlocutor, Zai Wo. This heightens the tension, which was already apparent when Zai Wo was present." And the source of this tension has to do with the question of whether or not one would feel comfortable doing this or that during a period of mourning. When asked whether he would feel comfortable "eating rice and wearing brocade" after observing only one year of mourning, Zai Wo replies that he would. To this, Confucius says, "Then go ahead." But privately he tells the others that Zai Wo is lacking in humaneness (*buren*). This may seem unreasonably critical, but then humaneness, in Confucius' view, has its grounding in the relationship one has with one's parents, and it is for this reason that Confucius stresses the importance of proper mourning after the parents die. He believed that the mourning should take the person to the beginning of that bond—to his first three years, when he was holding on to his parents for dear life. But the three-year mourning is not just a repayment of parental love. It allows the child time for reflection and for planning what is needed because he is entering the next stage of his life. Zengzi reports in 19.17, "I have heard the Master say that [on no occasion] does a person give his utmost. If there must be one exception, it would be mourning the death of a parent." But Zai Wo also offered valid reasons against prolonging the mourning beyond one year. He said that rites and music would suffer as a consequence and that since nature, whether in the form of grain or of fire, takes only a year to renew itself, so should human life. Confucius, however, was not convinced. For him, there could be no logical argument against a practice that was meant to assuage a loss so large and so deep as the death of one's parents.

17.22 The Master said, "To spend the whole day stuffing yourself and not to put your mind to use at all—this is hopeless behavior. Are there not such games as *bo* and *yi*? It would be better to play these games [than to do nothing at all]."

This is Confucius' diatribe against loafers and idlers. Why not take up board games like *bo* and *yi*? he says. At least they can keep the mind in use, which is better than letting it go to waste. *Bo* is *liubo*, which, scholars believe, is an early version of chess or of a game based on chance called *shuanglu*. *Yi* is *weiqi* (in Japanese, *go*), a game played with black and white pieces on a board of 289 squares in early China, 361 squares nowadays.

17.23 Zilu asked, "Does the gentleman [*junzi*] think highly of courage?"

The Master said, "The gentleman [*junzi*] puts rightness at the top. If a man of high status [*junzi*] has courage but not a sense of rightness, he will create political upheaval. If a lowly man has courage but not a sense of rightness, he will turn to banditry."

Qian Mu, in his commentary, calls attention to the double meaning of *junzi* in Confucius' remark. When Confucius first speaks about the *junzi*, Qian observes, he is referring to a man of moral cultivation, but in his second statement, he has in mind someone with an elevated social status. Liu Baonan, in his commentary, draws on the *Book of Rites* and the *Xunzi* to explain Confucius' response to Zilu.

The *Book of Rites* says, "If a man who is strong and brave wins his battles through conflicts, not through the force of his moral principle and ritual propriety, he is a troublemaker." Xunzi describes the kind of courage that is "on the side of what is right and just and will not be swayed by circumstances" as "the courage of a gentleman," and the kind of courage that is most evident in a fight for personal advantage and material gain, "where yielding is out of the question," as "the courage of a bandit."

17.24 Zigong asked, "Does the gentleman have his dislikes?"

The Master said, "He does have his dislikes. He dislikes those who call attention to the negative traits of others. He dislikes those who slander their superiors from an inferior position. He dislikes those who have courage but not ritual propriety and those who are resolute but have minds that block all light [*zhi*]."

The Master then added, "Si [Zigong], do you have your dislikes?"

"I dislike those who appropriate other people's ideas as their own [*yao*] and then think of themselves as smart. I dislike those who take impertinence as courage. I dislike those who believe that exposing other people's dark secrets [*jie*] is being forthright."

This conversation almost needs no comment. What Confucius and Zigong each say discloses a side of human nature that is relevant to all ages but perhaps even more so in our times. Traditional commentaries, especially those collected by Liu Baonan, helped me unpack the meaning of *zhi*, *yao*, and *jie*, words that seem to have stories of their own to tell.

17.25 The Master said, "Women and servants [*xiaoren*] are the most difficult to look after. They become insolent if you get too close to them. They complain if you keep your distance."

This is the comment that got Confucius into serious trouble with women in the twentieth century. Many called him a misogynist, but then, without a context, it is difficult to know whether this remark accurately reflects his attitude toward women. Confucius, of course, was wary of the power of women both at home and in the ruler's court, but then he would be watchful of anyone—woman or man, concubine or courtier—who, by the circumstances of her position, found that in order to have any influence in her world, she would have to resort to charm and wiles in small or large quantities. It is also possible to understand what he says here as simply a statement about what it was like to be at close quarters with the women (wives and concubines) and *xiaoren* (servants or lowly men).

17.26 The Master said, "If a man, by the age of forty, is still being disliked by others, that perception will remain until the end of his life."

Confucius expresses a similar sentiment in 9.23, but there he says, "If a man is forty or fifty and has not done anything to distinguish himself, then he is not worthy of our respect." So while he suggests in both statements that by the time a man is forty his character is formed and so it is nearly impossible for him to change, here he stresses other people's perception of such a man—that they will not alter their view of him and start liking him. This led the Qing scholar Yu Yue to conclude that Confucius could be speaking about himself.

BOOK EIGHTEEN

Book Eighteen stands out because, unlike other chapters in the *Analects*, which are characterized by their lack of organization, it follows a tight structure and sticks to its subject. The first entry introduces the subject, and it mentions three names—all of them names of virtuous men living toward the end of the Shang dynasty. These men's fate, which foreshadowed Confucius' own, signaled the futility of moral persuasion in the political world. And should that world become too dangerous to live in, their stories also suggested a few ways out. One could run away or feign madness, two options Confucius must have considered before rejecting them in the end. These strategies never went out of date in China's long history, but in the second half of the twentieth century the tactics and technologies of repression became so sophisticated that they closed nearly all the escape routes, thus rendering the way of the recluse and the way of the madman obsolete.

18.1 The Viscount of Wei left him. The Viscount of Ji became his slave. Bi Gan remonstrated with him and, because of it, was put to death. Confucius said, "The Shang had these three humane men."

The point of reference here is King Zhou, the last ruler of the Shang dynasty. The Viscount of Wei was his older brother; the Viscount of Ji and and Bi Gan were his uncles. Wei and Ji were the states that the first two men were enfeoffed in. The Viscount of Wei and the Viscount of Ji should have been at home, looking after the affairs of their states, but the behavior of their relative, King Zhou, had become so out of control that they felt they had to come to the royal court and see what they could do to bring some relief to the situation. This is the story one finds in the early histories. But just how did the events unfold? Which of the three was the first to act and which was the last? And what was Confucius' judgment of the three? He called them "humane men," but did he rate their humaneness as best, next best, and third? These are the questions that interested the traditional scholars. Sima Qian in his *History of the Grand Historian* offers two versions of how the narrative developed. In the first version, we are told that the Viscount of Wei, having witnessed for himself that his younger brother was beyond reform, "left him." This departure was followed by Bi Gan's more direct, and more daring, attempt to reprimand King Zhou, for which it was ordered that Bi Gan be cut open so that the king could "examine the heart of a sage." But this was not the kind of conclusion the Viscount of Ji wanted for his life, and so he "feigned madness and let himself be enslaved to the king." In the second version, we are told that the Viscount of Wei left the royal court after he saw what had happened to the Viscount of Ji and Bi Gan. According to Sima Qian, this man kept himself alive because he could not bear the thought of letting the sacrifices to the royal ancestors of the Shang come to an end.

And what about Confucius' judgment of the three? Confucius himself did not say who best embodied the idea of humaneness, but some scholars say that he would have put the Viscount of Wei first, followed by the Viscount of Ji and then Bi Gan. The Han scholar Xu Gan writes:

In the Yin [Shang] dynasty there were three men who realized humaneness. The virtue of the viscount of Wei was firmer than rock and he acted promptly. Although confronted by adversity, the viscount of Ji was able to keep his aims squarely on course. Bi Gan remonstrated and had his heart cut out. The gentleman [Confucius] considered the viscount of Wei's behavior as most exemplary, followed by that of the viscount of Ji, and Bi Gan's being the least so. Hence in the *Spring and Autumn Annals*, all those counselors who were killed for remonstrating with their rulers are criticized for not using their wisdom to escape death.

Xu Gan is probably right about how Confucius would have ranked these three men. For, in his teachings, Confucius emphasizes how to live or, in the words of the Qing Confucian Jiao Xun, "how to make the right choices about life and death." And to sacrifice one's life in order "to have humaneness fulfilled" would have been a person's last option, chosen only when keeping himself alive would come at the expense of humaneness. This is Confucius' point in 15.9.

18.2 Liuxia Hui was an official of criminal justice. He was dismissed three times. Others said to him, "Isn't it about time for you to leave for another state?" Liuxia Hui said, "If I serve another in an upright way, where can I go and not end up being dismissed three times? If I serve another by bending the way, what need is there for me to leave the state of my parents?"

Liuxia Hui offers another option for men who possessed a strong sense of moral and political responsibility. Remain in office, he tells them, and do not feel humiliated if you are pushed aside or dismissed. Mencius describes Liuxia Hui in this way:

> Liuxia Hui was not ashamed of a prince with a tarnished reputation, neither was he disdainful of a modest post. When in office he did not conceal his worthiness and always acted in accordance with the Way. When he was passed over, he harbored no grudge, nor was he distressed in straitened circumstances. That is why he said, 'you are you and I am I. Even if you were stark naked by my side, how could you defile me?' . . . Thus he felt it would be beneath his dignity to leave.

In Mencius' opinion, "Liuxia Hui lacked respect." Confucius, however, is more generous toward him, if we assume that he is the speaker in 18.2.

18.3 Duke Jing of Qi was considering how to treat Confucius, and he said, "I am unable to treat him the way the head of the Jisun family is treated [in Lu]. I will treat him as if his position is somewhere between the head of the Jisuns and the head of the Mengsuns." Later he told others privately, "I am too old. I will not able to use him in my government." Confucius left Qi [after he heard about this].

It makes sense that this entry should follow 18.1 and 18.2. In 18.1, it is said that "the Viscount of Wei left" the royal court of Shang. In 18.2, we learn that Liuxia Hui would not leave even after he was dismissed three times, because, he said, no matter where he went, his career would follow the same pattern if he insisted on serving a ruler "in an upright way." But here in 18.3, we are told that "Confucius left" the state of Qi because he realized that Duke Jing of Qi simply had no intention of employing him. (Duke Jing's insincerity was patent. Anyone could have seen it, for who could have believed that he might offer a professional-for-hire, a man of Confucius' status, a position equal in power and pay to that of the head of a hereditary family of Lu?) As for Confucius' visit to Qi and the background of this meeting, see my commentary on 12.11.

18.4 The men of Qi made a present of singing and dancing girls. Ji Huanzi accepted the girls [on behalf of Duke Ding], and court was not held for the next three days. Confucius left Lu.

I discussed at length in *The Authentic Confucius* the reason Confucius left Lu. He had weathered crises much more serious than what is described here, where the ruler and his chief counselor took a three-day break from their routine duties to enjoy the company of these singing and dancing girls. So why did Confucius leave? Mencius thinks that Confucius' departure had to do with not being given a portion of the sacrificial meat after he had participated in an official sacrifice. Mencius says, "Those who did not understand him thought that Confucius was begrudging not getting a share of the meat. But those who understood him knew that he had to go because [the ruling elite of] Lu had acted contrary to the rites." The Han historian Sima Qian puts the two accounts together and offers his own version: The ruler and his chief counselor came under the spell of the girls first; Confucius was disappointed but was willing to give them another chance, and when he was not offered a portion of the sacrificial meat, he thought that it was time for him to go. I, however, am not persuaded by these arguments. I feel that there was a more pressing reason for him to leave, and for that we have to return to the events of 498 BC, the year before Confucius' departure. In 17.5, we learn that Confucius for a while was tempted to use the muscle of the family retainers to get rid of the hereditary families. By 498, he seems to have given up the idea. Instead, he and his disciple Zilu were trying to persuade the hereditary families to destroy their own strongholds and start anew. But the retainers rebelled anyway. They took their arms to the streets of the capital of Lu, and Confucius, as the minister of crime, managed to beat the insurgents back with his band of men. His effort, however, went unsung because the hereditary families had suspected all along that Confucius, whenever he had a chance, would always try to work against them, since he wanted nothing more than to see that the political authority be returned to the legitimate ruler of Lu, who at that time was Duke Ding. Thus when he was not offered a piece of the sacrificial meat, it was, to use our vernacular, a vote of no confidence. He knew that Ji Huanzi, the head of the Jisuns and de facto ruler of Lu, was signaling him to leave. And as for the singing and dancing girls of Qi, the scandal they caused could have given Confucius further reason to pack up and go.

18.5 As Jie Yu, the Madman of Chu, went past Confucius' carriage, he sang:

> "Phoenix, phoenix,
> How your virtue has declined!
> What has gone by cannot be made right.
> What is to come still can be pursued.
> Leave off, leave off,
> Dangerous are those in office today."

Confucius got down from his carriage, hoping to have a word with the madman, but Jie Yu scampered away, to avoid him. Thus Confucius did not have a chance to speak to him.

I wrote in *The Authentic Confucius*, "In this song, Confucius is the phoenix—not a phoenix in full splendor but one whose power 'has declined'—from years of travel, perhaps, and the lonely chase of things good and noble. The madman tells Confucius, 'Leave off, leave off,' for one cannot correct the mistakes in the past nor anticipate new ones in the future. He warns also of the perils of politics: 'Dangerous are those in office today.'" To which I would add that the madman asks Confucius to consider his path, his way of life, for we hear him sing, "What is to come still can be pursued."

Another version of this meeting is found the *Book of Zhuangzi*. In it the madman reveals more of his enigmatic self and draws a sharper distinction between himself and Confucius. He says to the latter, "Phoenix, phoenix, how your virtue has declined! . . . In times like the present, it is already hard work just to avoid punishment. . . . Enough, enough, this looking after people with the force of your integrity. / Dangerous, dangerous, this picking your path and then setting off. / Bramble, bramble, don't spoil my walk. / I walk a crooked path—don't hurt my feet." Here, in Jie Yu's view, "Confucius was phoenix and bramble: supremely noble and a menace," as I wrote in my previous study. "He chose too carefully and pushed too far, in a time when it was 'already hard work just to avoid punishment.' And Confucius? What did he think of Jie Yu? He knew, of course, that Jie Yu was not raving mad, just so spirited that he could not walk a straight line. He knew also that Jie Yu had something to offer: a way out of his despair and a way out of the dangers humans created in a human world." The desire to go with him was strong, but Confucius resisted it, as he did with all the other temptations like this.

18.6 Chang Ju and Jie Ni were yoked together as they plowed the field. [Confucius went past them.] He then sent Zilu to find out where the ford might be.

Chang Ju asked, "Who is that man driving the carriage?"

Zilu replied, "It's Kong Qiu [Confucius]."

"Is it Kong Qiu of Lu?"

"Yes.'

"Then he knows where the ford is."

Zilu then tried [the other man,] Jie Ni.

Jie Ni asked, "Who are you?"

"Zhong You [Zilu]."

"Then you must be a disciple of Kong Qiu of Lu."

"I am."

"[Look at the water,] it keeps on moving forward. Everywhere in the world is the same. So why bother to seek another [ruler] when you have given up this one? Why change? Moreover, why do you want to follow someone who keeps running away from men [who turned out to be the wrong ones to serve]? Why not follow those who have run away from the world altogether?" He then went back to planting his seeds, burying them one by one without stopping.

Zilu went to tell Confucius what these two men had said. Confucius seemed lost in thought for a while. Then he spoke: "We cannot flock with birds and beasts, can we? Whom can I be with if not with other human beings? The world has a moral way, [I know,] so I will not change places with those two."

The Song scholar Jin Lüxiang thought that Chang Ju and Jie Ni could not be these men's birth names. "Chang Ju" means "the tall and lean one from the wetland," and "Jie Ni" means "the tall and well-built one with his feet covered in mud." These are, therefore, nicknames or descriptive names like *hekui*, "the man carrying a bamboo basket," in 14.39. And since these men lived near the water, as their names suggest, it seems reasonable for Confucius to send Zilu to ask them "where the ford might be." Chang Ju's response could be meant to say that if it is Confucius, the Confucius of Lu, who asks this question, then he should already know where the ford is, because he had been wandering around this part of the country for so long. Jie Ni, his companion in the field, is not any more helpful, but he makes a strong argument for giving up the world as most men find it. That world is shaped by the state, and no matter where you may be in that world, he says, you will find the same kind of ruler. And, as in the examples in 18.1 and 18.2, if you serve such a ruler honestly, you will be dismissed or, worse, have your body torn apart and your heart cut out. So, Jie Ni says to Zilu, why bother "to seek another when you have given up this one?" And why bother following a man who has done this repeatedly and found nothing but disappointment—why not join us, "who have run away from the world altogether"? This is one of the earliest calls of an agrarian partisan against the state, and it is the voice of a contentious man, not a simple farmer but someone who knows his opponent and has once lived at the other side of the divide. And Confucius' response—"We cannot flock with birds and beasts, can we?"—is equally emotional. Confucius accepts the human world and the existence of the state, and no matter how dejected he may feel, he believes that a moral way can be found in the murkiness of the situation.

18.7 While accompanying Confucius on the journey, Zilu happened to fall behind. He met an old man carrying a bamboo basket suspended from his staff. Zilu asked, "Have you seen my master?"

The old man said, "You look like someone who hasn't labored with his four limbs and cannot tell the difference between this kind of grain and that. Just who could be your master?" He then planted his staff on the ground and started weeding.

Zilu stood, cupping one hand in the other, showing his respect.

The old man stopped Zilu [from continuing his travels] and invited him home to spend the night. He killed a chicken and cooked millet for his guest to eat, and he introduced him to his two sons.

The next day, Zilu resumed his journey, [and when he caught up with Confucius,] he told him what had happened. Confucius said, "[The old man] must be a recluse." He then sent Zilu back to find him. When Zilu got there, the old man had already left for somewhere else. Zilu thereupon remarked, "There is no way of acquiring a sense of what is right if one does not enter public life. If a person knows not to abandon the measures of propriety between old and young, why, then, does he let go the moral responsibility between ruler and subject? By keeping himself unsullied, he has helped to bring chaos to an important human relationship. A gentleman takes office in order to understand the rightness in that relationship. As for putting the moral way into practice, he knows all along that it is not possible."

Here Zilu takes a clear stance regarding the human world—that it is here to stay—and he says that the political relationships in that world are as important as the relationships in a family and the relationship between friends; in fact, they put more demands on us, forcing us to work even harder to do the right thing. Thus to stay away from them—because we want to keep ourselves clean—is not only a sign of moral weakness, but, more important, it is something that will help to throw these relationships into disorder when they have already become an irrevocable part of our existence. And Zilu makes another point, which is more of a revelation than a pronouncement. He says that the gentleman plunges into the messy world of public service and the uncertain life of an official not because he feels that he is able to put "the moral way into practice." "He knows all along that it is not possible," Zilu tells us; rather, the gentleman does this "in order to understand the rightness" in those relationships. Most scholars believe that Zilu was simply repeating what Confucius had taught him, for he did not possess the subtlety and the moral acumen these words reflect. Still, one is grateful to have him play out the series of events that led to this coda and to have him register the right emotions as the story unfolds.

Confucius in this account, as in 18.5, did not have a chance to talk to the recluse, but the text implies that he was drawn to him and had respect for his way of life even though he made it clear through Zilu that it was not the life for him. And the recluse, like the madman in 18.5, was also cautious about Confucius' bidding, and so he disappeared before the invitation arrived, which could mean that he did not want to come under Confucius' influence and find himself back in the world of men. Some scholars say that the narrative style of 18.7—and also of 18.6—is a least a century ahead of its time, and so the record cannot be authentic. This may be true, but the spirit of the account reflects the spirit of the *Analects* and the Confucius we have come to know.

18.8 Men of integrity who relinquished their rightful positions and became recluses include Bo Yi, Shu Qi, Yu Zhong, Yi Yi, Zhu Zhang, Liuxia Hui, and Shao Lian. The Master said, "Unwilling to lower their aim and bring disgrace upon themselves—that would be Bo Yi and Shu Qi. Liuxia Hui and

Shao Lian were willing to lower their aim and bring disgrace upon themselves, but their words were morally sound and their conduct never wandered from their thought—this much is true. Yu Zhong and Yi Yi lived in reclusion and said whatever they liked; they were immaculate in character, and in giving up the world they acted with expediency. But I am different from all these men. I have no preconceptions about what one can or cannot do."

Since Bo Yi, Shu Qi, and Liuxia Hui had already been discussed in earlier entries and almost nothing was known about Yi Yi, Zhu Yang, and Shao Lian, most of the commentaries have focused on the identity of Yu Zhong. The search narrowed to two men in early history, Tai Bo's brother Yu Zhong, or a later descendent of this Yu Zhong, also named Yu Zhong. Tai Bo was the oldest son of the Zhou chieftain Tai Wang, and uncle of King Wen and granduncle of King Wu. Confucius commended Tai Bo in 8.1 as someone who "may be said to embody the highest virtue" because he "yielded his right to the empire three times" and sought no recognition for his action. And Yu Zhong was the brother who accompanied him to the untamed regions in the east when Tai Bo decided to relinquish his title as the heir to his father's position. These two older brothers wanted their youngest brother to be the next chieftain so that this man's son and grandson would be able to fulfill their potential as founders of a new dynasty. These fragments of Yu Zhong's life seemed to fit the Yu Zhong in Confucius' description: he left his home for somewhere in the wild; his character, if it was at all like Tai Bo's, was irreproachable; and "in giving up the world, he acted with expediency." Some scholars, however, say that Yu Zhong could also be a descendant of the older Yu Zhong. But their argument produces no evidence that bears a direct relationship to Confucius' comments about him. And regarding Zhu Zhang, Wang Bi, the third-century scholar of the *Laozi* and the *Book of Changes*, says that this man was Confucius' disciple Zhonggong. This, however, remains speculative, and since Confucius said nothing about Zhu Zhang, we should perhaps do the same until more evidence comes to light, and the same could be said of Yi Yi. What about Shao Lian? There is a Shao Lian in the *Book of Rites*, who was from the Lu region. Confucius thought that he and his brother "were good at observing the mourning rites," but there is no mention there or in other sources about his leaving the civilized world for the wild.

More important than the identity of these men is Confucius' final statement. One could read it as a companion to his assertion in 9.4 about the four things he stays away from and as a summing-up of what he has been saying all along about himself—in this chapter and throughout the *Analects*—that he does not approach life with preconceived notions and will not let his thought and action be the vehicle of an overarching principle. This meant, of course, that for each step of the way, he would have to look at the world anew and rely on his learning of a lifetime to help him see clearly what he "can or cannot do."

18.9 Zhi, the Grand Musician, left for Qi; Gan, musician for the second course of the banquet, left for Chu; Liao, musician for the third course, left for Cai; Jue, musician for the fourth course, left for Qin; Fang Shu the drummer walked down to the Yellow River; Wu, player of the hand drum, walked down to the River Han; Yang, the Grand Musician's deputy, and Hsiang, who played the stone chimes, walked down to the sea.

Zhi was the Grand Musician at the court of Lu. In 8.15, Confucius says of his performance, "how the superabundant music fills our ears!" From this slip of information, most scholars conclude that it is reasonable to assume that all the musicians on this roster were Confucius' contemporaries. Their exodus, to Confucius' mind, is a further indication of the moral decline of Lu. A few scholars, however, believe that these musicians could have lived in the last years of the Shang dynasty, because it is stated in several early histories that "the blind court musicians, clasping the instruments in their arms, dispersed in all directions. Some sought the patronage of regional rulers; others went to the edge of the sea." But there is a problem with this conjecture, Liu Baonan says, because the regional states some of the musicians fled to, Qi, Chu, Cai, and Qin, were Zhou states, and so could not have existed during the Shang.

18.10 The Duke of Zhou said to the Duke of Lu, "A person in a ruling position does not forget his nearest and dearest. He also does not give his officials occasion for complaint because he has failed to employ their skills [or consider their advice]. He does not abandon old friends and relations unless they have committed serious transgressions. He does not ask for perfection in anyone."

Most scholars think that this was what the Duke of Zhou said to his son, Boqin, before Boqin journeyed to the east to establish a settlement, which, in time, became the state of Lu. I wrote in the *The Authentic Confucius*: "Here, the Duke of Zhou appears to be fully aware of the delicate nature of human relationships. He tells his son to be considerate of those who are 'nearest and dearest' to him and those who work with him in politics; and he asks his son to be mindful of matters of greater importance so as not to let things of lesser importance spoil those relationships that should have constancy." I observed, "The Duke of Zhou offered guidelines but no theory, not here and not in any of his official speeches and proclamations. . . . Yet the words that were attributed to him in the early records could easily add up to a vision of political relationships and social arrangement that, for the sensitive mind, carried a deep moral resonance."

18.11 There were eight learned officials in the Zhou: Boda and Bokuo, Zhongtu and Zhonghu, Shuye and Shuxia, Jisui and Jigua.

According to traditional commentaries, these eight illustrious officials were four sets of twins born to the same woman in early Zhou, either during the reign of King Wu or that of his son King Cheng. The names Bo, Chong, Shu, and Ji indicate the order of their birth, with Bo being the oldest and Ji the youngest. The fact that they all had brilliant careers in government portended good fortune for the young dynasty. At a time when everything that mattered was on the decline, Qian Mu explains, it was natural for people to be nostalgic about those distinguished men from a glorious era in the past. Such is the case here, but no one knows who assembled the list of the four pairs of brothers or how the brothers found their way into the *Analects*.

BOOK NINETEEN

Book Nineteen belongs to the disciples, to those that survived Confucius and had already attracted students to their side. Scholars have noted the absence of Youzi, who, given his strong presence in Book One, was thought of as an early compiler of the *Analects* and who, for a while, had others believing that he could fill the void Confucius had left behind. How, then, do we explain his absence? Is he absent because he did not do enough to cultivate a following of his own? The legalist thinker Hanfeizi says that after Confucius' death his disciples split ten ways, each professing to be their teacher's most accurate interpreter. The tension is evident in this chapter. Confucian scholars, however, see a silver lining in the discordance. They believe that the sparring kept the teachings alive and vigorous.

19.1 Zizhang said, "[I would think that] a man is good enough to join the official ranks if he is ready to lay down his life when faced with danger, is mindful of what is right when he sees a chance for gain, and turns his thoughts to respectfulness during a sacrifice and to sorrow when in mourning."

We are told in 2.18 that "Zizhang was studying with the hope of obtaining an official position." In fact, most of the questions he had for Confucius, even those about keen perception and clouded judgment, can be understood as his attempt to find out what would make a good official. Here he seems to be offering his own assessment of who is qualified "to join the official ranks," but, in Qian Mu's view, Zizhang is merely repeating what Confucius says in 14.12 about how such a man should respond when "faced with danger" and when he "sees [a chance for] profit," and what Confucius says in 3.26 about a man's mental state during a sacrifice and when in mourning.

19.2 Zizhang said, "Holding on to virtue but not making it grand; having trust in the Way but not with full conviction— can we say such a man has gotten it or not?"

Some scholars feel that what Zizhang says here about virtue—that in order to possess it, one must make it grand—is a reflection of himself, of his grand presence and of his preference for a grand presentation of a lofty idea. A fellow disciple, Zengzi, said that Zizhang's presence was so imposing that it was "hard to work side by side with him on the practice of humaneness." This description stuck, especially for scholars who followed Zengzi, of whom there were many. But if this reading is correct—if to make virtue grand is simply to give virtue a grand presence—why then does one need to have complete trust in the moral way? Qian Mu thinks that the two ideas in Zizhang's statement are related: a person's virtue can expand only when he is committed to living a moral life. And in the case of those who hold on to this idea narrowly and unimaginatively, Zizhang asks, Have they gotten it or not?

19.3 Followers of Zixia asked Zizhang about the way of making friends [*jiao*]. Zizhang said, "What did Zixia say?" They responded, "Zixia said, 'Associate with those who are acceptable. Reject those who are not.'"

Zizhang said, "This is not what I have heard. [I have heard that] the gentleman respects the worthy and is charitable to the common lot. He applauds the good and is compassionate toward those who have a hard time trying to be good. If I am a person of great worth, why would I not be charitable to people? If I am not a person of worth, others for sure will reject me, and so how can I reject them?"

Two Han scholars, Bao Xian and Zheng Xuan, understand *jiao* to mean social interactions, and so, they say, when Zixia and Zizhang talk here about *jiao*, Zixia is referring to friendship while Zizhang is referring to "a wide range of relations," from one's relationship to "men of great worth" to one's relationship to "the common lot." Zixia and Zizhang each claimed that he had learned about the correct way in social relations from their teacher, Confucius. They both could be right if we accept the explanation of the Han scholars. For Confucius says in 1.8 and 9.25 that one "should stay close to those who do their best and are trustworthy" and "should not befriend those who are not one's equals," yet he also says in 1.6 that in one's youth one should be taught to "cherish all people" but to "stay close to the most humane." It is also possible to read Zizhang's statement here as an elaboration of what he says in 19.2, because to invite the common lot into the idea of friendship could be seen as an example of making virtue grand. What this implies, of course, is that Zixia's idea of friendship is smaller and narrower, and that Zixia himself is overly scrupulous, which is consistent with how we find him in the *Analects*.

19.4 Zixi said, "There must be a lot to see along the byways, but do not wander off, because you might get bogged down if you have to journey a long way. This is why the gentleman does not take the byways."

"Byways," *xiaodao*, could mean any of these things: heterodox ways, trivial diversions, or training in the technical skills of, say, a farmer, an artisan, a diviner, or a doctor. Zixia does not deny the fact that there are merits in these "byways," but, he says, a gentleman, having set his goal high, will stay on his course because he knows that he cannot afford to be "bogged down" by interests on the side or interests that might take him to the wrong path.

19.5 Zixia said, "To be aware each day of what you still don't know and to remember after a month what you were able to absorb—this is proof of your love for learning."

A person who wants to learn has to be aware of his deficiencies all the time, every day, if he intends to make progress. And to have a real love for learning, he must not forget what he has learned even after a month. In the words of the Ming dynasty scholar Liu Zong-zhou, the proof of one's love for learning is in what he fears, that "he will never learn enough" and that "he will forget what he has learned."

19.6 Zixia said, "Learn broadly and be constant in your effort. [With the knowledge you have gained,] ask questions that are pressing to you, and reflect on things close at hand—humaneness is found in this."

As in 19.5, Zixia emphasizes the importance of embodying the knowledge you have acquired. Make it your own, he says, so that you are able to call upon what you have learned and to reflect on questions that are immediate to you—"humaneness is found in this."

19.7 Zixia said, "Artisans live in their shops in order to master their craft; the gentleman steeps himself in learning in order to perfect the Way."

One could read Zixia's comment here as a restatement of 19.5 and 19.6, that a person must steep himself in learning "in order to perfect the Way" just as artisans need to live in their shop "to master their craft." This remark could also suggest that Zixia was an artisan kind of gentleman—that he rarely left the shop of learning; that he rarely came up for air.

19.8 Zixia said, "When a petty man makes a mistake, it's certain that he will try to gloss it over."

Everyone makes mistakes, even the Duke of Zhou, Mencius observes, but "the gentleman of antiquity would let his mistake be seen by all the people like the eclipse of the moon and the sun," and "when he corrected his mistake, people looked up to him." Men of today are another matter, Mencius says: they not only "persist in their mistakes," but they will "try to explain the mistakes away."

19.9 Zixia said, "The gentleman has three changes of appearance. From a distance, he is respectful and dignified. When you see him more closely, he is gentle and affable. When you listen to his words, [you realize that] he is forceful and perceptive."

The gentleman does not really change, but as we move closer to him, we begin to see the depth and range of his character, which only adds to but does not contradict our first impression of him.

19.10 Zixia said, "The gentleman earns the trust of his people first, before he subjects them to arduous labor. If he does not have their trust, they will think that he is trying to abuse them. He earns the trust [of his ruler] before he remonstrates with him. If he does not have [this man's trust], the ruler will think that he is trying to malign him."

The sixth-century scholar Huang Kan says, "People will have complete trust in a person who insists on conducting himself with integrity, and they will know that the labor and the hardship asked of them are not meant to serve his private interests. But if they do not trust their superior, then they will consider his demands as a form of abuse and as part of his attempt to have them serve his interests." Huang also says, "A person who has not gained the trust of his ruler will not be able to carry out his remonstrance; moreover, when seeing this man in the evening light, one would often find him pressing his hand against his sword." Thus, Huang concludes, "it only goes to show that without the other person's complete trust one should not give remonstrance lightly." The Ming scholar Lin Xiyuan points out that without trust, "people could be intolerant of their superior even when he does not subject them to arduous labor," and without trust, "a ruler could be intolerant of his counselor even when the counselor chooses not to remonstrate with him."

19.11 Zixia said, "Do not overstep the line when it comes to matters that involve important principles of integrity. But allow yourself some leeway in matters that involve minor infringements."

Confucius' judgment of Guan Zhong in 14.16 and 14.17 illustrates Zixia's point here. The counselor Zichan from the state of Zheng is another example. Confucius described him as generous and fair and a skillful administrator, but we know from the history of the Spring and Autumn period that when Zichan first assumed his position as the prime minister of Zheng, he bribed the powerful to keep them happy so that they would be willing to work for him. But there is no uniform view in the early Chinese sources, not even in the Confucian canon, about matters involving major and minor principles. Liu Baonan sees a gradual transformation: the founders of the Zhou, he says, taught that there should be consistency in one's conduct irrespective of the moral weight of a question; a thousand years later, in the Western Han, the Confucian thinker Dong Zhongshu wrote that in certain situations it was all right "to act against constant principles [*jing*] because of expediency [*quan*]"; and between the founders of the Zhou and Dong Zhongshu, there was Confucius, who, speaking through Zixia here, thought that it was important to allow oneself "some leeway," "some coming and going," "in matters that involve minor infringements" of integrity.

19.12 Ziyou said, "Followers of Zixia are capable of such tasks as sprinkling and sweeping, responding to calls and replying to questions, advancing and retiring [when there are guests]. But these are only details. Ask them about the fundamentals, they do not seem to know anything. How can that be?" When Zixia heard this, he said, "Ah, Yan You [Ziyou] is mistaken! As for the way of the gentleman, [how would a teacher know] who is ready to understand it at the beginning [of the lesson] and who [will get frustrated if it is introduced too early and thereby] will lose interest after a while? As with planting grass and trees [in a garden], one has to separate [the students] into different categories. How can one mishandle [the transmission of] the way of the gentleman? Only the sage is able to tackle it [whether he is introduced to the teaching] at the beginning or toward the end."

Some scholars understand the second sentence of Zixia's response to say: "As for the way of the gentleman, how can it be right to introduce [the fundamentals] at the beginning, and then to leave to the end details that one is too tired to teach?" Teaching is the subject in this interpretation, not disciples, as in my translation; yet both readings converge on the same point: human intelligence varies from one person to the next; therefore, if a person wants to transmit "the way of the gentleman" to a whole group of students, why not start with simple skills so that no one will be left behind? This, the scholars agree, is what Zixia tried to tell Ziyou.

Since Confucius considered both Ziyou and Zixia "accomplished in cultural pursuits," Qian Mu says, "how could Ziyou not know that sprinkling and sweeping, responding to calls and replying to questions, advancing and retiring, were part of the early stage of learning? He only feared that Zixia in his teaching might not give enough attention to the fundamentals and let his disciples get bogged down by these simple skills. In the same way, how could Zixia not know that beyond sprinkling and sweeping, responding to calls and replying to questions, advancing and retiring, there were the larger questions of rites and music, which he could not have overlooked?" Ziyou and Zixia may have meant well in their comments, each regarding what he said as a corrective to the other person's way of teaching. This is Qian Mu's view. I, however, feel that there was genuine division between the two. Each also wanted to be regarded as the best instructor in cultural things.

19.13 Zixia said, "A man in office, if he has energy to spare, should pursue learning. A man devoted to learning, if he has energy to spare, should take office."

Zixia's statement here does not apply to Confucius, who, because of his "humble station," had to learn and to acquire "many menial skills" in order to be considered for office. Confucius, therefore, was not someone who took office because he had "energy to spare." He had no choice. He needed a government job in order to make a living. Also, he probably would not have articulated the relationship of learning (*xue*) and taking office (*shi*) in the way that Zixia had, which alluded neither to the tension between the two nor to the reason why learning had to be tested in office.

19.14 Ziyou said, "The mourning ritual should come to a stop when grief is fully expressed."

Mourning is not about giving the deceased a lavish sendoff: rituals should not outdo what is fully expressed through feelings. And feelings, too, should not go beyond the point where they can become harmful to one's physical health and mental well-being.

19.15 Ziyou said, "It is difficult to emulate my friend Zhang [Zizhang]. Still, he has not fully realized humaneness."

19.16 Master Zeng [Zengzi] said, "What a grand presence Zizhang has! I find it hard to practice humaneness side by side with him."

Ziyou does not say in 19.15 just what aspect of Zizhang is "difficult to emulate." It could be his smartness and his mental acuity. But since Zengzi tells us in the next entry that Zizhang has "a grand presence," in fact, so much so that it is "hard to practice humaneness side by side with him," the Qing scholar Jiao Xun thinks that it must have been Zizhang's "grand presence" that was difficult for Ziyou to emulate. If Jiao Xun is right, one might say that it was also because of such a presence, which could seem overpowering, that Zengzi found Zizhang a difficult partner in the practice of humaneness. One could go further and ask whether this was also the reason why Zizhang could not fully realize his humaneness.

19.17 Master Zeng [Zengzi] said, "I have heard the Master say that [on no occasion] does a person give his utmost. If there must be one exception, it would be mourning the death of a parent."

Mencius, being a third-generation disciple of Zengzi, repeated this when he told someone who had just lost his father, "Mourning a parent must be the occasion during which one gives one's utmost." But just what did Zengzi, or rather Confucius, mean by "giving one's utmost" (*zizhi*)? It could mean doing one's best and complying with the rites in burying the parent and in sacrificing to him. Or it could mean giving full expression to one's feelings on such an occasion. The first reflects Mencius' explanation, and the second, that of Zhu Xi and his Song precursors.

19.18 Master Zeng [Zengzi] said, "I have heard the Master say that it is possible to match the filiality exemplified in Meng Zhuangzi in most respects. But as for the fact that he did not discharge the officials who had worked with his father and he did not veer from his father's way of conducting government— that would be hard to match."

Meng Zhuangzi and his father, Meng Xianzi, were members of the Mengsun family. Meng Zhuangzi succeeded Meng Xianzi as a chief counselor in the Lu government in 554 BC after the latter's death, but this was a short stint, for he died four years later. Traditional commentaries suggest that we read this entry together with 1.11, where Confucius says, "If for three years [after your father died] you refrained from altering your father's ways, you can be called filial." But should you inherit his government position, would your father's ways include the officials and the policies he favored? This question complicates the idea of being filial because the son's action in the political world would have serious consequences for the welfare of the state. If the father made mistakes and the son refrains from correcting them, then the son is doing a disservice to the public. But if his father was a capable counselor, then by holding himself back from appointing the men he wants in office and the policies he wants to put in place, the son not only shows filial respect but is also continuing his father's ways for the greater good.

19.19 The Meng family appointed Yang Fu as a legal officer [*shishi*], and he asked Master Zeng [Zengzi] for advice. Master Zeng said, "Those at the top have lost the Way, and people for a long time have been adrift [without any moral guidance]. If you are able to gather the facts and circumstances of their offenses, sorrow and compassion will weigh [in your judgment], but do not gloat about what you are able to achieve."

Yang Fu, according to some sources, was a disciple of Zengzi. After he was appointed a legal officer, a *shishi*, a position with the power to decide whether a criminal should live or die, he went to see his teacher to seek his advice about how to handle his responsibilities. And Zengzi's answer reflects what Confucius taught him about the moral duties of those who are at the top. When a counselor asked him about how to govern, Confucius said, in 12.17, "When you set an example by correcting your mistakes, who will dare not to correct his mistakes?" He told another counselor, in 12.19, "As head of the government, why would you need to kill anyone [to bring about moral order]?" But even Confucius recognized that "only after good men have been in government for a hundred years is there the possibility of winning the war against cruelty and doing away with capital punishment." Here, however, Zengzi is talking about a state where the ruling elite "have lost the Way, and people for a long time have been adrift." And so Zengzi has to confront the question of how to bring criminals to justice. He tells Yang Fu to find out the facts and circumstances (*qing*) of a crime, and once Yang Fu has fuller and more accurate knowledge of what happened, Zengzi believes that he will be more compassionate in his judgment. But he warns at the end against self-congratulation—this, Zengzi feels, will take away whatever empathy a judge may have had toward a criminal whose life is in his hands.

19.20 Zigong said, "Zhou could not have been as immoral as people say he was. Thus the gentleman loathes to find himself in a low and disreputable place, for all that is vile in the world tends to end up there."

King Zhou was the last ruler of the Shang dynasty, a man who, by reputation, was capable of every form of cruelty and moral depravity. And this is Zigong's point: Do not seek a low reputation or all the mean and despicable acts in the world will be lumped together with your name. A fourth-century text, the *Book of Liezi*, says, "All the admiration of the world went to Emperor Shun and Emperor Yu, the Duke of Zhou and Confucius; all the condemnation of the world went to the rulers Jie and Zhou." And of these last two men, the *Liezi* goes on to say, "Truly the reality was not what their reputation deserved."

19.21 Zigong said, "The mistake made by a gentleman is like the eclipse of the moon and the sun. When he errs, all the people can see what he has done, and when he corrects it, they look up to him."

Zigong's remark here, together with Zixia's in 19.8, comes very close to what Mencius says in 2B:9. See my commentary on 19.8.

19.22 Gongsun Chao [a counselor] of Wei asked Zigong, "From whom did Zhongni [Confucius] learn?"

Zigong replied, "The way of King Wen and King Wu has not yet fallen to the ground. It exists in all human beings. The worthy ones have grasped its essential points. The lesser ones have understood its minor attributes. There is no one who does not possess the way of King Wen and King Wu. So from whom did our Master not learn? And how could he have had just one particular teacher?"

The achievements of the Zhou could have disappeared in the dynasty's long history, and a large part of them did, but not her cultural tradition. The way of King Wen and King Wu—the culture they helped to shape—lived on because it had become the daily habits and rituals of ordinary people and it also had gotten a boost and strong reinforcement from men such as Confucius. Confucius makes it quite clear in 9.5 that King Wen's cultural vestiges are invested in him. But according to Zigong, Confucius also knew that every person possessed some of the same cultural vestiges. Thus Confucius learned from everyone, and he had no set idea about who should be his teacher. This was the reason why, Liu Baonan explains, "he asked Laozi about the rites, he had a discussion with Chang Hong about music, he had questions for Master Yan about the bureaucratic offices, and he studied the zither with Master Xiang."

19.23 Shusun Wushu, speaking to the counselors at court, said, "Zigong is worthier than Zhongni [Confucius]." Zifu Jingbo later told Zigong about this.

Zigong said, "Let us use the outer walls as an analogy. My

walls are shoulder high, and so it is possible to peer in [from outside the walls] and see the elegance of the rooms inside the house. The walls of the Master are several *ren* high, and so unless you let yourself in through the gate, you will not be able to see the magnificence of the ancestral temples or the splendor of the official buildings. It is no wonder that the gentleman you mentioned spoke as he did."

Shusun Wushu was a chief counselor in the court of Lu and a member of the hereditary Shusun family. Zifu Jingbo also appeared in 14.36, where he played a similar role. There, he told Confucius that Zilu might be in trouble because someone had spoken "ill of Zilu to the head of the Jisuns." The outer walls of a residence or a compound, Zigong says, could be "shoulder high" or several *ren* high. Later scholars worked out that a *ren* is a measure of either seven or eight feet. Lower walls were meant to enclose the living quarters of ordinary people and of the educated professionals, men like Zigong. Only kings and regional rulers were entitled to have their palaces, their ancestral temples, and their official buildings surrounded by walls that were several *ren* tall.

The important information that can be gleaned from this entry and the next two is how the ruling elite in Lu perceived Confucius immediately after his death and how they went about assessing his worth. And, it seems, these counselors liked to put Zigong on the spot: they stated outright that Zigong was superior to Confucius. These men could have acted out of malice, but they could have actually believed that Zigong was the greater man. And Zigong, I feel, could not have cared about their intentions. He simply wanted to put an end to such talk, and so he used exaggerated words and exaggerated ideas to characterize Confucius and to sharpen the difference between himself and his teacher. It could not have been his plan to elevate Confucius to a position beyond human reach.

19.24 Shusun Wushu spoke disparagingly of Zhongni [Confucius]. Zigong said, "There is no point in doing this. Zhongni is above disparagement. Great men in other people's estimation are like the hills—one can still reach beyond them. Zhongni is like the sun and the moon—he is insurmountable. Even if people wanted to estrange themselves from the sun and the moon, what harm would it do to either? This only goes to show that they have overestimated themselves."

When you disparage someone, you feel that others can surpass him, but this is not the case with Confucius, Zigong says, because he is like the sun and the moon. And, again, as in the case of the sun and the moon, if you alienate yourself from him, he does not cease to shine, and so you are the one who loses when you choose not to take in his radiance.

19.25 Chen Ziqin said to Zigong, "Surely you are being respectful [to your own teacher]. For how can Zhongni [Confucius] be superior to you?"

Zigong replied, "A gentleman can tell whether or not a person has knowledge just from a single remark he has made. Therefore, one cannot be too careful about what one says. The Master cannot be equaled, just as the sky [*tian*] cannot be scaled. Were he to become the head of a state or of a hereditary family, he would be like the man described in the saying 'He only has to help them stand on their own, and they will stand on their own; he only has to steer them [toward the right direction], and they will forge ahead; he only has to set them at ease, and they will gravitate toward him; he only has to mobilize them, and they will work in harmony.' He was honored when he was alive and mourned when he died. How can he be equaled?"

I wrote in *The Authentic Confucius*: "Here it was Zigong who was boastful. Confucius might have been as tall as the firmament, but he could not have made good the magic Zigong said he could in an earthly kingdom like Lu. His record in politics did not support Zigong's claim, and even if he had risen to a position of authority, the world in the last years of the Spring and Autumn had already swung too far from the path for magic—any kind of magic—to work."

BOOK TWENTY

Various scholars, for some time now, have felt that the *Analects* should conclude with Book Nineteen, with Zigong's passionate defense of his teacher. What could be more appropriate than to finish the work in this way, to have Zigong put an end to any suggestion that there might be other men of worth who could prove themselves to be better and more capable than Confucius? Thus, to these scholars, Book Twenty looks like an interloper. The voice in 20.1 and even in 20.2 could not have been that of Confucius, they argue: the ideas and the manner of expression are from a much later period, they say, either that of the late Warring States or that of the early Han. Sources from the received tradition allow their theory some support, but more evidence has been coming to light in last thirty years from the excavated materials of the Warring States period, which, I believe, is able to make this case even stronger. In my commentaries, I have tried to explain how my reading of 20.1 and 20.2 is influenced by what I have learned from these recently discovered bamboo texts.

20.1A Yao said, "Ah, you Shun! The order of succession, by Heaven's calculation, falls on your shoulders. Hold faithfully to the middle [*zhong*] [, to rightness and that perfect balance]. If all within the four seas find themselves in a dire condition, Heaven will withdraw its blessings." Shun instructed Yu with the same command.

Tang said, "I, Lü, the little one, dare to sacrifice a black ox and dare to make this declaration plainly to the most august

Lord [on High]. I dare not pardon those who have committed a crime. I will not hide anything, since we are subjects of our august Lord. The choice rests with our Lord. If I am guilty of a crime, do not let the ten thousand regions be entangled in it [and suffer as a consequence]. If the ten thousand regions are guilty of a crime, I am the one to blame."

The Zhou was greatly rewarded, having had in her service an abundance of good men.

[King Wu] said, "Even though I have my relatives, it is better to employ humane men. If the people transgressed, let the blame rest on me alone."

Scholars from as early as the third century believed that 20.1 stood as a separate chapter in the Ancient Text of the *Analects*, a version of the *Analects* that had disappeared by the end of the Han. What makes this section seem cut off and strangely out of place in the *Analects* is the chronology of kingship we find in the first half plus the idea that Yao's injunction—that Shun should "hold faithfully to the middle"—was passed on from Shun to the founders of the next three dynasties, Xia, Shang, and Zhou. Scholars note that Confucius did not speak about history in long disquisitions and certainly not about kings in this orderly fashion. Names such as Yao, Shun, Yu, Wen, and Wu came up in his conversations with others, and, on the whole, his comments there were spontaneous and to the point. And there is also the question of Yao's command. Those words of Yao do not appear in "The Canon of Yao" of the *Book of Documents*, which is the earliest account we have of the transfer of power from Yao to Shun. And the command itself—"hold . . . to the middle"—was expressed in a way that could not be earlier than the Warring States period, scholars say. One recently excavated text, "Treasured Instructions" (*Baoxun*), from the Tsinghua University collection of Warring States materials, has, I believe, direct bearing on these questions. The work begins with a scene in which King Wen was giving his final instruction to his successor, the future King Wu, as King Wen was lying on his deathbed. And the dying king told his son that when Emperor Shun was "a farmer at the foot of the Li Mountain, he sought to understand the middle [*zhong*]," and that after the emperor "had grasped the middle," he "did not confuse names with reality" and he "became even more vigilant and trustworthy." King Wen also told the future King Wu a second story, about the early ancestors of King Tang, and in it the idea of "the middle" also played a crucial role; and because King Tang inherited the instruction of "the middle," King Wen said, "he was given the great mandate" to become the founder of the Shang dynasty.

But what is "the middle"? Here, my feeling is that what King Tang and King Wu asked from Heaven—that they should take the blame for their people's transgressions—could be one way of understanding the concept of "the middle." And King Wu's remark that it is "better to employ humane men" than his own relatives offers another way of arriving at what is right and fair. And what about the prayer King Tang uttered to the Lord on High? Was he referring to some extreme adversity during his reign? According to one Warring States text, after King Tang completed his conquest of the Xia dynasty, the weather turned cruel—there was a drought—and King Tang said this prayer with the hope that if he put the blame on himself, Heaven might send down rain and relieve the people from their suffering.

20.1B Be careful and precise in setting the standards for weights and measures; give a thorough evaluation of the legal models and regulations; and restore the offices that have been abolished. Revive states that are about to perish and lineages that are about to come to an end. [Locate] men of worth who have gone into hiding, and elevate them to positions of prominence. [In this way,] people in the empire will gravitate toward you. What is important: food for the people, mourning and sacrificial rites.

If you are large-minded, you will win the hearts of the people. If you are trustworthy, people will have confidence in you. If you are quick in response, you will get things done. If you are just, people will be pleased.

Some scholars believe that the speaker in this second half of 20.1 is Confucius. Others feel that it is best not to give these words any attribution since the authenticity of this whole record is in doubt, except for the last passage, which is a repetition of what Confucius tells Zizhang in 17.6, with this slight discrepancy: in 17.6 Confucius stresses the virtue of being generous (*hui*), while here the speaker talks about the virtue of being just (*gong*).

20.2 Zizhang asked Confucius, "What must a man be like before he is able to serve in government?"

The Master said, "Respect the five beautiful traits and shun the four abhorrent ones, and then he is able to serve in government."

Zizhang asked, "What are the five beautiful traits?"

The Master said, "A gentleman is generous but is not wasteful. He works the people hard but does not incur their resentment. He has desires but is not covetous. He has breadth of character but is not arrogant. He is dignified but is not fierce."

Zizhang asked, "What does it mean to be generous but not wasteful?"

The Master said, "Benefit the people by letting them understand how they can best take advantage of their situation—is this not being generous without being wasteful? Push people to work harder on projects they are capable of carrying out—who will be resentful? Desire humaneness and obtain it—how is this covetous? The gentleman dares not be disrespectful whether he is dealing with a few or with many, with people big or small—is this not having breadth of character without being arrogant? The gentleman straightens his robe and cap and takes on a thoughtful gaze, and, seeing his stately presence, people are in awe—is this not being dignified without being fierce?"

Zizhang asked, "What are the four abhorrent traits?"

The Master said, "To execute people without first instructing them—this is cruelty. Not to give people warning and then suddenly expect results—this is tyranny. To be slow in issuing orders and then to be inflexible about the deadline—this is being harmful. Knowing that you have to give something to a person, but in the process of handing it over, behaving parsimoniously—this is like being a petty clerk."

Qian Mu, in his commentary, says that some scholars believe that this entry and 20.1 came from the hands of Zizhang's later followers, who had intended to draw together a collection devoted just to Zizhang's conversations with Confucius about government. And so the volume began with the subject of kingship. But either the work never took off or most of it was lost, and so, by the early Han, these two records found themselves at the end of the three standardized versions of the *Analects*. To support their claim, they point out that though Confucius had much to say about government, he never tried to give a long and prepared speech on the topic, which is the case here. And I would add that, just like the entries from Book Sixteen, the record here is more characteristic of the late Warring States writings, where enumerations and classifications and warnings of dos and don'ts often appear within the discursive text. Examples of this kind of disquisition would include the works of Hanfeizi and essays such as the "Confucius in Retirement" (*Kongzi xianju*) of the *Book of Rites* and the excavated bamboo manuscript "Father and Mother of His People" (*Min zhi fumu*).

20.3 The Master said, "A person will have no way to become a gentleman if he does not understand destiny. He will have no way to find his balance if he does not know the rites. He will have no way to assess people's character if he does not have insight into words."

If we accept the need to have a Book Twenty, this entry is a much better choice than 20.1 or 20.2 to conclude the *Analects*. Qian Mu believes that the record reflects "the essential teachings of Confucius." Does it? We know that Confucius in the *Analects* avoided talking about destiny, *ming*, but here he says that a man will not be able to become a gentleman if he does not understand destiny. And on the question of how to assess someone's character, he says in 2.10, "Observe what a person does. Look into what he has done. Consider where he feels at home. How then can he hide his character? How then can he hide his character?" There, Confucius makes no mention of "having an insight into words [*zhiyan*]" in order to gauge a person's character. In fact, "having an insight into words" was Mencius' strength—he told his disciple Gongsun Chou, "I have insight into words [*zhiyan*] and I am good at cultivating my flood-like *qi*." And destiny, *ming*, was Mencius' final teaching. He says toward the end of the *Book of Mencius*, "Though nothing happens that is not due to destiny, one accepts willingly only what is proper destiny. That is why he who understands destiny does not stand under a wall on the verge of collapse. He who dies after having done his best in following the Way dies according to proper destiny." So Confucius' last remark in this collection could have been a Mencian conclusion to the *Analects*, but followers of Zizhang also managed to stake out a claim in 20.2 as the work drew to a close.

學而第一

【一·一】子曰. 學而時習之. 不亦說乎. 有朋自遠方來. 不亦樂乎. 人不知而不慍.
不亦君子乎.

【一·二】有子曰. 其為人也孝弟而好犯上者. 鮮矣. 不好犯上而好作亂者. 未之有
也. 君子務本. 本立而道生. 孝弟也者. 其為仁之本與.

【一·三】子曰. 巧言令色. 鮮矣仁.

【一·四】曾子曰. 吾日三省吾身. 為人謀而不忠乎. 與朋友交而不信乎.
傳不習乎.

【一·五】子曰. 道千乘之國. 敬事而信. 節用而愛人. 使民以時.

【一·六】子曰. 弟子入則孝. 出則弟. 謹而信. 汎愛眾. 而親仁. 行有餘力.
則以學文.

【一·七】子夏曰. 賢賢易色. 事父母能竭其力. 事君能致其身. 與朋友交. 言而有
信. 雖曰未學. 吾必謂之學矣.

【一·八】子曰. 君子不重則不威. 學則不固. 主忠信. 無友不如己者. 過則勿憚改.

【一·九】曾子曰. 慎終追遠. 民德歸厚矣.

【一·十○】子禽問於子貢曰. 夫子至於是邦也. 必聞其政. 求之與. 抑與之與. 子
貢曰. 夫子溫良恭儉讓以得之. 夫子之求之也. 其諸異乎人之求之與.

【一·十一】子曰. 父在. 觀其志. 父沒. 觀其行. 三年無改於父之道. 可謂孝矣.

【一·十二】有子曰. 禮之用. 和為貴. 先王之道斯為美. 小大由之. 有所不行. 知和
而和. 不以禮節之. 亦不可行也.

【一·十三】有子曰. 信近於義. 言可復也. 恭近於禮. 遠恥辱也. 因不失其親.
亦可宗也.

【一·十四】子曰. 君子食無求飽. 居無求安. 敏於事而慎於言. 就有道而正焉. 可
謂好學也已.

【一·十五】子貢曰. 貧而無諂. 富而無驕. 何如. 子曰. 可也. 未若貧而樂. 富而好
禮者也. 子貢曰. 詩云如切如磋. 如琢如磨. 其斯之謂與. 子曰. 賜也. 始可
與言詩已矣. 告諸往而知來者.

【一·十六】子曰. 不患人之不己知. 患不知人也.

為政第二

【二‧一】子曰. 為政以德. 譬如北辰. 居其所而眾星共之.

【二‧二】子曰. 詩三百. 一言以蔽之. 曰思無邪.

【二‧三】子曰. 道之以政. 齊之以刑. 民免而無恥. 道之以德. 齊之以禮.
　　有恥且格.

【二‧四】子曰. 吾十有五而志于學. 三十而立. 四十而不惑. 五十而知天命. 六十
　　而耳順. 七十而從心所欲不踰矩.

【二‧五】孟懿子問孝. 子曰. 無違. 樊遲御. 子告之曰. 孟孫問孝於我. 我對曰.
　　無違. 樊遲曰. 何謂也. 子曰. 生事之以禮. 死葬之以禮. 祭之以禮.

【二‧六】孟武伯問孝. 子曰. 父母唯其疾之憂.

【二‧七】子游問孝. 子曰. 今之孝者是謂能養. 至於犬馬皆能有養. 不敬.
　　何以別乎.

【二‧八】子夏問孝. 子曰. 色難. 有事. 弟子服其勞. 有酒食. 先生饌.
　　曾是以為孝乎.

【二‧九】子曰. 吾與回言終日. 不違. 如愚. 退而省其私. 亦足以發. 回也不愚.

【二‧十】子曰. 視其所以. 觀其所由. 察其所安. 人焉廋哉. 人焉廋哉.

【二‧十一】子曰. 溫故而知新. 可以為師矣.

【二‧十二】子曰. 君子不器.

【二‧十三】子貢問君子. 子曰. 先行其言. 而後從之.

【二‧十四】子曰. 君子周而不比. 小人比而不周.

【二‧十五】子曰. 學而不思則罔. 思而不學則殆.

【二‧十六】子曰. 攻乎異端. 斯害也已.

【二‧十七】子曰. 由. 誨女知之乎. 知之為知之. 不知為不知. 是知也.

【二‧十八】子張學干祿. 子曰. 多聞闕疑. 慎言其餘. 則寡尤. 多見闕殆. 慎行其
　　餘. 則寡悔. 言寡尤. 行寡悔. 祿在其中矣.

【二‧十九】哀公問曰. 何為則民服. 孔子對曰. 舉直錯諸枉則民服. 舉枉錯諸直
　　則民不服.

【二‧二十】季康子問. 使民敬忠以勸. 如之何. 子曰. 臨之以莊則敬. 孝慈則忠. 舉
　　善而教不能則勸.

【二‧二一】或謂孔子曰. 子奚不為政. 子曰. 書云. 孝乎惟孝. 友於兄弟. 施於有
　　政. 是亦為政. 奚其為為政.

【二‧二二】子曰. 人而無信. 不知其可也. 大車無輗. 小車無軏. 其何以行之哉.

【二‧二三】子張問. 十世可知也. 子曰. 殷因於夏禮. 所損益可知也. 周因於殷禮.
　　所損益可知也. 其或繼周者. 雖百世. 可知也.

【二‧二四】子曰. 非其鬼而祭之. 諂也. 見義不為. 無勇也.

八佾第三

【三・一】孔子謂. 季氏八佾舞於庭. 是可忍也. 孰不可忍也.

【三・二】三家者以雍徹. 子曰. 相維辟公. 天子穆穆. 奚取於三家之堂.

【三・三】子曰. 人而不仁. 如禮何. 人而不仁. 如樂何.

【三・四】林放問禮之本. 子曰. 大哉問. 禮. 與其奢也寧儉. 喪. 與其易也寧戚.

【三・五】子曰. 夷狄之有君. 不如諸夏之亡也.

【三・六】季氏旅於泰山. 子謂冉有曰. 女弗能救與. 對曰. 不能. 子曰. 嗚呼. 曾謂泰山不如林放乎.

【三・七】子曰. 君子無所爭. 必也射乎. 揖讓而升. 下而飲. 其爭也君子.

【三・八】子夏問曰. 巧笑倩兮. 美目盼兮. 素以為絢兮. 何謂也. 子曰. 繪事後素. 曰. 禮後乎. 子曰. 起予者商也. 始可與言詩已矣.

【三・九】子曰. 夏禮. 吾能言之. 杞不足徵也. 殷禮吾能言之. 宋不足徵也. 文獻不足故也. 足則吾能徵之矣.

【三・十】子曰. 禘自既灌而往者. 吾不欲觀之矣.

【三・十一】或問禘之說. 子曰. 不知也. 知其說者之於天下也. 其如示諸斯乎. 指其掌.

【三・十二】祭如在. 祭神如神在. 子曰. 吾不與祭. 如不祭.

【三・十三】王孫賈問曰. 與其媚於奧. 寧媚於竈. 何謂也. 子曰. 不然. 獲罪於天. 無所禱也.

【三・十四】子曰. 周監於二代. 郁郁乎文哉. 吾從周.

【三・十五】子入大廟. 每事問. 或曰. 孰謂鄹人之子知禮乎. 入大廟. 每事問. 子聞之. 曰. 是禮也.

【三・十六】子曰. 射不主皮. 為力不同科. 古之道也.

【三・十七】子貢欲去告朔之餼羊. 子曰. 賜也. 爾愛其羊. 我愛其禮.

【三・十八】子曰. 事君盡禮. 人以為諂也.

【三・十九】定公問. 君使臣. 臣事君. 如之何. 孔子對曰. 君使臣以禮. 臣事君以忠.

【三・二十】子曰. 關雎樂而不淫. 哀而不傷.

【三・二一】哀公問社於宰我. 宰我對曰. 夏后氏以松. 殷人以柏. 周人以栗. 曰. 使民戰栗. 子聞之曰. 成事不說. 遂事不諫. 既往不咎.

【三・二二】子曰. 管仲之器小哉. 或曰. 管仲儉乎. 曰. 管氏有三歸. 官事不攝. 焉得儉. 然則管仲知禮乎. 曰. 邦君樹塞門. 管氏亦樹塞門. 邦君為兩君之好. 有反坫. 管氏亦有反坫. 管氏而知禮. 孰不知禮.

【三・二三】子語魯太師樂. 曰. 樂其可知也. 始作. 翕如也. 從之. 純如也. 皦如也. 繹如也. 以成.

【三・二四】儀封人請見. 曰. 君子之至於斯也. 吾未嘗不得見也. 從者見之. 出. 曰. 二三子何患於喪乎. 天下之無道也久矣. 天將以夫子為木鐸.

【三·二五】子謂韶盡美矣. 又盡善也. 謂武盡美矣. 未盡善也.
【三·二六】子曰. 居上不寬. 為禮不敬. 臨喪不哀. 吾何以觀之哉.

里仁第四

【四·一】子曰. 里仁為美. 擇不處仁. 焉得知.
【四·二】子曰. 不仁者不可以久處約. 不可以長處樂. 仁者安仁. 知者利仁.
【四·三】子曰. 唯仁者能好人. 能惡人.
【四·四】子曰. 苟志於仁矣. 無惡也.
【四·五】子曰. 富與貴. 是人之所欲也. 不以其道得之. 不處也. 貧與賤. 是人之所惡也. 不以其道得之. 不去也. 君子去仁. 惡乎成名. 君子無終食之間違仁. 造次必於是. 顛沛必於是.
【四·六】子曰. 我未見好仁者. 惡不仁者. 好仁者無以尚之. 惡不仁者. 其為仁矣. 不使不仁者加乎其身. 有能一日用其力於仁矣乎. 我未見力不足者. 蓋有之矣. 我未之見也.
【四·七】子曰. 人之過也. 各於其黨. 觀過. 斯知仁矣.
【四·八】子曰. 朝聞道. 夕死可矣.
【四·九】子曰. 士志於道而恥惡衣惡食者. 未足與議也.
【四·十】子曰. 君子之於天下也. 無適也. 無莫也. 義之與比.
【四·十一】子曰. 君子懷德. 小人懷土. 君子懷刑. 小人懷惠.
【四·十二】子曰. 放於利而行. 多怨.
【四·十三】子曰. 能以禮讓為國乎. 何有. 不能以禮讓為國. 如禮何.
【四·十四】子曰. 不患無位. 患所以立. 不患莫己知. 求為可知也.
【四·十五】子曰. 參乎. 吾道一以貫之. 曾子曰. 唯. 子出. 門人問曰. 何謂也. 曾子曰. 夫子之道. 忠恕而已矣.
【四·十六】子曰. 君子喻於義. 小人喻於利.
【四·十七】子曰. 見賢思齊焉. 見不賢而內自省也.
【四·十八】子曰. 事父母幾諫. 見志不從. 又敬不違. 勞而不怨.
【四·十九】子曰. 父母在. 不遠遊. 遊必有方.
【四·二十】子曰. 三年無改於父之道. 可謂孝矣.
【四·二一】子曰. 父母之年不可不知也. 一則以喜. 一則以懼.
【四·二二】子曰. 古者言之不出. 恥躬之不逮也.
【四·二三】子曰. 以約失之者鮮矣.
【四·二四】子曰. 君子欲訥於言而敏於行.
【四·二五】子曰. 德不孤. 必有鄰.
【四·二六】子游曰. 事君數. 斯辱矣. 朋友數. 斯疏矣.

公冶長第五

【五‧一】子謂公冶長. 可妻也. 雖在縲絏之中. 非其罪也. 以其子妻之.

【五‧二】子謂南容. 邦有道. 不廢. 邦無道. 免於刑戮. 以其兄之子妻之.

【五‧三】子謂子賤. 君子哉若人. 魯無君子者. 斯焉取斯.

【五‧四】子貢問曰. 賜也何如. 子曰. 女器也. 曰. 何器也. 曰. 瑚璉也.

【五‧五】或曰. 雍也仁而不佞. 子曰. 焉用佞. 禦人以口給. 屢憎於人.
　　　　不知其仁. 焉用佞.

【五‧六】子使漆雕開仕. 對曰. 吾斯之未能信. 子說.

【五‧七】子曰. 道不行. 乘桴浮于海. 從我者其由與. 子路聞之喜. 子曰. 由也好
　　　　勇過我. 無所取材.

【五‧八】孟武伯問. 子路仁乎. 子曰. 不知也. 又問. 子曰. 由也千乘之國可使治其
　　　　賦也. 不知其仁也. 求也何如. 子曰. 求也千室之邑百乘之家可使為之宰也. 不
　　　　知其仁也. 赤也何如. 子曰. 赤也束帶立於朝. 可使與賓客言也. 不知其仁也.

【五‧九】子謂子貢曰. 女與回也孰愈. 對曰. 賜也何敢望回. 回也聞一以知十. 賜
　　　　也聞一以知二. 子曰. 弗如也. 吾與女弗如也.

【五‧十〇】宰予晝寢. 子曰. 朽木不可雕也. 糞土之牆不可杇也. 於予與何誅. 子曰.
　　　　始吾於人也. 聽其言而信其行. 今吾於人也. 聽其言而觀其行. 於予與改是.

【五‧十一】子曰. 吾未見剛者. 或對曰. 申棖. 子曰. 棖也欲. 焉得剛.

【五‧十二】子貢曰. 我不欲人之加諸我也. 吾亦欲無加諸人. 子曰. 賜也.
　　　　非爾所及也.

【五‧十三】子貢曰. 夫子之文章可得而聞也. 夫子之言性與天道. 不可得而聞也.

【五‧十四】子路有聞. 未之能行. 惟恐有聞.

【五‧十五】子貢問曰. 孔文子何以謂之文也. 子曰. 敏而好學. 不恥下問.
　　　　是以謂之文也.

【五‧十六】子謂子產有君子之道四焉. 其行己也恭. 其事上也敬. 其養民也惠. 其
　　　　使民也義.

【五‧十七】子曰. 晏平仲善與人交. 久而敬之.

【五‧十八】子曰. 臧文仲居蔡. 山節藻梲. 何如其知也.

【五‧十九】子張問曰. 令尹子文三仕為令尹. 無喜色. 三已之. 無慍色. 舊令尹之
　　　　政必以告新令尹. 何如. 子曰. 忠矣. 曰. 仁矣乎. 曰. 未知. 焉得仁. 崔子弑齊
　　　　君. 陳文子有馬十乘. 棄而違之. 至於他邦. 則曰. 猶吾大夫崔子也. 違之.
　　　　之一邦. 則又曰. 猶吾大夫崔子也. 違之. 何如. 子曰. 清矣. 曰. 仁矣乎. 曰.
　　　　未知. 焉得仁.

【五‧二〇】季文子三思而後行. 子聞之. 曰. 再. 斯可矣.

【五‧二一】子曰. 甯武子邦有道則知. 邦無道則愚. 其知可及也. 其愚不可及也.

【五‧二二】子在陳. 曰. 歸與. 歸與. 吾黨之小子狂簡. 斐然成章. 不知所以裁之.

【五‧二三】子曰. 伯夷. 叔齊不念舊惡. 怨是用希.

【五‧二四】子曰. 孰謂微生高直. 或乞醯焉. 乞諸鄰而與之.

【五・二五】子曰. 巧言. 令色. 足恭. 左丘明恥之. 丘亦恥之. 匿怨而友其人. 左丘明恥之. 丘亦恥之.

【五・二六】顏淵. 季路侍. 子曰. 盍各言爾志. 子路曰. 願車馬衣裘. 與朋友共. 敝之而無憾. 顏淵曰. 願無伐善. 無施勞. 子路曰. 願聞子之志. 子曰. 老者安之. 朋友信之. 少者懷之.

【五・二七】子曰. 已矣乎. 吾未見能見其過而内自訟者也.

【五・二八】子曰. 十室之邑. 必有忠信如丘者焉. 不如丘之好學也.

雍也第六

【六・一】子曰. 雍也可使南面.

【六・二】仲弓問子桑伯子. 子曰. 可也簡. 仲弓曰. 居敬而行簡. 以臨其民. 不亦可乎. 居簡而行簡. 無乃大簡乎. 子曰. 雍之言然.

【六・三】哀公問. 弟子孰為好學. 孔子對曰. 有顏回者好學. 不遷怒. 不貳過. 不幸短命死矣. 今也則亡. 未聞好學者也.

【六・四】子華使於齊. 冉子為其母請粟. 子曰. 與之釜. 請益. 曰. 與之庾. 冉子與之粟五秉. 子曰. 赤之適齊也. 乘肥馬. 衣輕裘. 吾聞之也. 君子周急不繼富.

【六・五】原思為之宰. 與之粟九百. 辭. 子曰: "毋! 以與爾鄰里鄉黨乎!"

【六・六】子謂仲弓曰. 犁牛之子騂且角. 雖欲勿用. 山川其舍諸.

【六・七】子曰. 回也其心三月不違仁. 其餘則日月至焉而已矣.

【六・八】季康子問. 仲由可使從政也與. 子曰. 由也果. 於從政乎何有. 曰. 賜也可使從政也與. 曰. 賜也達. 於從政乎何有. 曰. 求也可使從政也與. 曰. 求也藝. 於從政乎何有

【六・九】季氏使閔子騫為費宰. 閔子騫曰. 善為我辭焉. 如有復我者. 則吾必在汶上矣.

【六・十】伯牛有疾. 子問之. 自牖執其手. 曰. 亡之. 命矣. 夫斯人也而有斯疾也. 斯人也而有斯疾也.

【六・十一】子曰. 賢哉回也. 一簞食. 一瓢飲. 在陋巷. 人不堪其憂. 回也不改其樂. 賢哉回也.

【六・十二】冉求曰. 非不說子之道. 力不足也. 子曰. 力不足者中道而廢. 今女畫.

【六・十三】子謂子夏曰. 女為君子儒. 無為小人儒.

【六・十四】子游為武城宰. 子曰. 女得人焉耳乎. 曰. 有澹臺滅明者. 行不由徑. 非公事未嘗至於偃之室也.

【六・十五】子曰. 孟之反不伐. 奔而殿. 將入門. 策其馬. 曰. 非敢後也. 馬不進也.

【六・十六】子曰. 不有祝鮀之佞. 而有宋朝之美. 難乎免於今之世矣.

【六・十七】子曰. 誰能出不由戶. 何莫由斯道也.

【六・十八】子曰. 質勝文則野. 文勝質則史. 文質彬彬. 然後君子.

【六・十九】子曰. 人之生也直. 罔之生也幸而免.

【六·二十】子曰. 知之者不如好之者. 好之者不如樂之者.

【六·二一】子曰. 中人以上可以語上也. 中人以下不可以語上也.

【六·二二】樊遲問知. 子曰. 務民之義. 敬鬼神而遠之. 可謂知矣. 問仁. 曰. 仁者先難而後獲. 可謂仁矣.

【六·二三】子曰. 知者樂水. 仁者樂山. 知者動. 仁者靜. 知者樂. 仁者壽.

【六·二四】子曰. 齊一變至於魯. 魯一變至於道.

【六·二五】子曰. 觚不觚. 觚哉. 觚哉.

【六·二六】宰我問曰. 仁者雖告之曰. 井有仁焉. 其從之也. 子曰. 何為其然也. 君子可逝也. 不可陷也. 可欺也. 不可罔也.

【六·二七】子曰. 君子博學於文. 約之以禮. 亦可以弗畔矣夫.

【六·二八】子見南子. 子路不說. 夫子矢之曰. 予所否者. 天厭之. 天厭之.

【六·二九】子曰. 中庸之為德也. 其至矣乎. 民鮮久矣.

【六·三十】子貢曰. 如有博施於民而能濟眾. 何如. 可謂仁乎. 子曰. 何事於仁. 必也聖乎. 堯舜其猶病諸. 夫仁者己欲立而立人. 己欲達而達人. 能近取譬. 可謂仁之方也已.

述而第七

【七·一】子曰. 述而不作. 信而好古. 竊比於我老彭.

【七·二】子曰. 默而識之. 學而不厭. 誨人不倦. 何有於我哉.

【七·三】子曰. 德之不修. 學之不講. 聞義不能徙. 不善不能改. 是吾憂也.

【七·四】子之燕居. 申申如也. 夭夭如也.

【七·五】子曰. 甚矣吾衰也. 久矣吾不復夢見周公.

【七·六】子曰. 志於道. 據於德. 依於仁. 遊於藝.

【七·七】子曰. 自行束修以上. 吾未嘗無誨焉.

【七·八】子曰. 不憤不啟. 不悱不發. 舉一隅不以三隅反. 則不復也.

【七·九】子食於有喪者之側. 未嘗飽也.

【七·十】子於是日哭. 則不歌.

【七·十一】子謂顏淵曰. 用之則行. 舍之則藏. 惟我與爾有是夫. 子路曰. 子行三軍則誰與. 子曰. 暴虎馮河. 死而不悔者. 吾不與也. 必也臨事而懼. 好謀而成者也.

【七·十二】子曰. 富而可求也. 雖執鞭之士. 吾亦為之. 如不可求. 從吾所好.

【七·十三】子之所慎. 齊. 戰. 疾.

【七·十四】子在齊聞韶. 三月不知肉味. 曰. 不圖為樂之至於斯也.

【七·十五】冉有曰. 夫子為衛君乎. 子貢曰. 諾. 吾將問之. 入曰. 伯夷、叔齊何人也. 曰古之賢人也. 曰. 怨乎. 曰. 求仁而得仁. 又何怨. 出. 曰. 夫子不為也.

【七·十六】子曰. 飯疏食. 飲水. 曲肱而枕之. 樂亦在其中矣. 不義而富且貴. 於我如浮雲.

【七‧十七】子曰．加我數年．五十以學易．可以無大過矣．

【七‧十八】子所雅言．詩．書．執禮．皆雅言也．

【七‧十九】葉公問孔子於子路．子路不對．子曰．女奚不曰．其為人也發憤忘食．樂
以忘憂．不知老之將至云爾．

【七‧二十】子曰．我非生而知之者．好古．敏以求之者也．

【七‧二一】子不語．怪．力．亂．神．

【七‧二二】子曰．三人行．必有我師焉．擇其善者而從之．其不善者而改之．

【七‧二三】子曰．天生德於予．桓魋其如予何．

【七‧二四】子曰．二三子以我為隱乎．吾無隱乎爾．吾無行而不與二三
子者．是丘也．

【七‧二五】子以四教．文．行．忠．信．

【七‧二六】子曰．聖人吾不得而見之矣．得見君子者斯可矣．子曰．善人吾
不得見之矣．得見有恆者斯可矣．亡而為有．虛而為盈．約而為泰．
難乎有恆矣．

【七‧二七】子釣而不綱．弋不射宿．

【七‧二八】子曰．蓋有不知而作之者．我無是也．多聞．擇其善者而從之．多見而
識之．知之次也．

【七‧二九】互鄉難與言．童子見．門人惑．子曰．與其進也．不與其退也．唯何甚．
人潔己以進．與其潔也．不保其往也．

【七‧三十】子曰．仁遠乎哉．我欲仁．斯仁至矣．

【七‧三一】陳司敗問．昭公知禮乎．孔子曰．知禮．孔子退．揖巫馬期而進之．曰．
吾聞君子不黨．君子亦黨乎．君取於吳．為同姓．謂之吳孟子．君而知禮．孰不
知禮．巫馬期以告．子曰．丘也幸．苟有過．人必知之．

【七‧三二】子與人歌而善．必使反之．而後和之．

【七‧三三】子曰．文莫吾猶人也．躬行君子．則吾未之有得．

【七‧三四】子曰．若聖與仁．則吾豈敢．抑為之不厭．誨人不倦．則可謂云爾已矣．
公西華曰．正唯弟子不能學也．

【七‧三五】子疾病．子路請禱．子曰．有諸．子路對曰．有之．誄曰．禱爾於上下神
祇．子曰．丘之禱久矣．

【七‧三六】子曰．奢則不孫．儉則固．與其不孫也．寧固．

【七‧三七】子曰．君子坦蕩蕩．小人長戚戚．

【七‧三八】子溫而厲．威而不猛．恭而安．

泰伯第八

【八‧一】子曰．泰伯其可謂至德也已矣．三以天下讓．民無得而稱焉．

【八‧二】子曰．恭而無禮則勞．慎而無禮則葸．勇而無禮則亂．直而無禮則絞．君子
篤於親．則民興於仁．故舊不遺則民不偷．

【八・三】曾子有疾. 召門弟子. 曰. 啟予足. 啟予手. 詩云. 戰戰兢兢. 如臨深淵. 如履薄冰. 而今而後. 吾知免夫. 小子.

【八・四】曾子有疾. 孟敬子問之. 曾子言曰. 鳥之將死. 其鳴也哀. 人之將死. 其言也善. 君子所貴乎道者三. 動容貌. 斯遠暴慢矣. 正顏色. 斯近信矣. 出辭氣. 斯遠鄙倍矣. 籩豆之事則有司存.

【八・五】曾子曰. 以能問於不能. 以多問於寡. 有若無. 實若虛. 犯而不校. 昔者吾友嘗從事於斯矣.

【八・六】曾子曰. 可以託六尺之孤. 可以寄百里之命. 臨大節而不可奪也. 君子人與. 君子人也.

【八・七】曾子曰. 士不可以不弘毅. 任重而道遠. 仁以為己任. 不亦重乎. 死而後已. 不亦遠乎.

【八・八】子曰. 興於詩. 立於禮. 成於樂.

【八・九】子曰. 民可使由之. 不可使知之.

【八・一〇】子曰. 好勇疾貧. 亂也. 人而不仁. 疾之已甚. 亂也.

【八・十一】子曰. 如有周公之才之美. 使驕且吝. 其餘不足觀也已.

【八・十二】子曰. 三年學. 不至於穀. 不易得也.

【八・十三】子曰. 篤信好學. 守死善道. 危邦不入. 亂邦不居. 天下有道則見. 無道則隱. 邦有道. 貧且賤焉. 恥也. 邦無道. 富且貴焉. 恥也.

【八・十四】子曰. 不在其位. 不謀其政.

【八・十五】子曰. 師摯之始. 關雎之亂. 洋洋乎盈耳哉.

【八・十六】子曰. 狂而不直. 侗而不愿. 悾悾而不信. 吾不知之矣.

【八・十七】子曰. 學如不及. 猶恐失之.

【八・十八】子曰. 巍巍乎舜禹之有天下也. 而不與焉.

【八・十九】子曰. 大哉堯之為君也. 巍巍乎唯天為大. 唯堯則之. 蕩蕩乎民無能名焉. 巍巍乎其有成功也. 煥乎其有文章.

【八・二十】舜有臣五人而天下治. 武王曰. 予有亂臣十人. 孔子曰. 才難. 不其然乎. 唐虞之際. 於斯為盛. 有婦人焉九人而已. 三分天下有其二. 以服事殷. 周之德其可謂至德也已矣.

【八・二一】子曰. 禹. 吾無間然矣. 菲飲食而致孝乎鬼神. 惡衣服而致美乎黻冕. 卑宮室而盡力乎溝洫. 禹. 吾無間然矣.

子罕第九

【九・一】子罕言利與命與仁.

【九・二】達巷黨人曰. 大哉孔子. 博學而無所成名. 子聞之. 謂門弟子曰. 吾何執. 執御乎. 執射乎. 吾執御矣.

【九・三】子曰. 麻冕. 禮也. 今也純. 儉. 吾從眾. 拜下. 禮也. 今拜乎上. 泰也. 雖違眾. 吾從下.

【九・四】子絕四. 毋意. 毋必. 毋固. 毋我.

【九・五】子畏於匡. 曰. 文王既沒. 文不在茲乎. 天之將喪斯文也. 後死者不得與
於斯文也. 天之未喪斯文也. 匡人其如予何.

【九・六】大宰問於子貢曰. 夫子聖者與. 何其多能也. 子貢曰. 固天縱之將聖. 又多
能也. 子聞之. 曰. 大宰知我乎. 吾少也賤. 故多能鄙事. 君子多乎哉. 不多也.

【九・七】牢曰:"子云:'吾不試. 故藝.'"

【九・八】子曰. 吾有知乎哉. 無知也. 有鄙夫問於我. 空空如也. 我叩其兩
端而竭焉.

【九・九】子曰. 鳳鳥不至. 河不出圖. 吾已矣夫.

【九・十】子見齊衰者. 冕衣裳者與瞽者. 見之. 雖少. 必作. 過之必趨.

【九・十一】顏淵喟然歎曰. 仰之彌高. 鑽之彌堅. 瞻之在前. 忽焉在後. 夫子循循然
善誘人. 博我以文. 約我以禮. 欲罷不能. 既竭吾才. 如有所立. 卓爾. 雖欲從
之. 末由也已.

【九・十二】子疾病. 子路使門人為臣. 病間. 曰. 久矣哉由之行詐也. 無臣而為有
臣. 吾誰欺. 欺天乎. 且予與其死於臣之手也. 無寧死於二三子之手乎. 且予縱
不得大葬. 予死於道路乎.

【九・十三】子貢曰. 有美玉於斯. 韞匵而藏諸. 求善賈而沽諸. 子曰. 沽之哉. 沽之
哉. 我待賈者也.

【九・十四】子欲居九夷. 或曰陋. 如之何. 子曰. 君子居之. 何陋之有.

【九・十五】子曰:"吾自衛反魯, 然後樂正, 雅頌各得其所。"

【九・十六】子曰. 出則事公卿. 入則事父兄. 喪事不敢不勉. 不為酒困.
何有於我哉.

【九・十七】子在川上曰. 逝者如斯夫. 不舍晝夜.

【九・十八】子曰. 吾未見好德如好色者也.

【九・十九】子曰. 譬如為山. 未成一簣. 止. 吾止也. 譬如平地. 雖覆一簣.
進. 吾往也.

【九・二○】子曰. 語之而不惰者. 其回也與.

【九・二一】子謂顏淵曰. 惜乎. 吾見其進也, 未見其止也.

【九・二二】子曰. 苗而不秀者有矣夫. 秀而不實者有矣夫.

【九・二三】子曰. 後生可畏. 焉知來者之不如今也. 四十. 五十而無聞焉. 斯亦
不足畏也已.

【九・二四】子曰. 法語之言. 能無從乎. 改之為貴. 巽與之言. 能無說乎. 繹之為
貴. 說而不繹. 從而不改. 吾末如之何也已矣.

【九・二五】子曰. 主忠信. 毋友不如己者. 過則勿憚改.

【九・二六】子曰. 三軍可奪帥也. 匹夫不可奪志也.

【九・二七】子曰. 衣敝縕袍與衣狐貉者立而不恥者. 其由也與. 不忮不求. 何用不
臧. 子路終身誦之. 子曰. 是道也. 何足以臧.

【九・二八】子曰. 歲寒. 然後知松柏之後彫也.

【九・二九】子曰. 知者不惑. 仁者不憂. 勇者不懼.

【九‧三十】子曰．可與共學．未可與適道．可與適道．未可與立．可與立．
　　未可與權．

【九‧三一】唐棣之華．偏其反而．豈不爾思．室是遠而．子曰．未之思也夫．
　　何遠之有．

鄉黨第十

【十‧一】孔子於鄉黨．恂恂如也．似不能言者．其在宗廟朝廷．便便言．唯謹爾．

【十‧二】朝與下大夫言．侃侃如也．與上大夫言．誾誾如也．君在．踧踖如也．
　　與與如也．

【十‧三】君召使擯．色勃如也．足躩如也．揖所與立．左右手．衣前後襜如也．趨
　　進．翼如也．賓退．必復命曰．賓不顧矣．

【十‧四】入公門．鞠躬如也．如不容．立不中門．行不履閾．過位．色勃如也．足躩如
　　也．其言似不足者．攝齊升堂．鞠躬如也．屏氣似不息者．出．降一等．逞顏色．
　　怡怡如也．沒階．趨進．翼如也．復其位．踧踖如也．

【十‧五】執圭．鞠躬如也．如不勝．上如揖．下如授．勃如戰色．足蹜蹜如有循．享
　　禮．有容色．私覿．愉愉如也．

【十‧六】君子不以紺緅飾．紅紫不以為褻服．當暑．袗絺綌．必表而出之．緇衣．羔
　　裘．素衣．麑裘．黃衣．狐裘．褻裘長．短右袂．必有寢衣．長一身有半．
　　狐貉之厚以居．去喪無所不佩．非帷裳．必殺之．羔裘玄冠不以弔．吉月．必
　　朝服而朝．

【十‧七】齊必有明衣布．齊必變食．居必遷坐．

【十‧八】食不厭精．膾不厭細．食饐而餲．魚餒而肉敗不食．色惡不食．臭惡不食．
　　失飪不食．不時不食．割不正不食．不得其醬不食．肉雖多．不使勝食氣．唯酒
　　無量．不及亂．沽酒市脯不食．不撤薑食．不多食．

【十‧九】祭於公．不宿肉．祭肉不出三日．出三日．不食之矣．

【十‧一〇】食不語．寢不言．

【十‧十一】雖疏食菜羹．瓜祭必齊如也．

【十‧十二】席不正不坐．

【十‧十三】鄉人飲酒．杖者出．斯出矣．

【十‧十四】鄉人儺．朝服而立於阼階．

【十‧十五】問人於他邦．再拜而送之．

【十‧十六】康子饋藥．拜而受之．曰．丘未達．不敢嘗．

【十‧十七】廄焚．子退朝．曰．傷人乎．不問馬．

【十‧十八】君賜食．必正席先嘗之．君賜腥．必熟而薦之．君賜生．必畜之．侍食
　　於君．君祭先飯．

【十‧十九】疾．君視之．東首．加朝服．拖紳．

【十‧二〇】君命召．不俟駕行矣．

【十‧二一】入太廟. 每事問.

【十‧二二】朋友死. 無所歸. 曰. 於我殯.

【十‧二三】朋友之饋. 雖車馬非祭肉. 不拜.

【十‧二四】寢不尸. 居不客.

【十‧二五】見齊衰者. 雖狎必變. 見冕者與瞽者. 雖褻必以貌. 凶服者式之. 式負版者. 有盛饌. 必變色而作. 迅雷風烈. 必變.

【十‧二六】升車. 必正立執綏. 車中. 不內顧. 不疾言. 不親指.

【十‧二七】色斯舉矣. 翔而後集. 曰. 山梁雌雉. 時哉時哉. 子路共之. 三嗅而作.

先進第十一

【十一‧一】子曰. 先進於禮樂. 野人也. 後進於禮樂. 君子也. 如用之. 則吾從先進.

【十一‧二】子曰. 從我於陳蔡者. 皆不及門也.

【十一‧三】德行. 顏淵閔子騫冉伯牛仲弓. 言語. 宰我子貢. 政事. 冉有季路. 文學. 子游子夏.

【十一‧四】子曰. 回也. 非助我者也. 於吾言無所不說.

【十一‧五】子曰. 孝哉閔子騫. 人不閒於其父母昆弟之言.

【十一‧六】南容三復白圭. 孔子以其兄之子妻之.

【十一‧七】季康子問弟子孰為好學. 孔子對曰. 有顏回者好學. 不幸短命死矣. 今也則亡.

【十一‧八】顏淵死. 顏路請子之車. 以為之槨. 子曰. 才不才. 亦各言其子也. 鯉也死. 有棺而無槨. 吾不徒行以為之槨. 以吾從大夫之後. 不可徒行也.

【十一‧九】顏淵死. 子曰. 噫. 天喪予. 天喪予.

【十一‧一〇】顏淵死. 子哭之慟. 從者曰. 子慟矣. 曰. 有慟乎. 非夫人之為慟而誰為.

【十一‧十一】顏淵死. 門人欲厚葬之. 子曰. 不可. 門人厚葬之. 子曰. 回也. 視予猶父也. 予不得視猶子也. 非我也. 夫二三子也.

【十一‧十二】季路問事鬼神. 子曰. 未能事人. 焉能事鬼. 敢問死. 曰. 未知生. 焉知死.

【十一‧十三】閔子侍側. 誾誾如也. 子路. 行行如也. 冉有. 子貢. 侃侃如也. 子樂. 若由也. 不得其死然.

【十一‧十四】魯人為長府. 閔子騫曰. 仍舊貫. 如之何. 何必改作. 子曰. 夫人不言. 言必有中.

【十一‧十五】子曰. 由之瑟. 奚為於丘之門. 門人不敬子路. 子曰. 由也. 升堂矣. 未入於室也.

【十一‧十六】子貢問師與商也. 孰賢. 子曰. 師也過. 商也不及. 曰. 然則師愈與. 子曰. 過猶不及.

【十一・十七】季氏富於周公. 而求也為之聚斂. 而附益之. 子曰. 非吾徒也. 小子
鳴鼓而攻之. 可也.

【十一・十八】柴也愚. 參也魯. 師也辟. 由也喭.

【十一・十九】子曰. 回也. 其庶乎. 屢空. 賜不受命. 而貨殖焉. 億則屢中.

【十一・二〇】子張問善人之道. 子曰. 不踐跡. 亦不入於室. 子曰. 論篤是與. 君子
者乎. 色莊者乎.

【十一・二一】子路問聞斯行諸. 子曰. 有父兄在. 如之何其聞斯行之. 冉有問聞斯
行諸. 子曰. 聞斯行之. 公西華曰. 由也問聞斯行諸. 子曰. 有父兄在. 求也問
聞斯行諸. 子曰. 聞斯行之. 赤也惑. 敢問. 子曰. 求也退. 故進之. 由也兼
人. 故退之.

【十一・二三】子畏於匡. 顏淵後. 子曰. 吾以女為死矣. 曰. 子在. 回何敢死.

【十一・二四】季子然問仲由. 冉求. 可謂大臣與. 子曰. 吾以子為異之問. 曾由
與求之問. 所謂大臣者. 以道事君. 不可則止. 今由與求也. 可謂具臣矣. 曰.
然則從之者與. 子曰. 弒父與君. 亦不從也.

【十一・二五】子路使子羔為費宰. 子曰. 賊夫人之子. 子路曰. 有民人焉. 有社稷
焉. 何必讀書. 然後為學. 子曰. 是故惡夫佞者.

【十一・二六】子路. 曾晳. 冉有. 公西華. 侍坐. 子曰. 以吾一日長乎爾. 毋吾以也.
居則曰. 不吾知也. 如或知爾. 則何以哉. 子路率爾而對曰. 千乘之國. 攝乎大
國之間. 加之以師旅. 因之以饑饉. 由也為之. 比及三年. 可使有勇. 且知方
也. 夫子哂之. 求. 爾何如. 對曰. 方六七十. 如五六十. 求也為之. 比及三年.
可使足民. 如其禮樂. 以俟君子. 赤. 爾何如. 對曰. 非曰能之. 願學焉. 宗廟之
事. 如會同. 端章甫. 願為小相焉. 點. 爾何如. 鼓瑟希. 鏗爾. 舍瑟而作. 對
曰. 異乎三子者之撰. 子曰. 何傷乎. 亦各言其志也. 曰. 莫春者. 春服既成. 冠
者五六人. 童子六七人. 浴乎沂. 風乎舞雩. 詠而歸. 夫子喟然歎曰. 吾與點
也. 三子者出. 曾晳後. 曾晳曰. 夫三子者之言何如. 子曰. 亦各言其志也已
矣. 曰. 夫子何哂由也. 曰. 為國以禮. 其言不讓. 是故哂之. 唯求. 則非邦也
與. 安見方六七十. 如五六十. 而非邦也者. 唯赤. 非邦也與. 宗廟會同. 非諸
侯而何. 赤也為之小. 孰能為之大.

顏淵第十二

【十二・一】顏淵問仁. 子曰. 克己復禮. 為仁. 一日克己復禮. 天下歸仁焉. 為仁由
己. 而由人乎哉. 顏淵曰. 請問其目. 子曰. 非禮勿視. 非禮勿聽. 非禮勿言.
非禮勿動. 顏淵曰. 回雖不敏. 請事斯語矣.

【十二・二】仲弓問仁. 子曰. 出門如見大賓. 使民如承大祭. 己所不欲. 勿施於人.
在邦無怨. 在家無怨. 仲弓曰. 雍雖不敏. 請事斯語矣.

【十二・三】司馬牛問仁. 子曰. 仁者. 其言也訒. 曰. 其言也訒. 斯謂之仁矣乎. 子
曰. 為之難. 言之得無訒乎.

【十二‧四】司馬牛問君子. 子曰. 君子不憂不懼. 曰. 不憂不懼. 斯謂之君子已乎.
子曰. 內省不疚. 夫何憂何懼.

【十二‧五】司馬牛憂曰. 人皆有兄弟. 我獨無. 子夏曰. 商聞之矣. 死生有命.
富貴在天. 君子敬而無失. 與人恭而有禮. 四海之內. 皆兄弟也. 君子何患乎
無兄弟也.

【十二‧六】子張問明. 子曰. 浸潤之譖. 膚受之愬. 不行焉. 可謂明也已矣. 浸潤之
譖. 膚受之愬. 不行焉. 可謂遠也已矣.

【十二‧七】子貢問政. 子曰. 足食. 足兵. 民信之矣. 子貢曰. 必不得已而去. 於斯三
者何先. 曰. 去兵. 子貢曰. 必不得已而去. 於斯二者何先. 曰. 去食. 自古皆有
死. 民無信不立.

【十二‧八】棘子成曰. 君子質而已矣. 何以文為. 子貢曰. 惜乎. 夫子之說君子也.
駟不及舌. 文猶質也. 質猶文也. 虎豹之鞟. 猶犬羊之鞟.

【十二‧九】哀公問於有若曰. 年饑. 用不足. 如之何. 有若對曰. 盍徹乎. 曰. 二.
吾猶不足. 如之何其徹也. 對曰. 百姓足. 君孰與不足. 百姓不足.
君孰與足.

【十二‧一〇】子張問崇德辨惑. 子曰. 主忠信. 徙義. 崇德也. 愛之欲其生. 惡之欲
其死. 既欲其生. 又欲其死. 是惑也. 誠不以富. 亦祇以異.

【十二‧十一】齊景公問政於孔子. 孔子對曰. 君君. 臣臣. 父父. 子子. 公曰. 善哉.
信如君不君. 臣不臣. 父不父. 子不子. 雖有粟. 吾得而食諸.

【十二‧十二】子曰. 片言可以折獄者. 其由也與. 子路無宿諾.

【十二‧十三】子曰. 聽訟. 吾猶人也. 必也使無訟乎.

【十二‧十四】子張問政. 子曰. 居之無倦. 行之以忠.

【十二‧十五】子曰. 博學於文. 約之以禮. 亦可以弗畔矣夫.

【十二‧十六】子曰. 君子成人之美. 不成人之惡. 小人反是.

【十二‧十七】季康子問政於孔子. 孔子對曰. 政者. 正也. 子帥以正. 孰敢不正.

【十二‧十八】季康子患盜. 問於孔子. 孔子對曰. 苟子之不欲. 雖賞之不竊.

【十二‧十九】季康子問政於孔子. 曰. 如殺無道以就有道. 何如. 孔子對曰. 子為政.
焉用殺. 子欲善. 而民善矣. 君子之德風. 小人之德草. 草上之風必偃.

【十二‧二〇】子張問士何如. 斯可謂之達矣. 子曰. 何哉. 爾所謂達者. 子張對曰.
在邦必聞. 在家必聞. 子曰. 是聞也. 非達也. 夫達也者. 質直而好義. 察言
而觀色. 慮以下人. 在邦必達. 在家必達. 夫聞也者. 色取仁而行違. 居之不
疑. 在邦必聞. 在家必聞.

【十二‧二一】樊遲從遊於舞雩之下. 曰. 敢問崇德. 脩慝. 辨惑. 子曰. 善哉問. 先
事後得. 非崇德與. 攻其惡. 無攻人之惡. 非修慝與. 一朝之忿. 忘其身. 以及
其親. 非惑與.

【十二‧二二】樊遲問仁. 子曰. 愛人. 問知. 子曰. 知人. 樊遲未達. 子曰. 舉直錯諸
枉. 能使枉者直. 樊遲退. 見子夏曰. 鄉也吾見於夫子而問知. 子曰. 舉直錯諸
枉. 能使枉者直. 何謂也. 子夏曰. 富哉言乎. 舜有天下. 選於眾. 舉皋陶. 不
仁者遠矣. 湯有天下. 選於眾. 舉伊尹. 不仁者遠矣.

【十二・二三】子貢問友. 子曰. 忠告而善道之. 不可則止. 毋自辱焉.

【十二・二四】曾子曰. 君子以文會友. 以友輔仁.

子路第十三

【十三・一】子路問政. 子曰. 先之勞之. 請益. 曰. 無倦.

【十三・二】仲弓為季氏宰. 問政. 子曰. 先有司. 赦小過. 舉賢才. 曰. 焉知賢才而舉之. 曰. 舉爾所知. 爾所不知. 人其舍諸.

【十三・三】子路曰. 衛君待子而為政. 子將奚先. 子曰. 必也正名乎. 子路曰. 有是哉. 子之迂也. 奚其正. 子曰. 野哉由也. 君子於其所不知. 蓋闕如也. 名不正. 則言不順. 言不順. 則事不成. 事不成. 則禮樂不興. 禮樂不興. 則刑罰不中. 刑罰不中. 則民無所措手足. 故君子名之必可言也. 言之必可行也. 君子於其言. 無所苟而已矣.

【十三・四】樊遲請學稼. 子曰. 吾不如老農. 請學為圃. 曰. 吾不如老圃. 樊遲出. 子曰. 小人哉. 樊須也. 上好禮. 則民莫敢不敬. 上好義. 則民莫敢不服. 上好信. 則民莫敢不用情. 夫如是. 則四方之民. 襁負其子而至矣. 焉用稼.

【十三・五】子曰. 誦詩三百. 授之以政. 不達. 使於四方. 不能專對. 雖多. 亦奚以為.

【十三・六】子曰. 其身正. 不令而行. 其身不正. 雖令不從.

【十三・七】子曰. 魯衛之政. 兄弟也.

【十三・八】子謂衛公子荊善居室. 始有. 曰. 苟合矣. 少有. 曰. 苟完矣. 富有. 曰. 苟美矣.

【十三・九】子適衛. 冉有僕. 子曰. 庶矣哉. 冉有曰. 既庶矣. 又何加焉. 曰. 富之. 曰. 既富矣. 又何加焉. 曰. 教之.

【十三・一〇】子曰. 苟有用我者. 期月而已可也. 三年有成.

【十三・十一】子曰. 善人為邦百年. 亦可以勝殘去殺矣. 誠哉是言也.

【十三・十二】子曰. 如有王者. 必世而後仁.

【十三・十三】子曰. 苟正其身矣. 於從政乎何有. 不能正其身. 如正人何.

【十三・十四】冉子退朝. 子曰. 何晏也. 對曰. 有政. 子曰. 其事也. 如有政. 雖不吾以. 吾其與聞之.

【十三・十五】定公問一言而可以興邦. 有諸. 孔子對曰. 言不可以若是其幾也. 人之言曰. 為君難. 為臣不易. 如知為君之難也. 不幾乎一言而興邦乎. 曰. 一言而喪邦. 有諸. 孔子對曰. 言不可以若是其幾也. 人之言曰. 予無樂乎為君. 唯其言而莫予違也. 如其善而莫之違也. 不亦善乎. 如不善而莫之違也. 不幾乎一言而喪邦乎.

【十三・十六】葉公問政. 子曰. 近者說. 遠者來.

【十三・十七】子夏為莒父宰. 問政. 子曰. 無欲速. 無見小利. 欲速. 則不達. 見小利. 則大事不成.

【十三·十八】葉公語孔子曰. 吾黨有直躬者. 其父攘羊. 而子證之. 孔子曰. 吾黨
之直者. 異於是. 父為子隱. 子為父隱. 直在其中矣.

【十三·十九】樊遲問仁. 子曰. 居處恭. 執事敬. 與人忠. 雖之夷狄. 不可棄也.

【十三·二〇】子貢問曰. 何如斯可謂之士矣. 子曰. 行己有恥. 使於四方. 不辱君
命. 可謂士矣. 敢問其次. 曰. 宗族稱孝焉. 鄉黨稱弟焉. 曰. 敢問其次.
曰. 言必信. 行必果. 硜硜然. 小人哉. 抑亦可以為次矣. 曰. 今之從政者. 何
如. 子曰. 噫. 斗筲之人. 何足算也.

【十三·二一】子曰. 不得中行而與之. 必也狂狷乎. 狂者進取. 狷者有所不為也.

【十三·二二】子曰. 南人有言曰. 人而無恆. 不可以作巫醫. 善夫. 不恆其德. 或承
之羞. 子曰. 不占而已矣.

【十三·二三】子曰. 君子和而不同. 小人同而不和.

【十三·二四】子貢問曰. 鄉人皆好之. 何如. 子曰. 未可也. 鄉人皆惡之. 何如. 子
曰. 未可也. 不如鄉人之善者好之. 其不善者惡之.

【十三·二五】子曰. 君子易事而難說也. 說之不以道. 不說也. 及其使人也器之.
小人難事而易說也. 說之雖不以道. 說也. 及其使人也. 求備焉.

【十三·二六】子曰. 君子泰而不驕. 小人驕而不泰.

【十三·二七】子曰. 剛. 毅. 木. 訥. 近仁.

【十三·二八】子路問曰. 何如斯可謂之士矣. 子曰. 切切偲偲. 怡怡如也. 可謂士
矣. 朋友切切偲偲. 兄弟怡怡.

【十三·二九】子曰. 善人教民七年. 亦可以即戎矣.

【十三·三〇】子曰. 以不教民戰. 是謂棄之.

憲問第十四

【十四·一】憲問恥. 子曰. 邦有道穀. 邦無道穀. 恥也. 克. 伐. 怨. 欲. 不行焉. 可
以為仁矣. 子曰. 可以為難矣. 仁. 則吾不知也.

【十四·二】子曰. 士而懷居. 不足以為士矣.

【十四·三】子曰. 邦有道. 危言危行. 邦無道. 危行言孫.

【十四·四】子曰. 有德者必有言. 有言者不必有德. 仁者必有勇. 勇者不必有仁.

【十四·五】南宮适問於孔子曰. 羿善射. 奡盪舟. 俱不得其死然. 禹稷躬稼. 而有
天下. 夫子不答. 南宮适出. 子曰. 君子哉若人. 尚德哉若人.

【十四·六】子曰. 君子而不仁者. 有矣夫. 未有小人而仁者也.

【十四·七】子曰. 愛之能勿勞乎. 忠焉能勿誨乎.

【十四·八】子曰. 為命. 裨諶草創之. 世叔討論之. 行人子羽修飾之. 東里子
產潤色之.

【十四·九】或問子產. 子曰. 惠人也. 問子西. 曰. 彼哉彼哉. 問管仲. 曰. 人也. 奪
伯氏駢邑三百. 飯疏食. 沒齒無怨言.

【十四·一〇】子曰. 貧而無怨. 難. 富而無驕. 易.

【十四‧十一】子曰. 孟公綽為趙魏老. 則優. 不可以為滕薛大夫.

【十四‧十二】子路問成人. 子曰. 若臧武仲之知. 公綽之不欲. 卞莊子之勇. 冉求
之藝. 文之以禮樂. 亦可以為成人矣. 曰. 今之成人者. 何必然. 見利思義. 見
危授命. 久要不忘平生之言. 亦可以為成人矣.

【十四‧十三】子問公叔文子於公明賈曰. 信乎. 夫子不言不笑不取乎. 公明賈對
曰. 以告者過也. 夫子時然後言. 人不厭其言. 樂然後笑. 人不厭其笑. 義然後
取. 人不厭其取. 子曰. 其然. 豈其然乎.

【十四‧十四】子曰. 臧武仲以防求為後於魯. 雖曰不要君. 吾不信也.

【十四‧十五】子曰. 晉文公譎而不正. 齊桓公正而不譎.

【十四‧十六】子路曰. 桓公殺公子糾. 召忽死之. 管仲不死. 曰. 未仁乎. 子曰. 桓
公九合諸侯. 不以兵車. 管仲之力也. 如其仁. 如其仁.

【十四‧十七】子貢曰. 管仲非仁者與. 桓公殺公子糾. 不能死. 又相之. 子曰. 管仲
相桓公. 霸諸侯. 一匡天下. 民到于今受其賜. 微管仲. 吾其被髮左衽矣. 豈
若匹夫匹婦之為諒也. 自經於溝瀆. 而莫之知也.

【十四‧十八】公叔文子之臣大夫僎. 與文子同升諸公. 子聞之曰. 可以為文矣.

【十四‧十九】子言衛靈公之無道也. 康子曰. 夫如是. 奚而不喪. 孔子曰. 仲叔圉
治賓客. 祝鮀治宗廟. 王孫賈治軍旅. 夫如是. 奚其喪.

【十四‧二〇】子曰. 其言之不怍. 則為之也難.

【十四‧二一】陳成子弒簡公. 孔子沐浴而朝. 告於哀公曰. 陳恆弒其君. 請討之.
公曰. 告夫三子. 孔子曰. 以吾從大夫之後. 不敢不告也. 君曰. 告夫三子者.
之三子告. 不可. 孔子曰. 以吾從大夫之後. 不敢不告也.

【十四‧二二】子路問事君. 子曰. 勿欺也而犯之.

【十四‧二三】子曰. 君子上達. 小人下達.

【十四‧二四】子曰. 古之學者為己. 今之學者為人.

【十四‧二五】蘧伯玉使人於孔子. 孔子與之坐而問焉. 曰. 夫子何為. 對曰. 夫子
欲寡其過而未能也. 使者出. 子曰. 使乎. 使乎.

【十四‧二六】子曰. 不在其位. 不謀其政. 曾子曰. 君子思不出其位.

【十四‧二七】子曰. 君子恥其言. 而過其行.

【十四‧二八】子曰. 君子道者三. 我無能焉. 仁者不憂. 知者不惑. 勇者不懼. 子貢
曰. 夫子自道也.

【十四‧二九】子貢方人. 子曰. 賜也. 賢乎哉. 夫我則不暇.

【十四‧三〇】子曰. 不患人之不己知. 患其不能也.

【十四‧三一】子曰. 不逆詐. 不億不信. 抑亦先覺者. 是賢乎.

【十四‧三二】微生畝謂孔子曰. 丘何為是栖栖者與. 無乃為佞乎. 孔子曰. 非敢
佞也. 疾固也.

【十四‧三三】子曰. 驥不稱其力. 稱其德也.

【十四‧三四】或曰. 以德報怨. 何如. 子曰. 何以報德. 以直報怨. 以德報德.

【十四‧三五】子曰. 莫我知也夫. 子貢曰. 何為其莫知子也. 子曰. 不怨天. 不尤
人. 下學而上達. 知我者其天乎.

【十四・三六】公伯寮愬子路於季孫. 子服景伯以告. 曰. 夫子固有惑志於公伯寮.
吾力猶能肆諸市朝. 子曰. 道之將行也與. 命也. 道之將廢也與. 命也. 公伯
寮其如命何.

【十四・三七】子曰. 賢者辟世. 其次辟地. 其次辟色. 其次辟言. 子曰.
作者七人矣.

【十四・三八】子路宿於石門. 晨門曰. 奚自. 子路曰. 自孔氏. 曰. 是知其不可而
為之者與.

【十四・三九】子擊磬於衛. 有荷蕢而過孔氏之門者. 曰. 有心哉. 擊磬乎. 既而曰.
鄙哉硜硜乎. 莫己知也. 斯已而已矣. 深則厲. 淺則揭. 子曰. 果哉. 末之難矣.

【十四・四〇】子張曰. 書云高宗諒陰. 三年不言. 何謂也. 子曰. 何必高宗. 古之人
皆然. 君薨. 百官總己. 以聽於冢宰三年.

【十四・四一】子曰. 上好禮. 則民易使也.

【十四・四二】子路問君子. 子曰. 修己以敬. 曰. 如斯而已乎. 曰. 修己以安人. 曰.
如斯而已乎. 曰. 修己以安百姓. 修己以安百姓. 堯舜其猶病諸.

【十四・四三】原壤夷俟. 子曰. 幼而不孫弟. 長而無述焉. 老而不死. 是為賊. 以
杖叩其脛.

【十四・四四】闕黨童子將命. 或問之曰. 益者與. 子曰. 吾見其居於位也. 見其與
先生並行也. 非求益者也. 欲速成者也.

衛靈公第十五

【十五・一】衛靈公問陳於孔子. 孔子對曰. 俎豆之事. 則嘗聞之矣. 軍旅之事. 未
之學也. 明日遂行.

【十五・二】在陳絕糧. 從者病. 莫能興. 子路慍見曰. 君子亦有窮乎. 子曰. 君子固
窮. 小人窮斯濫矣.

【十五・三】子曰. 賜也. 女以予為多學而識之者與. 對曰. 然. 非與. 曰. 非也. 予
一以貫之.

【十五・四】子曰. 由. 知德者鮮矣.

【十五・五】子曰. 無為而治者. 其舜也與. 夫何為哉. 恭己正南面而已矣.

【十五・六】子張問行. 子曰. 言忠信. 行篤敬. 雖蠻貊之邦. 行矣. 言不忠信. 行不
篤敬. 雖州里行乎哉. 立則見其參於前也. 在輿則見其倚於衡也. 夫然後行.
子張書諸紳.

【十五・七】子曰. 直哉史魚. 邦有道. 如矢. 邦無道. 如矢. 君子哉蘧伯玉. 邦有道.
則仕. 邦無道. 則可卷而懷之.

【十五・八】子曰. 可與言而不與之言. 失人. 不可與言而與之言. 失言. 知者不失
人. 亦不失言.

【十五・九】子曰. 志士仁人. 無求生以害仁. 有殺身以成仁.

【十五‧一〇】子貢問為仁. 子曰. 工欲善其事. 必先利其器. 居是邦也. 事其大夫
之賢者. 友其士之仁者.

【十五‧十一】顏淵問為邦. 子曰. 行夏之時. 乘殷之輅. 服周之冕. 樂則韶舞. 放
鄭聲. 遠佞人. 鄭聲淫. 佞人殆.

【十五‧十二】子曰. 人無遠慮. 必有近憂.

【十五‧十三】子曰. 已矣乎. 吾未見好德如好色者也.

【十五‧十四】子曰. 臧文仲其竊位者與. 知柳下惠之賢. 而不與立也.

【十五‧十五】子曰. 躬自厚而薄責於人. 則遠怨矣.

【十五‧十六】子曰. 不曰如之何. 如之何者. 吾末如之何也已矣.

【十五‧十七】子曰. 羣居終日. 言不及義. 好行小慧. 難矣哉.

【十五‧十八】子曰. 君子義以為質. 禮以行之. 孫以出之. 信以成之. 君子哉.

【十五‧十九】子曰. 君子病無能焉. 不病人之不己知也.

【十五‧二〇】子曰. 君子疾沒世而名不稱焉.

【十五‧二一】子曰. 君子求諸己. 小人求諸人.

【十五‧二二】子曰. 君子矜而不爭. 羣而不黨.

【十五‧二三】子曰. 君子不以言舉人. 不以人廢言.

【十五‧二四】子貢問曰. 有一言而可以終身行之者乎. 子曰. 其恕乎. 己所不欲.
勿施於人.

【十五‧二五】子曰. 吾之於人也. 誰毀誰譽. 如有所譽者. 其有所試矣. 斯民也. 三
代之所以直道而行也.

【十五‧二六】子曰. 吾猶及史之闕文也. 有馬者. 借人乘之. 今亡矣夫.

【十五‧二七】子曰. 巧言亂德. 小不忍. 則亂大謀.

【十五‧二八】子曰. 眾惡之. 必察焉. 眾好之. 必察焉.

【十五‧二九】子曰. 人能弘道. 非道弘人.

【十五‧三〇】子曰. 過而不改. 是謂過矣.

【十五‧三一】子曰. 吾嘗終日不食. 終夜不寢. 以思. 無益. 不如學也.

【十五‧三二】子曰. 君子謀道不謀食. 耕也. 餒在其中矣. 學也. 祿在其中矣. 君
子憂道不憂貧.

【十五‧三三】子曰. 知及之. 仁不能守之. 雖得之. 必失之. 知及之. 仁能守之. 不
莊以涖之. 則民不敬. 知及之. 仁能守之. 莊以涖之. 動之不以禮. 未善也.

【十五‧三四】子曰. 君子不可小知. 而可大受也. 小人不可大受. 而可小知也.

【十五‧三五】子曰. 民之於仁也. 甚於水火. 水火. 吾見蹈而死者矣. 未見蹈仁
而死者也.

【十五‧三六】子曰. 當仁. 不讓於師.

【十五‧三七】子曰. 君子貞而不諒.

【十五‧三八】子曰. 事君敬其事而後其食.

【十五‧三九】子曰. 有教無類.

【十五‧四〇】子曰. 道不同. 不相為謀.

【十五‧四一】子曰. 辭達而已矣.

【十五‧四二】師冕見. 及階. 子曰. 階也. 及席. 子曰. 席也. 皆坐. 子告之曰. 某在
　　斯. 某在斯. 師冕出. 子張問曰. 與師言之道與. 子曰. 然. 固相師之道也.

季氏第十六

【十六‧一】季氏將伐顓臾. 冉有季路見於孔子曰. 季氏將有事於顓臾. 孔子曰.
　　求. 無乃爾是過與. 夫顓臾. 昔者先王以為東蒙主. 且在邦域之中矣. 是社稷
　　之臣. 何以伐為. 冉有曰. 夫子欲之. 吾二臣者. 皆不欲也. 孔子曰. 求. 周任
　　有言曰. 陳力就列. 不能者止. 危而不持. 顛而不扶. 則將焉用彼相矣. 且爾言
　　過矣. 虎兕出於柙. 龜玉毀於櫝中. 是誰之過與. 冉有曰. 今夫顓臾固而近於
　　費. 今不取. 後世必為子孫憂. 孔子曰. 求. 君子疾夫. 舍曰欲之. 而必為之
　　辭. 丘也聞有國有家者. 不患寡而患不均. 不患貧而患不安. 蓋均無貧. 和無
　　寡. 安無傾. 夫如是. 故遠人不服. 則脩文德以來之. 既來之. 則安之. 今由與
　　求也. 相夫子. 遠人不服. 而不能來也. 邦分崩離析. 而不能守也. 而謀動干
　　戈於邦內. 吾恐季孫之憂. 不在顓臾. 而在蕭牆之內也.

【十六‧二】孔子曰. 天下有道. 則禮樂征伐. 自天子出. 天下無道. 則禮樂征伐. 自
　　諸侯出. 自諸侯出. 蓋十世希不失矣. 自大夫出. 五世希不失矣. 陪臣執國命.
　　三世希不失矣. 天下有道. 則政不在大夫. 天下有道. 則庶人不議.

【十六‧三】孔子曰. 祿之去公室. 五世矣. 政逮於大夫. 四世矣. 故夫三桓
　　之子孫微矣.

【十六‧四】孔子曰. 益者三友. 損者三友. 友直. 友諒. 友多聞. 益矣. 友便辟. 友
　　善柔. 友便佞. 損矣.

【十六‧五】孔子曰. 益者三樂. 損者三樂. 樂節禮樂. 樂道人之善. 樂多賢友. 益
　　矣. 樂驕樂. 樂佚游. 樂宴樂. 損矣.

【十六‧六】孔子曰. 侍於君子. 有三愆. 言未及之而言. 謂之躁. 言及之而不言. 謂
　　之隱. 未見顏色而言. 謂之瞽.

【十六‧七】孔子曰. 君子有三戒. 少之時. 血氣未定. 戒之在色. 及其壯也. 血氣
　　方剛. 戒之在鬭. 及其老也. 血氣既衰. 戒之在得.

【十六‧八】孔子曰. 君子有三畏. 畏天命. 畏大人. 畏聖人之言. 小人不知天命而
　　不畏也. 狎大人. 侮聖人之言.

【十六‧九】孔子曰. 生而知之者. 上也. 學而知之者. 次也. 困而學之. 又其次也.
　　困而不學. 民斯為下矣.

【十六‧一〇】孔子曰. 君子有九思. 視思明. 聽思聰. 色思溫. 貌思恭. 言思忠. 事
　　思敬. 疑思問. 忿思難. 見得思義.

【十六‧十一】孔子曰. 見善如不及. 見不善如探湯. 吾見其人矣. 吾聞其語矣. 隱
　　居以求其志. 行義以達其道. 吾聞其語矣. 未見其人也.

【十六・十二】齊景公有馬千駟. 死之日. 民無德而稱焉. 伯夷叔齊. 餓於首陽之下.
民到於今稱之. 其斯之謂與.

【十六・十三】陳亢問於伯魚曰. 子亦有異聞乎. 對曰. 未也. 嘗獨立. 鯉趨而過庭.
曰. 學詩乎. 對曰. 未也. 不學詩. 無以言. 鯉退而學詩. 他日. 又獨立. 鯉趨而
過庭. 曰. 學禮乎. 對曰. 未也. 不學禮. 無以立. 鯉退而學禮. 聞斯二者. 陳
亢退而喜曰. 問一得三. 聞詩聞禮. 又聞君子之遠其子也.

【十六・十四】邦君之妻. 君稱之. 曰夫人. 夫人自稱. 曰小童. 邦人稱之. 曰君夫
人. 稱諸異邦. 曰寡小君. 異邦人稱之. 亦曰君夫人.

陽貨第十七

【十七・一】陽貨欲見孔子. 孔子不見. 歸孔子豚. 孔子時其亡也. 而往拜之.
遇諸塗. 謂孔子曰. 來. 予與爾言. 曰. 懷其寶而迷其邦. 可謂仁乎. 曰不可. 好
從事而亟失時. 可謂知乎. 曰不可. 日月逝矣. 歲不我與. 孔子曰. 諾.
吾將仕矣.

【十七・二】子曰. 性相近也. 習相遠也. 子曰. 惟上知與下愚不移.

【十七・四】子之武城. 聞弦歌之聲. 夫子莞爾而笑. 曰. 割雞焉用牛刀. 子游對曰.
昔者偃也聞諸夫子曰. 君子學道則愛人. 小人學道則易使也. 子曰. 二三子.
偃之言是也. 前言戲之耳.

【十七・五】公山弗擾以費畔. 召. 子欲往. 子路不說曰. 末之也已. 何必公山氏之之
也. 子曰. 夫召我者. 而豈徒哉. 如有用我者. 吾其爲東周乎.

【十七・六】子張問仁於孔子. 孔子曰. 能行五者於天下. 為仁矣. 請問之. 曰. 恭.
寬. 信. 敏. 惠. 恭則不侮. 寬則得眾. 信則人任焉. 敏則有功. 惠則足以使人.

【十七・七】佛肸召. 子欲往. 子路曰. 昔者由也聞諸夫子曰. 親於其身為不善者.
君子不入也. 佛肸以中牟畔. 子之往也. 如之何. 子曰. 然. 有是言也. 不曰堅
乎. 磨而不磷. 不曰白乎. 涅而不緇. 吾豈匏瓜也哉. 焉能繫而不食.

【十七・八】子曰. 由也. 女聞六言六蔽矣乎. 對曰. 未也. 居. 吾語女. 好仁不好學.
其蔽也愚. 好知不好學. 其蔽也蕩. 好信不好學. 其蔽也賊. 好直不好學. 其
蔽也絞. 好勇不好學. 其蔽也亂. 好剛不好學. 其蔽也狂.

【十七・九】子曰. 小子何莫學夫詩. 詩可以興. 可以觀. 可以羣. 可以怨. 邇之事
父. 遠之事君. 多識於鳥獸草木之名.

【十七・一〇】子謂伯魚曰. 女為周南召南矣乎. 人而不為周南召南. 其猶正牆
面而立也與.

【十七・十一】子曰. 禮云禮云. 玉帛云乎哉. 樂云樂云. 鐘鼓云乎哉.

【十七・十二】子曰. 色厲而內荏. 譬諸小人. 其猶穿窬之盜也與.

【十七・十三】子曰. 鄉愿. 德之賊也.

【十七・十四】子曰. 道聽而塗說. 德之棄也.

【十七·十五】子曰. 鄙夫. 可與事君也與哉. 其未得之也. 患得之. 既得之. 患失之. 苟患失之. 無所不至矣.

【十七·十六】子曰. 古者民有三疾. 今也或是之亡也. 古之狂也肆. 今之狂也蕩. 古之矜也廉. 今之矜也忿戾. 古之愚也直. 今之愚也詐而已矣.

【十七·十八】子曰. 惡紫之奪朱也. 惡鄭聲之亂雅樂也. 惡利口之覆邦家者.

【十七·十九】子曰. 予欲無言. 子貢曰. 子如不言. 則小子何述焉. 子曰. 天何言哉. 四時行焉. 百物生焉. 天何言哉.

【十七·二十】孺悲欲見孔子. 孔子辭以疾. 將命者出戶. 取瑟而歌. 使之聞之.

【十七·二一】宰我問三年之喪. 期已久矣. 君子三年不為禮. 禮必壞. 三年不為樂. 樂必崩. 舊穀既沒. 新穀既升. 鑽燧改火. 期可已矣. 子曰. 食夫稻. 衣夫錦. 於女安乎. 曰. 安. 女安. 則為之. 夫君子之居喪. 食旨不甘. 聞樂不樂. 居處不安. 故不為也. 今女安則為之. 宰我出. 子曰. 予之不仁也. 子生三年. 然後免於父母之懷. 夫三年之喪. 天下之通喪也. 予也有三年之愛於其父母乎.

【十七·二二】子曰. 飽食終日. 無所用心. 難矣哉. 不有博弈者乎. 為之猶賢乎已.

【十七·二三】子路曰. 君子尚勇乎. 子曰. 君子義以為上. 君子有勇而無義為亂. 小人有勇而無義為盜.

【十七·二四】子貢曰. 君子亦有惡乎. 子曰. 有惡. 惡稱人之惡者. 惡居下流而訕上者. 惡勇而無禮者. 惡果敢而窒者. 曰. 賜也亦有惡乎. 惡徼以為知者. 惡不孫以為勇者. 惡訐以為直者.

【十七·二五】子曰. 唯女子與小人為難養也. 近之則不孫. 遠之則怨.

【十七·二六】子曰. 年四十而見惡焉. 其終也已.

微子第十八

【十八·一】微子去之. 箕子為之奴. 比干諫而死. 孔子曰. 殷有三仁焉.

【十八·二】柳下惠為士師. 三黜. 人曰. 子未可以去乎. 曰. 直道而事人. 焉往而不三黜. 枉道而事人. 何必去父母之邦.

【十八·三】齊景公待孔子. 曰. 若季氏. 則吾不能. 以季孟之間待之. 曰. 吾老矣. 不能用也. 孔子行.

【十八·四】齊人歸女樂. 季桓子受之. 三日不朝. 孔子行.

【十八·五】楚狂接輿歌而過孔子. 曰. 鳳兮鳳兮. 何德之衰. 往者不可諫. 來者猶可追. 已而已而. 今之從政者殆而. 孔子下. 欲與之言. 趨而辟之. 不得與之言.

【十八·六】長沮桀溺. 耦而耕. 使子路問津焉. 長沮曰. 夫執輿者為誰. 子路曰. 為孔丘. 曰. 是魯孔丘與. 曰. 是也. 曰. 是知津矣. 問於桀溺. 桀溺曰. 子為誰. 曰. 為仲由. 曰. 是魯孔丘之徒與. 對曰. 然. 曰. 滔滔者. 天下皆是也. 而誰以易之. 且而與其從辟人之士也. 豈若從辟世之士哉. 耰而不輟. 子路行以告. 夫子憮然曰. 鳥獸不可與同羣. 吾非斯人之徒與. 而誰與. 天下有道. 丘不與易也.

【十八·七】子路從而後. 遇丈人以杖荷蓧. 子路問曰. 子見夫子乎. 丈人曰. 四體不勤. 五穀不分. 孰為夫子. 植其杖而芸. 子路拱而立. 止子路宿. 殺雞為黍而食之. 見其二子焉. 明日. 子路行以告. 子曰. 隱者也. 使子路反見之. 至. 則行矣. 子路曰. 不仕無義. 長幼之節. 不可廢也. 君臣之義. 如之何其廢之. 欲潔其身. 而亂大倫. 君子之仕也. 行其義也. 道之不行. 已知之矣.

【十八·八】逸民. 伯夷. 叔齊. 虞仲. 夷逸. 朱張. 柳下惠. 少連. 子曰. 不降其志. 不辱其身. 伯夷叔齊與. 謂柳下惠少連. 降志辱身矣. 言中倫. 行中慮. 其斯而已矣. 謂虞仲夷逸. 隱居放言. 身中清. 廢中權. 我則異於是. 無可無不可.

【十八·九】太師摯適齊. 亞飯干適楚. 三飯繚適蔡. 四飯缺適秦. 鼓方叔入於河. 播鼗武入於漢. 少師陽擊磬襄入於海.

【十八·一〇】周公謂魯公曰. 君子不施其親. 不使大臣怨乎不以. 故舊無大故. 則不棄也. 無求備於一人.

【十八·十一】周有八士. 伯達. 伯适. 仲突. 仲忽. 叔夜. 叔夏. 季隨. 季騧.

子張第十九

【十九·一】子張曰. 士見危致命. 見得思義. 祭思敬. 喪思哀. 其可已矣.

【十九·二】子張曰. 執德不弘. 信道不篤. 焉能為有. 焉能為亡.

【十九·三】子夏之門人. 問交於子張. 子張曰. 子夏云何. 對曰. 子夏曰. 可者與之. 其不可者距之. 子張曰. 異乎吾所聞. 君子尊賢而容眾. 嘉善而矜不能. 我之大賢與. 於人何所不容. 我之不賢與. 人將距我. 如之何其距人也.

【十九·四】子曰. 雖小道. 必有可觀者焉. 致遠恐泥. 是以君子不為也.

【十九·五】子夏曰. 日知其所亡. 月無忘其所能. 可謂好學也已矣.

【十九·六】子夏曰. 博學而篤志. 切問而近思. 仁在其中矣.

【十九·七】子夏曰. 百工居肆. 以成其事. 君子學以致其道.

【十九·八】子夏曰. 小人之過也必文.

【十九·九】子夏曰. 君子有三變. 望之儼然. 即之也溫. 聽其言也厲.

【十九·一〇】子夏曰. 君子信而後勞其民. 未信. 則以為厲己也. 信而後諫. 未信. 則以為謗己也.

【十九·十一】子夏曰. 大德不踰閑. 小德出入可也.

【十九·十二】子游曰. 子夏之門人小子. 當洒掃. 應對. 進退. 則可矣. 抑末也. 本之則無. 如之何. 子夏聞之曰. 噫. 言游過矣. 君子之道. 孰先傳焉. 孰後倦焉. 譬諸草木. 區以別矣. 君子之道. 焉可誣也. 有始有卒者. 其惟聖人乎.

【十九·十三】子夏曰. 仕而優則學. 學而優則仕.

【十九·十四】子游曰. 喪致乎哀而止.

【十九·十五】子游曰. 吾友張也. 為難能也. 然而未仁.

【十九·十六】曾子曰. 堂堂乎張也. 難與並為仁矣.

【十九·十七】曾子曰. 吾聞諸夫子. 人未有自致者也. 必也親喪乎.

【十九・十八】曾子曰. 吾聞諸夫子. 孟莊子之孝也. 其他可能也. 其不改父之臣與
父之政. 是難能也.

【十九・十九】孟氏使陽膚為士師. 問於曾子. 曾子曰. 上失其道. 民散久矣. 如得
其情. 則哀矜而勿喜.

【十九・二十】子貢曰. 紂之不善. 不如是之甚也. 是以君子惡居下流. 天下之
惡皆歸焉.

【十九・二一】子貢曰. 君子之過也. 如日月之食焉. 過也. 人皆見之. 更也. 人皆仰之.

【十九・二二】衛公孫朝問於子貢曰. 仲尼焉學. 子貢曰. 文武之道. 未墜於地. 在
人. 賢者識其大者. 不賢者識其小者. 莫不有文武之道焉. 夫子焉不學. 而亦
何常師之有.

【十九・二三】叔孫武叔語大夫於朝曰. 子貢賢於仲尼. 子服景伯以告子貢. 子貢
曰. 譬之宮牆. 賜之牆也及肩. 窺見室家之好. 夫子之牆數仞. 不得其門而入.
不見宗廟之美. 百官之富. 得其門者或寡矣. 夫子之云. 不亦宜乎.

【十九・二四】叔孫武叔毀仲尼. 子貢曰. 無以為也. 仲尼不可毀也. 他人之賢者. 丘
陵也. 猶可踰也. 仲尼. 日月也. 無得而踰焉. 人雖欲自絕. 其何傷於日月乎.
多見其不知量也.

【十九・二五】陳子禽謂子貢曰. 子為恭也. 仲尼豈賢於子乎. 子貢曰. 君子一言以
為知. 一言以為不知. 言不可不慎也. 夫子之不可及也. 猶天之不可階而升
也. 夫子之得邦家者. 所謂立之斯立. 道之斯行. 綏之斯來. 動之斯和. 其生也
榮. 其死也哀. 如之何其可及也.

堯曰第二十

【二十・一】堯曰. 咨. 爾舜. 天之曆數在爾躬. 允執厥中. 四海困窮. 天祿永終. 舜亦
以命禹. 曰. 予小子履. 敢用玄牡. 敢昭告於皇皇后帝. 有罪不敢赦. 帝臣不
蔽. 簡在帝心. 朕躬有罪. 無以萬方. 萬方有罪. 罪在朕躬. 周有大賚. 善人是
富. 雖有周親. 不如仁人. 百姓有過. 在予一人. 謹權量. 審法度. 修廢官. 四方
之政行焉. 興滅國. 繼絕世. 舉逸民. 天下之民歸心焉. 所重. 民食. 喪. 祭. 寬
則得眾. 信則民任焉. 敏則有功. 公則說.

【二十・二】子張問於孔子曰. 何如斯可以從政矣. 子曰. 尊五美. 屏四惡. 斯可以從
政矣. 子張曰. 何謂五美. 子曰. 君子惠而不費. 勞而不怨. 欲而不貪. 泰而不
驕. 威而不猛. 子張曰. 何謂惠而不費. 子曰. 因民之所利而利之. 斯不亦惠而
不費乎. 擇可勞而勞之. 又誰怨. 欲仁而得仁. 又焉貪. 君子無眾寡. 無小大.
無敢慢. 斯不亦泰而不驕乎. 君子正其衣冠. 尊其瞻視. 儼然人望而畏之. 斯
不亦威而不猛乎. 子張曰. 何謂四惡. 子曰. 不教而殺. 謂之虐. 不戒視成. 謂
之暴. 慢令致期謂之賊. 猶之與人也. 出納之吝. 謂之有司.

【二十・三】孔子曰. 不知命. 無以為君子也. 不知禮. 無以立也. 不知言.
無以知人也.

Appendix 1A

DISCIPLES OF CONFUCIUS

The list includes all the disciples that appear in the *Analects*, with their personal names. One should consider the text together with the commentaries for a more nuanced description of the principal disciples.

Boniu 伯牛 (Ran Boniu 冉伯牛; Ran Geng 冉耕)	6.10, 11.3
Fan Chi 樊遲 (Fan Xu 樊須)	2.5, 6.22, 12.21, 12.22, 13.4, 13.19
Gongxi Hua 公西華 (Gongxi Chi 公西赤)	5.8, 6.4, 7.34, 11.22, 11.26
Gongye Chang 公冶長	5.1
Min Ziqian 閔子騫 (Min Sun 閔損)	6.9, 11.3, 11.5, 11.13, 11.14
Nan Rong 南容 (Nangong Tao 南宮縚)	5.2, 11.6
Qidiao Kai 漆彫開	5.6
Ran Qiu 冉求 (Ran You 冉有)	3.6, 5.8, 6.4, 6.8, 6.12, 7.15, 11.3, 11.13, 11.17, 11.22, 11.24, 11.26, 13.9, 13.14, 14.12, 16.1
Shen Cheng 申棖 (Zhou 周)	5.11
Tantai Mieming 澹臺滅明 (Ziyu 子羽)	6.14
Wuma Qi 巫馬旗 (Wuma Shi 巫馬施)	7.31
Yan Hui 顏回 (Yan Yuan 顏淵)	2.9, 5.9, 5.26, 6.3, 6.7, 6.11, 7.11, 9.11, 9.20, 9.21, 11.3, 11.4, 11.7, 11.8–11.11, 11.19, 11.23, 12.1, 15.11

Appendix 1B

HISTORICAL FIGURES

The list includes only the major figures that appear in the *Analects*; in most cases, the words and actions of these individuals are also found in the records of China's early history. The names of all other historical figures mentioned may be found in the Index.

Appendix 2A

CHINESE TERMS

Below is a find-list of key Chinese terms with variants of their translation. One should refer to the commentaries for their broader meanings. It is important to note that sometimes, instead of the Chinese term, a variant of its translation appears in the entry.

cai 才	talent, material (5.7, 8.20)
chi 耻	shameful, having a sense of shame (1.13, 2.3, 13.20, 14.1)
dao 道	Way, way, moral way, path, road (4.8, 6.17, 6.27, 7.6, 8.13, 15.29, 15.32, 15.40, 17.14, 18.7, 19.2 19.4, 19.7, 19.22)
de 德	virtue, integrity, power, kindness (1.9, 2.1, 4.25, 6.29, 7.3, 7.6, 7.23, 8.20, 9.18, 12.10, 12.21, 14.4, 14.33, 14.34, 15.4, 15.13, 15.27, 17.13, 17.14, 19.2)
e 惡	morally culpable, vile (4.4)
he 和	harmony (1.12, 13.23)
hui 誨	to teach by way of imparting light (7.2, 7.7, 14.7)
jing 敬	respect, respectful attitude, reverence (1.5, 13.19, 14.42, 15.6, 15.38, 19.1)
juan 狷	overly cautious (13.21)
junzi 君子	a gentleman (2.12, 2.13, 2.14, 4.10, 4.16, 5.3, 6.18, 6.26, 6.27, 7.26, 7.33, 8.6, 9.14, 11.21, 12.4, 12.5, 12.15, 12.16, 12.24, 13.23, 13.25, 13.26, 14.6, 14.23, 14.26, 14.27, 14.28, 14.42, 15.2, 15.7, 15.18, 15.19, 15.21, 15.22, 15.23, 15.34, 15.37, 16.8, 16.10, 16.13, 17.23, 17.24, 19.7, 19.9, 19.10, 19.12, 19.21, 19.25, 20.3); men in the ruling position, men born with hereditary status (1.8, 4.11, 12.19)

kuang 狂	wildly spirited (5.22, 13.21, 17.16)
li 利	suitability, profit (9.1)
li 禮	rites, ritual propriety (1.12, 1.13, 2.3, 2.5, 2.23, 3.6, 3.7, 3.8, 3.9, 3.11, 3.12, 3.15, 3.17, 3.22, 3.26, 4.13, 6.27, 7.13, 8.2, 8.8, 9.3, 9.11, 11.26, 12.1, 12.2, 12.18, 13.4, 14.41, 15.18, 15.33, 16.13, 17.11, 20.3)
ming 命	destiny (6.10, 9.1, 12.5, 14.36, 20.3)
ning 佞	glib (11.25, 14.32, 15.11, 16.4); skillful in speech (5.5, 6.16)
qi 器	vessel, implement (2.12, 5.4)
quan 權	exercising moral discretion (9.30)
ren 仁	humane, humaneness (1.2, 4.1, 4.2, 4.3, 4.4, 4.5, 4.6, 5.5, 5.8, 5.19, 6.7, 6.22, 6.30, 7.6, 7.34, 8.2, 8.7, 9.1, 9.29, 12.2, 12.3, 12.22, 12.24, 13.12, 13.19, 13.27, 14.1, 14.4, 14.5, 14.16, 14.28, 15.8, 15.10, 15.33, 15.35, 15.36, 17.1, 17.6, 17.8, 17.17, 18.1, 19.6, 19.16); character (4.7)
ru 儒	ritual specialists and professional men with textual knowledge (6.13). Confucius was a *ru*. Later the term refers to his followers and ideas associated with him.
shan 善	goodness (16.11)
shanren 善人	a good man (7.26, 11.20, 13.11, 13.29)
sheng 聖	sage (6.30, 7.26, 7.34, 9.6, 16.8, 19.12)
shengui 神鬼	gods and spirits (7.21, 8.21, 11.12)
shi 詩	odes, poems, poetry (1.15, 2.2, 3.2, 3.8, 3.20, 8.8, 8.15, 13.5, 16.13, 17.9, 17.10)
shi 士	a man of education and professional aspiration, a man good enough to be in government, a common gentleman (4.9, 8.7, 12.20, 13.20, 13.28, 14.2, 15.10, 19.1)
shi 時	timely, timeliness (1.1, 10.27)
shu 恕	treating others with and awareness that they, too, are alive with humanity; putting oneself in the other person's place (4.15, 15.24)
si 思	to think (2.15, 9.31, 15.31)

tian 天   heaven meaning nature (8.19, 17.19);
                    Heaven meaning the supreme moral force and
                       that which decides human destiny (3.24, 5.13,
                       6.28, 7.23, 9.5, 9.6, 9.12, 11.9, 12.5, 14.35, 20.1);
                    heaven meaning the sky (19.25)

tianming 天命   what Heaven decreed, what Heaven intended
                       (2.4, 16.8)

wen 文   culture, cultural refinement, literature, written
                       works (1.6, 3.14, 5.13, 5.15, 6.27, 7.1, 7.25,
                       8.19, 9.4, 9.11, 11.3, 12.18, 12.24)

xi 習   practice (1.1, 17.2)

xian 賢   worthiness, worthy (14.31, 14.37)

xiao 孝   filial, filiality (1.2, 1.6, 1.11, 2.5, 2.6, 2.7, 2.8,
                       4.18, 4.20, 4.21, 8.3, 9.18)

xiaoren 小人   a petty man (2.14, 4.16, 13.4, 13.25, 13.26, 14.6,
                       14.23, 15.2, 15.21, 15.34, 16.8, 17.23, 19.8); a
                       commoner, common people (4.11, 12.19); a
                       servant (17.25)

xin 信   trust, trustworthy (1.8, 1.13, 5.28, 7.25, 8.13,
                       9.25, 12.7, 12.10, 13.4, 15.6, 15.18, 17.8,
                       19.10)

xing 性   human nature (5.13, 7.2, 17.2)

xing 行   deed, action, conduct, to act (7.22, 7.25, 7.33,
                       11.3, 12.3, 12.22, 14.3, 14.27, 15.6, 18.8)

xue 學   learning, to learn, to study (1.1, 2.15, 5.28, 6.3,
                       7.2, 7.3, 8.12, 8.13, 8.17, 9.30, 11.7, 14.24, 15.3,
                       15.31, 15.32, 17.8, 19.5, 19.6, 19.7, 19.13)

yan 言   words, speech, to speak (4.22, 4.24, 5.25, 9.24,
                       11.3, 12.3, 14.3, 14.4, 14.20, 15.6, 15.8, 15.23,
                       17.19, 18.8, 20.3)

yi 義   what is right, rightness, fairness (1.13, 4.10, 6.22,
                       7.3, 12.10, 13.4, 15.17, 15.18, 16.10, 16.11,
                       17.23, 18.7, 19.1)

yong 勇   courage, courageous, brave (2.24, 9.29, 14.4,
                       14.28, 17.8, 17.23)

yue / le 樂   *yue*: music (3.3, 3.23, 7.14, 8.8, 8.15, 9.15, 15.11,
                       16.13, 17.11); *le*: joy, pleasure (1.1, 6.11, 6.20,
                       16.5)

zheng 政   to govern, to rule, government (1.10, 2.1, 11.3,
                     11.26, 12.7, 12.11, 12.14, 12.17, 12.19, 13.1,
                     13.2, 13.3, 13.6, 13.14, 13.16, 13.17, 16.2)
zheng 正   to correct, to rectify, upright (12.17, 13.6, 13.13)
zhengming 正名   rectifying names (12.27, 13.3)
zhi 知   to know, to understand, knowledge, all-knowing
                     cognizance (2.17, 6.20, 7.20, 8.9, 9.8, 12.22,
                     14.35, 15.33, 15.34, 16.9, 17.8); wise, wisdom
                     (4.2, 6.22, 9.29, 14.28, 15.8)
zhi 直   upright, uprightness (6.19, 12.22, 13.18, 14.34,
                     15.7, 15.26, 16.4, 17.8)
zhong 忠   to do one's best (1.8, 5.19, 5.28, 7.25, 9.25, 12.10,
                     12.14, 13.19, 14.7, 15.6)

Appendix 2B

MAJOR TOPICS

Many topics are cross-listed with their Chinese terms. One should go to the discussion in the commentaries for references in square brackets, and to Appendix 2A for the transliterated terms.

action, conduct	See *xing* 行.
archery	3.7, 3.16
barbarians	3.5, 9.14, 13.19
Confucius' self-description	2.4, 7.1–7.8, 7.12, 7.19, 7.24, 7.28, 7.33, 7.34, 9.6, 9.7, 9.16, 14.28
courage	See *yong.*
culture, literature	See *wen.*
destiny	See *ming.*
doing one's best	See *zhong.*
fengjian enfeoffment system	[2.3, 7.5]
filial, filiality	See *xiao* and also 4.19, 17.21.
friend, friendship	12.23, 12.24, 16.4, 19.3
funeral/mourning	2.5, 3.2, 3.26, 7.9, 10.25, 12.8, 12.9, 12.10, 12.11, 17.21, 19.14, 19.17
gentleman	See *junzi.*
glib	See *ning.*
gods and spirits	See *shengui.*
good man	See *shanren.*
government/ruler	See *zheng* and also 1.5, 2.19, 2.20, 3.19, 13.15, 14.15, 18.10.
harmony	See *he.*
Heaven, heaven, nature	See *tian.*
Heaven's decree	See *tianming.*
human nature	See *xing* 性.

Appendix 3

CHINESE SCHOLARS AND THINKERS CITED IN THE COMMENTARIES

Liu Baonan 劉寶楠 (1791–1855)

1.3, 1.10, 1.12, 2.15, 2.18,
2.21, 3.21, 3.23, 4.2, 4.3,
4.7–4.13, 5.27, 6.21, 6.27,
7.17, 7.22, 7.25, 7.26, 7.36,
8.5, 8.9, 8.13, 9.1, 9.28,
11.1, 11.12, 11.18, 12.7,
15.3, 15.37, 15.41, 16.13,
17.3, 17.8, 17.10, 17.15,
17.19, 19.11

Liu Kai 劉開 (1784–1824)

4.21

Liu Zongzhou 劉宗周 (1578–1645)

15.22 19.5

Lu Longqi 陸隴其 (1630–1693)

12.6

Ma Rong 馬融 (79–166)

2.6, 3.1, 14.20

Mencius (Mengzi) 孟子 (fourth century BC)

1.1, 1.4, 1.11, 3.13, 3.23,
5.22, 6.26, 7.24, 8.11, 8.13,
9.17, 9.19, 9.29, 10.20,
11.12, 13.9, 13.29, 15.40,
16.7, 17.13, 18.2, 18.4,
19.8, 19.17, 20.3

Qian Daxin 錢大昕 (1728–1804)

1.11, 9.10

Qian Mu 錢穆 (1895–1990)

4.12, 4.13, 4.25, 5.11, 6.4,
6.8, 7.36, 8.9, 8.11, 9.10,
10.27, 14.35, 15.3, 15.12,
15.37, 16.6, 17.2, 19.1,
19.2, 19.12

Ruan Yuan 阮元 (1764–1849)

9.1

Sima Guang 司馬光 (1019–1086)

11.14

Sima Qian 司馬遷 (145?–85?)

5.23, 6.28, 7.24, 15.2, 15.20,
18.1, 18.4

Song Xiangfeng 宋翔鳳 (1779–1860)

2.1, 7.12, 13.2, 14.16

Sun Qifeng 孫奇逢 (1585–1675)

16.10

Wang Bi 王弼 (226–249)

7.21, 18.8

Wang Fuzhi 王夫之 (1616–1692)

3.5, 6.30

Wang Yangming 王陽明 (1472–1529)

1.4, 11.26

Wang Zhong 汪中 (1745–1794)

1.11

Wu Jiabin 吳嘉賓 (1803–1864)

1.10, 14.34, 15.27, 15.40

Xie Liangzuo 謝良佐 (1050–c. 1120)

9.18

Notes

The three commentaries on the *Chunqiu* (the *Spring and Autumn Annals*), *Chunqiu Zuozhuan*, *Chunqiu Gongyangzhuan*, and *Chunqiu Guliangzhuan*, are cited as *Zuozhuan*, *Gongyangzhuan*, and *Gulianzhuan*. Liu Baonan's *Lunyu zhengyi* (Collected commentaries on the *Analects*) is cited as Liu. Cheng Shude's *Lunyu jishi* (Collected glosses on the *Analects*) is cited as Cheng. Qian Mu's *Lunyu xinjie* (New explication of the *Analects*) is cited as Qian. Detailed information on items referenced in the notes may be found in the bibliography.

PREFACE

vii **He refrained from:** *Analects* 9.4.
vii **has "to knock at both sides":** *Analects*, 9.8.
xi **more and more scholars are giving up this theory:** *Beijing daxue cang XiHan zhushu* (Peking University Collection of the Western Han Bamboo Manuscripts), vol. 1, pp. 224–225; Edward Shaughnessy, *Rewriting Early Chinese Texts*, pp. 49–61.

BOOK ONE

1 **1.1:** Cheng Shude, *Lunyu jishi*, pp. 2–4 (unless otherwise noted, all Cheng citations refer to this work); Zhu Xi, *Lunyu jizhu* in *Sishu zhangju*, p. 47; *Mencius*, 5B:1.
2 **1.2:** *Mencius*, 3A:4 (slightly revised from Lau's translation, p. 61); Liu Baonan, *Lunyu zhengyi*, pp. 4–5 (unless otherwise noted, all Liu citations refer to this work); Cheng, pp. 10–12.
3 **1.3:** Cf. 5.5, 11.25, 16.4, 17.13; see also Liu, p. 5.
3 **1.4:** Cf. 8.7, 11.18.

4   1.5: *Zuozhuan*, Duke Zhao, 13th year (ed. Yang Bojun, p. 4);
     Liu, pp. 7–10; Zhu Xi, *Lunyu jizhu* in *Sishu zhangju*, p. 49.

4   1.6: *Liji xunzuan*, *Naize* ("Rules in the Inner Quarters"), pp.
     440–441; Zhu Xi, p. 49.

5   1.7: Liu, pp. 11–12.

6   1.8: Liu, pp. 12–13; Cheng, p. 33.

7   1.9: *Liji xunzuan*, *Jitong* ("Basic Principles of Sacrifice"), p.
     723; also quoted in Liu, p. 13.

7   1.10: Liu, pp. 14–15.

8   1.11: Liu, pp. 15–16; *Mencius*, 4A:19, 7B:36; Qian Daxin,
     Qianwen tang wen ji, quoted in Liu, p. 16.

9   1.12: Liu, pp. 16–17; Qian Mu, *Lunyu xinjie*, pp. 17–18 (unless
     otherwise noted, all Qian citations refer to this work); Cheng,
     pp. 46–47. See, for instance, the *Analects* translations of Sling-
     erland, Watson, and Huang.

9   1.13: Liu, pp. 17–18; Cheng, p. 51; *Zuozhuan*, Duke Xi, 4th
     year.

10   1.14: Cf. 6.11, 6.3, 9.11.

10   1.15: *Shijing zhuxi*, Ode 55, *Qiaoao*, pp. 155–158 (see Arthur
     Waley's translation, "Little Bay of Qi," in *The Book of Songs*,
     p. 46). See also Annping Chin, *The Authentic Confucius*, pp.
     69–74 (unless otherwise noted, all Chin citations refer to this
     work).

11   1.16: Zhu Xi, p. 53; Liu, pp. 19–20; Cheng, 59.

BOOK TWO

12   2.1: Cf. 15.5; see also Liu, pp. 20–21.

12   2.2: *Shijing zhuxi*, Ode 297, pp. 997–1001 (see Waley's transla-
     tion, "Stout," in *Book of Songs*, pp. 308–309); *Xunzi*, chapter
     27, *Dalüe* (27.92), quoted in Liu, p. 22. Cf. 3.20.

13   2.4: Cf. 2.1, 2.2.

14   2.5: Liu, pp. 25–26.

15   2.6: Liu, p. 26.

15   2.7: Liu, pp. 26–27; Zhu Xi, p. 56; *Analects of Confucius*, trans.
     Burton Watson, p. 21.

16   2.8: Liu, pp. 27–28.

16   2.9: Cf. 9.20, 11.4; see also Liu, pp. 28–29.

16   2.10: Cf. 5.8, 5.9, 5.16, 5.17, 5.18, 5.19; see also Liu, p. 29.

17   2.11: Liu, pp. 29–30.

17   2.12: Liu Baonan, pp. 30–31; Zhu Xi, p. 57; Zhang Xuecheng,
     Wenshi tongyi, *juan* 3, pp. 19–21.

18   2.13: Cheng, p. 97; *Liji xunzuan, Ziyi* ("Black Robes"), pp. 815–816.

18   2.14: Liu, p. 31.

18   2.15: The first sentence: *Mencius*, 6A:15; *Xunzi jijie, Quanxue* ("Encouraging Learning"), pp. 12–13 (slightly revised from Watson's translation in *Basic Writings*, p. 20). The second sentence: cf. 15.31; see also Liu, pp. 31–32.

19   2.16: Liu, pp. 32–33; Cheng, pp. 104–110.

20   2.17: Cf. 9.12, 9.27, 11.13, 11.23, 11.25, 11.26, 12.12; see also Cheng, p. 111–112; Liu, p. 33; *Xunzi jijie*, p. 140.

20   2.18: Cf. 12.10, 12.20, 19.15; see also Liu, pp. 34–35.

21   2.19: Liu, p. 35; Zhu Xi, p. 58.

22   2.20: Cf. 6.8, 11.7, 11.17, 12.17, 12.18, 12.19; see also *Zuozhuan*, Duke Ai, 11th year.

22   2.21: Liu, pp. 36–37; Cheng, pp. 126–123; *Zuozhuan*, Duke Ai, 11th year.

23   2.22: Cheng, p. 127.

23   2.23: The two readings: Liu, pp. 39–40; Cheng, pp. 129–130. The last sentence: see Gu Yanwu, *Rizhilu*, quoted in Cheng, p. 128.

24   2.24: Liu, p. 41.

BOOK THREE

25   3.1: Cf. 11.17; see also Liu, pp. 43–44; Cheng, pp. 136–139; *Zuozhuan*, Duke Xiang, 11th year (ed. Yang), pp. 984–987, and Duke Ai, 11th year (ed. Yang), p. 1668.

25   3.2: Chin, pp. 48–49.

26   3.3: *Liji xunzuan, Ruxing*, p. 864; quoted in Liu, p. 44.

27   3.4: Cf. 11.10; see also *Xunzi jijie*, chapter 17, *Tianlun*, p. 318 (cited in Liu, p. 44, but slightly different from the original); *Liji xunzuan, Liyun*, p. 355 (cited in Liu, p. 44).

27   3.5: Zhu Xi, p. 62; Gu Yan Wu and Wang Fuzhi were quoted in Cheng, p. 150.

28   3.6: Cf. 6.4, 6.12, 11.17, 11.24; see also *Zuozhuan*, Duke Ai, 11th year, pp. 1657–1660; Liu, p. 46.

28   3.7: *Mencius*, 7A:41, 2A:7; Cheng, p. 155.

29   3.8: Dai Zhen, *Mengzi ziyi shuzheng*, section 37, 8a–b; Liu, pp. 48–49; Cheng, 157–160.

30   3.9: Liu, pp. 49–50; Zheng Xuan, *Lunyu Zhengshi zhu jishu*, p. 312.

31   3.10: Liu Baonan, *Additional Comments on the Analects (Lunyu buzhu)* (quoted in Cheng, p. 171); Liu, pp. 50–53.

31   3.11: Liu, p. 53; Cheng, pp. 173–174.

32   3.12: *Liji xunzuan, Jiyi* ("The Meaning of the Sacrifice"), p. 702.

32   3.13: Cf. 6.28, 14.19; see also *Mencius*, 5A:8; Sima Qian, *Shiji (Records of the Grand Historian)*, 47:1920–1921; Liu, p. 56; Cheng, pp. 180–181.

33   3.14: Liu, p. 56.

34   3.15: Liu, pp. 56–57; Cheng, pp. 185–186.

34   3.16: *Liji Xunzuan, Sheyi* ("The Meaning of Archery"), p. 897; Cheng, pp. 188–189.

35   3.17: Cheng, pp. 191–195; Liu, pp. 59–62; *Gongyangzhuan*, Duke Wen, 6th and 16th years (SPPY), 13:8b–9a, 14:10a–11b.

36   3.18: Liu, p. 62.

36   3.19: Liu, p. 62; Cheng, p. 197.

37   3.20: Cf. 16.13, 2.2; *Shijing*, Ode 1 (Owen's translation in Stephen Owen, trans. and ed., *An Anthology of Chinese Literature*, pp. 30–31).

37   3.21: Cf. 5.10, 6.26, 11.3, 17.21; see also Cheng, pp. 200–206; Liu, pp. 63–66; Chin, 65–66.

38   3.22: Liu, pp. 68–70; Cheng Yaotian, *Lunxue xiaoji (Informal discussions about learning)*, quoted in Liu Baonan, p. 67.

39   3.23 playing of "metal instruments": Liu, pp. 70–71; Zheng Xuan, p. 22, also quoted in Liu, pp. 70–71. Mencius on Confucius and music: *Mencius*, 5B.1; Cheng, pp. 216–217.

40   3.24: Yang Bojun's commentary to *Zuozhuan*, Duke Xiang, 14th year, pp. 1017–1018; Liu, pp. 72–73.

41   3.25: Cf. 7.14; see also Sun Xingyan, *Shangshu jinguwen zhushu, Gaoyaomo*, part 3, pp. 123–133; Chin, 152–153.

41   3.26: Dong Zhongshu, *Chunqiu fanlu yizheng, Renyifa* ("Models of Humaneness and Rightness"), pp. 226–227; quoted in Liu, p. 74.

BOOK FOUR

43   4.1: Liu, pp. 74–75; Cheng, pp. 227–228; Mencius, 2A:7.

43   4.2: *Liji xunzuan, Fangji*, p. 758, and *Biaoji*, p. 784; Liu, p. 75.

44   4.3: Liu, p. 75.

44   4.4: Dong, *Chunqiu fanlu yizheng, Yuying*, p. 78; quoted in Liu, 75–76.

45   4.5: Liu, 76–77.

46   4.6: The second sentence: Liu, pp. 77–78; Zhu Xi, p. 70.

47   4.7: Zhu Xi, p. 71; Liu, p. 78.

47   4.8: Liu, p. 78.

48   **4.9 Liu Baonan says:** Liu, p. 78.

48   4.10: *Hou Hanshu*, "Biography of Liu Liang," quoted in Liu Baonan, p. 79; see also Cheng, pp. 247–249; Qian Mu, pp. 93–94.

49   4.11: On *xiaoren*: see Liu, pp. 79–80. On *junzi*: see Qian Mu, pp. 94–95; Cheng, p. 251.

49   4.12: Qian Mu, p. 95; Liu, p. 80; *Xunzi jijie*, p. 502.

50   4.13: Liu, p. 80; Qian, p. 96.

50   4.14: *Xunzi*, chapter 6; quoted in Liu, pp. 80–81.

51   4.15: On *zhong* and *shu*: Jiao Xun, *Diaogulou ji* (Collected essays from the Diaogu Pavilion), cited in Cheng Shude, pp. 259–260, and Liu Baonan, p. 81; see also *Mencius*, 2A:8 and 3A:4. On *zhong* (the middle): cf. 20.1; see also *Baoxun* ("Treasured Instructions"), in the *Qinghua daxue cang zhanguo zhujian* (Tsinghua University Collection of the Warring States Bamboo Texts), p. 143.

52   4.16: Dong is quoted in Qian Mu, p. 100; see also Liu, 82–83; Cheng, 267–268; *Xunzi*, section 9.

53   4.17: *Xunzi jijie, Xiushen*, pp. 20–21, quoted in Liu, p. 83.

53   **4.18 Scholars in their commentaries:** *Tangong* chapter and *Jiyi* chapter of *Liji Zhengzhu (The Book of Rites* with Zheng Xuan's commentary), quoted in Liu, pp. 83–84.

55   4.21: Cheng, p. 275.

55   4.22: *Liji xunzuan, Ziyi*, p. 815 (quoted in Liu, p. 85); *Liji xunzuan, Biaoji*, pp. 798–799.

56   4.23: Liu, p. 85; *Liji xunzuan, Biaoji*, pp. 787–788 (partially quoted in Liu).

57   4.25: Liu, pp. 85–86; Qian Mu, p. 106.

57   4.26: Cf. 2.7; see also Liu, p. 86; Qian Mu, p. 107; Zheng Xuan, *Lunyu Zhengshi zhu jishu*, p. 378.

BOOK FIVE

58   5.1: Cheng, pp. 285–286; Liu, p. 87. Xunzi on disgrace: *Xunzi jijie*, chapter 18, *Zhenglun* (see John Knoblock's translation, vol. 3, pp. 46–47).

59   5.2: Liu, pp. 87–88; Cheng, pp. 287–289; Sima Qian, *Shiji*, 47: 1907–1908; *Kongzi jiayu*, pp. 522–525; Ode 256, *Yang* ("Admiration"), *Shijing zhuxi*, pp. 559–560.

60   5.3: Liu Xiang, *Shuoyuan jiaozheng, Zhengli* ("Principles of Government"), pp. 158–159; *Lüshi chunqiu, Chaxian* ("Oberving the Worthy"), 21:277–278; Cheng, pp. 290–292.

60 5.4: Zhu Xi, p. 76; Herbert Fingarette, *Confucius*, pp. 71–76; Qian, p. 111.

61 5.5: Cheng, pp. 294–295. On the initial consonant of *ren* and *ning*, see Zhang Taiyan, *Guogu lunheng*, pp. 25–28.

62 5.6: Cf. 18.6; see also Liu, p. 90; Cheng, pp. 296–297.

62 5.7: Liu, pp. 91–92; Cheng, pp. 299–302.

64 5.9: Cf. 1:15, 2.9, 9.11; see also *Xunzi jijie*, chapter 8, *Xiaoru*, pp. 139–141.

65 5.10: Cf. 3.21, 6.26, 11.3, 17.21; see also *Zuozhuan*, Duke Ai, 14th year, pp. 1683–1685.

65 5.11: Qian Mu, p. 120; Liu, p. 97; Cheng, p. 316.

66 5.12: Qian Mu, pp. 121–122; Liu, pp. 97–98. For other English translations, see those by Slingerland, p. 44; Watson, p. 17; and Legge, p. 177.

66 5.13: Cf. 7.1, 9.11; see also Cheng, pp. 318–323; Liu, pp. 98–100.

67 5.14: Cf. 5.7, 7.11, 11.22, 12.12.

68 5.15: *Zuozhuan*, Duke Ai, 11th year (pp. 1665–1667), and Duke Zhao, 5th year (p. 1163); Cheng, pp. 325–326; Liu, p. 100; Chin, pp. 119–121.

68 5.16: Zichan: *Zuozhuan*, Xianggong, 30th year, and Zhaogong, 20th year; Liu, p. 101; Chin, pp. 56–57. Zhu Xi on Zichan: Zhu Xi, p. 79; *Zuozhuan*, Xiang, 30th year, p. 1181.

69 5.17: Qian, p. 125; Liu, p. 101.

69 5.18: Cheng, pp. 328–331; Liu, pp. 102–103; *Zuozhuan*, Duke Wen, 2nd year, pp. 525–526.

71 5.19: Liu, pp. 103–104; Cheng, pp. 331–335; Qian, p. 127; Ziwen: *Zuozhuan*, Xuan, 4th year, pp. 679–683; Zhuang, 30th year, p. 247; Xi, 23rd year, p. 402. Cuizi and Chen Wenzi: *Zuozhuan*, Xiang, 19th year, pp. 1048–1050, and Xiang, 25th year, pp. 1096–1099; see also Liu, pp. 104–105; Cheng, pp. 335–337. Cuizi (Cui Zhu) and historians of Qi: *Zuozhuan*, Xiang, 25th year, p. 1099; see also *Xinxu jiaoshi*, *Jieshi* ("Men of Integrity"), pp. 903–908.

73 5.20: *Zuozhuan*, Cheng, 16th year, p. 894; Xiang, 5th year, pp. 944–945; and Wen, 18th year, pp. 631–632. See also Cheng, pp. 337–340; Liu, p. 105.

74 5.21: Cheng, pp. 340–343; Qian, pp. 129–130; Liu, p. 106; see also *Zuozhuan*, Duke Wen, 4th year, where Ning Wuzi showed knowledge and wisdom on a visit to the court of Lu (pp. 535–536).

74 5.22: Cf. 6.18, 13.21; see also *Mencius*, 7B:37; Liu, pp. 402–406.

75 5.23: Qian, pp. 132–133; Cheng, pp. 345–346. Sima Qian on Bo

Yi and Shu Qi: *Shiji*, 61:2127, 2123 (Watson's translation, *Ssu-ma Ch'ien Grand Historian of China*, p. 188).

76 5.24: Cheng, pp. 346–348; Liu, p. 108.

77 5.25: *Liji xunzuan, Biaoji* ("Records of Exemplary Conduct"), p. 781; Cheng, p. 348; Liu, pp. 108–109. Identity of Zuoqiu Ming: see Cheng Shude's discussion, pp. 348–352.

78 5.26: Liu, pp. 109–110.

79 5.27: Liu, pp. 110–111.

79 5.28: Cf. 7.18, 7.32; see also Liu, p. 110; Cheng, pp. 358–359.

BOOK SIX

80 6.1: *Xunzi*, "Contra Twelve Philosophers" (*Fei shi'erzi*) in *Xunzi jijie*, pp. 60–66; *Shanghai Bowuguan cang Zhanguo Chu zhushu*, vol. 3, pp. 261–283; Liu Baonan, pp. 111–112.

80 6.2: Liu, 112–113; *Zhuangzi jishi*, "The Great and Venerable Teacher" (*Dazongshi*), "The Mountain Tree" (*Shanmu*), pp.44–45, pp. 125–126; *Chuci duben (Songs of Chu)*, "Crossing the River" (*Shejiang*), p. 99; *Shuoyuan jiaozheng*, "Refining Culture" (*Xiuwen*), pp. 498–499.

81 6.3: Cf. 11.8; see also Liu, pp. 113–114; Qian, pp. 140–141.

82 6.4: Cf. 7.34, 11.26; see also Liu, pp. 114–115; Qian Mu, p. 142; *Liji xunzuan, Tangong*, part 1, pp. 91–91.

82 6.5: Cf. 14.1; see also Liu, pp. 115–116; Qian, p. 143.

83 6.7: Qian, pp. 145–146.

84 6.8: Cf. 2.20; see also *Zuozhuan*, Duke Ai, 11th year, p. 1668; Chin, pp. 119–126.

84 6.9: Cf. 11.3, 11.5, 11.14, 17.5; see also *Zuozhuan*, Duke Xi, 1st year, pp. 278–279; Chin, pp. 29–36; Liu, p. 119.

85 6.10: Cf. 11.3, 11.9, 11.10, Liu, pp. 119–121; see also Zhu Xi, p. 87
  6.11: Cf. 9.11.
  6.12: Cf. 8.7, 19.7, 19.12; see also Liu, pp. 121–122; Chin, pp. 134–137.

86 6.13: Liu, p. 122; Cheng, pp. 389–391.

87 6.14: Liu, pp. 122–123; Zhu Xi, p. 88.

87 6.15: *Zuozhuan*, Duke Ai, 11th year, pp. 1657–1660.

88 6.16: Qian, pp. 153–154; Liu, p. 124.

88 6.17: Liu, pp. 124–125.

89 6.18: Liu, p. 125.

89 6.19: Liu, pp. 125–126.

90 6.20: Liu, p. 126.

90   **6.21:** Cf. 5.13, 9.11, 11.22, 19.3; see also Liu, p. 126.

90   **6.22:** Liu, pp. 126–127; cf. 12.22; Qian, pp. 157–158; *Sources of Chinese Tradition*, p. 596.

91   **6.23:** Qian, pp. 158–159; Liu, pp. 127–128; Cheng, pp. 410–411; cf. *Mencius*, 7A:1; 7A:2.

92   **6.24:** Liu, pp. 128–129.

93   **6.25:** Cheng, pp. 412–415.

93   **6.26:** *Mencius*, 5A:2.

94   **6.27:** Liu, pp. 130–131; Cheng Yaotian, *Lunxue xiaoji*, essay 2, *Bowen pian*, in *Tongyi lu*; Cheng Shude, pp. 417–419.

95   **6.28:** Cf. 3.13; see also Qian Mu, *Kongzi zhuan*, pp. 45–47; Chin, pp. 90–91; Sima Qian, *Shiji*, 47:1920–1921.

95   **6.29:** Qian, pp. 163–164; Cheng, pp. 425–427.

96   **6.30:** Cheng, pp. 427–430.

BOOK SEVEN

97   **7.1:** Liu, p. 135.

98   **7.2:** Cf. 15.3; see also Liu, p. 136; Cheng, pp. 438–439; Xu Shen, *Shuowen jiezi*, 3A:10a; 3B:41a (pp. 91, 128).

98   **7.3:** See Zheng Xuan's comments quoted in Liu, p. 137.

98   **7.4:** Qian, p. 169.

99   **7.5:** Cf. 17.5; see also Chin, pp. 41–48.

99   **7.6:** Liu, pp. 137–138.

100 **7.7:** Liu, pp. 138–139.

100 **7.8:** Chin, p. 144.

101 **7.9:** Qian, p. 173; Liu, pp. 139–140.

101 **7.10:** Qian, p. 173; Liu, pp. 139–140.

101 **7.11:** See *Laozi*, chapters 15, 26; *Mencius*, 6B:15; see also Zeng Guofan, *Zeng Wenzhenggong riji (The diary of Zeng Guofan)* (Taipei: Laogu wenhua shiye gongsi, 1979), pp. 55–56.

101 **7.12:** Cf. 9.6, 9.7; see also Liu, pp. 140–141; Cheng, pp. 454–455.

102 **7.13:** *Liji xunzuan*, *Jiyi* ("The Meaning of Sacrifice"), p. 701; Chin, 162.

102 **7.14:** Liu Xiang, *Shuoyuan jiaozheng*, "Refining Culture" (*Xiuwen*), p. 499; Chin, p. 153.

103 **7.15:** Liu, pp. 142–143.

104 **7.16:** Qian, pp. 178–179.

104 **7.17:** Liu, p. 144; Qian, p. 180.

105 **7.18:** Liu, pp. 145–146.

106 **7.19:** See *Zuozhuan*, Duke Ai, 2nd and 4th years, about the history of She (pp. 1618, 1625–1628), and also Duke Ding, 5th

year, and Duke Ai, 16th year, about the character of the Governor of She (p. 1552; pp. 1700–1704).

107 7.21: Liu, p. 146.

107 7.22: Liu, pp. 146–147.

107 7.23: *Zuozhuan*, Ding, 10th year (p. 1582); *Mencius*, 5A:8; Sima Qian, *Shiji*, 47:1921; Chin, pp. 100–102.

108 7.24: Cf. 7.8, 9.11, 17.19; see also Liu, p. 147.

109 7.25: Liu, p. 147.

109 7.26: Liu, p. 148.

110 7.27: Cf. *Mencius* 3B:1 (Lau's translation, p. 63); *Xunzi, Wangzhi* ("Regulations of a King"), Watson's translation, pp. 46–47; Liu, pp. 148–149.

111 7.29: Liu, pp. 149–150.

111 7.31: Liu, pp. 150–151.

113 7.33: Liu, p. 152; Qian, p. 194.

113 7.35: Liu, pp. 152–153; Qian, pp. 195–196; cf. 7.17.

114 7.36: Liu, p. 153; Qian, p. 197.

BOOK EIGHT

116 8.1: Liu, pp. 154–155; Qian, pp. 199–200.

117 8.2: Liu, pp. 155–156; Cheng, pp. 514–516.

117 8.3: Liu, pp. 156–157.

118 8.4: Liu, pp. 157–158.

119 8.5: Liu, pp. 158–159; Xu Gan, *Xu Dao* ("The Way of Humility"), in *Balanced Discourses (Zhonglun)* (revised from John Makeham's translation, pp. 50–53).

120 8.6: Liu, p. 159.

121 8.8: Chin, pp. 163–164.

121 8.9: Liu, pp. 162–163; Qian, p. 208.

122 8.10: For these scholars' commentaries, see Liu, p. 162.

122 8.11: Liu, p. 162; Qian, pp. 209–210; *Mencius*, 6B:13.

123 8.13: Cf. 14.1, 17.5, 17.7; see also *Mencius*, 7A:1, 7A:2; Liu, pp. 163–164; Chin, pp. 23–40.

124 8.14: *Mencius*, 5B:5 (Lau's translation, p. 117); Liu, p. 164.

124 8.15: Liu, pp. 164–165.

125 8.16: *Xunzi jijie*, chapter 3, *Bugou*, pp. 42–44, quoted in Liu, p. 165; Waley, trans., *Analects*, p. 135.

125 8.17: Liu, p. 165.

125 8.18: Qian, p. 215; Liu, pp. 165–166.

126 8.19: *Laozi* (Lau's translation, p. 82); *Xunzi jijie*, chapter 3, p. 46.

126 8.20: Liu, pp. 167–168; Qian, pp. 216–218.

BOOK NINE

129 9.1: Liu, p. 172; Zhu Xi, p. 109.

130 9.2: Cf. 8.19; see also Liu, pp. 172–173; Waley, trans., *Analects*, pp. 138, 244.

130 9.3: Liu, pp. 173–174.

131 9.4: Zhu Xi, pp. 109–110; *Lunyu Zhengshi zhu jishu*, pp. 128–129.

131 9.5: Cf. 17.1; see also Liu, pp. 176–177; *Zuozhuan*, Duke Ding, 6th year, pp. 1556–1557; *Hanshi waizhuan*, 6:21 (11b–12a); Chin, pp. 102–104.

132 9.6: Liu, pp. 177–178.

133 9.7: Cheng, pp. 583–584.

133 9.8: Cheng, p. 591; Qian, pp. 227–228.

134 9.9: Liu, pp. 179–180.

134 9.10: Cheng, p. 591; Qian, pp. 229–230.

135 9.11: Cf. 2.9, 5.9, 6.3; see also Chin, pp. 73–74.

135 9.12: Liu, p. 184; Qian, pp. 232–234; Chin, pp. 76–77.

136 9.13: Liu, pp. 184–185; Cheng, pp. 601–604.

137 9.14: Cheng, pp. 604–606; Liu, pp. 185–186.

138 9.15: Liu, pp. 186–188.

138 9.16: Cheng, pp. 609–610.

138 9.17: *Mencius*, 4B.18; Dong Zhongshu, chapter 73, "Hymn to Mountains and Rivers" (the *Mencius* and Dong are quoted in Liu, p. 188); Cheng, pp. 610–611.

139 9.18: Liu, pp. 188–189; Zhu Xi, *Lunyu jizhu, Sishu zhangju jizhu*, p. 114.

140 9.19: *Mencius*, 7A:29 (Lau's translation); Liu, p. 189.

140 9.20: Liu, p. 189.

140 9.21: Cf. 9.11, 11.8, 11.9, 11.10, 11.11.

140 9.22: Liu, p. 190.

141 9.23: Liu, p. 190; Cheng, pp. 616–617.

141 9.24: Liu, pp. 190–191.

142 9.26: Zheng Xuan, quoted in Liu, p. 191; Chin, p. 49; *Zuozhuan*, Duke Xiang, 11th year, pp. 984–987.

143 9.27: Liu, pp. 192–193; Chin, pp. 79–81; see *Ode* 33.

143 9.28: *Lunyu Zhengshi, zhu jishu*, p. 417; Liu, p. 193; *Zhuangzi, Rangwang* ("Giving Away a Throne") (revised from Watson's translation, p. 319).

144 9.29: Liu, p. 193; cf. *Analects*, 4.1, 4.2; *Mencius*, 2A:2 (D. C. Lau's translation, pp. 31–32).

144 9.30: Chin, pp. 169–170.

145 9.31: Liu, pp. 193–195.

BOOK TEN

146 10.2: Liu, pp. 197–198; Chin, p. 177.

147 10.3: Liu, p. 198; Chin, p. 177.

148 10.4: Liu, pp. 201–205; Qian, pp. 251–253.

149 10.5: Qian, pp. 253–255; Liu, pp. 205–208.

149 10.6: Liu, pp. 209–218; Qian, pp. 255–257; Chin, pp. 175–176.

150 10.7: Liu, pp. 218–220; Chin, p. 179; *Liji xunzuan, Jiyi*, pp. 702–703.

151 10.8: Liu, pp. 219–223; Cheng, pp. 692–693; *Zhuangzi*, chapter 3 (Watson's translation, pp. 50–51).

152 10.9: Liu, pp. 223–224.

153 10.11: Liu, pp. 225–226.

153 10.13: Liu, pp. 225–226; *Liji xunzuan, Xiangyinjiu yi*, pp. 883–887, and *Zaji* chapter, pp. 650–651.

154 10.14: Liu, pp. 226–227; Cheng, p. 709; Qian, p. 262.

154 10.15: Liu, p. 227.

155 10.17: Liu, p. 228.

155 10.18: Liu, pp. 228–230; Qian, pp. 264–265; *Liji xunzuan, Sangfu xiaoji* ("Record of Smaller Matters in the Dress of Mourning"), pp. 450–451.

156 10.19: Liu, pp. 230–231.

156 10.20: Liu, p. 231; *Mencius*, 5B:7; *Xunzi*, chapter 27, *Dalue* ("Great Compendium").

157 10.22: Liu, pp. 231–232; Qian, p. 266; translation of passage 10.22 in Chin, pp. 178–179; *Liji xunzuan, Tankong*, part 1, p. 114.

157 10.23: Liu, p. 232.

157 10.24: Liu, p. 232.

158 10.25: *Xie* and *ban*: Liu, pp. 232–233; Qian, pp. 267–268. A change of expression: cf. 7.21; see also Chin, pp. 179–180.

159 10.26: Liu, pp. 234–235; Chin, p. 179.

159 10.27: Qian, pp. 269–271; Liu, pp. 235–236; *Mencius*, 5B.1.

BOOK ELEVEN

161 11.1 "Before" and "after": Cf. 7.7, 9.6, 9.7; see also Liu, pp. 236–237; Qian, pp. 275–276. *Yeren* and *junzi*: Liu, pp. 236–237; Zhu Xi, p. 123; Qian Mu, pp. 275–276; Chin, p. 77.

162 11.2: Qian, pp. 276–277; *Mencius*, 7B:18; Liu, p. 238.

162 11.3: Liu, pp. 238–239; Qian, p. 277.

163 11.5: Liu, pp. 239–240; Ban Gu, *Hanshu*, biography of Du Ye, 85:3447; *Hanshi waizhuan*, 2:5 (4a).

163 11.6: Cf. 5.2.

164 11.8: Chin, pp. 74–76.

164 11.9: Chin, pp. 74–76.

164 11.10: Chin, pp. 74–76.

165 11.11: Chin, pp. 74–76.

165 11.12: Liu, p. 243; *Mencius*, 7A:2; Qian, pp. 285–286.

166 11.13: *Zuozhuan*, Duke Ai, 15th year, pp. 1694–1696; Liu, pp. 243–244; Chin, pp. 81–82.

166 11.14: Liu, pp. 244–245; *Zuozhuan*, Duke Zhao, 25th year, pp. 1456–1466; Chin, pp. 58–62.

167 11.15: Cf. 9.29, 12.12; see also Liu, p. 245; Cheng, pp. 770–772; Liu Xiang, *Shuoyuan jiaozheng*, chapter 19, *Xiuwen*, pp. 508–510; Chin, p. 80.

168 11.16: Liu, pp. 245–246; *Liji xunzuan*, p. 745; p. 773; Chin, pp. 131–136.

168 11.17: Liu, pp. 246–247; *Zuozhuan*, Duke Ai, 12th year; *Gongyangzhuan*, Duke Xuan, 12th year (SPPY), 16:8a–b; *Guliangzhuan*, Duke Xuan, 12th year (SPPY), 12:15a; *Mencius*, 3A:3; Chin, pp. 123–126.

169 11.18: Cf. 5.22, 7.15, 11.16, 13.21; see also *Mencius*, 7B:37; Liu, p. 247; Zhu Xi, p. 127; *Zuo Commentary*, Duke Ai, 15th year, pp. 1694–95; *Kongzi jiayu*, chapter 12, *Dizixing* ("Conduct of the Disciples").

170 11.19: Cf. 5.9, 6.11, 9.11, 11.6, 12.8 14.29.

170 11.20: Liu, p. 249.

171 11.21: Cf. 4.22, 4.24, 5.5, 12.20, 17.13; see also Cheng, pp. 786–787; Zhu Xi, p. 128.

171 11.22: Cf. 3.6, 5.7, 6.4, 6.12, 7.11, 11.17; see also Chin, pp. 77–83.

172 11.23: Cf. 7.11, 9.5; see aso Liu, p. 250.

173 11.24: Cheng, p. 792; Liu, pp. 250–251.

174 11.25: Cf. 5.5, 6.9, 11.18.

175 11.26: Chin, pp. 139–140; Wang Yangming, *Wang Yangming quanshu*, 1:12.

BOOK TWELVE

178 12.1: "If for one day . . .": Qian, p. 303; Cheng, pp. 817–821. "It is up to the self . . .": Cf. 17.11; see also Chin, pp. 167–168.

179 12.2: Chin, pp. 168–169.

180 12.3: Cf. 7.23; see also *Mencius*, 5A:8; Liu, pp. 263–264; *Zuozhuan*, Duke Ding, 10th year (p. 1582), and Duke Ai, 14th year (pp. 1686–1688); Chin, pp. 100–101.

181 12.4: Liu, p. 264; Qian, p. 307.

181 12.5: *Zuozhuan*, Duke Ai, 14th year (ed. Yang, pp. 1687–1688); Liu, pp. 264–265.

182 12.6: Lu Longqi, *Songyang jiangyi*, quoted in Cheng, p. 835.

182 12.7: Liu, pp. 266–267; Qian, pp. 310–311.

183 12.8: Chin, pp. 70–71.

184 12.9: Liu, pp. 268–270; *Xunzi jijie*, chapter 10, pp. 194–195; *Gongyangzhuan*, Duke Xuan, 15th year (SPPY), 16:8a–b; *Guliangzhuan*, Duke Xuan, 15th year (SPPY), 12:15a; *Zuozhuan*, Duke Xuan, 15th year, (ed. Yang, p. 766); cf. *Mencus*, 3A:3.

185 12.10: Cheng, pp. 853–855; Waley's translation, *Book of Songs*, p. 161.

186 12.11: Cf. 14.21, 16.12; Liu, pp. 271–272; *Zuozhuan*, Duke Zhao, 25th and 26th years; Duke Ai, 5th and 14th years.

187 12.12: Liu, pp. 272–273; Qian, pp. 315–316.

188 12.13: Cf. 2:3; see also Liu, p. 273.

188 12.14: Liu, p. 274; Cheng, p. 268.

189 12.16: *Dadai Liji*, chapter 49, *Zengzilishi* ("Master Zeng's Teachings"), p. 432.

189 12.17: Cf. 2.20, 12.18, 12.19, 13.13.

190 12.18: Cf. 12.19.

190 12.19: Liu, pp. 275–276; Qian, pp. 319–320.

191 12.20: Cf. 17.3; see also Liu, pp. 276–277.

192 12.21: The second sentence in Confucius' response: cf. 4.3, 12.6, 12.10; reason for this conversation: cf. 12.10; Liu, p. 277; Lau translation of *Analects*, p. 116; *Gongyangzhuan*, Duke Zhao, 25th year (SPPY), 24:4a; Qian, pp. 322–323.

193 12.22: Cf. 6.22; see also Liu, pp. 278–279; Qian, pp. 324–325.

195 12.24: Qian, p. 326.

BOOK THIRTEEN

196 13.1: Liu, pp. 279–280; *DaDai Liji*, chapter 65, *Zhangzi wen ruguan* ("Master Zhang Asked About How to Enter Government Service"), p. 802.

196 13.2: Liu, p. 280; *Lüshi chunqiu*, 17:198; *I Ching*, Lynn's translation, p. 206.

197 13.3: Liu, pp. 283–284; *Xunzi jijie*, chapter 22, p. 422.

198 13.4: Liu, pp. 284–285; *Mencius*, 3A:4 (slightly revised from Lau's translation, pp. 59–60).

199 13.5: Cf. 2.2, 3.20; see also *Zuozhuan*, Duke Xiang, 29th year (ed. Yang, pp. 1161–1166); and see David Schaberg's

discussion of Prince Jizha's performance in *A Patterned Past*, pp. 85–95.

200 13.6: Liu, p. 286; Qian, pp. 332–333; *Xunzi*, chapters 3 and 22.

200 13.7: Cf. 14.18, 15.7; see also Liu, p. 286; *Zuozhuan*, Duke Ai, 14th year (ed. Yang, pp. 1685–1686); Chin, pp. 87–89.

201 13.8: Cf. 3.4; 11.8, 11.11; see also Liu, pp. 286–287; *Zuozhuan*, Duke Xiang, 29th year (ed. Yang, p. 1166).

202 13.9: Liu, p. 287; *Mencius*, 1A:7 (revised from D. C. Lau's translation, p. 13); *Xunzijijie, Dalue* ("Great Compendium"), pp. 498–499.

203 13.10: Liu, pp. 287–288.

203 13.11: Liu, p. 288.

204 13.12: Liu, pp. 288–289; Cheng, p. 911.

204 13.14: Cf. 3.6, 6.12, 11.17; see also Liu, p. 289; Cheng, pp. 913–914; *Zuozhuan*, Duke Ai, 11th and 12th years (ed. Yang, p. 1658).

206 13.15: Liu, p. 290; *Shijing, zhuxi, Daming*, pp. 452–453 (Waley's translation in *Book of Songs*, p. 229); Sun Xingyan, *Shangshu jinguwen zhushu, Junshi*, p. 448; *Hanshi waizhuan*, 10:4 (3a–b) (see Hightower's translation, *Han Shih Wai Chuan*, pp. 321–322); *Guoyu, Wuyu*, vol. 2, p. 602.

207 13.16: Chin, p. 110; *Zuozhuan*, Duke Ai, 2nd and 4th years for the history of She (Fuhan) (ed. Yang, pp. 1618, 1625–1627); *Zuochuan*, Duke Ai, 16th year (ed. Yang, pp. 1700–1704) for Governor She's role in the court politics of Chu; see also Qian Mu's discussion of the history of She in his *Kongzi zhuan (Life of Confucius)*, pp. 54–55, and in his *Xianqin zhuzi xinian*, pp. 55–56.

208 13.17: *Xunzi jijie*, chapter 14, p. 174 (quoted in Liu, p. 291); *Lüshi chunqiu*, 15:164–165 (partly quoted in Liu, p. 291).

209 13.18: Zhu Xi, p. 146; Cheng Yaotian, *Shugong*, in *Lunxue xiaoji* ("Informal notes on the topic of learning"), found in his collected works, *Tongyi lu* (On understanding the art of things) (partly quoted in Liu, p. 292); Chin, pp. 110–112.

210 13.19: Cf. 12.14, 15.6, 17.6; see also Qian, p. 342.

210 13.20: Liu, pp. 293–294; Qian, pp. 343–344.

211 13.21: *Mencius*, 7B:37.

212 13.22: Liu, pp. 295–296; Cheng, pp. 932–935; *Yijing*, hexagram 32, *heng*; *Shijing*, Ode 195; *Liji xunzuan, Ziyi*, pp. 815–816; *Guodian chumu zhujian* (Guodian bamboo texts from a Chu tomb), *Ziyi*, p. 131.

213 13.23: Liu, pp. 296–297; *Zuozhuan*, Duke Zhao, 20th year (ed. Yang, pp. 1419–1420).

214 13.24: Cf. 12.20, 15.28; 17.18.

214 13.25: Cf. 18.10.

215 13.26: Cf. 13.20; see also Liu, p. 298; Qian Mu, *Zhuangzi zuan-jian*, chapter 17, p. 130.

215 13.27: Cf. 4.22, 4.24, 5.5, 5.11, 8.7, 10.1; see also Liu, p. 298.

216 13.28: Liu, pp. 298–299; *Mencius*, 4B:30 (slightly revised from Lau's translation, p. 96); see also *Mencius* 4A:18, 5A:1, 5A:2, 5A:3.

216 13.29: Liu, p. 299; Qian, p. 350; Zhu Xi, *Lunyu jizhu, Sishu zhangju jizhu*, p. 148; Zheng Xuan, *Lunyu zhengshi zhu jishu, Tangchaoben* (Tang manuscript), p. 347.

BOOK FOURTEEN

218 14.1: Cheng, pp. 946–950; Liu, p. 300.

219 14.2: Liu, p. 300.

220 14.3: *Zhuangzi, Renjianshi* ("In the World of Men") (revised from Watson's translation, p. 55); Liu, p. 301.

220 14.4: Liu, p. 301; *Xunzi jijie*, chapter 5, p. 83, and chapter 23, p. 447 (quoted in Liu, p. 301).

221 14.5: Liu, pp. 301–304; Cheng, pp. 952–957; *Zuozhuan*, Duke Xiang, 4th year, and Duke Ai, 1st year (ed. Yang, pp. 936–938, 1605–1606).

222 14.6: Cf. 8.7, 14.1; see also Liu, p. 303.

222 14.7: Liu, pp. 303–304.

223 14.8: Liu, pp. 304–305; *Zuozhuan*, Duke Xiang, 31st year (ed. Yang, p. 1191).

223 14.9: Liu, pp. 305–306; Cheng, pp. 962–963; cf. *Zuozhuan*, Duke Xiang, 30th and 31st years, and Duke Zhao, 20th year (ed. Yang, pp. 1180–1181, 1192, 1421–1422); *Mencius*, 4B:2, 2A:1; Chin, p. 15, pp. 56–57.

224 14.10: Liu, pp. 306–307.

225 14.11: Liu, p. 307.

225 14.12: A different reading: Liu, pp. 307–308; Cheng, pp. 969–975. The four men: Sima Qian, *Shiji*, 70:2302; *Hanshi waizhuan*, 10:13 (9b–10a) (see Hightower's translation, pp. 334–335); *Zuozhuan*, Duke Xiang, 23rd year (ed. Yang, pp. 1082–1085).

226 14.13: Liu, pp. 308–309; *Liji yijie, Tangong*, p. 134.

227 14.14: *Zuozhuan*, Duke Xiang, 23rd year (ed. Yang, pp. 1082–1084).

228 14.15: Liu, pp. 309–310.

229 14.16: Liu, pp. 311–313; *Zuozhuan*, Duke Huan, 18th year (ed.

Yang, pp. 152–153), and Zhuang, 8th and 9th years (ed. Yang, pp. 176–180); *Cambridge History of Ancient China*, pp. 553–557.

230   14.17: Liu, pp. 314–316; Qian, pp. 367–369; *Guanzi* (*Master Guan*), chapters 18 and 20; *Cambridge History of Ancient China*, pp. 553–557.

231   14.18: Liu, p. 316; Chin, p. 89.

232   14.20: Liu, p. 317.

232   14.21: Liu, pp. 317–318; *Zuozhuan*, Duke Ai, 14th year (ed. Yang, pp. 1682–1686, 1689); Chin, pp. 128–129.

234   14.22: Liu, p. 318.

234   14.23: Liu, p. 318.

234   14.24: *Xunzi jijie*, pp. 12–13 (revised from Watson's translation, p. 21), quoted in Liu, pp. 318–319.

235   14.25: Liu, p. 319; Qian, pp. 374–375; *Zhuangzi, Zeyang* (Watson's translation, p. 288); Chin, pp. 92–93.

236   14.28: Qian, p. 377.

237   14.29: Cf 5.9, 11.16, 11.19; see also Liu, p. 320; Qian, pp. 377–378.

237   14.30: Cf. 1.1, 14.24.

238   14.32: Cf. 14.2; see also Liu, pp. 320–321; Qian, pp. 379–380.

238   14.33: Liu, p. 321.

239   14.34: Liu, p. 321; *Liji xunzuan, Biaoji*, pp. 783–784; Wu Jiabin, *Lunyushuo* (quoted in Liu, p. 321).

239   14.35: Cf. 14.23, 17.19; see also Qian, pp. 382–383; *Xunzi jijie*, chapter 3, p. 28.

240   14.36: Liu, pp. 322–324.

241   14.37: Cf. 18.8; see also Liu, p. 324.

242   14.39: Cf. 14.37, 14.38, 18.5, 18.6, 18.7, 18.8; see also Liu, pp. 325–326; Chin, pp. 117–118.

243   14.40: On the three-year mourning period: Liu, pp. 326–329; *Liji xunzuan, Sannianwen* ("Questions About the Three-Year Mourning"), pp. 842–843, and chapter 22, *Sangdaji* ("The Greater Record of Mourning Rites") (revised from Legge's translation, p. 191); Sun Xingyan, *Shangshu jinguwen zhushu, Wuyi* ("Against Luxurious Ease"), pp. 435–438; on Gaozong and Fuyue: *Guoyu, Chu Yu*, p. 554; Sima Qian, *Shiji, Yin benji*, 3:103; *Qinghua zhujian, Yueming*, vol. 3, pp. 121–131.

244   14.41: Cf. 2.1, 12.17, 13.3, 14.40.

244   14.42: Liu, p. 329; Qian, pp. 391–392; *Liji xunzuan*, chapter 31, *Zhongyong*, p. 780.

245   14.43: Liu, pp. 329–330; Qian, pp. 392–393.

246   14.44: Liu, p. 330.

BOOK FIFTEEN

247 15.1: Cf. 3.13, 6.28, 12.17, 13.29, 13.30; see also Liu, p. 331; Chin, p. 96, 99–100.

247 15.2: Cf. 14.36; see also *Xunzi jijie*, chapter 28, *Youzuo*, pp. 345–346; Qian Mu, *Zhuangzi zuanjian*, chapter 20, *Shanmu*, pp. 159–160; Sima Qian, *Shiji*, 47:1930–1932; Chin, pp. 105–109.

248 15.3: Cf 2.2; see also Liu, pp. 333–334; Qian, pp. 397–398.

249 15.4: Qian, pp. 398–399.

249 15.5: Qian, pp. 399–400; *Laozi*, chapter three; *Xunzi jijie*, chapter 21, p. 400.

250 15.7: Liu, pp. 335–336; *Hanshi waizhuan*, 7:21; *Zuozhuan*, Duke Xiang, 14th and 26th years (ed. Yang, pp. 1012, 1112) (both quoted in Liu).

251 15.8: Liu, pp. 336–337; Qian, p. 402; Xu Gan, *Balanced Discourses (Zhonglun)*, chapter 6, *Guiyan* ("Valuing Words") (John Makeham's translation, pp. 72–77).

252 15.9: Liu, p. 336; Qian, pp. 402–403; *Mengzi zhengyi*, pp. 783–784; Annping Chin, "*Shigui huoshi wanggui: Mengzi yu Qi Xuan Wang de duihua*" (Is a *shi* nobler than a king: conversations between Mencius and King Xuan of Qi), *Mengzi sixiang de dangdai jiazhi guoji xueshu taolunhui* (International Conference on the Thought of Mencius), conference volume, 2006, pp. 445–449 (the essay's Chinese translation is in Zhongguo ruxue 2 (2006), pp. 67–78).

253 15.11: Cf. 3.25, 7.14, 17.18; see also Liu, pp. 337–340; Qian, pp. 404–406; *Cambridge History of Ancient China*, pp. 19–20; Chin, *Authentic Confucius*, pp. 149–151.

254 15.12: Qian, p. 406.

255 15.14: Cf. 18.2, 18.8; see also Qian, p. 407, Cheng, pp. 1094–1097.

255 15.15: Liu, pp. 340–341; Dong, *Chunqiu fanlu yizheng*, *Renyifa*, pp. 255–256; *Lüshi chunqiu*, 19:252.

256 15.16: Liu, p. 341.

257 15.20: Liu, p. 342;, Sima Qian, "Biography of Po Yi and Shu Qi," in *An Anthology of Chinese Literature*, trans. and ed. Stephen Owen, p. 144.

258 15.21: Cheng, pp. 1103–1104.

258 15.22: Cf. 4.10; see also Liu, p. 343.

259 15.23: Liu, p. 343.

259 15.24: Cf. 5.12.

260 15.25: Qian, pp. 413–414.

260 15.26: Liu, pp. 344–345; Ban Gu, *Hanshu, Yiwenzhi*, p. 1721 (quoted in Liu); Chin, p. 3.

261 15.27: Cf. 4.3, 7.8, 7.11; see also Liu, p. 345; Cheng, pp. 415–416; Zhu Xi, *Lunyu jizhu, Sishu zhangju jizhu*, p. 167.

261 15.29: Liu, pp. 345–346; *Liji xunzuan*, chapter 31, *Zhongyong* ("Doctrine of the Mean"), p. 778; Ban Gu, *Hanshu*, 56 *juan*, biography of Dong Zhongshu, pp. 2499–2500 (passages from the *Zhongyong* and the *Hanshu* are quoted in Liu).

262 15.30: Cf. 6.3; see also Liu, p. 346.

262 15.32: Liu, p. 346.

263 15.33: Qian, pp. 419–420.

264 15.34: Liu, p. 347; Zhu Xi, *Lunyu jizhu, Sishu zhangju jizhu*, p. 168.

264 15.35: Liu, p. 348; Cheng, pp. 1123–1124; *Mencius*, 7A:23.

265 15.36: Liu, p. 348; Dong, *Chunqiu fanlu yizheng, Zhulin* ("Bamboo Forest"), pp. 51–55; *Gongyangzhuan*, Duke Xuan, 15th year; Chin, pp. 145–146.

266 15.37: Liu, p. 348; Qian, p. 422; *Mencius*, 7A:26 (quoted in Liu).

266 15.38: Cf. 15.32; see also Liu, p. 348; Qian, p. 423; *Liji xunzuan, Biaoji*, p. 797.

266 15.39: Liu, pp. 348–349; Qian, p. 423; Cheng, p. 1126; Slingerland, trans., *Confucius Analects*, p. 189.

267 15.40: Liu, p. 349; *Mencius*, 5B:1.

268 15.41: Liu, p. 349.

268 15.42: Liu, p. 349; Chin, pp. 142–143.

BOOK SIXTEEN

269 16.1: Liu, pp. 350–354; Cheng, pp. 1130–1141; Qian, pp. 426–429; *Zuozhuan*, Duke Xi, 21st year (ed. Yang, pp. 391–392); Zhu Xi, *Lunyu jizhu, Sishu zhangju jizh*, pp. 169–171.

271 16.2: Liu, pp. 354–356; Chin, pp. 41–42.

273 16.3: Cf. 17.1, 17.5; see also Liu, pp. 353–354; *Zuozhuan*, Duke Wen, 18th year, and Duke Zhao, 32nd year (ed. Yang, pp. 631–633, 1519–1520.

273 16.4: Cf. 5.25; see also Liu, pp. 357–358.

274 16.6: Liu, p. 359; Qian, p. 433; *Xunzi jijie*, chapter 1, *Quanxue* ("Encouraging Learning"), pp. 17–18.

275 16.7: *Mencius*, 2A:2 (see Lau's translation, pp. 32–33); *Xunzi*, chapters 21, 22, 23 (see Watson's translation, pp. 121–171).

275 16.8: Liu, pp. 359–360.

276 16.9: Cf. 15.39, 17.2.

276 16.10: Liu, p. 361; *Mencius*, 6A:15.

277 16.11: Cf. 9.21, 11.7, 11.19; see also Qian, pp. 437–438.

277 16.12: Cf. 5.23, 7.15, 12.11, 18.3; see also Liu, pp. 362–363; Qian, pp. 438–439; Zhu Xi, *Lunyu jizhu, Sishu zhangju jizh*, p. 136.

278 16.13: Cf. 17.9, 17.10; see also Liu, pp. 364–365.

279 16.14: Cheng, pp. 1170–1173; Qian, p. 441.

BOOK SEVENTEEN

280 17.1: *Zuozhuan*, Duke Ding, 8th year (ed. Yang, pp. 1563, 1568–1570); Chin, pp. 32–35.

281 17.2: Cf. 15.39, 16.9; see also Qian, p. 444; Cheng, pp. 1177–1184.

281 17.3: Cf. 16.9; see also Liu, p. 368.

282 17.4: Liu, p. 369.

283 17.5: Cf. 17.1, 17.7; see also *Zuozhuan*, Duke Ding, 12th year (ed. Yang, pp. 1585–1587); Chin, pp. 29–36.

284 17.6: Liu, p. 371; Qian, pp. 447–448.

284 17.7: Liu, pp. 371–373; *Zuozhuan*, Duke Ding, 13th year, and Duke Ai, 3rd and 5th years (ed. Yang, pp. 1589–1591, 1622–1623, 1630).

285 17.8: Liu, pp. 373–374; *Xunzi jijie*, chapter 21, *Jiebi*, pp. 386–410 (Watson's translation, "Dispelling Obsessions," pp. 120–138).

286 17.9: Liu, pp. 374–375.

287 17.10: Liu, p. 375.

288 17.11: Liu, pp. 375–376.

288 17.13: *Mencius*, 7B:37; Chin, pp. 154–155.

289 17.14: Liu, p. 377; *Xunzi jijie*, chapter 1, *Quanxue*, pp. 12–13 and p. 509.

291 17.17: Liu, pp. 377–378.

291 17.18: Liu, p. 379.

291 17.19: Liu, pp. 379–380; *Xunzi jijie*, *Tianlun* ("A Discussion of Heaven") (slightly revised from Watson's translation, p. 80), and *Bugou* ("Nothing Indecorous"), p. 28.

292 17.20: Qian, pp. 458–459.

292 17.21: Cf. 14.40; see also Chin, p. 67.

294 17.22: Cf. 15.17; see also Liu, pp. 383–384; Qian, pp. 461–462.

294 17.23: Liu, p. 384; *Liji jijie*, chapter 48, p. 947; *Xunzi jijie*, chapter 4, *Ronru* ("Of Honor and Disgrace"), p. 56, quoted in Liu).

295 17.24: Liu, pp. 384–386.

295 17.25: Qian, p. 646; Chin, pp. 96–99.

296 17.26: Cheng, pp. 1245–1246.

BOOK EIGHTEEN

297 **18.1:** Liu, pp. 386–388; Xu Gan, *Balanced Discourses* (*Zhong-lun*) (John Makeham's translation, p. 117), also quoted in Liu.

299 **18.2:** Cf. 18.8; *Mencius*, 2A:9 (slightly revised from Lau's translation, p. 40).

299 **18.3:** Liu, pp. 388–389; *Mencius*, 5B:1 (see Lau's translation, pp. 111–113).

300 **18.4:** Chin, pp. 26–32, 39–40; *Mencius*, 6B:6; Sima Qian, *Shiji*, 47:1918; *Zuozhuan*, Duke Ding, 12th year (ed. Yang, pp. 1585–1587).

301 **18.5:** Liu, pp. 390–391; Chin, pp. 113–114; Qian Mu, *Zhuangzi zuanjian*, *Renjianshi* ("In the World of Men"), p. 38.

302 **18.6:** Liu, pp. 391–393.

304 **18.7:** Liu, pp. 393–395; Qian, pp. 473–475; Chin, pp. 115–116.

305 **18.8:** Cf. 5.23, 7.15, 16.12, 18.2; see also Liu, pp. 395–397; Qian, pp. 475–477; *Liji xunzuan*, *Zaji* ("Miscellaneous Records"), p. 634; Chin, pp. 116–117.

307 **18.9:** Liu, pp. 397–399; Chin, pp. 140–141.

307 **18.10:** Chin, p. 48.

308 **18.11:** Qian, pp. 479–480.

BOOK NINETEEN

309 **19.1:** Cf. 12.6, 12.10; see also Qian, p. 481.

310 **19.3:** Cf. 17.6, 19.4, 19.7, 19.12, 20.2; see also Liu, pp. 401–402.

311 **19.4:** Liu, p. 402; Qian, pp. 483–484.

311 **19.5:** Liu, p. 402.

312 **19.8:** Cf. 19.21; *Mencius*, 2B:9 (quoted in Liu, p. 403).

313 **19.9:** Qian, pp. 486–487.

313 **19.10:** Cheng, pp. 1315–1316.

313 **19.11:** Cf. 5.16, 14.8, 14.9; see also Liu, p. 404; *Book of Documents*, *Jiugao* ("The Announcement About Drunkenness"), in Sun Xingyan, *Shangshu jinguwen zhushu*, p. 376; Dong, *Chunqiu fanlu yizheng*, *Yuying*, pp. 79–80.

314 **19.12:** Cf. 9.7; see also Qian, pp. 488–490; Liu, pp. 404–405; Cheng, pp. 1319–1324.

315 **19.13:** Cf. 9.6, 9.7, 18.6, 18.7.

316 **19.14:** Cf. 11.8–11.11; see also Cheng, pp. 1325–1326; Qian, p. 491.

316 **19.16:** Cf. 2.18, 12.10, 12.20; see also Liu, p. 406.

316 **19.17:** Cf. 2.5; see also *Mencius*, 3A:2; Cheng, p. 1329.

317 19.18: Cf. 2.5; see also Qian, pp. 493–494.

317 19.19: Cf. 2.3, 12.17–12.19, 13.11, 13.12; see also Cheng, pp. 1330–1332.

318 19.20: Cf. 18.1; see also Liu, pp. 407–408; *Liezi* (slightly revised from A. C. Graham's translation in *The Book of Lieh-tzu*, pp. 150, 151).

319 19.22: Liu, p. 408.

319 19.23: Liu, pp. 408–409.

320 19.24: Liu, p. 410; Qian, pp. 498–499.

321 19.25: Chin, pp. 187–188.

BOOK TWENTY

322 20.1A: *Shanghsu, Yaodian; Baoxun* ("Treasured Instructions"), in the *Qinghua daxue cang zhanguo zhujian* (Tsinghua University Collection of the Warring States Bamboo Texts), Vol. 1B: 142–148; Liu, pp. 411–414; Qian, pp. 503–508.

324 20.1B: Liu, pp. 414–417.

325 20.2: Cf. 7.15, 7.38, 13.26, 19.10; see also Cheng, pp. 1370–1374; Qian, pp. 509–511.

326 20.3: *Mencius*, 2A:2 (Lau's translation, p. 33), and 7A:2 (Lau's translation, p. 145); Qian, pp. 511–512.

Bibliography

MAJOR COMMENTARIES CONSULTED

Liu Baonan was my guide from beginning to end. Cheng Shude gathered more materials and introduced more disparate interpretations in his four-volume edition, though much of his work was built on that of Liu Baonan. Qian Mu, being versed in the scholarship of the past, brought freshness—and often a surprising point of view—to the discussion.

Liu Baonan (劉寶楠). *Lunyu zhengyi* (論語正義) (Collected commentaries on the *Analects*). In *Xinbian zhuzi jicheng* (新編諸子集成) (New edition of the works of the early philosophers). Vol. 1. Taipei: Shijie shuju, 1974.

Cheng Shude (程樹德). *Lunyu jishi* (論語集釋) (Collected glosses on the *Analects*). 4 vols. Beijing: Zhonghua shuju, 1990.

Qian Mu (錢穆). *Lunyu xinjie* (論語新解) (New explication of the *Analects*). Beijing: Sanlian Shudian, 2002.

OTHER SOURCES

Ames, Roger, and Henry Rosemont, Jr., trans. *The Analects of Confucius: A Philosophical Translation.* New York: Ballantine Books, 1998.

Ban Gu (班固). *Hanshu* (漢書) (History of the former Han). Vol. 6. Beijing: Zhonghua shuju, 1962.

Beijing daxue cang Xi Han zhushu (The Peking University Collection of the Western Han Bamboo Manuscripts). Vol. 1, edited by Han Wei. Shanghai: Shanghai Guji shubanshe, 2012.

Brooks, E. Bruce, and A. Taeko Brooks, trans. and comm. *The*

Original Analects: Sayings of Confucius and His Successors.
New York: Columbia University Press, 1998.

The Cambridge History of Ancient China: From the Origins of Civilization to 221 B.C. Edited by Michael Loewe and Edward L. Shaughnessy. Cambridge: Cambridge University Press, 1999.

Cheng Yaotian (程瑤田). *Tongyi lu* (通藝錄) (On understanding the art of things). Yangzhou: *Jiangsu guangling guji,* 1991.

Chin, Annping. *The Authentic Confucius: A Life of Thought and Politics.* New York: Scribner, 2007.

Chuci duben (楚辭讀本) *(Songs of Chu).* Annotated by Fu Xiren 傅錫壬. Taipei: Sanmin shuju, 1976.

Chunqiu Gongyangzhuan zhushu (春秋公羊傳注疏) (The Gongyang commentary on the *Spring and Autumn Annals*). Annotated by He Xiu (何休). Sibu beiyao (四部備要) (SPPY) edition. Shanghai: Zhonghua paiyin ben, 1933.

Chunqiu Guliangzhuan (春秋穀梁傳) (The Guliang commentary on the *Spring and Autumn Annals*). Annotated by Fan Ning (范甯). Sibu beiyao (四部備要) (SPPY) edition. Shanghai: Zhonghua shuju, 1930.

Chunqiu Zuozhuan zhu (春秋左傳注) (The *Spring and Autumn Annals* with the *Zuo Commentary*), 4 vols. Edited by Yang Bojun (楊伯峻). Beijing: Zhonghua shuju, 1990.

Creel, Herrlee. *Confucius and the Chinese Way.* New York: Harper & Row, 1960.

DaDai Liji huijiao jijie (大戴戴禮記匯校集解) (Collected commentaries on the *Elder Dai's Book of Rites*). Edited by Fang Xiangdong. Beijing: Zhonghua shuju, 2008.

Dai Zhen (戴震). *Mengzi ziyi shuzheng* (孟子字義疏證) (An evidential study of the meaning of terms in the *Mencius*). Taipei: Guangwen shuju, 1978.

Dawson, Raymond, trans. *The Analects.* Oxford: Oxford University Press, 1993.

Dingzhou Han mu zhujian Lunyu (定州漢墓竹簡論語) (The bamboo-strip *Analects* manuscript from the Han tomb at Dingzhou). Edited by the Hebei wenwu yanjiusuo. Beijing: Wenwu chubanshe, 1997.

Dong Zhongshu (董仲舒). *Chunqiu fanlu yizheng* (春秋繁露義證) (Luxuriant gems of the *Spring and Autumn Annals* with annotations), edited by Su Yu (蘇輿). Beijing: Zhonghua shuju, 2002.

Eno, Robert. "The Background of the Kong Family of Lu and the Origins of Ruism." *Early China* 28 (2003): 1–41.

Falkenhausen, Lothar von. *Chinese Society in the Age of Confucius (1000–250 B.C.).* Los Angeles: Cotsen Institute of Archaeology, UCLA, 2006.

Fingarette, Herbert. *Confucius—the Secular as Sacred*. New York: Harper & Row, 1972.

Gao Shiqi (高士奇). *Zuozhuan jishi benmo* (左傳紀事本末) (The ins and outs of the events recorded in the *Zuo Commentary*). 3 vols. Beijing: Zhonghua shuju, 1979.

Graham, A. C., trans. *The Book of Lieh-tzu*. New York: Columbia University Press, 1990.

———. *Disputers of the Tao*. La Salle: Open Court, 1989.

Gu Derong (顧德融) and Zhu Shunlong (朱順龍). *Chunqiu shi* (春秋史) (History of the Spring and Autumn period). Shanghai: Renmin chubanshe, 2001.

Guanzi (管子). Edited by Dai Wang (戴望). Vol. 5 of *Xinbian zhuzi jicheng* (新編諸子集成) (New edition of the works of the early philosophers). Taipei: Shijie shuju, 1974.

Guodian chumu zhujian (郭店楚墓竹簡) (The Guodian bamboo texts from a Chu tomb). Edited by Jingmen Bowuguan (荊門博物館). Beijing: Wenwu chubanshe, 1998.

Guoyu (國語) (Sayings of the states). 2 vols. Shanghai: Guji chubanshe, 1978.

Hanfeiizi jijie (韓非子) (Collected commentaries on *Hanfeizi*). Edited by Wang Xianshen (王先慎). Vol. 5 of *Xinbian zhuzi jicheng* (新編諸子集成) (New edition of the works of the early philosophers). Taipei: Shijie shuju, 1974.

Hanshi waizhuan (韓詩外傳) (The outer chapters of Han Ying's commentary on the *Book of Poetry*). In *Jifu congshu* (畿輔叢書), 94:6–8. Taipei: Yiwen yinshuguan, 1966.

Hightower, James. *Han Shih Wai Chuan: Han's Ying's Illustration of the Didactic Application of the* Classic of Songs. Cambridge: Harvard University Press, 1952.

Hsu, Cho-yun. *Ancient China in Transition: An Analysis of Social Mobility, 722–222 B.C.* Stanford: Stanford University Press, 1965.

Huang, Chichung, trans. *The Analects of Confucius*. New York and Oxford: Oxford University Press, 1997.

I Ching. *The Classic of Changes: A New Translation of the* I Ching *as Interpreted by Wang Bi*. Translated by Richard John Lynn. New York: Columbia University Press, 1994.

Knoblock, John, trans. *Xunzi: A Translation and Study of the Complete Works*. 3 vols. Stanford: Stanford University Press, 1988–1994.

Kongzi jiayu (孔子家語) (Recorded conversations from the private collections of the Kong family). Commentary by Wang Su (王肅). Vol. 2 of *Xinbian zhuzi jicheng* (新編諸子集成) (New edition of the works of the early philosophers). Taipei: Shijie shuju, 1974.

Laozi Daodejing (老子道德經). Vol. 3 of *Xinbian zhuzi jicheng* (新編諸子集成) (New edition of the works of the early philosophers). Taipei: Shijie shuju, 1974.

Lau, D. C., trans. *The Analects (Lun yü) / Confucius.* Harmondsworth: Penguin Books, 1979.

———, trans. *Lao Tzu, Tao Te Ching.* Harmondsworth: Penguin Books, 1963.

———, trans. *Mencius.* Harmondsworth: Penguin Books, 1970.

Legge, James, trans. *The Chinese Classics. Vol. 1, Confucian Analects; The Great Learning; The Doctrine of the Mean. Vol. 2, The Works of Mencius. Vol. 3, The Shoo King (Shujing).* Oxford: Clarendon Press, 1893–1895. Reprint. Hong Kong: Hong Kong University Press, 1960.

———, trans. *Li Chi (Liji): The Book of Rites.* 2 vols. Oxford: Clarendon Press, 1885.

Leys, Simon, trans. *The Analects of Confucius.* New York: W. W. Norton, 1997.

Li, Feng. "'Feudalism' and Western Zhou China: A Criticism." *Harvard Journal of Asiatic Studies* 63, no. 1 (June 2003): 115–144.

———. *Landscape and Power in Early China: The Crisis and Fall of the Western Zhou, 1045–771 B.C.* Cambridge, MA: Cambridge University Press, 2006.

Li, Wai-yee. *The Readability of the Past in Early Chinese Historiography.* Cambridge, MA: Harvard University Asia Center, 2007.

Liji shijie (禮記釋解) (The *Book of Rites* with modern Chinese explication). Edited by Wang Wenjin (王文錦). 2 vols. Beijing: Zhonghua shuju, 2001.

Liji xunzuan (禮記訓纂) (Collected commentaries on the *Book of Rites*). Edited by Zhu Bin (朱彬). 2 vols. Beijing: Zhonghua Shuju, 1998.

Liji Zheng zhu (禮記鄭注) (The *Book of Rites* with Zheng Xuan's commentary). Edited, with commentary, by Zheng Xuan (鄭玄). Sibu beiyao (SPPY) edition. Shanghai: Zhonghua shuju, 1936.

Liu Xiang (劉向). *Shuoyuan jiaozheng* (說苑校證) (The *World of Stories* with annotations). Collated by Xiang Zonglu (向宗魯). Beijing: Zhonghua shuju, 1987.

Lü Simian (呂思勉). *Xianqin shi* (先秦史) (History before the Qin dynasty). Hong Kong: Taiping shuju, 1962.

Lunyu Zhengshi zhu jishu (論語鄭氏注輯述) (The *Analects* with Zheng Xuan's commentary based on the excavated manuscript from the Tang). Edited and annotated by Cheng Ching-jo, Taipei, Xuehai Chubanshe, 1981.

Lüshi Chunqiu xinjiaozheng (呂氏春秋) (Newly edited commentary on *Mr. Lü's Spring and Autumn Annals*). Collated by Bi Yuan (畢沅), with commentary by Gao You (高誘). Vol. 6 of *Xinbian zhuzi jicheng* (新編諸子集成) (New edition of the works of the early philosophers). Taipei: Shijie shuju, 1974.

Makeham, John. *Transmitters and Creators: Chinese Commentators and Commentaries on the* Analects. Cambridge, MA: Harvard University Asia Center, 2004.

Mengzi zhengyi (孟子正義) (Collected commentaries on the *Mencius*). Edited, with commentary, by Jiao Xun (焦循). Vol. 1 of *Xinbian zhuzi jicheng* (新編諸子集成) (New edition of the works of the early philosophers). Taipei: Shijie shuju, 1974.

Nivison, David. *The Life and Thought of Chang Hsüeh-ch'eng (Zhang Xuecheng)*. Stanford: Stanford University Press, 1966.

Owen, Stephen, trans. and ed. *An Anthology of Chinese Literature: Beginnings to 1911*. New York: W. W. Norton, 1996.

Pines, Yuri. *Foundations of Confucian Thought: Intellectual Life in the Chunqiu Period, 722–453 B.C.E.* Honolulu: University of Hawaii Press, 2002.

Qian Mu. (錢穆). *Kongzi zhuan* (孔子傳) (Life of Confucius). Beijing: Sanlian shudian, 2002.

———. *Xianqin zhuzi xinian* (先秦諸子繫年) (A study of the dates of events in the lives of the pre-Qin philosophers). Beijing: Shangwu Yinshuguan, 2001.

———. *Zhuangzi zuanjian* (莊子纂箋) (Commentary on the *Zhuangzi*). Taipei: Dongda tushu, 1985.

Qinghua daxue cang zhanguo zhujian (清華大學藏戰國竹簡) (The Tsinghua University Collection of the Warring States Bamboo Texts). Vols. 1 and 3, edited by Li Xueqin (李學勤). Shanghai: Zhongxi shuju, 2010–2013.

Schaberg, David. *A Patterned Past: Form and Thought in Early Chinese Historiography*. Cambridge, MA: Harvard University Asia Center, 2001.

Schwartz, Benjamin. *The World of Thought in Ancient China*. Cambridge, MA: Belknap Press of Harvard University Press, 1985.

Shanghai bowuguan cang zhanguo Chu zhushu (上海博物館藏戰國楚竹書) (The Shanghai Museum Collection of the Warring States Chu Bamboo Manuscripts). Edited by Ma Chengyuan (馬承源). 9 vols. Shanghai: Shanghai guji chubanshe, 2001–.

Shaughnessy, Edward. *Before Confucius: Studies in the Creation of the Chinese Classics*. Albany: State University of New York Press, 1997.

———. *Rewriting Early Chinese Texts*. Albany: State University of New York Press, 2006.

Shijing zhuxi (詩經注析) (The *Book of Poetry* with annotations and analysis). Edited by Cheng Junying (程俊英) and Jiang Jianyuan (蔣見元). 2 vols. Beijing: Zhonghua shuju, 2005.

Shirakawa, Shizuka (白川靜). *Kōshi den* (孔子傳) (Life of Confucius). Tokyo: Chuō kōronsha, 1991.

Sima Qian (司馬遷), (*Shiji* 史記) (*Records of the Grand Historian* with collected annotations). 10 vols. Beijing: Zhonghua chubanshe, 1959.

Slingerland, Edward, trans. *Confucius Analects, with Selections from Traditional Commentaries*. Indianapolis: Hackett Publishing, 2003.

Sources of Chinese Tradition. Compiled by Wm. Theodore de Bary and Irene Bloom. 2nd ed. Vol. 1. New York: Columbia University Press, 1999.

Sun Xingyan (孫星衍). *Shangshu jinguwen zhushu* (尚書今古文注疏) (Commentary on the *Book of Documents*). Beijing: Zhonghua shuju, 1986.

Waley, Arthur, trans. *The Analects of Confucius*. London: Allen & Unwin, 1938. Reprint. New York: Random House, n.d.

———, trans. *The Book of* Songs. Edited, with additional translations, by Joseph Allen. New York: Grove Press, 1996.

Wang Chong (王充). *Lun heng* (論衡) (Disquisitions weighed in the balance). Vol. 7 of *Xinbian zhuzi jicheng* (新編諸子集成) (New edition of the works of the early philosophers). Taipei: Shijie shuju, 1974.

Wang Yangming (王陽明). *Wang Yangming quanshu* (王陽明全書) (Complete works of Wang Yangming). Vol.1. Taipei: Zhengzhong shuju, n.d.

Watson, Burton, trans. *The Analects of Confucius*. New York; Columbia University Press, 2007.

———, trans. *Basic Writings of Mo Tzu (Mozi), Hsün Tzu (Xunzi), and Han Fei Tzu (Hanfeizi)*. New York: Columbia University Press, 1967.

———, trans. *The Complete Works of Chuang Tzu (Zhuangzi)*. New York: Columbia University Press, 1968.

———, *Ssu-ma Ch'ien Grand Historian of China*. New York: Columbia University Press, 1958.

Xu Gan (徐幹). *Balanced Discourses (Zhonglun)*, translated by John Makeham. New Haven: Yale University Press, 2002.

Xu Shen (許慎). *Shuowen jiezi* (說文解字) (Etymological dictionary), with annotations by Duan Yucai. Taipei: Shuming chuban gongsi, 1990.

Xunzi jijie (荀子集解) (Collected commentaries on the *Xunzi*). Edited by Wang Xianqian (王先謙). Vol. 2 of *Xinbian zhuzi jicheng* (新編諸子集成) (New edition of the works of the early philosophers). Taipei: Shijie shuju, 1974.

Zhang Taiyan (章太炎). *Guogu lunheng shuzheng* (國故論衡疏證). Beijing: Zhonghua shuju, 2008.

Zhang Xuecheng (章學誠). *Wenshi tongyi* (文史通義) (General principles of literature and history). Vol.1. Taipei: Guangwen shuju, 1967.

Zhu Xi (朱熹). *Sishu zhangju jizhu* (四書章句集注) (Commentaries on the Four Books). Beijing: Zhonghua shuju, 1986.

Zhuangzi jijie (莊子集釋) (Collected commentaries on the *Zhuangzi*). Edited by Wang Xianqian (王先謙). Vol. 3 of *Xinbian zhuzi jicheng* (新編諸子集成) (New edition of the works of the early philosophers). Taipei: Shijie shuju, 1974.

Zufferey, Nicholas. *To the Origins of Confucianism*. Bern: Peter Lang, 2003.